World Food, Population
and
Development

World Food, Population and Development

Edited by
Gigi M. Berardi

Rowman & Allanheld
PUBLISHERS

ROWMAN & ALLANHELD

Published in the United States of America in 1985
by Rowman & Allanheld, Publishers
(a division of Littlefield, Adams & Company)
81 Adams Drive, Totowa, New Jersey 07512

Library of Congress Cataloging-in-Publication Data
Main entry under title:

World food, population and development.

  1. Food supply. 2. Population. 3. Economic
development. 4. Food supply—Government policy.
5. Population policy. 6. Economic policy. I. Berardi,
Gigi M.
HD9000.5.W59 1985   338.1'9   85-14398
ISBN 0-8476-7455-X
ISBN 0-8476-7456-8 (pbk.)

85 86 87 / 10 9 8 7 6 5 4 3 2 1
Printed in the United States of America

In loving memory of
my parents

Contents

Foreword

Widespread hunger . . . death from starvation . . . nothing could seem more remote and depressing to most students in America's colleges and universities today. Yet, from my own experience, I am convinced that understanding the roots of world hunger can engender in us feelings of empowerment, an understanding that world hunger problems are within our control.

Fifteen years ago I began asking: What are the roots of world hunger? And what are the appropriate responses for those who want to help end the suffering of hunger? I was convinced that if I could just answer those questions I would have a powerful handle in tackling the most complex economic and political questions facing our world.

My hunch was right. Understanding the roots of hunger did prove a great awakening in my own life. Instead of a depressing subject to be avoided, I learned that understanding "why hunger" was a first step in grasping where my own self-interest—and that, I believe, of most Americans—lies.

But my learning had to begin with unlearning—the gradual peeling away of the many-layered myths that mislead and immobilize us with fear, guilt and hopelessness.

* The myth of scarcity—that the earth simply cannot provide for us all.
* The myth that greater production alone can alleviate hunger.
* The myth that hunger is caused by the greed of average Americans and that our perpetual responsibility is to feed the world.

In brief, I came to see that world hunger is needless—and therein lies the outrage to every person of conscience. While my sense of the needlessness of the tragedy grew, so did my respect for the dignity and innate capacities of those who now go hungry. I came to understand that I do not have to solve the problem of world hunger *for other people*. For all human beings can and will feed themselves, if they are allowed to do so. My responsibility is to make sure that the economic and military policies of the United States government and those of corporations based in this economy are not reinforcing social structures in the third world that prevent people from being able to feed themselves.

Through study and travel, I have constantly tested my "working hypotheses," learning to reformulate my views—admitting my mistakes—when new knowledge pushed me to new understanding. It is now clear to me that what became liberating discoveries developed only through grappling with contrasting, indeed contradictory perspectives. For this reason, I find *World Food, Population and Development* an invaluable, long overdue tool.

By its very formulation, this book encourages critical thinking. Introducing the social, political, economic and biological dimensions of nutrition, food production and agricultural development, the varied thinkers in *World Food, Population and Development* challenge the conventional wisdom offered for "food and population" problems. Perhaps more important, because it includes widely varying views, this book demonstrates that there are no "experts" up there who have the answers for us. Realizing that we cannot look to "them," we are called upon to take our own lives more seriously. We realize that we ourselves can begin to make sense out of contrasting perspectives and, in so doing, can contribute to the search for solutions to the terrible scourge of hunger.

The variety of the topics chosen for this volume carries another critical message—that the solution to world hunger, and other mammoth global problems, is to be found only as human beings learn to integrate knowledge of the social, political and biological worlds. Historically, texts on world hunger have focused on strictly agricultural issues, such as improved seeds and pesticides or narrowly on the technical economic questions of pricing and marketing. This volume, however, also takes on the less visible, but crucial, social questions of power—who controls decision making over resource use. It challenges students to ask the larger questions—to probe beneath the technical to the fundamental value questions for which there are no easy "right" or "wrong" answers.

In other words, *World Food, Population and Development* calls forth integrative thinking. It is an exceptionally useful resource for undergraduate students in political economy, international studies, regional planning, environmental studies, food and population, nutrition and science and technology courses, as well as, of course, for individuals outside the academic community.

I met the editor of this volume, Gigi Berardi, almost ten years ago when my own search was just beginning. I am grateful that she has continued to probe the roots of hunger, offering us this useful volume which builds on her many years of experience teaching about world hunger. The juxtaposition of the articles makes for engaging reading along with Dr. Berardi's insightful introductions to the selections, providing the reader with helpful context.

I enthusiastically recommend *World Food, Population and Development* as a foundation for critical thinking and the interdisciplinary study of world hunger and development.

Frances Moore Lappé

Preface

My interest in world food and population issues began in September 1974 when I enrolled as a graduate student at Cornell University. At that time, there was much concern about the "World Food Crisis." An ideology of scarcity had been developed in the mid- and late-1960s by such demagogues as Garrett Hardin and William and Paul Paddock. Treatises on overpopulation, limits to growth and food scarcity were rampant. *Famine 1975* (Paddock and Paddock) was written in 1967 followed shortly thereafter by *The Population Bomb* (Ehrlich) and "Tragedy of the Commons" (Hardin). Indeed, famines in the Indian subcontinent prompted a concern for resource shortage. This concern was reinforced in the early-1970s with dramatic decreases in world grain production, the Arab oil embargo, drought in sub-Sahara Africa, not to mention the Vietnam war.

What were the responses to this so-called world food crisis? Frances Moore Lappé wrote *Diet for a Small Planet* (1971). Oxfam America organized its first Thanksgiving fast (1974), a National University Conference on Hunger (I was one of two delegates from Cornell University) was held in Austin, Texas (1975), the first National Food Day was organized (1975) for which *Food For People Not For Profit* (Lerza and Jacobson) was written and various hunger/food/development organizations were initiated and/or strengthened (e.g., World Hunger Year, Bread for the World, Worldwatch Institute).

Amid this concern, some statistics were ignored, e.g., that per capita food production was increasing while the rate of world population growth was decreasing (although absolute increases in population numbers could be expected into the twenty-first century). Instead, world attention was focused on the dangers of relentless, exponential population growth despite the fact that researchers such as Roy Rappaport had published data showing that a given supply of food is not necessarily transformed into human protoplasm, some of it may be diverted to raising the standard of living (e.g., for increased meat production, use of draft animals, etc.). To do so, fertility is controlled.

When it was finally recognized that there was enough food available to feed the world's population, inequitable distribution of resources was given as the cause of resource shortage. Eventually, some scholars and critics began to focus on social institutions, production processes and the structure of society as starting points for investigations of the root causes of hunger. It was recognized that scarcity is a social, rather than a physical phenomenon (certainly not a new idea) and that "overpopulation" and food scarcity were symptoms rather than causes of "world food problems."

Unfortunately, substantial sums of money had been invested in population control programs where previously it had been thought that "overpopulation" was the most serious world problem and that people did not control their fertility because they did not know *how.* Needless to say, fertility control is an economic- and social-based decision and no amount of contraceptive inundation will affect the socio-economic forces that influence a couple's decision about when and how to procreate. Finally, it was realized that decreases in infant mortality was the most important precondition to fertility decline and some funds (e.g., from the World Bank) were diverted to infant and child nutrition programs, and to prenatal and postnatal care.

As with population control policy, the idea of "technological fix" prevailed in food production programs and thus there was considerable excitement about Single Cell Protein (SCP), Fish Protein Concentrate (FPC) and other "miracle" foods (not to mention the contribution of Norman Borlaug and his colleagues—the green revolutionists—their work, and the socio-eonomic impacts of it, pales in comparison to the harbingers of the "gene revolution"). Finally, after millions of research dollars had been wasted, it was realized that food production and consumption, too, were a political, social, economic as well as biological phenomenon. Indeed, interesting studies had been conducted in Cali, Colombia, showing that certain programs designed to prevent malnutrition by simply providing food were unsuccessful. Poor sanitation, poor diet and limited education prevented any nutrition intervention from being effective. Indeed, in Chile, over 60 million U.S. dollars each year for a period of 20 years had to be expended before it was realized that a free milk distribution program had resulted in no substantial changes in the nutritional status of the child population. (Probably U.S. dairy farmers were the primary beneficiaries.) Nutrition intervention programs succeed only as integrated programs, consisting of improved nutrition and health conditions, as well as changes in the socio-economic environment.

In the past decade several food- and population-worthy events have occurred that warrant mention:

1. The Nestle boycott, organized by INFACT (Infant Formula Action Coalition), was finally called off in 1984 after many years of hard work, shareholders' resolutions, United Nations meetings and conferences. Nestle no longer persists in certain marketing and promotion of infant formula activities. The target for boycott action is now U.S.-based infant formula companies.

2. Patrick Hughes and his friends, with a small grant from the National Council of Churches, produced a slide show on the activities of Gulf and Western (G+W) corporation in the Dominican Republic. G+W "fought" the slide show with millions of dollars and much public relations energy. My class (at Cornell University) and I were the recipients of some of the attention—G+W at one time wanted to fly an agronomist from the Dominican Republic to speak to my class of ten students in Ithaca, New York. Such fervor in refuting a slide show made on a shoestring budget was heartwarming. This Patrick Hughes-G+W interaction was really a case of the "Mouse that Roared." Patrick Hughes died several years ago, but the slide show remains to politicize and attempt to counter the on-going publicity assault by G+W (e.g., a 63-page advertising supplement in *Time* magazine).

3. In 1975-76, the price of coffee increased substantially—we boycotted coffee in the United States. Was this the appropriate action to take? Were we preventing small-scale landholders from increasing their income, or were we making a statement to absentee landlords and multinational corporations?

4. In the mid- to late-1970s, a forced sterilization campaign in India resulted in tremendous (international) public outrage and instability in Indira Ghandi's government, which eventually collapsed.

5. In the mid-1970s, doctors in New York City (New York professors of gynecology Gordon W. Douglas, Saul Gusberg, Irwin Kaiser, James Nelson, Martin Stone, Raymond Vande Wiele and two unidentified patients) filed suit, claiming that the rights of doctors were violated when (a) a doctor was not permitted to initiate a

sterilization procedure and (b) he or she must discuss sterilization in the context of alternative forms of birth control. The doctors sustained that the patient's right to know violated the doctor's right to free speech! Needless to say, this suit generated considerable controversy.

6. A transformation of U.S. agriculture occurred, from "famine to feast," jeopardizing the structure of agriculture. In the early-1970s, U.S. farmers capitalized (literally) on world hunger and overinvested and overproduced. The world market has experienced a period of overproduction for most grains for several years, despite billions of dollars spent on agricultural policy and price support systems in the U.S. and elsewhere. Low commodity prices, increasing production costs, decreasing land values and farm foreclosures all characterize a gloomy farm situation.

7. What of the quantity and quality of the U.S. food supply? A documentary made in the 1960s shocked America about our hunger problem. *Hunger in America* showed us that kwashiorkor (protein deficiency) and marasmus (calorie deficiency) exist here, as well as in the developing countries. A follow-up study conducted in 1977 showed that the gross malnutrition observed in the earlier study had been eliminated—due to food assistance programs rather than decreases in unemployment. Unfortunately, federal subsidies for those programs have been cut in recent years. Individual states and counties are responsible for food assistance programs and thus the effectiveness of the program varies with the commitment and sensitivity of the particular local government involved.

In terms of quality of the U.S. food supply, we are still concerned about additives—sulfur compounds are receiving more attention now. Nitrites and nitrates at one time were in the limelight. Gradually, we are becoming a more nutrition-conscious people. We are advised from practically every major public and private nutrition/health/medical organization that no more than one-third of our calories should be in the form of fat, and that we need to increase our intake of complex carbohydrates—whole-grain breads and cereals, fruits and vegetables—and limit consumption of sugar and salt. Furthermore, weight control must be established with a regular program of exercise rather than dieting.

8. Last, international nutritionists and medical scholars have made some impact on food scientists and international development researchers in convincing them that most of the malnutrition in developing countries is due simply to inadequate intake of food. Protein deficiency is not the most important diet-related disease in the world. To focus on protein deficiency to the neglect of calorie deficiency has resulted in disastrous consequences. Millions of dollars have been wasted on food and nutrition programs that have emphasized the provision of expensive protein sources (SCP, FPC, animal protein) when the major nutritional problem was calorie defiency. According to nutritionists, present trends indicate an increasing dominance of marasmus in the future.

These and other phenomena are discussed and presented in greater detail in this volume.

What, then, are some of the major food and resource problems/issues confronting us in the 1980s and 1990s? First, the hegemony of the superpowers, i.e., intervention by world superpowers (of immediate concern is intervention in Central America) in destabilizing democratic governments. Second, the huge balance-of-payments problems experienced by poor debtor countries (indeed, some of the "aid" we "give" to these countries is used to pay interest on the loan payments they owe us). And third, the "gene revolution" in agriculture by which there will be a complete integration of the chemical and seed industries, and thus total control over the agricultural production process. (For an in-depth treatment of development problems faced by poorer third world countries, using both Marxist and neo-Keynesian methods of analysis, see *Agricultural Development in the Third World*, edited by Carl K. Eicher and John M. Staatz [Baltimore: The Johns Hopkins University Press. 1984], and *The Political Economy of Underdevelopment*, by Amiya Kumar Bagchi [Cambridge, England: The Cambridge University Press. 1982].)

What are some solutions to the problems discussed above? Should we try to increase agricultural production (through multiple-cropping; see Chapter 49), decrease infant mortality, facilitate democratic decision making processes in developing countries? How? Do we use "appropriate technology" or high-energy technology which is beyond the reach of the small-scale landholder? Should we try and give foreign aid a "good name," as Richard Critchfield suggests in Chapter 47? What about programs such as the Caribbean Basin Initiative—should developing economies grow export crops or food crops? Perhaps there should be more support for development groups such as Oxfam America (see Chapter 50), World Hunger Year or the Plenty Project (see Chapter 51). We are also tempted to investigate "miracle foods." Now, the "winged bean." The winged bean is a high protein, high calorie food, its leaves are like spinach in taste and nutritive value, the immature pods are like green beans, the immature seeds are like green peas, the mature dry seeds are like soybeans and the roots of many varieties produce tubers like potatoes, but are much richer in protein than the potato. Truly, a "miracle" plant.

Or perhaps the solution lies in less intervention and more emphasis on the self-reliance of the developing countries. The Filipinos have already "turned back from the Green Revolution" (see Chapter 48) and India is "taking control of its own development" (see Chapter 54). Foreign involvement is limited in India, and there is little foreign ownership of certain businesses.

These ideas are not meant to be answers to the questions raised earlier in the Preface. In fact, these "solutions" are actually phrased as questions themselves. And that is all we can hope for—to develop an intellectual framework within which we ask questions and begin to think critically.

Gigi Berardi

Acknowledgments

Compiling a list of acknowledgments to friends and colleagues, students and teachers who have assisted me in my study of world food and population issues would be a project in itself. However, five colleagues in particular deserve special acknowledgment. First, I acknowledge the intellectual and moral support provided by Pierre Borgoltz. Together, we have explored food and population issues, examining them in their larger socio-economic context, debated different viewpoints and argued political economy. Arne Youngerman and Bach Vu are also acknowledged for their organizing (with Pierre Borgoltz) of a food activist group, the Coalition for the Right to Eat, at Cornell University, wherein it was possible to study food and population issues with friends and colleagues. Z.H. Przasnyski is also gratefully acknowledged for his support throughout all phases of this project. I thank all the teaching assistants who have helped me in preparing materials, but in particular Ms. Janis Boettinger, a soil scientist who is a scholar in the broadest sense of the word. Lastly, I thank the students I have taught. Everywhere I have worked—Cornell University, Hobart and William Smith Colleges, University of Maryland Baltimore County and Allegheny College—I have gained new insights and perspectives. For this, I am very grateful.

Acknowledgment is given to friends and colleagues at Cornell University, Ellen Bowmaster and Cheryl Hurwitz, for their assistance in the production of this work. Acknowledgment is also given to students and staff members at Allegheny College for their editing, typing and graphic arts skills, in particular Jody Bruckner, Alma Brown and her Printing Services staff including Roxanne Free, the library reference staff including Dorothy Smith, Cynthia Burton-Eldeeb and Donald Vrabel, and work study students Karen Becker, Annette Totten, Valezka Conde, John Dorries, Bryna Rosen and Jill Talbot. Jill Talbot deserves a special mention for her invaluable assistance in the initial style editing and copy preparation of the manuscript. I am especially grateful to Ms. Mimi Bean and her staff of Bright Typing, Inc. for their expert typing and editing skills, and the Department of Environmental Science and Office of the Provost at Allegheny College for their financial support.

Last, I wish to thank the previous editors of "food and population" readers: Dr. Joan Dye Gussow who edited *The Feeding Web: Issues in Nutritional Ecology* (Palo Alto: Bull Publishing Company. 1978) and Dr. Dorothy Blair who edited a reader for Science, Technology and Society 430 (offered at the Pennsylvania State University, University Park). I also thank Dr. Thomas T. Poleman for his food, population and employment bibliography. Some of their work appears in this volume.

Part I

OVERVIEW OF THE WORLD FOOD SITUATION

1

A Look to Not-So-Bad Times
George F. Will

In the first article included in this Overview section, George Will warns us that "the experts" are confused. The Club of Rome (composed of financiers and scholars alike) qualifies its limits-to-growth ideology and emphasizes limits on the developed world's growth, while organizations such as the Hudson Institute do not recognize a world resource problem. Will concludes by affirming that human behavior is more the cause of resources being in short supply than their supposedly finite nature. If human behavior is the problem, what are the tenable solutions with which we are left?

Some people argue that Western civilization is a blot on, well, Western civilization. They say Western consumption has caused the shadow of scarcity to fall across the entire globe, and that we must brace ourselves for the narrowing of wide horizons.

You may have noticed that many calls for asceticism come from tenured professors and others in whose eyes all sacrifices are beautiful as long as they are not required to make any. For example, four years ago the Club of Rome, a group of 100 businessmen, scientists and professors, published *The Limits of Growth*. Three million persons bought this book, a litany of forebodings about the austere future that was supposed to be bearing down upon us.

In 1972 the Club argued that only a prompt end to economic growth could forestall such calamities as famine, war and over-population. Well, the world turns and so does the Club of Rome, which has just executed a maneuver perfected by Rome's taxi drivers—a tight U-turn.

* * *

Last month the Club announced, as solemnly as it announced a contrary opinion four years ago, that, on second thought, we will not perish from economic growth after all if the growth includes poor nations.

So as we are getting used to the ashen taste of life's limits, we start hearing from optimists. The Hudson Institute has shoved in its oar, announcing that 200 years hence our children's children's children's children's children will be living in the lap of abundance.

It is dreadfully hard to cultivate a fashionable melancholy when the seers at Hudson are saying that by 2176 a declining rate of world population growth will mean an abundance of resources, including energy because coal and other fossil fuels are sufficient to last until the development of "virtually eternal energy sources," such as nuclear fusion.

But before you dash out to buy a Buick Electra with the money you had put aside for your great-great-great-grandchildren, remember one thing: Modern prophets generally look at least 200 years ahead because they know in their innermost hearts that they don't know what will befall us in the next 25 years. This utter uncertainty is understandable—mankind has had precious little experience with economic growth, which began approximately 200 years ago after 10,000 years of economic stagnation. Norman Macrae of "The Economist" says it well:

"The average Roman citizen in A.D. 1 seems to have had a slightly higher annual income . . . than his successor citizen in the next great republic (just under $200 a head for the U.S. in 1776). The man of 1776 used much the same energy sources as the man of A.D. 1 (animal muscle, wind and water); he could travel much the same tiny maximum distance per day; he had much the same materials for tools (wood and iron) . . ."

Since 1776, world population has increased sixfold, the real Gross World Product has increased eightyfold, the distance a man can travel a thousandfold. But man still cannot see far ahead: When one travels that fast the landscape is a blur.

* * *

One thing is clear. The most frightening shortage, food, may be the most remediable.

As Macrae notes, if the rest of the world would learn to cultivate land as efficiently as the Dutch do, the world could feed 60 billion people—15 times today's world population. Today only 3 per cent of the earth's surface is farmed. Seventy per cent of the crops in some poor nations are eaten by pests that could be easily controlled.

The most serious inefficiency in world food production is the conversion of grain into livestock. Today the world's pig population consumes seven times more primary protein than North Americans consume. Horses, many used only for recreation, consume more than the Chinese. Cows, a third of them in African and Asian countries and serving no nutritive purpose, consume more grain than all the world's humans.

It is an old story. Human behavior, which is changeable, is more important than the finiteness of the earth's resources as a cause of human problems. So there are grounds, however slight, for hoping that the future will not be quite as bad as some people have expected. But of course that still leaves a lot of room for badness.

2

The World Food Prospect

Lester R. Brown

Lester Brown, President of Worldwatch Institute, provides us with a perspective on world food prospects that is not optimistic. He argues that scarcity is more or less endemic, ecological degradation unavoidable with current production practices and population growth, "relentless." Although the article was written in 1975, Brown's perspective is still commonly held by many academicians in the 1980s.

The article is included in its entirety for its historical import (capturing the concern in 1975 generated by the decreases in food production a few years earlier) and for the discussion of "key actors on the global scene." Brown also discusses agricultural production and policy, and inefficiencies therein, in the Soviet Union that result in large fluctuations in world grain demand and supply. Note the neo-Malthusian ideology evident throughout the article.

As we make the transition from the third to the final quarter of this century, the world food economy appears to be undergoing a fundamental transformation. Two developments stand out. One, the comfortable reserve of surplus stocks and excess production capacity which the world has enjoyed over the past generation may now be a passing incident in its history. Two, the world is becoming overwhelmingly dependent on North America for food supplies. These two changes point to a new role and responsibility for North America.

Within a span of a few years the world's surplus stocks and excess production capacity have largely disappeared. Today the entire world is living hand to mouth, trying to make it from one harvest to the next.

Grain exports from North America, a measure of growing worldwide food deficits, have doubled during the 1970's, expanding from 56 million tons in 1970 to nearly 100 million tons during the current fiscal year. Of the 115 countries for which data are readily available, all but a few now import grain. Of the countries that remain significant exporters, two dominate: the United States and Canada. During the current fiscal year the two together will export enough grain to feed the 600 million people of India.

The reasons for growing dependence on North American food supplies include ecological deterioration of food systems because of growing population pressure,

Reprinted with permission from *Science* 190 (4219): 1053–1059 (12 December 1975). Copyright 1975 by the AAAS.

mismanagement of agriculture, soaring population-induced demands, and sharp increases in demand as a result of newfound wealth, as in the Organization of Petroleum Exporting Countries (OPEC). The causes of the growing deficits vary, and often a combination of factors is responsible, but the effects are the same— ever greater pressure on North American food supplies.

As a result of these trends, North America today finds itself with a near monopoly of the world's exportable grain supplies. In a world of food scarcity, where there may not be enough food to go around, North America must decide who gets how much food and on what terms. The governments of the United States and Canada have not consciously sought this responsibility, any more than the countries of the Middle East have planned their geographical location astride the world's richest oil field.

In recent years shortages of food have contributed to global double-digit inflation and to severe nutritional stress among low-income people everywhere. In some of the poorer countries, shortages have led to a rise in death rates, reversing postwar trends. National political leaders in the food-deficit countries, rich and poor alike, are becoming uneasy over future access to food supplies. Profound changes in the world food economy have brought into question the basic assumptions underlying North American food policies, particularly at the international level.

New Sources of Global Food Insecurity

Throughout much of the period since World War II, the world has had two major food reserves: stocks of grain held by the principal exporting countries and cropland idled under farm programs in the United States. During the 1960's and early 1970's some 50 million acres out of a total U.S. cropland base of 350 million acres was held out of production to support prices (1). Stocks of grain held by the exporting countries were readily available for use when needed. Cropland idled under farm programs in the United States could be brought back into production within a year. Together grain stockpiles and cropland reserves provided security for all mankind, a cushion against any imaginable food disasters.

As recently as early 1972, it seemed likely that surplus stocks and cropland idled under farm programs would be part of the landscape for the forseeable future. Then, suddenly, the global demand for food, fueled by the relentless growth of population and by rising affluence, began to outstrip the productive capacity of the world's farmers and fishermen. The world fish catch, which had tripled between 1950 and 1970 and had moved to a new high each year, turned downward for three consecutive years. Although most of the idled U.S. cropland was released for use in 1973 and the remainder thereafter, food reserves have not been rebuilt.

In 1961, the combination of reserve stocks of grain in exporting countries and idle cropland in the United States amounted to the equivalent of 105 days of world grain consumption. In 1972 stocks still equaled 69 days of world consumption. Then reserves began to drop rather abruptly—to 55 days in 1973 and still further to 33 days in 1974. The 1975 carry-over stocks remain precariously low, and all hopes for rebuilding them to safe levels have vanished with the poor 1975 Soviet harvest. Current U.S. Department of Agriculture estimates of carry-over stocks in 1976, already largely determined by the 1975 harvest, indicate an even lower level then in 1975 (2) (Table 2.1).

A third factor leading to global food insecurity and instability in the mid-1970's is the near total dependence of the entire world on one region, North America, for food supplies. Both countries within the region are affected by the same climatic

TABLE 2.1. Index of World Food Security, 1961 to 1976

Reserves (million metric tons)

Year	Grain*	Grain Equivalent of Idled U.S. Cropland	Total	Reserves as Days of World Grain Consumption
1961	163	68	231	105
1962	176	81	257	105
1963	149	70	219	95
1964	153	70	223	87
1965	147	71	218	91
1966	151	78	229	84
1967	115	51	166	59
1968	144	61	205	71
1969	159	73	232	85
1970	188	71	259	89
1971	168	41	209	71
1972	130	78	208	69
1973	148	24	172	55
1974	108	0	108	33
1975#	111	0	111	35
1976	100	0	100	31

*Based on carry-over stocks of grain at beginning of crop year in individual countries for year shown. The USDA has recently expanded the coverage of reserve stocks to include importing as well as exporting countries, thus the reserve levels are slightly higher than those heretofore published (2)
#
 Preliminary estimates by USDA.

cycles, with a poor crop in one all too often associated with a poor crop in the other.

A fourth factor contributing to instability was a decision made by Soviet political leaders to offset crop shortfalls with imports. Since recent year-to-year fluctuations in the Soviet grain harvest have exceeded the average annual gains in the world grain crop, their decision further destabilizes the world food economy. This policy, apparently made in early 1972, may not be irreversible, but neither will it be easily abandoned. Soviet herds and flocks have been building steadily throughout the 1970's as a result of this policy. So too have the expectations and appetites of Soviet consumers.

The high costs of this food price instability are economic, political, and social. Consumers, particularly the poor, suffer. Most families do not find it easy to adjust to wide fluctuations in food prices. These same fluctuations, in turn, make it more difficult for producers to decide how much to plant and how much to invest in inputs. Dairymen and cattlemen everywhere have been caught in a bind between the price of milk or beef and the cost of grain. Thousands of these producers have been driven out of business, leading to erratic flows of milk and meat to market, and to discontent among consumers.

TABLE 2.2. The Changing Pattern of World Grain Trade

	Grain Exports (+) and Imports (-)* (million metric tons)				#
Region	1934-38	1948-52	1960	1970	1976
North America	+ 5	+23	+39	+56	+94
Latin America	+ 9	+ 1	0	+ 4	- 3
Western Europe	-24	-22	-25	-30	-17
Eastern Europe and U.S.S.R.	+ 5		0	+ 1	-25
Africa	+ 1	0	- 2	- 5	-10
Asia	+ 2	- 6	-17	-37	-47
Australia and New Zealand	+ 3	+ 3	+ 6	+12	+ 8

*Data are from FAO (3) and USDA (2).

#

Author's estimates for fiscal year are derived from preliminary USDA data (2).

Governments also find it difficult to operate in a world of violent fluctuations in food prices. Unstable markets wreak havoc with foreign exchange budgets, particularly those of developing countries heavily dependent on food imports, and undermine government efforts to combat inflation.

Emergence of the North American Breadbasket

North America has emerged as the world's breadbasket only since World War II. Its rise is best measured by examining the net grain trade flows among various geographic regions. An aggregate of all grains is a useful indicator of food trends, since grains supply more than half of man's food energy supply when consumed directly, and a sizable segment of the remainder when consumed indirectly. On the production side, they occupy more than 70 percent of the world's cropland area. Net regional data, which exclude trade among countries within a region, are used in order to isolate more clearly the basic trends in the world food economy.

Prior to World War II, all geographic regions, except Western Europe, were net exporters. North America was not the only exporter nor even the leading one. From 1934 to 1938, Latin America was exporting an average of 9 million tons per year, while North America exported only 5 million tons. Eastern Europe, including the Soviet Union, was exporting 5 million tons annually, exactly the same as North America (3).

All this has now changed. Asia has developed a massive deficit. It is now importing some 50 million tons of grain per year, most of it taken by three countries—Japan, China, and India. Africa, Latin America, and Eastern Europe (including U.S.S.R.) have all become food-deficit regions. Western Europe, continually a major importer, has been the only stable element through the period; its imports rarely moved outside the range of 20 to 30 million tons.

North America's unchallenged dominance as a global food supplier began in the 1940's. The scale of exports expanded gradually during the 1950's and 1960's. During the 1970's, North American grain exports have nearly doubled in response to the explosive growth in import demand from around the world (Table 2.2).

Most countries today obtain part of their food supplies from North America. Dependence has increased rapidly over the past decade and shows every indication of continuing to grow. The worldwide movement of countries outside of North America from export to import status is a one-way street. No country has gone against this trend over the past quarter century. Scores of countries have become important food importers, but not one new country has emerged as a major cereal exporter during this period.

Not only are more and more countries becoming importers, but the degree of dependence on outside supplies by the food deficit countries is growing. More and more countries, both industrial and developing, are actually importing more food than they produce. Among the countries which now import more than half of their grain supply are Japan, Belgium, Senegal, Libya, Saudi Arabia, Venezuela, Lebanon, Switzerland, and, at least temporarily, Algeria. Other countries rapidly approaching primary dependence on imported foodstuffs include Portugal, Costa Rica, Sri Lanka, South Korea, and Egypt (2).

This rate of ever-growing dependence on North America by the rest of the world cannot continue for much longer. North America has doubled its grain exports within the past decade, but the world should not count on a repeat performance during the next decade. Unless recent dependence trends are altered, the restriction of grain imports from North America will become commonplace. In mid-July the Canadian Wheat Board banned further exports of wheat until the size of the 1972 harvest was known. Political pressure forced the United States to limit exports of grain to the Soviet Union and Poland in the late summer of 1975. This pattern is beginning to repeat itself—first in 1972, then in 1974, and again in 1975—three out of the past four years. It occurred in the last two years despite the release of 5 million acres of idle cropland in the United States for production.

As we enter the fourth year of precariously balanced food supplies, the international community must at least prepare for the possibility that the current situation may not be temporary. The obvious question is: Why has one region emerged as a supplier of food to the rest of the world? If I were to select the single dominant factor reshaping world trade patterns in recent decades, it would be varying rates of population growth. Certainly the conversion of Asia, Africa, and Latin America to deficit status was closely related to population growth. This factor has been less influential in Eastern Europe, and one of the keys to Western Europe's stability as a food importer has been its modest population growth.

A comparison of North America and Latin America with respect to world food trade illustrates the effects of rapid population growth. In 1950, North America and Latin America had roughly equal populations, 163 and 168 million, respectively. While North America's population growth has slowed substantially since the late 1950's, Latin America's has exploded. For example, Mexico, Venezuela, Peru, and Brazil have population growth rates of about 3 percent per year, a rate which, if it continues, would lead to a 19-fold population increase within a century. If North America's 1950 population had expanded 3 percent per year, it would now be 341 million rather than the actual 236 million. At current per capita consumption levels, those additional 105 million people would absorb virtually all exportable supplies and North America would be struggling to maintain self-sufficiency.

Some Key Actors on the Global Scene

Japan. Japan is the world's largest grain importer, importing more than any other two countries combined. The government there is upgrading diets for a population equal to nearly half that of North America and squeezed into an area smaller than

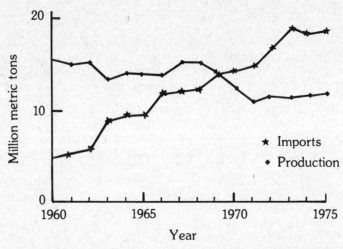

Figure 2.1. Japan: production and imports of all grains, 1960 to 1975 (2).

California. This year Japan will import nearly 20 million tons of grain, mostly feed grains and wheat, making it more dependent on imports of grain than on its own production (Fig. 2.1).

Japan was formerly able to restrict its cereal imports. As population pressure began to mount several decades ago, the Japanese began to reserve their limited land resources for the intensive production of rice and turned to the oceans for their animal protein in the form of fish. As a result, they now grow the rice they need, but make increased claims on the world's fisheries.

Postwar prosperity has enabled Japanese consumers to enrich their diets, but, as a result, they now make increased claims on the world's grain supply. As their incomes and purchasing power have risen, many Japanese consumers have begun to develop a taste for livestock products. Japanese production and consumption of pork and poultry products are now on a par with that of other industrial countries, and still expanding (4). Beef consumption has been nominal (only 9 pounds per capita per year) and could expand substantially.

Japanese economic projections for the coming decades show food imports continuing to rise as a result of further moderate population growth and rising incomes. If prices remain reasonable it seems safe to predict that Japanese consumers will continue to increase their purchases of livestock products. Speculation about when Japan's cereal imports might level off is problematical, contingent as it is upon their future prosperity and rate of population growth.

On the population front, Japan received a great deal of credit for the sharp reduction in its birth rate during the years immediately after World War II. Since then, however, its population has continued to grow at 1 percent or more per year, and is now nearly double the North American rate of natural increase. Recent signs suggest that the Japanese are again preparing to actively discourage population growth, and they could quite reasonably move toward population stability over the next decade if they decide to do so.

China. Recent visitors to China almost always comment on the excellent nutritional condition of the population. Journalists, economists, scientists, and doctors all come away with the same impression. The obvious clinical signs of malnutrition, present in almost every other low-income country, appear to be almost wholly absent in China.

The success of Chinese efforts in nutrition is probably due more to improvements in distribution than to production gains. The latter have been creditable but not spectacular. China has imported several million tons of grain per year since 1960, a total of 78 million tons from 1960 to 1975. In fact, from 1970 to 1975 it imported more grain than India (2). The difference is that China has apparently achieved both a higher per capita production and availability of grain and a more equitable distribution.

Chinese success in agriculture cannot be viewed apart from the social reforms and regimentation that have resulted in a rare degree of social equity, not only within the rural sector but between the rural and urban sectors as well. Another strength of the Chinese system is that the production teams are organized to permit the mobilization of excess or seasonally idle labor for rural road construction, reforestation, and the construction of terraces and irrigation reservoirs and canals. Enormous earthfilled irrigation dams have been built almost entirely by human muscle power.

Nevertheless, pressures on agricultural resources are evident in the shift of land from soybeans to cereals. As recently as the 1930's, China has supplied 90 percent of the soybeans entering the world market. Within the last few years it has not only lost this exportable surplus, but has even begun to import soybeans, almost exclusively from the United States.

The seriousness with which the Chinese leaders view the agricultural problem is evident in their willingness to compromise ideologically and turn to foreign engineering firms, primarily American, to build fertilizer plants for them. The 13 massive new nitrogen fertilizer complexes under construction should virtually eliminate China's heavy dependence on imported fertilizer. Nonetheless, returns on additional fertilizer use in China are dependent on comparable increases in other inputs and on further progress in basic agronomic research. Without these, the returns on additional massive quantities of fertilizer will diminish rapidly.

China may ultimately solve its food problem, but probably as much by its aggressive action on the population front as on the food front. Rough estimates of current population growth (not even the Chinese seem to have precise data) hover around 1.4 percent per year, and this rate appears to be declining. If it is 1.4 percent per year, it is comparable to that of the United States in the late 1950's.

The Chinese leaders have been among the first to perceive the need to sharply curtail population growth. With the possible exception of Singapore, no government has confronted the population threat so directly as that of China. The leadership has not only provided family planning services, but it has also reshaped important economic and social policies in order to discourage large families. The birth rate appears to be dropping sharply and, if it continues, China's population growth rate could dip to 1 percent by the end of this decade or shortly thereafter. If China can continue to move toward the clearly defined goal of population stability, then it could ultimately solve its food problem, and, by eliminating the need for imports, contribute to solving the world's food problem.

India. The outlook for India's future food situation appeared bleak in the mid-1960's until the government reshaped its food policies and priorities, giving agriculture the support it deserved. This reshaping of economic policies, combined with the availability of the high-yielding strains of wheat and rice, gave Indian agriculture a dramatic boost. During the six-year span between 1966 and 1971, India succeeded in doubling its wheat crop, a performance unmatched by any other major country. By 1972, India was on the brink of being self-sufficient in cereals (Fig. 2.2). Malnutrition

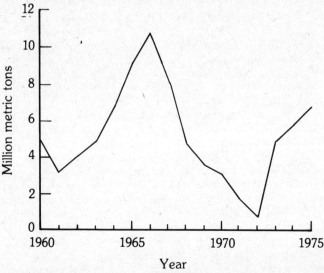

Figure 2.2. India: grain imports, 1960 to 1975 (2).

was still rampant among the poor, but India's farmers were producing about all that the market would absorb. It actually provided substantial food aid to refugees from Bangladesh and to the newly independent nation itself.

Since that high watermark for Indian agriculture, in the early 1970's, there have been numerous setbacks, some external to the Indian economy. In the spring of 1975, the U.S. Department of Agriculture estimated that the Indian wheat crop was reduced by a million tons simply because of a shortage of fuel to operate irrigation pumps. Then too, India, more than most other countries, has been adversely affected by the short supply and high price of fertilizer. Heavy dependence on fertilizer imports is due in part to the inefficiency of India's domestic fertilizer plants. The problem is not lack of agricultural potential; India is capable of producing far more food than is now produced. But India has not been able to put together the resources, the priorities, and the policies to maintain its earlier agricultural momentum.

The economic problems of the 1970's are exacerbated by the negative effects of ecological abuse. Deforestation, overgrazing, desert encroachment, and increased flooding due to the destruction of natural vegetation are beginning to take their toll on India's food production. The productivity of a vast semiarid area, covering a fifth of the country, is threatened by these forces. Soil erosion and the silting of irrigation reservoirs are having a perceptible negative effect on food output.

India has succeeded in modestly reducing its birth rate, but it still has a long way to go. It remains to be seen whether India can reduce its dependence on imported foodstuffs or whether this dependence will become absolute and crippling in the years ahead as a result of continuing high birth rates, unfavorable economic forces, and negative ecological trends.

The U.S.S.R. The agricultural production potential of the Soviet Union is severely constrained both by its natural environment and by the organization of its agriculture. Soviet agriculture is, by and large, low rainfall agriculture comparable to that of the Great Plains of Canada and the United States. The U.S.S.R. has severe winters

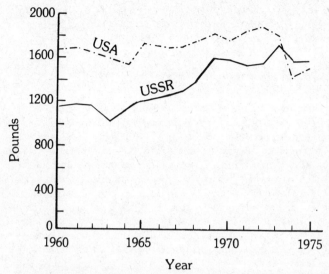

Figure 2.3. United States and Soviet Union: per capita annual grain use, 1960 to 1975 (2).

and a short growing and grazing season. It has no choice region like the U.S. corn belt that combines rich soils and high, dependable rainfall.

On top of these natural constraints Soviet agriculture is confronted with some basic institutional inefficiencies. Among these are the weaknesses of central agricultural planning, a lack of management skills at the local level, poor equipment maintenance, the inefficient use of the vast agricultural labor force, and an overall lack of incentives for those working on the land. Planting and harvesting often lag behind schedule, resulting in reduced yield and in crop losses. Perhaps the most telling statistic is the grain-meat ratio. Beginning in 1974, Soviet per capita grain use (both that consumed directly and that consumed indirectly, in the form of livestock products) moved above that of the United States (Fig. 2.3). Nonetheless, despite great demand, per capita meat consumption in the Soviet Union is scarcely half that in the United States. In addition to the natural handicaps such as the short growing season, inefficiency in the livestock industry is compounded by reliance on dual purpose breeds of livestock for milk and meat.

The Soviet decision to offset crop shortfalls with massive imports rather than with belt tightening is the most destabilizing single factor in the world food economy today, because of its enormous cost to consumers everywhere. The instability derives not so much from the scale of Soviet grain imports as from the erratic occurrence of their demands. The question now before the international community is how to reconcile the erratic need for imports with the urgent need to maintain some semblance of stability in the world grain market.

There are signs that the Soviet Union will be importing grain for the foreseeable future. A recent speech by Soviet spokesman and agricultural leader, Fedor Kerbkov, which was published in full in both *Pravda* and *Izvestia*, suggests that the return on heavy investment in Soviet agriculture over the past decade has been much lower than the leadership had hoped. Indeed, the Soviets may be contemplating a shift in investment emphasis toward the exploitation of minerals and other raw materials for export. Even after a decade of heavy investment in agriculture, they still find that satisfying consumer needs requires large grain imports. There is little to suggest any reduction in Soviet dependence on food imports in the years ahead, so that North America must gear both its production and export policies to the new reality of heavy Soviet dependence on imported grain (1).

Brazil. For at least a generation, writings on world food prospects have alluded to the potential of Brazil and particularly of the Amazon Basin as a source of food for the world (5). Unfortunately, as we face global food shortages and are forced to reassess reality, it is becoming clear that Brazil is by no means a cornucopia. Although it is now exporting soybeans in significant quantities, it is far from fulfilling its once promising potential as a major supplier of food for the world. Indeed, in 1973 Brazil imported more grain than any country in the Western Hemisphere. Even with food from abroad, Brazil's northeast still contains one of the largest areas of abject poverty, hunger, and malnutrition found anywhere in the world.

What has happened to the notion that Brazil could someday feed the world? First, only a minute percentage of the area of the vast Amazon Basin is potentially cultivable with present food prices and prospective farming technologies. Even development of the pockets of agriculturally promising land will require extensive investment in transportation, drainage, research, and credit and marketing facilities. The problem is not so much that Brazil has not been able to expand its food production; it has, and at a fairly impressive rate. But Brazil is faced with an unprecedented growth in the demand for food, because the population of Brazil grows at nearly 3 percent per year. In addition, its economy has been growing at an impressive 8 to 10 percent yearly over the past decade. Together these two sources of growth in demand are increasing food needs by some 4 percent per year (2).

This means that to be self-sufficient Brazil needs to increase agricultural output far more rapidly than any major country has yet succeeded in doing. A sustained 4 percent annual growth in food production makes essential a heavy continuing investment in agriculture. In addition, it requires rapid innovation in agriculture which in turn requires the development of new technologies, and their rapid dissemination and acceptance by farmers. With an agricultural research system that is underdeveloped and underfinanced and a rural population which is still partly illiterate, the problems involved here are evident. And finally, with land holdings highly concentrated among a small percentage of the population, a redistribution of land is urgently needed to give those who work it a stronger incentive to raise its productivity.

But even all this is not enough. At its present growth rate of nearly 3 percent, Brazil's population (now 108 million) will be nearly 2 billion in a century, just four generations hence. Brazil could have to contend with a population larger than that of China and India combined well before this time in the next century. Without a strong commitment to family planning, Brazil is not likely to be a major supplier of grain to the world.

OPEC: New Claimants on Food Supplies

The unprecedented accretion of wealth and purchasing power in oil-exporting countries over the past few years is now reflected in their expanding food imports. Not only is the increase in purchasing power a very sharp one, but the number of people involved also represents a substantial portion of the world's population. The 13 OPEC countries have a combined population of 268 million, nearly half this number being in Indonesia. Per capita food consumption, especially of high protein foods, among OPEC country populations is modest. Thus, much of the new income and purchasing power will be spent on food.

In countries where oil exports are large and populations relatively small, as in Iraq, Iran, or Venezuela, food consumption per person is likely to rise in a meteoric fashion. Overall, the scale of food imports into OPEC countries seems certain to increase dramatically in the years ahead. If oil prosperity begins to spread beyond the urban elite, diets will be rapidly upgraded. In view of the longtime neglect of agriculture in most of these countries, any sharp increase in demand will have to be satisfied initially by imports.

Most OPEC countries are semiarid and many face the effects of severe ecological stresses in agriculture. Both Algeria and Nigeria suffer from overgrazing, deforestation, and the spread of the Sahara Desert. Nigeria, with a population variously estimated at from 60 to 80 million people, is confronted with intense population pressures at a time when the system of traditional slash-and-burn cultivation is being over-exploited in some areas. As recovery periods between plantings are shortened to keep pace with the demand for food, soils are no longer able to regenerate their fertility.

One of the most important uses of the new oil wealth is investment in agriculture. Ecuador, Nigeria, Iran, and Iraq are intensifying their investment in agriculture severalfold. But continuing rapid growth in food output requires more than capital. The support system for agriculture must include an indigenous research capacity, technical advisory services, farm credit services, roads and markets, and, in many instances, reforms in land tenure.

The rate of expansion in agricultural output of the OPEC countries will accelerate, but the question is how fast the acceleration will be relative to that of the demand for food. Nearly all OPEC countries have food deficits, and in some they are substantial. Algeria, for example, relies heavily on imported wheat to sustain its population. The poor 1975 wheat harvest of 700,000 tons may result in an import need of close to 2 million tons, more than double the average of the past ten years (6) (Fig. 2.4).

As increased purchasing power in OPEC countries converts into greater demand for livestock products, including poultry, many countries are implementing programs of rapid expansion of food production. Some expect to double poultry and egg output within a period of two or three years; Iraq, for example, which has not traditionally imported feed grains, is projected to import nearly a million tons annually by the end of the current decade in order to support its burgeoning poultry and livestock industry (7).

Ecuador has expanded its food output only 5 percent over the past three years. Yet, while production limps along, the demand for food is soaring, both because of population growth and the infusion of oil money into the economy. The result, as of mid-1975, is an acute domestic shortage of food and a need for a sharp increase in imports.

One of the unknowns in the food outlook in OPEC countries is Indonesia. If the oil dollars begin to filter down to the lower-income groups, they will convert almost immediately into a demand for additional food. Can the Indonesian agricultural economy respond to this growth in demand? In the short run at least it is doubtful. Because Indonesia supports a large population, even modest increases in per capita food import requirements would result in a large market demand for food imports.

From a social point of view, increasing the purchasing power of more than a quarter of a billion of the world's lower-income people is unquestionably desirable. New buying power would enhance both the quantity and quality of food intake and greatly reduce malnutrition. From an analytical point of view, the claims on

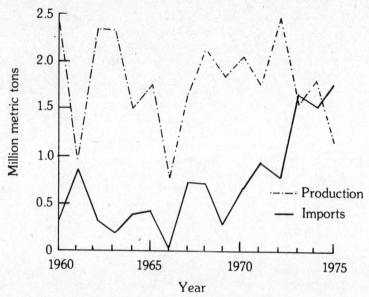

Figure 2.4. Algeria: production and imports of all grains, 1960 to 1975 (2).

the world's exportable food supplies are very steep and abrupt, and they come at a time when there is little slack in the world farm economy.

Green Revolution Countries: Population Overrunning Technology

The so-called Green Revolution countries deserve special attention. The mid 1960's witnessed the launching of a remarkable effort to expand food production in the food-deficit poor countries, an effort centered around the development and international dissemination of high-yielding dwarf wheats and rices. Highly responsive to fertilizer, these new strains were capable of doubling yields of indigenous varieties if managed properly.

Coming at a time when per capita food production in the developing world was declining and requests for food aid were beginning to pour in, the Green Revolution was heralded as an exciting advance. India doubled its wheat crop in a six-year period, a feat unmatched by any major country in history. Mexico, the Philippines, Pakistan, and Turkey all increased cereal production dramatically.

The Green Revolution enabled many countries to cut back grain imports and some to become exporters. India, riding the crest of the Green Revolution, was on the verge of cereal self-sufficiency in the early 1970's. Mexico exported 10 percent of its grain crop between 1965 and 1969, but the production gains were overwhelmed by one of the world's fastest population growth rates (Fig. 2.5).

By the mid-1970's, Mexico was importing one-fifth of its grain needs. The Green Revolution enabled the Philippines to end a half century of dependence on imported rice and to become a net exporter of rice during the late 1960's. Today it is again importing rice on a large scale. The advances made in these countries were being eaten up by the relentless growth in population.

During the early years of the Green Revolution many of those involved in launching it, including Norman Borlaug, the originator of the dwarf wheats, and

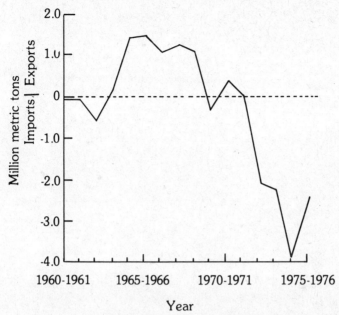

Figure 2.5. Mexico: net grain trade, 1960 to 1976 (2).

myself, cautioned that the new seeds should not be viewed as a solution to the food problem. The only ultimate solution to the food problem in these countries was to put the brakes on population growth. The new seeds were simply buying time, perhaps another 15 to 20 years, to get population growth under control. Half of that time has now passed. Although there has been some progress in family planning, the above data indicate that it is not nearly enough, and that time will not be bought so cheaply again.

A Disturbing Reversal

One of the most disturbing trends in the world food economy during the 1970's has been the downturn in grain output per hectare (Fig. 2.6). This new trend shows up in recent U.S. Department of Agriculture data on all grains except rice, for which reliable yield data are not yet available. If the average world grain yield during the period from 1960 to 1975 is plotted as a three-year sliding average in order to smooth out the fluctuations associated with weather, a disturbing trend emerges. From 1960 until 1972 this three-year average increased each year, but then in 1973 it turned downward, dropping further in 1974 and still further in 1975. At its peak in 1972, the average grain yield per hectare was 1.91 metric tons, but over the next three years it dropped to 1.84 metric tons, a decline of 4 percent.

Aside from weather, which may have been a major factor, there are at least five other factors which may have contributed to this downturn in world grain yields per acre: (i) the release for production of the 50 million acres of U.S. idled cropland, most of it below average fertility; (ii) the high cost and tight supply of energy; (iii) the high cost and tight supply of fertilizer; (iv) the shortening of the slash-and-burn cycle in some densely populated areas thus preventing soil regeneration; and (v) the increasing use of animal dung as fuel rather than as fertilizer.

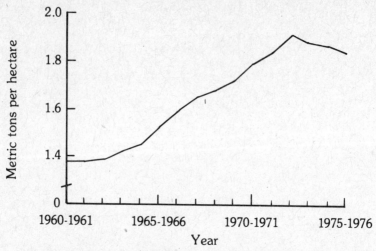

Figure 2.6. World grain yield per hectare, 1960 to 1976 (2) (excludes rice; plotted as three-year sliding averages).

Assessing Future Food Prospects

The conditions under which the world's farmers and fishermen will attempt to expand food output during the final quarter of this century are quite different from those prevailing during most of the quarter century just ending. In most respects it will be more difficult to increase food production than it was in the past. None of the basic resources required to expand food output—land, water, energy, fertilizer— could be considered abundant today. The enormous growth of both economic and agricultural output during the second quarter of this century depended largely on a seemingly boundless supply of cheap energy. There is no prospect of a return to cheap energy in the foreseeable future.

Expanding the cultivated land area is also becoming more difficult and costly. Indeed, in some countries, the area under cultivation is actually declining as a result of desert encroachment, soil erosion, or urban sprawl. There are only a few places in the world where fertile new land awaits the plow: the Republic of Sudan, the tsetse fly belt in sub-Saharan Africa (assuming the tsetse fly can be eradicated), and parts of the interior of Latin America.

Scarce though new land is, the lack of water may be the principal constraint for future efforts to expand world food output. From 1950 to 1970 there was a great expansion in irrigated areas as large new irrigation projects were undertaken in China, India, and numerous other developing countries. The total irrigated area was expanding by nearly 3 percent per year, but the annual increase from now until the end of the century will be scarcely 1 percent since most of the choice dam sites have already been exploited.

The real cost of fertilizer, particularly widely used nitrogen fertilizer, declined substantially throughout most of the period since World War II. Cheap fertilizer played a major role in the impressive expansion of food production in the industrial countries of North America, Europe, and Japan, but because the cost of fertilizer is closely tied to the cost of energy, we cannot expect a return to cheap fertilizer.

At mid-century the world fishing industry was brimming with optimism. Seemingly inexhaustible supplies of fish could be netted as fast as fishing technologies improved and capital investment expanded. This optimism was well founded. The world fish catch expanded from 22 million tons in 1950 to 70 million in 1970. Then suddenly, with little warning, the world fish catch declined for two consecutive years, at least partly as a result of overfishing. An increasingly common phenomenon, overfishing now affects oceanic fisheries as widely separated as the haddock fishery in the North Atlantic and anchovy fishery in the South Pacific (1). Some marine biologists think the world catch of table-grade fish may be approaching its maximum sustainable limit. Others envision brighter prospects, but not even the most hopeful foresee future gains even remotely approaching those of the past 25 years.

In a number of oceanic fisheries, efforts to expand the catch further have led to overfishing, depletion of stocks, and an actual decline in catch. Additional investment in fishing capacity for many fisheries today brings not merely a diminishing return per unit of investment, but an actual negative return. What is not yet widely realized is that a similar predicament may engulf agriculture in parts of the world where population pressure is building. Extending food production onto marginal land is already leading to overgrazing, deforestation, desert expansion, soil erosion, silting of irrigation reservoirs, and increased flooding (8).

In some developing countries, these negative forces may soon override the drive to step up food output by means of additional capital investment and technological innovation. We may witness in the not too distant future sustained absolute declines in national food production in some developing countries, namely those with the most rapid population growth, because of these ecological stresses. This backsliding will be without precedent in the modern world and, I dare say, our success in anticipating such a reversal may not be any greater than our success in anticipating the declining catch in some of the major oceanic fisheries.

In the industrial countries, diminishing returns on key agricultural inputs such as fertilizer and energy may severely constrain efforts to expand food output rapidly. In the early 1950's, each additional pound of fertilizer in the American corn belt raised corn yields by 15 to 20 pounds. Today an additional pound of fertilizer applied in the same cornfield may yield only an additional 5 pounds of grain. The use of chemical fertilizer has not yet reached the saturation point in any of the industrial countries, but for some the point may not be far off. By contrast the production response to fertilizer in the developing countries, where usage rates are low, is still quite high.

Summary

The scarcity of the basic resources required to expand food output, the negative ecological trends that are gaining momentum year by year in the poor countries, and the diminishing returns on the use of energy and fertilizer in agriculture in the industrial countries lead me to conclude that a world of cheap, abundant food with surplus stocks and a large reserve of idled cropland may now be history. In the future, scarcity may be more or less persistent, relieved only by sporadic surpluses, of a local and short-lived nature. The prospects are that dependence on North America will be likely to continue to increase, the increase probably being limited only by the region's export capacity.

Notes

1. L.R. Brown and E.P. Eckholm, *By Bread Alone* (Praeger, New York, 1974).
2. U.S. Department of Agriculture, Foreign Agricultural Service Grain Division, R & D computer printout of 14 July 1975. This printout contains country-by-country figures for the 1960 to 1975 period on area harvested, yields, beginning stocks, total production, imports,

exports, feed consumption, and total consumption of wheat and coarse grains (barley, corn, rye, oats, sorghum).

3. United Nations Food and Agricultural Organization, *Production Yearbook* (Food and Agriculture Organization, Rome, 1960).

4. U.S. Department of Agriculture, Foreign Agricultural Service, *Foreign Agriculture Circular FLM-7-75—Livestock and Meat* (U.S. Department of Agriculture, Washington, D.C., 1975).

5. C.F. Marbut and C.V. Manifold, "The soils of the Amazon Basin in relation to agricultural possibilities," *Geographical Review* 16, No.3(1926).

6. H.S. Steiner, "Maghreb grain crops decline—Import needs on the rise," *U.S. Dep. Agric., Foreign Agriculture* 13(42), 2(1975).

7. J.D. Parker, Jr., "Rapid growth continues in U.S. farm exports to Iraq," *ibid.* 13(15), 2(1975).

8. E.P. Eckholm, *Losing Ground: Environmental Stress and World Food Prospects* (Norton, New York, in press).

3

Food First

Frances Moore Lappé
and Joseph Collins

Frances Moore Lappé, who is perhaps best known for her earlier work *Diet for a Small Planet* (New York: Ballantine Books. 1971), and Joseph Collins, who had worked previously on *Global Reach* (edited by Richard J. Barnet and Ronald E. Muller. New York: Simon & Schuster. 1974), a book on multinational corporations, are the co-founders of the Institute For Food and Development Policy (San Francisco, California). Lappé has formally chronicled her "journey" from a concern about the "scarcity" of world food supplies (as discussed by Lester Brown in Chapter 2) and inefficiencies in livestock protein conversion to disclosing the "myths" about hunger and developing a set of "food first principles." Lappé and Collins' arguments contrast sharply with those of Lester Brown. The authors maintain that hunger is due neither to food or land scarcity nor overpopulation. Rather, the structure of production is to blame. (The reader is referred to pp. 7-29 and 99-117 of *Food First* for further discussion, and is encouraged to read the text in its entirety.)

For the last several years we have struggled to answer the question "why hunger?" Analyses that call for more aid or for reducing our consumption so that the hungry might eat left us with gnawing doubts.

Here we want to share the six myths that kept us locked into a misunderstanding of the problem as well as the alternative view that emerged once we began to grasp the issues. Our hope is to help anchor the hunger movement with an unequivocal and cogent analysis. Only then will our collective potential no longer be dissipated.

Myth One: People are hungry because of scarcity—both of food and agricultural land.

Can scarcity seriously be considered the cause of hunger when even in the worst years of famine in the early 70's there was plenty to go around—enough in grain alone to provide everyone in the world with 3000 to 4000 calories a day, not counting all the beans, root crops, fruits, nuts, vegetables, and non-grain-fed meat?

And what of land scarcity?

We looked at the most crowded countries in the world to see if we could find a correlation between land density and hunger. We could not. Bangladesh, for example, has just half the people per cultivated acre that Taiwan has. Yet Taiwan has no starvation while Bangladesh is thought of as the world's worst basketcase. China has twice as many people for each cultivated acre as India. Yet in China people are not hungry.

Finally, when the pattern of *what* is grown sank in, we simply could no longer subscribe to a "scarcity" diagnosis of hunger. In Central America and in the Caribbean, where as much as 70 percent of the children are undernourished, at least half of the agricultural land, and the best land at that, grows crops for export, not food for the local people. In the Sahelian countries [of] Sub-Saharan Africa, exports of cotton and peanuts in the early 1970's actually *increased* as drought and hunger loomed.

Next we asked: What solution emerges when the problem of hunger is defined as scarcity?

Most commonly, people see greater production as the answer. So techniques to increase production become the central focus: supplying the "modern" inputs—large scale irrigation, chemical fertilization, pesticides, machinery and the seeds dependent on these other outputs. All of this is designed to make the land produce more. But when a new agricultural technology enters a system shot through with power inequalities, it brings greater profit only to those who already have some combination of land, money, credit "worthiness" and political influence. This alone has barred most of the world's rural population and all the world's hungry from the benefits of 'producing more.'

More Production, More Hunger

Once agriculture is viewed as a growth industry in which the control of the basic inputs guarantees big money, a catastrophic chain of events is set into motion. Competition for land sends land values soaring (land values have jumped three to five times in the "Green Revolution" areas of India). Higher rents force tenants and sharecroppers into the ranks of the landless. With the new profits the powerful buy out small farmers who have gone bankrupt (in part through having been forced to double or triple their indebtedness trying to partake of the new technology). Moreover, faced with a short planting and harvest time for vast acreages planted uniformly with the most profitable crop, large commercial growers mechanize to avoid the troublesome mobilization of human labor. Those made landless by the production focus, finding ever fewer agricultural jobs, join an equally hopeless search for work in urban slums.

Fewer and fewer people gain control over more and more land. In Sonora, Mexico, the average farm before the Green Revolution was 400 acres. After 20 years of publicly funded modernization, the average has climbed to 2000 acres with some holdings running as large as 25,000 acres.

The poor pay the price. Total production per capita may be up yet so are the numbers who face hunger. A strategy to solve hunger by increasing production has led directly to increased inequality, in fact to the absolute decline in the welfare of the majority. A study now being completed by the ILO shows that in the very South Asian countries—Pakistan, India, Thailand, Malaysia, Philippines and Indonesia—where the focus has been on production and where the GNP has risen, the majority of the rural population are worse off than before.

But if the scarcity diagnosis, with the implied solution of increasing production, by technical inputs, has taken us not forward but backward, what is the right diagnosis?

We could answer that question only after our research at IFDP led us to conclude that there is *no* country without sufficient agricultural resources for the people to feed themselves and then some. And if they are not doing so, you can be sure there are powerful obstacles in the way. The prime obstacle is not, however, inadequate production to be overcome by technical inputs. The obstacle is that the people do not control the productive resources. When control is in the hands of the producers, people will no longer appear as liabilities—as a drain on resources. People are potentially a country's most under-utilized resource and most valuable capital. People who know they are working for themselves will not only make the land produce but through their labor make it ever more productive.

Myth Two: A hungry world simply cannot afford the luxury of justice for the small farmer.

We are made to believe that, if we want to eat, we had better rely on the large landowners. Thus governments, international lending agencies and foreign assistance programs have passed over the small producers, believing that concentrating on the large holders was the quickest road to production gains. A study of 83 countries, revealing that just over 3 percent of the land holders control about 80 percent of the farmland; gave us some idea of how many of the world's farmers would be excluded by such a concentration.

Yet a study of Argentina, Brazil, Chile, Colombia, Ecuador and Guatemala found the small farmer to be three to fourteen times more productive per acre than the larger farmer. In Thailand plots of two to four acres yield almost 60 percent more rice per acre than farms of 140 acres or more. Other proof that justice for the small farmer increases production comes from the experience of countries in which the redistribution of land and other basic agricultural resources like water has resulted in rapid growth in agricultural production: Japan, Taiwan, and China stand out.

But where has the grip of this myth led? As the large holders are reinforced, often with public subsidies, the small holders and laborers have been cut out of production through the twin process of increasing land concentration and mechanization. *To be cut out of production is to be cut out of consumption.*

Flowers not Food

As fewer and fewer have the wherewithal either to grow food or to buy food, the internal market for food stagnates or even shrinks. But large commercial farmers have not worried. They orient their production to high-paying markets—a few strata of urban dwellers and foreign consumers. Farmers in Sinaloa, Mexico, find they can make 20 times more growing tomatoes for Americans than corn for Mexicans. Development funds have irrigated the desert in Senegal so that multinational firms can grow eggplant and mangoes for air freighting to Europe's best tables. Colombian landholders shift from wheat to carnations that bring 80 times greater return per acre. In Costa Rica the lucrative export beef business expands as the local consumption of meat and dairy products declines. Throughout the non-socialist countries we find a consistent pattern. Agriculture, once the livelihood for millions of self-provisioning farmers, is being turned into the production site of high-value non-essentials for the minority who can pay.

Moreover, entrusting agricultural production to the large farmers means invariably the loss of productive reinvestment in agriculture. Commonly profits of the large holders that might have gone to improve the land are spent instead on conspicuous consumption, investment in urban consumer industries or job-destroying mechanization. The control of the land by large holders for whom the land is not the basis of daily sustenance often means its underutilization. In Colombia, for example, the largest land owners control 70 percent of all agricultural land but actually cultivate only 6 percent.

It is not enough simply to deflate the myth that justice and production are incompatible. We must come to see clearly that the only solution to hunger is a conscious plan to reduce inequality at every level. The reality is that not only will the re-distribution of control of agricultural resources boost production but it is the only guarantee that today's hungry—the rural poor and the urban refugees—will eat.

Myth Three: We are now faced with a sad trade-off. A needed increase in food production can come only at the expense of the ecological integrity of our food base. Farming must be pushed onto marginal lands at the risk of irreparable erosion. And the use of pesticides will have to be increased even if the risk is great.

Is the need for food for a growing population the real pressure forcing people to farm lands that are easily destroyed?

Haiti offers a shocking picture of environmental destruction. The majority of the utterly impoverished peasants ravage the once-green mountain slopes in near-futile efforts to grow food to survive. Has food production for Haitians used up every easily cultivated acre so that only the mountain slopes are left? No. These mountain peasants must be seen as exiles from their birthright—some of the world's richest agricultural land. The rich valley lands belong to a handful of elites, who seek dollars in order to live an imported lifestyle, and to their American partners. These lands are thus made to produce largely low-nutrition and feed crops (sugar, coffee, cocoa, alfalfa for cattle) and exclusively for export. Grazing land is export oriented too. Recently, U.S. firms began to fly Texas cattle into Haiti for grazing and re-export to American franchised hamburger restaurants.

A World Bank study of Colombia states that "large numbers of farm families . . . try to eke out an existence on too little land, often on slopes of 45 degrees or more. As a result, they exploit the land very severely, adding to erosion and other problems, and even so are not able to make a decent living." Overpopulation? No. Colombia's good level land is in the hands of absentee landlords who use it to graze cattle, raise animal feed and even flowers for export to the United States ($18 million worth in 1975).

During the Sahelian drought media coverage highlighted over-grazing as a cause of the encroachment of the desert. Too much demand for meat? No. Suppressed FAO reports show that, while more than enough grain for everyone in the Sahel was produced during the drought, much of it was hoarded for speculation. Nomads found that one month they could exchange one head of cattle for four bags of millet while the next month one head was "worth" only a single bag of millet. One reason, therefore, the pastoralists tried to increase their herds was to survive in a food speculation economy. The tragedy was that everyone trying to have a herd large enough to survive resulted in the destruction of the means by which anyone could have any herd at all.

The Amazon is being rapidly deforested. Is it the pressure of Brazil's exploding population? Brazil's ratio of cultivatable land to people (and that excludes the Amazon Forest) is slightly better than that of the United States. The Amazon Forest is being destroyed not because of a shortage of farm land but because the military government refuses to break up the large estates that take up over 43 percent of the country's farmland. Instead the landless are offered the promise of future new frontiers in the Amazon basin even though most experts feel the tropical forest is not suited to permanent cropping. In addition, multinational corporations like Anderson Clayton, Goodyear, Volkswagen, Nestle, Liquigas, Borden, Mitsubishi and multibillionaire Daniel Ludwig's Universe Tank Ship Co. can get massive government subsidies to turn the Amazon into a major supplier of beef to Europe, the U.S. and Japan.

It is not, then, people's food needs that threaten to destroy the environment by other forces: land monopolizers that export non-food and luxury crops forcing the rural majority to abuse marginal lands; colonial patterns of cash cropping that continue today; hoarding and speculation on food; and irresponsible profitseeking by both local and foreign elites. Cutting the number of the hungry in half tomorrow would not stop any of these forces.

The Real Pests

Still we found ourselves wondering whether people's legitimate need to grow food might not require injecting even more pesticides into our environment. In the emergency push to grow more food, won't we have to accept some level of damage from deadly chemicals?

First, just how pesticide-dependent is the world's current food production? In the U.S. about 1.2 billion pounds, a whopping six pounds for every American and 30 percent of the world's total, are dumped into the environment every year. Surely, we thought, such a staggering figure means that practically every acre of the nation's farmland is dosed with deadly poisons. U.S. food abundance therefore, appeared to us as the plus that comes from such a big minus. The facts, however, proved us wrong.

Fact one: Nearly half the pesticides are used not by farmland but by golf courses, parks and lawns.

Fact two: Only about 10 percent of the nation's cropland is treated with insecticides, 30 percent with weedkillers and less than 1 percent with fungicides (the figures are halved if pastureland is included).

Fact three: Non-food crops account for over half of all insecticides used in U.S. agriculture. (Cotton alone received almost half of all insecticides used. Yet half of the total cotton acreage receives no insecticides at all.)

Fact four: The U.S. Department of Agriculture estimates that, even if all pesticides were eliminated, crop loss due to pests (insects, pathogens, weeds, mammals and birds) would rise only about seven percentage points, from 33.6 percent to 40.7 percent.

Fact five: Numerous studies show that where pesticides are used with ever greater intensity crop losses due to pests are frequently *increasing*.

What about the underdeveloped countries? Do pesticides there help produce food for hungry people?

In underdeveloped countries most pesticides are used for export crops, principally cotton, and to a lesser extent fruits and vegetables grown under plantation conditions for export. In effect, then, these enclaves of pesticide use in the underdeveloped world function as mere extensions of the agricultural systems of the industrialized countries. The quantities of pesticides injected into the world's environment have very little to do with the hungry's food needs.

The alternatives to chemical pesticides—crop rotation, mixed cropping, mulching, hand weeding, hoeing, collection of pest eggs, manipulation of natural predators, and so on are numerous and proven effective. In China, for example, pesticide use can be minimized because of a nationwide early warning system. In Shao-tung county in Honan Province, 10,000 youths make up watch teams that patrol the fields and report any sign of pathogenic change. Appropriately called the "barefoot doctors of agriculture," they have succeeded in reducing the damage of wheat rust and rice borer to less than 1 percent and have the locust invasions under control. But none of these safe techniques for pest control will be explored as long as the problem is in the hands of profit-oriented corporations. The alternatives require human involvement and the motivation of farmers who have the security of individual or collective tenure over the land they work.

Myth Four: Hunger is a contest between the Rich World and the Poor World.

Rather than seeing vertical stratified societies with hunger at the lower rungs in both so-called developed and underdeveloped countries, terms like "hungry world" and "poor world" make us think of uniformly hungry masses. Hunger becomes a place—and usually a place over there. Rather than being the result of a social process, hunger becomes a static fact, a geographic given.

Worse still, the all-inclusiveness of these labels leads us to assume that everyone living in a "hungry country" has a common interest in eliminating hunger. Thus we look at an underdeveloped country and assume its government officials represent the hungry majority. Well-meaning sympathizers in the industrialized countries then believe that concessions, to these governments, e.g. preference schemes or increased foreign investment, represent progress for the hungry when in fact the "progress" may be only for the elites and their partners—the multinational corporations.

Moreover, the "rich world" versus "poor world" scenario makes the hungry appear as a threat to the material well-being of the majority in the metropolitan countries. To average Americans or Europeans the hungry become the enemy who, in the words of Lyndon Johnson, "want what we got." In truth, however, hunger will never be addressed until the average citizen in the metropolitan countries can see that the hungry abroad are their allies, not their enemies.

The Grip of Agribusiness

What are the links between the plight of the average citizen in the metropolitan countries and the poor majority in the underdeveloped countries? There are many. One example is multinational agribusiness shifting production of luxury items— fresh vegetables, fruits, flowers and meat—out of the industrial countries in search of cheap land and labor in the underdeveloped countries. The result? Farmers and workers in the metropolitan countries lose their jobs while agricultural resources in the underdeveloped countries are increasingly diverted away from food for local people. The food supply of those in the metropolitan countries is being made dependent on the active maintenance of political and economic structures that block hungry people from growing food for themselves.

Nor should we conclude that consumers in the metropolitan countries at least get cheaper food. Are Ralston Purina's and Green Giant's mushrooms grown in Korea and Taiwan cheaper than those produced stateside? Not one cent, according to a U.S. government study. Del Monte and Dole Philippine pineapples actually cost the U.S. consumers more than those produced by a small company in Hawaii.

The common threat is the worldwide tightening control of wealth and power over the most basic human need, food. Multinational agribusiness firms right now are creating a single world agricultural system in which they exercise integrated control over all stages of production from farm to consumer. Once achieved, they will be able to effectively manipulate supply and prices for the first time on a world wide basis through well-established monopoly practices. As farmers, workers and consumers, people everywhere already are beginning to experience the cost in terms of food availability, prices and quality.

Myth Five: An underdeveloped country's best hope for development is to export those crops in which it has a natural advantage and use the earnings to import food and industrial goods.

There is nothing "natural" about the underdeveloped countries concentration on a few, largely low-nutrition crops. The same land that grows cocoa, coffee, rubber, tea and sugar could grow an incredible diversity of nutritious crops—grains, high-protein legumes, vegetables and fruits.

Nor is there any advantage. Reliance on a limited number of crops generates economic as well as political vulnerability. Extreme price fluctuations associated with tropical crops combine with the slow-maturing nature of plants themselves (many, for example, take two to ten years before the first harvest) to make development planning impossible.

Often-quoted illustrations showing how much more coffee or bananas it takes to buy one tractor today than 20 years ago have indeed helped us appreciate that the value of agricultural exports have simply not kept pace with the inflating price of imported manufactured goods. But even if one considers only agricultural trade, the underdeveloped countries still come out the clear losers. Between 1961 and 1972 half of the industrialized countries increased their earnings from agricultural exports by 10 percent each year. By contrast, at least 18 underdeveloped countries are earning less from their agricultural exports than they did in 1961.

Another catch in the natural advantage theory is that the people who need food are not the same people who benefit from foreign exchange earned by agricultural exports. Even when part of the foreign earnings is used to import food, the food is not basic staples but items geared toward the eating habits of the better-off urban classes. In Senegal the choice land is used to grow peanuts and vegetables for export to Europe. Much of the foreign exchange earned is spent to import wheat for foreign-owned bakeries that turn out European-style bread for the urban dwellers. The country's rural majority goes hungry, deprived of land they need to grow millet and other traditional grains for themselves and local markets.

The very success of export agriculture can further undermine the position of the poor. When commodity prices go up, small self-provisioning farmers may be pushed off the land by cash crop producers seeking to profit on the higher commodity prices. Moreover, governments in underdeveloped countries, opting for a development track dependent on promoting agricultural exports, may actively suppress social reform. Minimum wage laws for agricultural laborers are not enacted, for example, because they might make the country's exports uncompetitive. Governments have been only too willing to exempt plantations from land reform in order to encourage their export production.

Finally, export-oriented agricultural operations invariably import capital-intensive technologies to maximize yields as well as to meet product and processing specifications. Relying on imported technologies then makes it likely that the production will be used to pay the bill—a vicious circle of dependency.

Land for Food

Just as export-oriented agriculture spells the divorce of agriculture and nutrition, food first policies would make the central question: How can this land best feed people? As obvious as it may seem, this policy of basing land use on nutritional output is practiced in only a few countries today; more commonly, commercial farmer and national planners make hit-and-miss calculations of which crop might have a few cents edge on the world market months or even years hence. With food first policies industrial crops (like cotton and rubber) and feed crops would be planted only after the people meet their basic needs. Livestock would not compete with people but graze on marginal lands or, like China's 240 million pigs, recycle farm and household wastes while producing fertilizer at the same time.

In most underdeveloped countries the rural population contributes much more to the national income than it receives. With food first policies agricultural development would be measured in the welfare of the people, not in export income. Priority would go to de-centralized industry at the service of labor-intensive agriculture. A commitment to food self-reliance would close the gap between rural and urban well-being, making the countryside a good place to live. Urban dwellers, too, like those volunteering to grow vegetables in Cuba's urban "green belts," would move toward self-reliance.

Food self-reliance is not isolationist. But trade would be seen, not as the one desperate hinge on which survival hangs, but as a way to widen choices once the basic needs have been met.

Myth Six: Hunger should be overcome by redistributing food.

Over and over again we hear that North America is the world's last remaining breadbasket. Food security is invariably measured in terms of reserves held by the metropolitan countries. We are made to feel the burden of feeding the world is squarely on us. Our overconsumption is tirelessly contrasted with the deprivation elsewhere with the implicit message being that we cause their hunger. No wonder that North Americans and Europeans feel burdened and thus resentful. "What did we do to cause their hunger?" they rightfully ask.

The problem lies in seeing redistribution as the solution to hunger. We have come to a different understanding. Distribution of food is but a reflection of the control of the resources that produce food. Who controls the land determines who can grow food, what is grown and where it goes. Who can grow: a few or all who need to? What is grown: luxury non-food or basic staples? Where does it go: to the hungry or the world's well-fed?

Thus redistribution programs like food aid or food stamps will never solve the problem of hunger. Instead we must face up to the real question: How can people everywhere begin to democratize the control of food resources?

Six Food First Principles

We can now counter these six myths with six positive principles that could ground a coherent and vital movement:
1. There is no country in the world in which the people could not feed themselves from their own resources. But hunger can only be overcome by the transformation of social relationships and is only made worse by the narrow focus on technical inputs to increase production.
2. Inequality is the greatest stumbling block to development.
3. Safeguarding the world's agricultural environment and people feeding themselves are complementary goals.
4. Our food security is not threatened by the hungry masses but by elites that span all capitalist economies profiting by the concentration and internationalization of control of food resources.

5. Agriculture must not be used as the means to export income but as the way for people to produce food first for themselves.

6. Escape from hunger comes not through the redistribution of food but through the redistribution of control over food-producing resources.

What would an international campaign look like that took these truths to be self-evident?

If we begin with the knowledge that people can and will feed themselves if allowed to so, the question for all of us living in the metropolitan countries is not "What can we do for them" but "How can we remove the obstacles in the way of people taking control of the production process and feeding themselves?"

Since some of the key obstacles are being built with our taxes, in our name, and by corporations based in our economies, our task is very clear:

Stop any economic aid—government, multilateral or voluntary—that reinforces the use of land for export crops. Stop support for agribusiness penetration into food economies abroad through tax incentives and from governments and multilateral lending agencies. Stop military and counter-insurgency assistance to any underdeveloped country; more often than not it goes to oppose the changes necessary for food self-reliance.

Work to build a more self-reliant food economy at home so that we become even less dependent on importing food from hungry people. Work for land reform at home. Support worker-managed producers, and distributors to counter the increasing concentration of control over our food resources.

Educate, showing the connections between the way government and corporate power works against the hungry abroad and the way it works against the food interests of the vast majority of people in the industrial countries.

Counter despair. Publicize the fact that 40 percent of all people living in underdeveloped countries live where hunger has been eliminated through common struggle. Learn and communicate the efforts of newly liberated countries in Africa and Asia to reconstruct their agriculture along the principles of food first self-reliance.

Most fundamentally, we all must recognize that we are not a "hunger" movement. Rather we all can become moulders of the future who have chosen to seize this historical moment. We have chosen to use the visible tragedy of hunger to reveal the utter failure of our current economic system to meet human needs.

4

On Scholarship, Hunger, and Power
Susan George

In this excerpt from her foreword to Nicole Ball's bibliography, *World Hunger: A Guide to the Economic and Political Dimensions* (Santa Barbara: ABC-Clio, Inc. 1981), Susan George presents three models of development. (For an in-depth treatment of rival theoretical frameworks in which to understand development problems, see *Rural Development: Theories of Peasant Economy and Agrarian Change*, edited by John Harriss [London: Hutchinson University Library for Africa. 1982].) As discussed by Lappé and Collins (see Chapter 3), George also argues that self-reliance is the key word in development. Basic needs must be satisfied; people must participate in their economy's development. They must not only participate, they must be in control of their resource base.

Knowledge costs money, and money is not thrown away by those who dispose of it. It is no accident that our libraries are filled with studies on the hungry and poverty-stricken of the Third World. Cynically but realistically put, the more one knows about those who may, in desperation, become restive and dangerous, the better tools one possesses for keeping them in check.

Scholarship may also, wittingly or unwittingly, serve purely commercial interests. One fears, for instance, that the current vogue for studying "appropriate technology" may become a vehicle for introducing new dependency-creating products in societies where incomes are inadequate for the purchase of expensive high-technology goods, but which can contribute to Western corporate interests at their own level.

Social scientists can also function as promoters of particular ideologies and help to create a climate in which development strategies devised by the powerful may be pursued without hindrance or criticism. Intellectuals, as Noam Chomsky has put it, are "experts in legitimation" and in packaging concepts so that they will sell, even if the wrappings conceal shoddy and adulterated merchandise.

There are basically three paradigms or models in the literature of development and hunger alleviation. The first is the "growth/trickle-down" model, which seeks the increase of gross national product through industrialization and by concentrating on those elements of society supposedly most "modern" or "entrepreneurial" (poor peasants, in contrast, are "backward" or "traditional," although it is no longer

Reprinted from the Community Nutrition Institute 12(26):4-5 (1 July 1982) by permission of ABC-Clio, Inc. Copyright 1981 by ABC-Clio, Inc.

considered fashionable to say so). The accumulated wealth of these "modernizing elites" will, eventually, also benefit the worse-off.

This model encourages the import of foreign capital and technology (as well as the implantation of transnational corporations) and assumes that the development process in the Third World should be imitative of the one that occurred in the now industrialized western countries. Economic and social control is concentrated in the hands of the classes which act as motors of growth.

This paradigm presupposes harmony: harmony at the national level (the elites will somehow want to share their advantages with their poorer compatriots, toward whom their attitude is essentially benevolent); harmony at the international level, also called "interdependence" (the present world system is beneficial to all nations which should trade according to the principles of "comparative advantage").

Due to its generally recognized failure, this first model has lately been perceived as badly in need of a facelift. This has been undertaken but is largely rhetorical. New keywords are *basic needs* and *participation*, but as defined by experts, mostly from developed countries. Deprived people are neither to be consulted as to their needs nor allowed to participate to the degree that they might demand fundamental changes in existing patterns of income or power distribution.

Dependency Theory

The second model is based on "dependency theory" which holds that there is a center (the rich countries, with the U.S. as the center of the center) and a periphery (the Third World); and that the former has consistently exploited the latter since colonial times. The goal of development is thus to correct this historic and ongoing imbalance through the use of measures summed up in the New International Economic Order (NIEO) strategy; fair and stable prices for Third World raw materials, free access to Northern markets for industrial goods, state control over transnational corporations' practices, alleviation of debt, etc.

This model also rests on an assumption of global interdependence, but stresses that serious adjustments will have to be made in the world system so that all nations can benefit and achieve that mutuality of interests which does not yet exist. This is the stance from which nearly all Third World governments (the so-called Group of 77) argue in international negotiations.

The third model does not deny the need for an NIEO, but tries to enrich this concept with a class analysis. The world is not merely divided into rich/powerful and poor/relatively powerless nations: all countries, including the rich ones, are characterized by a dominating and a dominated class (each, of course, with its own subdivisions). The NIEO is an incomplete solution to the problems of hunger and underdevelopment because nothing guarantees that increased national revenues will benefit the poor more than marginally.

In the third model, the goal of development is not merely greater equality between states, but the decent livelihood and dignity of all human beings. Unlike the first model, this approach assumes not harmony but conflict. Third World elites will not give up their privileges without a struggle and will meanwhile prevent any substantial advantages from trickling down. Rich nations will continue to exploit poor ones, but industrialized country elites will also support their Third World counterparts so that this exploitation may more conveniently continue.

Three Propositions

People who work and write from the third model are convinced (frequently from field experience in underdeveloped countries) of the logic of the following propositions:

1. Development (strategies, projects, innovations, etc.) which benefits the least favored classes or nations will not be acceptable to the dominant classes or nations unless their interests are also adequately served.

2. Development (. . .) which benefits only the poor will be ignored, sabotaged, or otherwise suppressed by the powerful.

3. Development (. . .) which serves the interests of the elites while doing positive harm to the poor will still be put into practice and if necessary maintained by violence so long as no basic change in the balance of social and political forces takes place.

Advocates of the third model see hope for the Third World not in the greater integration of the less developed countries into the world system but in their greater independence from it. They call for self-reliance—the full use of all local material and human resources—before asking for outside help, and for a fundamental redistribution of power as the only way to end hunger and misery. *Basic needs*, yes, but as defined by the communities concerned; not so much *participation* as *empowerment*—the capacity to control those decisions which most affect one's life.

Has scholarship anything to contribute to the emergence and the enforcement of the third model (for which my own bias will be obvious)? Development students, researchers, and writers must address the needs of the most deprived and must be accountable for the work they produce. Students who see such accountability as an intellectual and moral imperative can begin by approaching the material listed here with their critical faculties on full alert and by asking the kinds of questions we have sketched here: Is the study part of the "conventional wisdom," or does it try to take an opposing or unpopular point of view? Where does it stand in relation to the above three models, i.e., to power? Does it presume harmony and proceed in a social and political vacuum? Could the work contribute to increasing the knowledge—and thus the manipulative capacity—of national or international elites?

The reader, and especially the writer, should not forget that researchers, too, stand somewhere in the power structure. Their work can be used by the rich against the poor, but, one may also hope, vice versa. Why not turn our sights toward those who hold control, with a view to giving a clearer understanding of their activities to those whose lives they affect? This is often a difficult task, for the well-endowed are less vulnerable to scholarly scrutiny than those who have no choice but to let themselves be studied; we should accept this as a challenge.

The mass of scholarship represents an incalculable number of man/woman hours devoted to examining various aspects of world hunger, and while all of us have been writing, the relative and absolute numbers of hungry and destitute people have vastly increased. It is time we ask ourselves why, as scholars, we are still discussing poverty and want, and apply ourselves to transforming the contents of future bibliographies into explosive devices and instruments of liberation.

5

Malthusians, Marxists, and Missionaries
(excerpts)
Nick Eberstadt

In an earlier work entitled "Food Crisis—Myths that Paralyze Us" (*Washington Star*, 15 February 1976), Eberstadt argued that there is a misinformation network promoting the idea of a "food crisis." Indeed, there are many myths about starvation and hunger that "paralyze us" into inaction. Malnutrition is in fact very difficult to define, let alone diagnose. Nutritional "requirement" is a dynamic concept. Some researchers argue that people can have substandard anthropometry as well as low dietary intake, and not be functionally impaired. (For further discussion, see "The 'Small but Healthy' Hypothesis: An Inquiry into the Meaning and Measurement of Malnutrition" by David Seckler and "Auto-regulatory Homeostatic Nature of Energy Balance" by P.V. Sukhatme and Sheldon Margen in *Newer Concepts in Nutrition and Their Implications for Policy*, P.V. Sukhatme, ed. Pune, India: 127-137, 101-116.) In this recent work, Eberstadt takes both Lester Brown and Susan George to task, while at the same time reinforcing points made in his earlier article. Today, he argues, three ideological positions dominate the post-mid 1970s literature on food and hunger: Malthusian (as represented, for example by Lester Brown in Chapter 2), Marxist (as represented, for example, by Susan George) and Modern Missionary (as represented, for example, by Sterling Wortman and Ralph Cumming in *To Feed This World* [Baltimore: The Johns Hopkins University Press. 1978]). Eberstadt examines the answers to basic questions about world hunger from each of these ideological perspectives presented.

Three ideological positions dominate the new (which is to say, post-food-crisis) literature on food and hunger. The first is the Malthusian. It contends that the world is endangered by growing numbers of people, especially poor people; they are consuming more, and producing more children, than the world's fixed resource base can accommodate. The only way of saving the poor is by regulating them, by forcing them to live "sensibly." The second ideological position is the Marxist. From this perspective, hunger and other forms of human misery are testimony to the unavoidable damage the capitalist system wreaks as the forces of exploitation and class conflict work themselves through. Because misery is set in the very foundations of capitalism, anything less than the overthrow of the system will not get at the heart of the problem. The third position might be called the Modern Missionary. Drawing heavily on Enlightenment thought, it holds that hunger and other forms of misery are largely the result of ignorance and regressive, but correctable, attitudes. Consequently, the best medicine for human suffering is knowledge and the power of reason, especially as embodied in importable packages of applied science or "good government."

Lester Brown's *The Twenty-Ninth Day* has been heavily influenced by Malthusianism; and Susan George's *How the Other Half Dies*, by Marxism; while Sterling Wortman and Ralph Cumming's *To Feed the World* is representative of the Modern Missionary approach. These three books are the best work from each of the different ideological camps. They are full of information, and each makes many important points, yet at critical points, each misinterprets events in a way which suits its specific viewpoint.

The hunger problem can best be analyzed by trying to answer three questions. 1) What is the extent of world hunger, who suffers from it, and how severely? 2) What are the social and ecological causes of various manifestations of hunger? 3) Within the narrow confines of the administratively possible, how could we most effectively use our scarce financial, intellectual, and governmental resources to accelerate the elimination of hunger? By examining the ways in which these books answer these questions, we may not only get a better idea of the limitations which adherence to fixed, ideological viewpoints places on analysts of the hunger problem, but also see the basic parameters of the food and hunger situations more clearly, and thereby, we might hope, be able to help the poor and hungry more effectively.

Extent of Hunger

To attack a social problem effectively, it is necessary to have a good idea of its nature, extent, and severity. If we are attempting to alleviate malnutrition, this means we should want to know as much as we can about the people who suffer from hunger. We must try to learn something about the incidence of hunger by age and sex: what proportion of the hungry are weanlings and small children, pregnant mothers, old people, teenagers, working fathers? We must try to learn where it is the hungry live: what proportions are in Latin America, Africa, and Asia? What proportions live in villages, towns, cities, and suburban slums? We must try to learn how these people try to pay for their food; is it through day labor in the field, odd jobs in the city, tenant farming, begging, or borrowing from relatives? Finally, we must get some idea of how many people are afflicted by hunger of different levels of severity. If by "hungry" we mean all people who experience physical discomfort from lack of food for some portion of the year, how many people would be hungry? How many would be so hungry in the sense that they cannot perform their duties, be it work or housework? How many would be so hungry in the sense that they risk potentially irreversible physical or mental damage for want of food? How many would be so hungry in the sense that they are actually threatened by death? Insisting on having questions such as these answered may seem obfuscatory or even inhumane when perhaps millions of people around the globe are literally starving to death; in point of fact, however, taking the time to address such questions would save many more lives than it would endanger. There are at least two reasons for this.

First, our perception of the hunger problem focuses our efforts; the better we understand the extent and severity of hunger, the more effective our actions against it are likely to be. It is not enough to say, as is the current vogue, that hunger is an income problem, which will be surmounted as the poor become more affluent. Affluence will arrive in the long term; hunger, however, is by its very nature a short-term problem, for people cannot average their appetites over their lifetimes, or even from season to season. The efforts of governments, organizations, and individuals, on the other hand, can make a critical difference in the short run, and are all the more likely to do so if their actions are backed up by useful information. Children will need different sorts of help from old men. Rural and urban hunger cannot be tackled through the same policies. A nation in which five percent of the population, by some definition, is seriously underfed will probably need to use different sorts of development strategies from a nation where the at-risk proportion is fifteen percent.

Second, our perception of the hunger problem affects the vigor of our efforts. Underestimating the severity of malnutrition will encourage half-hearted efforts rather than the major mobilizations which may be necessary. Deliberate and cynical downplaying of the hunger situation in Ethiopia and elsewhere during the early 1970s cost many tens of thousands of helpless and unrepresented people their lives. On the other hand, exaggerating the severity of nutritional problems may cause governments simply to ignore them. Bureaucracies are much more likely to take on problems which they think they have a chance of solving than those which are likely to result in defeat or humiliation, especially when the constituency to be served is weak and helpless.

Important though it may be to quantify the extent and severity of hunger, the authors of these three books make little effort to do so. Lester Brown's only specific comment on the extent and severity of hunger in the poor world is that death rates in Bangladesh and India were abnormally high during the years 1972-74; he takes this as proof that the world, and in particular, the poor, must "accommodate" their demands to the limited bounty which the world can be expected to provide. Brown seems to feel that hunger is to be expected, and that its quantification is therefore irrelevant. Susan George also feels that hunger is to be expected, although for entirely different reasons. Hunger in a world of bounty is proof of the failure of the capitalist system; as a consequence, she *is* looking for numbers, and for big ones. Referring to the World Food Conference position paper, she says, "the UN claims that one of every eight people in the world is literally starving." Not all of these wretches, of course, live in capitalist nations of the Third World; in her view ten to twelve million people are starving or sick from want of food in the United States, the leading capitalist nation. Wortman and Cummings, who are seasoned agricultural experts, are far more knowledgeable about the facts of hunger than either Brown or George. Unfortunately, they choose not to assess the dimensions of the hunger problem. In their entire treatise there is a single mention of the extent of malnutrition, a short reference to a Food and Agriculture Organization (FAO) estimate that in 1970, 462 million people "had an insufficient supply of calories and proteins," of which 94 percent lived in less developed countries. Unlike George, Wortman and Cummings have the integrity to warn us that "the accuracy of such estimates is controversial"; they do not, however, follow up this observation. This figure resulted from a basic failure in approach. FAO estimates were computed by comparing available food supplied against estimated nutritional needs. There is no reason to assume that available food goes to those who need it most, if anything, the evidence is to the contrary. The figure of 462 million, therefore, is actually a meaningless number.

Perhaps one of the reasons that discussions of the extent of hunger seem to be avoided is that hunger itself turns out to be a surprisingly difficult thing to quantify. It comes in many different shades, and those who suffer from its most severe manifestations can be extremely difficult to locate. For example, nutritional experts have returned from China ready to vouch for the Maoist claim that hunger had been eliminated in the People's Republic; a change in political sentiment in the Politburo, however, has let slip the announcement that somewhere between one hundred and two hundred million Chinese are still "hungry." Even in situations where gracious hosts are not inclined to mislead the experts, recognizing a hunger problem is not always easy. During the depth of the Sahelian crisis, for example, Western relief organizations could get no decent estimates of the extent of the human suffering; the figure cited most frequently turned out to be an extrapolation made by a young relief worker based on his experience in a single refugee camp. The magnitude of the problem remained infuriatingly elusive.

The fact that it is difficult, in both conceptual and practical terms, to map out hunger should not deter us from attempting to do so. If we were willing to look for answers, we would find that a number of biometric and socioeconomic indicators already at our disposal, if properly used, could tell us at least something about the nutritional plight of a community or a nation, and a number of other indicators, not in common use today, might help us further.

Among the most frequently used (and the least useful) indices are estimates of food availability per capita. These do not speak to the crucial issue of food distribution; instead, they lump together the diets of the hungry and the well fed. The nutritional status of a people may improve even as the amount of food available to them delines, as seems to have happened in China; conversely, as Susan George rightly points out, an increase in availability may coincide with a deterioration in the diet of the common people, as may have happened, for example, in El Salvador.

Of greater use is the dietary survey, which breaks down food consumption by region, occupation, or income level. When properly conducted, even a small sample can represent accurately the eating patterns of a large population. But it will give us the false impression of the hunger situation unless we remember three things. First, because trained manpower is scarce and expensive, such surveys are conducted as quickly as possible—usually over the course of a week, sometimes only on a single day. This means a tendency to exaggerate the extent of both under- and overnutrition, for at any given point in time one is quite likely to be eating either under or over one's longer term average. (Susan George does not understand this: armed with results from an Indian survey which shows poor people subsisting on 940 calories a day, she wonders how they could stay alive. The answer, of course, is that they probably could not if they were actually living on such meager portions continuously.) Second, the poorer strata eat less not only because of their lower income, but because of lower physical needs. They are making less money because they are doing less work, and as a consequence, they do not need to burn as much fuel. Finally, we must remember that nutritional needs vary: the fact that someone is eating less than the estimated "average" requirement does not necessarily mean he or she is undernourished in any normal population, after all, fifty percent will need less than the average.

A fact that hunger experts often seem to forget is that, at least with respect to nutrition, food is only a *means*: what we are really concerned with is the *end*, which is a strong, healthy body and an active, unimpaired mind. For this reason, anthropometric measures may be more useful than dietary surveys; they would seem to give a clearer impression of the results of food consumption. Even these, unfortunately, are fraught with problems. A typical anthropometric test will mark off a child's height against the "normal" measure for his or her age or weight vis-a-vis height, and if the child's score is significantly lower than the "normal" median, the child will be considered malnourished. But this begs the question: what should the "normal" measure be? As it turns out, "normality" tends to be represented as a typical population drawn from Sweden, Great Britain, or the United States—the countries of the world where children tend to be tallest and heaviest for their age.

Hunger becomes serious at the point that it impairs the normal functioning of the body; as it becomes progressively more serious, it causes enfeeblement, sickness, and finally death. When properly differentiated, mortality statistics can give a stark picture of the hunger situation in any community. Life expectancy figures, infant mortality rates, death rates for children one to four years old, and breakdowns by the apparent causes of death for the poulation at large are all useful in slightly different ways. In assessing the magnitude of a hunger problem from mortality statistics, however, one must remember two things. First, not every death from a hunger-related disease should necessarily be attributed to hunger; gastrointestinal diseases and tuberculosis were killers in the United States in the early part of this century even among the well nourished, and may strike down people in the poor world today who suffer less from lack of food than lack of access to decent medical services. Second, mortality statistics obviously show us only the deadly tip of an iceberg of hunger, if a certain number of people are dying from lack of food, a much larger number are physically threatened by malnutrition. What is necessary is to be able to determine just how many more these may be.

Other methods of determining the location, extent, and severity of hunger could surely be constructed. Hazy, but readily obtainable, indications could be garnered from comparing wage and earnings statistics against prices for food. Such comparisons, unfortunately, are likely to be most difficult and least reliable where hunger is most severe, for a paucity of social information is one of the hallmarks of poverty. Comparative figures on ages at menarche may give an impression of the nutritional plight of populations in a way which is as yet unresearched. The onset of menstruation, it seems, is delayed if the proportion of fat to body weight is low, and hunger clearly lowers this ratio. Figures from Bangladesh indicate that the age of menarche for girls in the cities is about a year and a half lower than for girls in the countryside, though we are not yet in a position to judge just what this difference means in terms of relative nutrition, the implications of this gap are clear. Statistics could presumably be gathered for working populations to show the elasticity of response to an improvement in diet, if a one percent increase in caloric intake led to, say, a two percent increase in physical activity, it would be safe to assume that a worker was getting less to eat than he or she would willingly choose. Other indicators of varying degrees of sophistication could be put together to map out hunger more fully, for hunger is a complex thing, and its incidence probably cannot be captured by any single number.

The point of this digression on hunger statistics is simply to show that our information about malnutrition is based upon a rather limited—indeed, an unduly limited—number of crude, sometimes unreliable, and widely misinterpreted indicators. Not only do we have too little information about, say, the social characteristics of the victims of "chronic" malnutrition, but it is not even clear that we can determine unambiguously, or even satisfactorily, what "chronic" malnutrition is. But even with the few feeble tools currently at our disposal, it is possible to point out two general, but terribly significant, developments in the hunger picture.

First, although Brown, George, and Wortman and Cummings state or imply that the hunger problem is becoming more acute, it is almost certain that this is not so. Death rates, and the incidence of hunger, may have risen tragically during the "food crisis" of the early 1970s; even more tragically, it is virtually certain that this will not be the last such man-made disaster. But social and economic spasms such as this stand essentially as temporary aberrations in a trend which is seeing an ever greater proportion of the world's population decently fed. A lower proportion of the world's total population, in all likelihood, is *desperately* hungry today than at any previous time in history. More food is reaching the poorest strata of poor societies than ever before, in part because of general (though by no means even) growth in the power of productive resources in their hands, in part because of a spreading (though at this point hardly universal) recognition on the part of the world's political elites of some sort of obligation to attempt to improve the material circumstances of their people, and in part because of the emergence of powerful and sophisticated state apparatuses which could make good that obligation (although the growth of state power cuts both ways for the poor and the hungry).

A general improvement in world nutrition is reflected, albeit imperfectly, in the postwar revolution life chances. In 1950 the life expectancy of the less developed countries, excluding China, was something like 40 years; today, it is something like 53 years, nearly a third higher. In the poorest countries of the world, according to the World Bank, life expectancy may have increased by about 20 percent from 1960 to 1977. Not all of this can be passed off as the result of improvements in civil order, medical care, and sanitation; on the contrary, it is rather unlikely that a rise of this magnitude could have occurred without a pronounced concomitant improvement in nutrition. Mortality figures for the most nutritionally vulnerable age group, the 1- to 4-year-olds, would seem to bear this out. By the World Bank's estimate, death rates for this age group in the poorest countries fell by almost half from 1960 to 1977. To be sure, hunger and ill health still stalk the people of the poor world; the 20-year gap in life expectancies between rich and poor peoples of the world is grim testimony to this. The fact that much remains to be done, however, should not blind us to the progress which has been made. In relative terms, and probably in absolute terms as well, the incidence of serious hunger has been declining.

The second important point is that the number of seriously hungry people in the world today is not nearly so large as FAO figures are sometimes used to suggest. Calculations I have made elsewhere, which were based on admittedly scanty data, suggested that the number of critically hungry people in the world—those who might be considered starving—would not be more than 70 million. In light of the new information on hunger in China, this figure should be revised upwards; nonetheless, it would still be well under 100 million. The world's population today is something like 4,200 million; the critically hungry would constitute just over 2 percent of this. We should not conclude from this that critical hunger is a problem small enough to ignore. For starvation to exist at all in our world of abundance is morally unacceptable. What we should realize, however, is that the problem of critical hunger is of manageable proportions. Concerted international action on this front could conceivably eliminate the most horrifying manifestations of hunger in a matter of years (of course, this would leave a great number of hungry people in this world). If instead we insist on promoting inflated figures on world hunger, which for the most part have lost their shock-value, we risk making the problem of controlling critical hunger seem hopelessly large.

Astonishing though it may seem, at the end of the Second Development Decade we still know more about the life rhythms of certain species of insects than about those of our hungriest fellow human beings. Unless this situation changes, interventions on their behalf are likely to continue to be unnecessarily weak and inept. Sadly, there seems to be no indication on the part of our hunger experts, be they

Malthusians, Marxists, or Modern Missionaries, of any conviction that even the most basic questions about the extent and severity of hunger should be pursued. Our experts have already answered these questions for themselves, it seems, and to their own satisfaction. They have also diagnosed the causes of hunger. According to the Malthusians, hunger is caused by the unavoidable scarcity which results from the collision of "excessively" high rates of population growth against a fixed and dwindling resource base. To the Marxist, the cause of hunger is capitalism, whose mechanisms of immiseration deprive the poor of the power to feed themselves. To the Modern Missionaries, it is a combination of population growth, which raises food requirements, and an inability (presumably due to a lack of research and improper government policies) to produce large quantities of food. Each of these competing theories about the real causes of hunger leaves something to be desired.

6

Resources, Population, Environment: An Oversupply of False Bad News

Julian L. Simon

Julian Simon is one of many authors in this volume whose writings are controversial. Like Lappé and Collins (Chapter 3), he exposes popular myths about population and resources. Like Eberstadt (Chapter 5), Simon is concerned about the proliferation of information about population and resources based on flimsy evidence or no evidence at all. Both he and Eberstadt accuse Worldwatch Institute scholars of making sweeping statements based on very little data. Simon refutes most of the popularly held myths about food and population using existing data from "recognized" sources (U.N. Food and Agricultural Organization Production Yearbook, U.S. Environmental Protection Agency, U.S. Geological Survey, etc.). He confronts the ideology of neo-Malthusians Paul Ehrlich (*The Population Bomb*. New York: Ballantine Books. 1968) and Paul and William Paddock (*Famine, 1975*. Boston: Little, Brown and Company. 1967), the "gospel" according to the World Bank and the U.S. Agency for International Development and the models of the Limits-to-Growth group. In doing so, he is often accused of being guilty of the same behavior of which he accuses other researchers: manipulating data and data sources to support biased statements (although he is basing those statements on published data, the sources of which can be verified). Simon discusses at some length the work of Ansley Coale and Edgar Hoover who were responsible in large part for the "population growth in less-developed countries is bad for the world" propaganda which in turn led to questionable population control programs. Lastly, Simon speculates on why the public is constantly exposed to sensational "bad news."

In September 1977 *Newsweek* reported that "more than 100,000 West Africans perished of hunger" in the Sahel between 1968 and 1973 because of drought (1). Upon inquiry, the writer of the account, Peter Gwynne, informed me that the estimate came from Kurt Waldheim's message to the United Nations' Desertification Conference. I therefore wrote to Waldheim asking for the source of the estimate.

Three mutually contradictory documents came back from the United Nations' Public Inquiries Unit: (i) Waldheim's message to the conference, saying, "Who can

Reprinted with permission from *Science* 208 (4451): 1431-1437 (27 June 1980). Copyright 1980 by the AAAS.

forget the horror of millions of men, women and children starving, with more than 100,000 dying, because of an ecological calamity that turned grazing land and farms into bleak desert?" (ii) A two-page excerpt from a memo by the U.N. Sahelian Office, dated 8 November 1974, saying, "It is not possible to calculate the present and future impact of this tragedy, on the populations. . . . Although precise figures are not available, indeed unobtainable . . . certainly there has been an extensive and tragic loss of life. . . ." (iii) A one-page memo written for the United Nations by Helen Ware, an Australian expert on African demography, who was a visiting fellow at the University of Ibadan in March 1975 when she wrote it. From calculations of the normal death rate for the area, together with "the highest death rate in any group of nomads" during the drought, she estimated "an absolute, and most improbable, upper limit [of] a hundred thousand. . . . Even as a maximum [this estimate] represents an unreal limit."

Ware's statement which makes nonsense of Waldheim's well-publicized assessment, was on page one of a document written for the United Nations well before the Desertification Conference. Apparently it was the only calculation the United Nations had, and it was grossly misinterpreted.

More recently, the U.N. press releases have retreated to the more modest assertion that "tens of thousands" died in the Sahelian drought (2). But even this assertion is undocumented. "The problem with deaths in the Sahel," Ware says, "is precisely that there was so little evidence of them—rather like the photograph of the dead cow which kept turning up in illustration to every newspaper story" (3). A recent summary of the scientific evidence on the drought's effects by John Caldwell, a demographer who was familiar with the area prior to the drought and spent 1973 there, says, "One cannot certainly identify the existence of the drought in the vital statistics . . . nutritional levels, although poor, were similar to those found before the drought in other parts of Africa. The only possible exception was that of very young children" (4).

It is an example of a common phenomenon: Bad news about population growth, natural resources, and the environment that is based on flimsy evidence or no evidence at all is published widely in the face of contradictory evidence.

Another example comes from the same *Newsweek* piece: "More than one-third of all the land is desert or near-desert. And deserts are spreading inexorably, turning arable land into stony waste or heaps of drifting sand . . . annually destroying twelve million to seventeen million acres" (1). The headline on a front-page story in the *New York Times* said, "14 Million Acres a Year Vanishing as Deserts Spread Around Globe" (5).

Some arable land surely is deteriorating. But these news stories, and the many others originating from the book *Losing Ground* (6), by Erik Eckholm of Worldwatch Institute, clearly imply a more general proposition: that the world's supply of arable land is decreasing. Yet the truth is exactly the opposite: Joginder Kumar made a country-by-country survey of the changes in arable land from 1950 to 1960 (7). His finding: There was 9 percent more total arable land in 1960 than in 1950 in the 87 countries for which he could find data (constituting 73 percent of the land area of the world)—a gain of almost 1 percent per year (Table 6.1). And the more recent Food and Agriculture Organization data show a rise in "arable and permanent cropland" from 1403 to 1507 million hectares in the world as a whole from 1961-65 to 1974, an annual increase of roughly 0.7 percent. In the developing countries the area increased by 1.1 percent annually over the decade 1960 to 1970 (8).

The increase in the quantity of land that is cultivated rose even faster than 1 percent per year—from 8.9 percent of the total area to 9.9 percent during 1950 to 1960 (Table 6.1). And the increase in effective crop area was greater yet, because

TABLE 6.1. Land Use, 1950 and 1960. [Data from (6, p. 107)]

Region	Arable as % of total		Cultivated as % of arable		Cultivated as % of total		Arable plus pasture as % of total	
	1950	1960	1950	1960	1950	1960	1950	1960
Africa	14.27	15.30	36.21	42.72	5.2	6.5	46.50	49.02
Middle East	12.87	13.91	52.11	57.88	6.7	8.1	13.06	17.34
Asia	19.03	20.78	82.06	86.17	15.6	17.9	46.35	49.60
Frontier countries (North and South America, U.S.S.R., Australia, New Zealand)	6.88	7.75	82.85	82.96	5.7	6.4	34.27	38.59
Europe	30.79	30.98	89.02	90.06	27.4	27.9	45.63	46.10
All Regions	10.73	11.73	82.74	83.99	8.9	9.9	37.35	41.07

of the increase in multiple cropping in Asia and elsewhere. In some places the extension of cultivation has reduced the quality of land, of course, but in other places the process has improved the quality of land (9).

But does not a larger population necessarily mean "more pressure" on the land, so that ultimately everyone will be scratching out three skimpy meals from 18 hours of work a day on a plot the size of a window box? There has been such a trend in countries that have not yet entered into modernization and industrialization. For example, farm size declined as population increased in Poland from 1787 to 1937 and in China from 1870 to 1930 (10). But the more general trend points in the opposite direction. In all the higher-income industrialized countries in Europe and North America, and in Japan, a smaller absolute number of farmers are producing much more food and feeding much larger populations than in the past. An extrapolation of this benign trend carried to the same absurdity as the nightmare above, would suggest that eventually one person will be farming all the cropland in the United States and feeding everyone. The less-developed countries have not begun this trend, though the relative proportions of their populations that are in agriculture are falling rapidly. We may expect that as they get richer smaller absolute numbers of persons will be doing the farming for larger populations, on ever-larger farm units.

Some Other Myths About Population and Resources

Here are some other examples of publicized, false, bad news and the unpublicized, good-news truth:

Statement: The food situation in less-developed countries is worsening. "Serious World Food Gap Is Seen Over the Long Run" is a typical New York Times headline.

Perhaps most influential in furthering that idea was Paul Ehrlich's best-selling book The Population Bomb, which begins: "The battle to feed all of humanity is over. In the 1970's the world will undergo famines—hundreds of millions of people are going to starve to death" (11). Many writers view the situation as so threatening that they call for strong measures to restrict population growth—"compulsion if voluntary methods fail," as Ehrlich put it (11). Some, such as Paul and William Paddock, authors of the 1967 book Famine—1975!, find warrant in these assertions for such policies as "triage—letting the least fit die in order to save the more robust victims of hunger" (12). "My [one of the Paddocks] own opinion as the triage

TABLE 6.2. Per Capita Food Production in the World,
1948 to 1976 [Data from (40)]

Year	Excluding Mainland China (1952-56 = 100)	Including Mainland China (1961-65 = 100)	Combined index (1948-52 = 100)
1948-50	93		100
1952	97		104
1953	100		108
1954	99		106
1955	101		109
1956	103		111
1957	102		110
1958	106		114
1959	106		114
1960	107		115
1961	106		114
1962	108		116
1963	108		116
1964	109	102	118
1965	108	100	116
1966	111	103	119
1967	113	105	121
1968		106	123
1969		105	119
1970		106	123
1971		107	125
1972		104	120
1973		108	126
1974		107	125
1975		108	126
1976		110	128

classification of these sample nations is: Haiti, Can't-be-saved; Egypt, Can't-be-saved; The Gambia, Walking Wounded; Tunisia, Should Receive Food; Libya, Walking Wounded; India, Can't-be-saved; Pakistan, Should Receive Food" (13).

Fact: Per capita food production has been increasing at roughly 1 percent yearly—25 percent during the last quarter century (Table 6.2). Even in less-developed countries food production has increased substantially. World food stocks are high now, and even India has large amounts of food in storage. In the United States farmers are worrying about disaster from too much food.

Some countries have done far worse than the average, and have even had declining production, often because of war or political upheaval. And progress in food production has not been steady. But there has been no year, or series of years, so bad as to support a conclusion of long-term retrogression. Some readers might wonder whether my assertions are overly influenced by recent events, but the first draft of this material, for publication in my technical book (14), was written in 1971 and 1972, when food production was having its worse time in recent decades.

What about the data the other fellows quote to support their worried forecasts? In simple fact there are no other basic data. The data shown in Table 6.2 were published by the United Nations, collected from the individual countries. Of course the data are less reliable than one would like; economic data usually are. But these are the only official data, and data that would show a worsening trend in recent decades simply do not exist.

Statement: The danger of famine is increasing. The U.N. Economic and Social Commission for Asia and the Pacific predicts "500 million starvation deaths in Asia between 1980 and 2025" (15).

Contrary evidence: The course of famines is difficult to measure quantitatively. But D. Gale Johnson, an agricultural economist who has studied the history of famines intensively, estimates that since World War II there has been a "dramatic decline" in famines. Only a tenth as many people died of famine in the third quarter of the 20th century as in the last quarter of the 19th century, despite the much larger population now (16). A key cause of the decline in famine deaths has been the improvements in road systems, which allow food to be moved from regions of plenty to regions of shortage. The road-system improvements are themselves a product of increased population density (17) as well as of improvements in technology.

Statement: Higher population growth implies lower per capita economic growth. This has been almost gospel for the World Bank, the State Department's Agency for International Development (AID), and other development agencies.

Contrary evidence: Empirical studies find no statistical correlation between countries' population growth and their per capita economic growth either over the long run or in recent decades. Decadal growth rates of population and output per capita for those countries where long-run data are available are shown in Fig. 6.1. No strong relationship appears. Contemporary cross-national comparisons of current rates of population growth and economic growth are another source of evidence. Many such studies have been done by now, and they agree that population growth does not have a negative effect upon economic growth in either more-developed or less-developed countries (18). These overlapping empirical studies do not show that fast population growth increases per capita income, but they certainly imply that one should not confidently assert that population growth decreases economic growth.

Statement: Sophisticated computer models show that for the next 30 years an increase in population causes a decrease in per capita income.

Phyllis Piotrow (19) documented the decisive impact upon the late 1960's policy of AID and the U.N.'s Fund for Population Activities that was exerted by the first of these models, created in 1958 by Ansley Coale and Edgar Hoover (20). Largely founded on the Coale-Hoover simulation, the belief that population growth in less-developed countries is bad for the world led the State Department to greatly increase its spending for fertility reduction in poor countries, hand-in-hand with relatively lower spending on mortality reduction and other health programs, as seen in Table 6.3 (21). Along with the hundreds of millions of dollars for fertility reduction, the United States has put pressure on foreign governments to adopt fertility reduction programs.

Response: At the heart of all these models is simply an arithmetical truth: When considering the ratio (total income)/persons and assuming the numerator (income) to be fixed, an increase in the denominator (persons) implies a decrease in income per capita. That is, an added child with all sharing a given amount of goods means there is less to go around. As Wilfred Beckerman remarked, the instant a calf is born, per capita income and wealth go up, but the instant a child is born, per capita income and wealth go down. This truth was well recognized by Coale and Hoover with respect to their model and findings: "The inauspicious showing of the

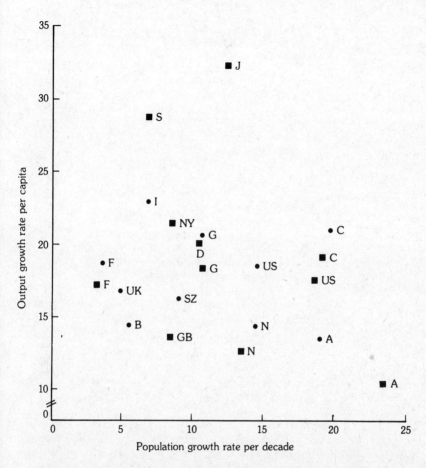

Figure 6.1. The nonrelationship between population growth and growth of living standards over half a century (●) and a century (■). A, Australia (1900–04 to 1963–67 and 1861–69 to 1963–67); B, Belgium (1900–04 to 1963–67); C, Canada (1920–24 to 1963–67 and 1870–74 to 1963–67); D, Denmark (1865–69 to 1963–67); F, France (1876 to 1963–66 and 1861–70 to 1963–66); G, Germany (1910–13 to 1963–67 and 1850–59 to 1963–67); GB, Great Britain (1855–64 to 1963–67); I, Italy (1895–99 to 1963–67); J, Japan (1874–79 to 1963–67); N, Netherlands (1900–09 to 1963–67 and 1860–70 to 1963–67); NY, Norway (1865–69 to 1963–67); S, Sweden (1861–69 to 1963–67); SZ, Switzerland (1910 to 1963–67); UK, United Kingdom (1920–24 to 1963–67); US, United States (1910–14 to 1963–67 and 1859 to 1963–67). [Data from (38)]

TABLE 6.3. Monies Obligated (loans and disbursements)
for Population and Health Programs by the
Agency for International Development, 1965
to 1977 (in millions of U.S. dollars)
[Data from (41)]

Fiscal Year	Population	Health	Total
1965	1.9	32.4	34.3
1966	3.8	58.7	62.5
1967	4.3	98.1	102.4
1968	34.4	131.3	165.7
1969	43.9	38.3	82.0
1970	73.1	37.1	110.2
1971	94.0	57.7	151.7
1972	120.9	35.4	156.3
1973	121.7	42.9	164.6
1974	100.1	81.5	181.6
1975	100.0	54.5	154.5
1976	103.0	54.4	157.4
1977*	143.4	93.6	237.0

*Estimated.

high-fertility case . . . in levels of living is traceable entirely to the accelerated growth in the number of consumers" (20). The point was crystal-clear to Malthus even without a complex model. He noted that an increase in population "increases the number of people before the means of subsistence are increased. The food therefore which before supported eleven millions, must now be divided among eleven millions and a half" (22).

Once the children grow up, however, and become producers as well as consumers, their impact on per capita income reverses. Eventually the income of other people is higher because of the additional children, as my own technical work (14) has argued. But this takes more than the 25 or 30 years covered by the well-known models.

Another point of view: The main new element in my model for more-developed countries (MDC's) is the contribution of additional people to increasing productivity (14). This occurs partly through larger market and economies of scale. But more important are an additional person's contributions to increased knowledge and technical progress. People bring not only mouths and hands into the world but also heads and brains. The source of improvements in productivity is the human mind, and the human mind is seldom found apart from the human body. This is an old idea, going back at least as far as William Petty (23):

As for the Arts of Delight and Ornament, they are best promoted by the greatest number of emulators. And it is more likely that one ingenious curious man may rather be found among 4 million than 400 persons. . . . And for the propagation and improvement of useful learning, the same may be said concerning it as above-said concerning . . . the Arts of Delight and Ornaments. . . .

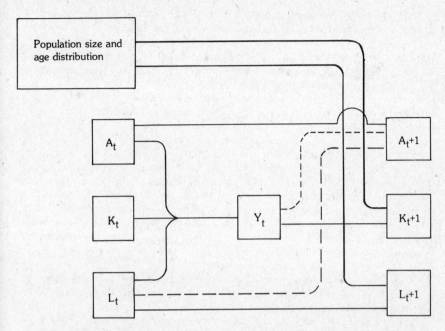

Figure 6.2. Schematic of MDC model. A_t, level of technology in year t; K_t, capital; L_t, labor; Y_t, national income. The model is run for 160 periods, the output from each year becoming the input for year t + 1. The model was run with various specifications of the technical progress function.

Population growth and productivity increase are not independent forces running a race. Rather, additional persons cause technological advances by inventing, adapting, and diffusing new productive knowledge.

Technical progress, which is the main source of long-run economic growth in MDC's, arises partly from organized scientific R & D and partly from people who are not especially educated and do not work in science—the supermarket manager who finds a method to display more merchandise in a given space, the supermarket clerk who develops a quicker way to stamp the prices on cans, the market researcher who experiments to learn more efficient and cheaper means of advertising the store's prices and sale items, and so on. This is the "learning by doing" phenomenon which has been all-important in raising our standard of living from what it was 20,000 years ago, 200 years ago, 20 years ago, to what it is now. The aggregate economic importance of the technological knowledge factor has clearly emerged in two well-known studies, one by Robert Solow and the other by Edward Denison (24).

I have added this effect of additional people on productivity to a standard economic model in several variants of Fig. 6.2. The result is that additional persons, instead of being a permanent drag, lead to an increase in per worker output starting 30 to 70 years after birth—that is, 10 to 50 years after entry into the labor force. (Economics can therefore be a cheerful science rather than the dismal science Malthus thought it to be.)

Babies do not create knowledge and improve productivity while still in their cradles. And though the family bears most of the cost, society must also unpurse to bring the baby to productive adulthood. This means that if you do not look as far ahead as the next 25 years, the knowledge benefits of someone else's baby born today do not interest you, and that baby therefore appears to be a poor social investment for your taxes. But if you feel some interest in, and obligation for, the longer-run future—perhaps because you yourself are today enjoying the fruits of the investment that someone paid for 25 or 50 or 100 years ago, or because you have children whose future is important to you—then you will view the knowledge produced by today's children as being of great benefit to you (25).

The mechanism is different in less-developed countries (LDC's). Offsetting the negative capital-dilution force of more people, there are the positive forces of increased work done by parents, extra stimulus to agricultural and industrial investment, increased social infrastructure, and other economies of scale. When all these forces are combined into my LDC simulation model, an additional child comes to have a positive net effect on the general standard of living after the better part of a century. But this positive net effect is much larger than the negative net effect early on (14). Once again, most of the cost is borne by the immediate family rather than the rest of society. And the immediate family apparently feels that the benefits from the additional child outweigh the costs in the early years, because they choose to bear the children and the expenses.

In short, economic theory that includes key elements left out of previous models, together with the empirical data, suggests that additional children have positive long-run effects upon the standard of living.

It is true that the long run—30 to 70 years—is far from now, and therefore is of less importance to us than is the short run. But our long run will be someone else's short run, just as our short run was someone else's long run. Some measure of unselfishness should impel us to keep this in mind as we make our decisions about population policy.

Statement: Urban sprawl is paving over the United States, including much "prime agricultural land" and recreational areas.

Fact: All the land used for urban areas plus roadways totals less than 3 percent of the area of the United States. And the increase over the half-century starting in 1920 was only 0.00025 percent of total land annually (26). The U.S. Department of Agriculture says "we are in no danger of running out of farmland" (27).

Each year 1.25 million acres are converted to efficient cropland by draining swamps and irrigating desserts, while 0.9 million acres are converted to urban and transportation use. The rest of the 2.2 million acres of rural land which goes out of use yearly is abandoned not because of "paving over" but because it has "low soil fertility and a terrain unsuited to efficient use of modern machinery" (28). A million acres yearly goes into additional wilderness recreation areas and wildlife refuges, and another 300,000 acres goes for reservoirs and flood control (27). The danger to agriculture from "paving over" is another bogeyman.

About wildlife areas, state and national parks: these increased from 8 million acres in 1920 to 73 million acres in 1974 and are still increasing (26). The number of visits to these recreation areas has risen sharply because of improved transportation and increased income. From 1946 to 1960, for example, visits increased from 780 to 2,184 per thousand people yearly.

Statement: We are running out of natural resources and raw materials. "Entering an age of scarcity" is [so] commonplace that it is simply assumed and asserted in public discussion by people ranging from B.F. Skinner to Solzhenitzyn (29).

Response: The only meaningful measure of scarcity in peacetime is the cost of the good in question (30). The cost trends of almost every natural resource—whether measured in labor time required to produce the energy, in production costs, in the proportion of our incomes spent for energy, or even the goods—have been downward over the course of recorded history.

An hour's work in the United States has bought increasingly more of copper, wheat, and oil (representative and important raw materials) from 1800 to the present. And the same trend has almost surely held throughout human history. Calculations of expenditures for raw materials as a proportion of total family budgets make the same point even more strongly. These trends imply that the raw materials have been getting increasingly available and less scarce relative to the most important and most fundamental element of life, human work time. The prices of raw materials have even been falling relative to consumer goods and the Consumer Price Index. All the items in the Consumer Price Index have been produced with increasing efficiency in terms of labor and capital over the years, but the decrease in cost of raw materials has been even greater than that of other goods, a very strong demonstration of progressively decreasing scarcity and increasing availability of raw materials.

The relative fall in the prices of raw materials understates the positive trend, because as consumers we are interested in the services we get from the raw materials rather than the raw materials themselves. And we have learned to use less of given raw materials for given purposes, as well as to substitute cheaper materials to get the same services. Consider a long-ago copper pot for cooking. The consumer is interested in a container which can be put over heat. After iron and aluminum were discovered, quite satisfactory cooking pots—almost as good as, or perhaps better than, pots of copper—could be made of those materials. The cost that interests us is the cost of providing the cooking service, rather than the cost of copper.

A dramatic example of how the service that copper renders can be supplied much more cheaply by a substitute process: A single communications satellite in space provides intercontinental telephone connections that would otherwise require thousands of tons of copper.

Statement: Energy is getting scarcer.

Response: The facts about the cost of energy are much the same as the facts about other raw materials. The new strength of the OPEC cartel to control oil price obscures the cost of production. But the production cost of a barrel of oil has not risen, and probably has fallen, in deflated dollars; even after the "oil crisis" of 1973 it was still $0.05 to $0.15 per barrel in the Persian Gulf, which was perhaps a hundredth of the market price (31). It is reasonable to expect that eventually the price of oil will again return nearer its economic cost of production, and the long-run downward trend in the price of oil will resume its course.

The price of electricity is an interesting measure of the consumer cost of energy, and it is largely unaffected by cartels and politics (though the price of electricity did rise after 1973 because all energy sources, including coal and uranium, jumped in price when the price of oil went up, on account of the improved market power of coal and uranium suppliers). But the long-run cost of electricity clearly has been downward.

In short, the data show that energy has not been getting scarcer in basic economic terms, but rather has been getting more plentiful.

Statement: The supplies of natural resources are finite. This apparently self-evident proposition is the starting point and the all-determining assumption of such models as *The Limits to Growth* and of much popular discussion.

Response: Incredible as it may seem at first, the term "finite" is not inappropriate but is downright misleading in the context of natural resources, from both the practical and the philosophical points of view. As with so many of the important arguments in this world, this is "just semantic." Yet the semantics of resource scarcity muddle public discussion and bring about wrongheaded policy decisions.

A definition of resource quantity must be operational to be useful. It must tell us how the quantity of the resource that might be available in the future could be calculated. But the future quantities of a natural resource such as copper cannot be calcuated even in principle, because of new lodes, new methods of mining copper, and variations in grades of copper lodes; because copper can be made from other metals; and because of the vagueness of the boundaries within which copper might be found—including the sea, and other planets. Even less possible is a reasonable calculation of the amount of future services of the sort we are now accustomed to get from copper, because of recycling and because of the substitution of other materials for copper, as in the case of the communications satellite.

Even the total weight of the earth is not a theoretical limit to the amount of copper that might be available to earthlings in the future. Only the total weight of the universe—if that term has a useful meaning here—would be such a theoretical limit, and I don't think anyone would like to argue the meaningfulness of "finite" in that context.

With respect to energy, it is particularly obvious that the earth does not bound the quantity available to us; our sun (and perhaps other suns) is our basic source of energy in the long run, from vegetation (including fossilized vegetation) as well as fron solar energy. As to the practical finiteness and scarcity of resources—that brings us back to cost and price, and by these measures history shows progessively decreasing rather than increasing scarcity.

Why does the word "finite" catch us up? That is an interesting question in psychology, education, and philosophy; unfortunately there is no space to explore it here.

In summary, because we find new lodes, invent better production methods, and discover new substitutes, the ultimate constraint upon our capacity to enjoy unlimited raw materials at acceptable prices is knowledge. And the source of knowledge is the human mind. Ultimately, then, the key constraint is human imagination and the exercise of educated skills. Hence an increase of human beings constitutes an addition to the crucial stock of resources, along with causing additional consumption of resources.

Statement: The old trends no longer apply. We are at a moment of discontinuity now.

Response: One cannot logically dispute assertions about present or impending discontinuity. And one can find mathematical techniques suggesting discontinuities that will be consistent with any trend data. We can say scientifically, however, that if in the past one had acted on the belief that the long-run price trend was upward rather than downward, one would have lost money on the average.

Statement: The nation's "overall environmental well-being" is declining, according to the Environmental Quality Index (EQI).

Fact: This widely reported index is, according to the National Wildlife Federation, which prepares and disseminates it, "a subjective analysis . . . judgment [which] represents collective thinking of the editors of the National Wildlife Federation Staff." That is, the EQI represents casual observation rather than hard statistical facts. It includes such subjective judgments as that the trend of "living space" is "down . . . vast stretches of America are lost to development yearly" (32). But the objective statistical facts indicate that the environment is getting better. Earlier we saw that "living space" is not declining, and recreational areas are increasing rapidly. The official data of the Council on Environmental Quality concerning major air pollutants show sharp improvements in the last decade (Fig. 6.3). With respect to

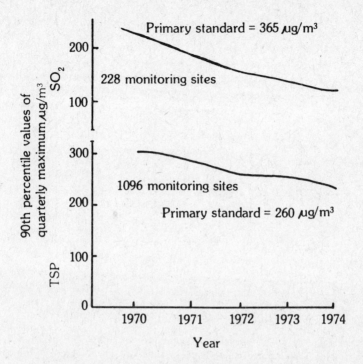

Figure 6.3. Overall national trends in daily observed levels of sulfur dioxide (*upper curve*) and total suspended particulates (*lower curve*). [Reproduced from (33, p. 226); data from U.S. Environmental Protection Agency]

water, "major improvements in the quality of polluted streams have been documented" (33, p.285) (see Fig. 6.4). The fish catch in Lake Erie, long ago said to be "dead" by Barry Commoner, has been increasing. The most important indicator of environmental quality is life expectancy; it continues to rise, and at an increasing rate: a gain of 2.1 years from 1970 to 1976, compared with a gain of only 0.8 year in the entire decade of the 1960's (34).

Statement: "[E]ven if the family size drops gradually—to the two-child average— there will be no year in the next two decades in which the absolute number of births will be less than in 1970," said the President's Commission on Population Growth, 1972 (35).

Fact: In 1971—the year before this forecast by the President's Commission was transmitted to the President and then published—the absolute number of births (not only the birth rate) was less than in 1970. By 1975, the absolute number of births was barely higher than in 1920, and the number of white births was actually lower than in most years from 1914 to 1924. This scientific fiasco shows how flimsy are the demographic forecasts upon which arguments about growth policy are based. In this case the Commission did not even "backcast" correctly, let alone forecast well.

Another peculiar forecasting episode: Between 1969 and 1978, U.N. and other standard estimates of the world's population in the year 2000 fell from around 7.5 billion to around 5.5 billion people. This is a difference of 2 billion people—equal to about half the world's present population—for a date only 30 years or less in

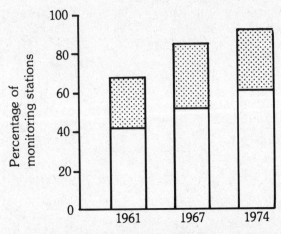

Drinking water suitability

Figure 6.4. Summary of water quality observations related to drinking water suitability, 1961, 1967, and 1974. Unshaded, "good"; dotted, "fair." [Adapted from (39); data from U.S. Geological Survey]

the future. There is also grave disagreement even among estimates of current magnitudes. An important example is the population growth rate of China, a fifth of the entire world population: 2.4 percent per year according to the Environmental Fund, 0.8 percent per year according to AID, these estimates correspond to doubling times of about 30 years and about 90 years respectively, estimates with entirely different implications (36).

Why Do We Hear Phony Bad News?

Why do false statements of bad news dominate public discussion of these topics? Here are some speculations.

1) There is a funding incentive for scholars and institutions to produce bad news about population, resources, and the environment. The AID and the U.N.'s Fund for Population Activities disburse more than a hundred million dollars each year to bring about fertility decline. Much of this money goes to studies and publications that show why fertility decline is a good thing. There are no organizations that fund studies having the opposite aim.

2) Bad news sells books, newspapers, and magazines; good news is not half so interesting. Is it a wonder that there are lots of bad-news best-sellers warning about pollution, population growth, and natural resource depletion but none telling us the facts about improvement?

3) There are a host of possible psychological explanations for this phenomenon about which I am reluctant to speculate. But these two seem reasonably sure: (i) Many people have a propensity to compare the present and the future with an ideal state of affairs rather than with the past or with some other feasible state; the present and future inevitably look bad in such a comparison. (ii) The cumulative nature of exponential growth models has the power to seduce and bewitch.

4) Some publicize dire predictions in the idealistic belief that such warnings can mobilize institutions and individuals to make things even better; they think that

nothing bad can come of such prophecies. But we should not shrug off false bad news as harmless exaggeration. There will be a loss of credibility for real threats as they arise, and loss of public trust in public communication. As Philip Handler, president of the National Academy of Sciences, testified to congressmen in the midst of the environmental panic of 1970: "The nations of the world may yet pay a dreadful price for the public behavior of scientists who depart from . . . fact to indulge . . . in hyperbole" (37).

The question, then, is: Who will tell us the good-and-true news? How will it be published for people to learn?

Notes

1. *Newsweek*, 19 September 1977, p. 80.
2. Associated Press, in Champaign-Urbana *News Gazette*, 10 January 1978, p. A-5.
3. H. Ware, personal communication, 20 March 1978.
4. J. Caldwell, in *Drought in Africa No. 2 (African Environment Special Report No. 6)*, D. Dalby, R.J.H. Church, F. Bezzaz, Eds. (UNEP-IDEP-SIDA, London, 1977), pp. 93-100. For a full and judicious assessment of the situation and the area see Caldwell's *The Sahelian Drought and Its Demographic Implications* (Overseas Liaison Committee, American Council on Education, Washington, D.C., 1975).
5. *New York Times*, 28 August 1977, p. 1.
6. E. P. Eckholm, *Losing Ground: Environmental Stress and World Food Prospects* (Norton, New York, 1976).
7. J. Kumar, *Population and Land in World Agriculture* (Univ. of California Press, Berkeley, 1973).
8. *FAO Production Yearbook* (United Nations, New York, 1975), vol. 29, p. 3; *Foreign Agricultural Economic Report No. 98* (Department of Agriculture, Washington, D.C., 1974).
9. When I submitted a letter to the editor containing these facts, *Newsweek* did not print it but replied: "Dear Mr. Simon: We can only say that, in preparing the Sept. 19, 1977 story to which you refer, we used what we thought were the best available sources. The different figures you have obtained are of course disturbing. But all we can say at this point is that we will add this information to our files and take it into account in future stories. We appreciate the concern that prompted you to write to *Newsweek*."
10. W. Stys, *Popul. Stud.* 11, 136 (1957); R. H. Myers, *The Chinese Peasant Economy* (Harvard Univ. Press, Cambridge, Mass., 1970), originally from J. L. Buck, *Land Utilization in China Statistical Supplement* (Nanking Univ. Press, Nanking, 1937), p. 288.
11. P. Ehrlich, *The Population Bomb* (Ballantine, New York, 1968), p. xi.
12. *Newsweek*, 11 November 1974, p. 16.
13. P. Paddock, *Famine—1975!* (Little, Brown, Boston, 1967), p. 222.
14. J. L. Simon, *The Economics of Population Growth* (Princeton Univ. Press, Princeton, N.J., 1977).
15. Associated Press, 12 February 1975.
16. D. G. Johnson, *Am. Stat.* 28, 89 (1974). For more details, see Johnson's article "Famine" in the *Encyclopedia Brittanica*, 1973 edition.
17. "The effect of population density upon infrastructure: The case of roadbuilding," *Econ. Dev. Cultural Change* 23, No. 3 (1975).
18. Summarized in (14, pp. 139-140). To ensure that earlier studies were not flawed by employing only population growth as an independent variable, R. Gobin and I regressed the economic growth rate in various cross-sections of less-developed countries from 1950 to 1970 on population density and population size together with population growth. Population growth continued to show no effect. Interestingly, however, population density shows a pronounced positive influence on economic growth. See J. L. Simon and R. Gobin, in *Research in Population Economics*, J. Simon and J. DaVanzo, Eds. (JAI Press, Greenwich, Conn., 1979), vol. 2.
19. P. Piotrow, *World Population Crisis: The United States Response* (Praeger, New York, 1973).
20. A. J. Coale and E. M. Hoover, *Population Growth and Economic Development in Low-Income Countries* (Princeton Univ. Press, Princeton, N.J., 1958).

21. Ehrlich caught the spirit of this policy thus: ". . . we should see that the majority of federal support of bio-medical research goes into the broad areas of population regulation, environmental sciences and behavioral sciences, rather than into short-sighted programs of death control" [P. Ehrlich, *Reader's Dig.* 94, 137 (1969)]. Or as an economist then of the Coale-Hoover school put it, "To diminish mortality and morbidity . . . where underemployment of labor is the critical characteristic . . . serves markedly to retard rates of general economic growth" [quoted in W. Petersen, *Population* (Macmillan, New York, ed. 2, 1969), p. 572].

22. T. R. Malthus, *An Essay on the Principle of Population, or a View of its Past and Present Effects on Human Happiness* (J. Johnson, London, "A new edition," 1803).

23. W. Petty, "Another Essay in Political Arithmetic" (1682), reprinted in *The Economic Writings of Sir William Petty*, C. H. Hull, Ed. (Cambridge Univ. Press, Cambridge, 1899), p.474.

24. R. Solow, *Rev. Econ. Stat.* 39, 312 (1957); E. F. Denison, *The Sources of Economic Growth in the United States and the Alternatives Before Us* (Committee for Economic Dev., New York, 1962).

25. For a comprehensive discussion, see H. J. Barnett, *Econ. Dev. Cultural Change* 19, 545 (1971).

26. R. Barlowe, *Land Resource Economics: The Economics of Real Property* (Prentice-Hall, Englewood Cliffs, N.J., 1978), p.50.

27. *Our Land and Water Resources: Current Prospective Supplies and Uses* (Miscellaneous Publication No. 1290, Economic Research Service, Department of Agriculture, Washington, D.C., 1974); p. vi; H.T. Frey, "Cropland for Today and Tomorrow" (USDA Economic Report No. 291, Washington, D.C., 1975); "Major Uses of Land in the United States: Summary for 1969" (USDA Economic Report No. 247, Washington D.C., p1973).

28. M. L. Cotner, M.D. Skold, O. Krause, *Farmland: Will There Be Enough?* (Economic Research Service, Department of Agriculture, Washington, D.C., 1975), p. 10.

29. G. Homans, *Harv. Mag.* July-August 1977, p. 58; A. Solzhenitsyn, quoted in *Newsweek*, 18 March 1974, p. 122.

30. H. J. Barnett and C. Morse [*Scarcity and Growth* (Johns Hopkins Press, Baltimore, 1963)] give the classic argument for this point of view, accompanied by a wealth of data. My discussion was inspired by their treatment and follows in their spirit, which in turn has roots in the Paley Commission of the early 1950's and in J. S. Davis, *J. Polit. Econ.* 61, 369 (1953). The data in *Scarcity and Growth* cover 1870 to 1957. Barnett has recently extended his analysis from 1957 to 1970 and found that the downward trends in real costs of extractive materials continue [H. J. Barnett in *Scarcity and Growth Reconsidered*, V.K. Smith, Ed. (Resources for the Future, Washington, D.C., in press)]. A provocative but convincing technologically based argument for continuation of these downward cost trends for minerals is H. E. Goeller and Alvin M. Weinberg, *Science* 191, 683 (1976).

31. *Jerusalem Post*, 3 January 1978, p. 5; M. Zonis, *Univ. Chicago Mag.*, March 1976, p. 14.

32. "Environmental quality index," *Natl. Wildlife* 15 (No. 2) (1977).

33. *Environmental Quality—1976*, seventh annual report of the Council on Enviornmental Quality, Washington D.C., p. 285.

34. *Stat. Bull. Metrop. Life Insur. Co.* 58, 9 (May 1977).

35. E. R. Morse and R. H. Reed, Eds., *Economic Aspects of Population Change* (Government Printing Office, Washington, D.C., 1972), p. 4 [as quoted by Larry Neal, *Ill. Bus. Rev.* 35, No. 2 (1978)].

36. R. Kramer and S. Baum, "Comparison of recent estimates of world population growth," presented at a meeting of the Population Association of America, 1978.

37. P. Handler, interview in *U.S. News World Rep.*, 18 January 1971, p. 30.

38. S. Kuznets, *Economic Growth of Nations* (Norton, New York 1971), pp. 11–14.

39. *Sixth Annual Report* (Council on Environmental Quality, Washington, D.C., 1975), p. 352.

40. *FAO Production Yearbook* (United Nations, New York, 1968, 1975, 1976).

41. L. E. Bradshaw, D. Pitty, C. P. Green, *Popul. Rep. Ser. J* (1977), p. J272.

42. This article is drawn from the author's forthcoming book, *The Ultimate Shortage* (Princeton Univ. Press, Princeton, N.J., in press). I thank S. Friedman, E. Satinoff, and R. Simon for their useful comments. D. Love assisted me ably.

Part II
POPULATION

7

World Food: Myth and Reality
(excerpts)
Thomas T. Poleman

To include the readings in Part II under the title "Population" is actually creating an artificial distinction between resource use and population growth according to neo-Malthusian scholars. To them, overpopulation is the (or soon-to-be) single most important cause of world resource "scarcity" (see Lester Brown's article in Part I, Chapter 2). What is the Malthusian syllogism which forms the basis of the neo-malthusian argument today? Thomas Poleman discusses Malthus' "theory" as cogently and succinctly as he dismisses it.

III. The Myth of the Food-Population Race

The doomsayers' silence on population control is symptomatic of the widespread acceptance of a second myth encouraged by the hunger/starvation distortion: the old Malthusian one of a (losing) race between food and mouths to feed. One calls it Malthusian with reluctance, because it is impossible to believe that Malthus, had he today's evidence on matters about which he could only theorize 175 years ago, would have had much truck with what is said in his name. Few have paid so high a price for original thought.

Malthus wrote at a time when very little was known about population trends. Censuses had only begun to be taken and the good Reverend seemed quite prepared to go along with Bishop Ussher's timing of the Creation at 4004 B.C.[1] Evidence on food production was even sketchier. None the less Malthus was bold enough to perceive in them tendencies sufficiently strong to upset the then prevailing notions of man's perfectability.

His theory was most succinctly stated in the first edition of his famous *Essay*:[2]

I think I may fairly make two postulata. First, that food is necessary to the existence of man.

Secondly, that the passion between the sexes is necessary, and will remain nearly in its present state. . .

Assuming then, my postulata as granted, I say, that the power of population is indefinitely greater than the power in the earth to produce subsistence for man.

Reprinted with permission from *World Development*, 5: 389–394: Thomas T. Poleman, "World Food: Myth and Reality." Copyright 1977, Pergamon Press, Ltd.

Population, when unchecked, increases in a geometrical ratio. Subsistence increases only in an arithmetical ratio. A slight acquaintance with numbers will show the immensity of the first power as compared with the second.

By that law of our nature which makes food necessary to the life of man, the effects of these two unequal powers must be kept equal.

This implies a strong and constantly operating check on population from the difficulty of subsistence. . . . The race of plants, and the race of animals shrink under this great restrictive law. And the race of man cannot, by any efforts of reason, escape from it. Among plants and animals its effects are waste of seed, sickness, and premature death. Among mankind, misery and vice. The former, misery, is an absolutely necessary consequence of it. Vice is a highly probable consequence . . . I see no way by which man can escape from the weight of this law which pervades all animated nature. . .

Such was the (uncommon) wisdom of his youth. In later editions, as Malthus grappled with the question of how populations controlled their size, the argument expanded and became less tidy. As with most prolific writers and thinkers, he at one time or another seemed to be on most sides of most questions. But it was his original perception that first captured the world's attention and it is this perception which has been used by so many to dramatize the problems posed by the current spurt in population.

We are all familiar with drawings which indicate that the world's population remained essentially stable from biblical times to about 1650. Such drawings are valid in that they drive home the magnitude of the current explosion in numbers, some 80% of which is taking place in the LDCs, but they mislead in several important respects. The current upturn is not unique, and growth (and contraction) prior to 1650 took place not gradually but in spurts.

This is of fundamental importance and is perhaps most easily appreciated when visualized in terms of a simplified graphing conceived by E.S. Deevey. The drawing, which is plotted on logarithmic scales to make great differences in time and magnitude manageable, summarizes much of what we have learned since Malthus' time. The present upsurge in numbers is not the first but the third in a sequence of bursts that have been associated with major breakthroughs in man's ability to cope with his environment. The first occurred several million years ago—Deevey plotted it at one million, although today he would no doubt move it back—and attended man's emergence from the primate line into a maker of tools able to hunt and gather over a range of conditions. The second marked his domestication of plants and animals some 10,000 years ago and the beginnings of agriculture—the 'Neolithic Revolution'.

These breakthroughs, of course, did not take place simultaneously around the world, but were staggered in their impact. Just as the industrial and scientific revolution occurred first in Europe, food gatherers and hunters first became agriculturists in the Fertile Crescent and Southeast Asia. Still, the effect in a particular locality was rapid and profound. For example,[3]

Twenty thousand people would probably be an extreme estimate of the population of hunter-gatherers the Egyptian section of the Nile valley could have supported at the end of paleolithic times. The population of the Old Kingdom two thousand years later has been variously estimated at from three to six millions.

That such epochal technological breakthroughs would be accompanied by rapid population rises seems obvious. What is less obvious is the nature of the forces that ultimately acted to force a leveling off. Malthus' food supply, together with

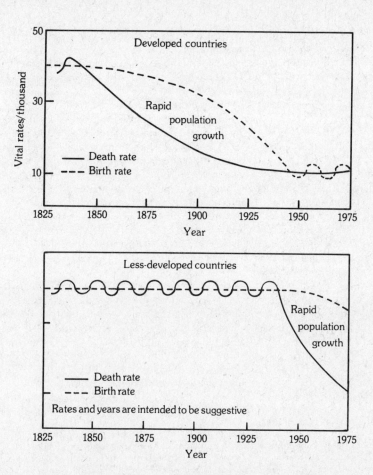

Figure 7.1. The demographic transition schematized.

such other essentials as space, water and air, clearly set an upper limit, but one wonders how frequently an operative one. The long-term population equilibria of the past would seem to have been at levels below those associated with marginal starvation. Thus, a 'Paleolithic man who stuck to business should have found enough food on two square kilometers, instead of [the] 20 or 200' believed to have been available *per capita*, respectively, in the Upper and Lower Paleolithic ages.[4] And it is not weather but changed political circumstances that are most clearly linked to the great swings in China's population over the last two millennia.

If the parameters of the demographic transition associated with the Neolithic remain to be satisfactorily generalized, those associated with the third of the great upheavals, the industrial and scientific revolution, would seem fairly clear cut (Fig. 7.1). Initial population stability is characterized by high birth and death rates. Then, as public health measures are introduced, the death rate drops. Birth rates, however, remain at their old level, and a period of population 'explosion' sets in. Then birth rates in their turn fall, and the population again approaches stability, but at a much higher level.

Most of the industrialized states of the West have passed through this transition and seem fairly near the new level of stability—'zero population growth' in the idiom. For them the transition averaged between 50 and 100 years. Virtually all the LDCs have passed through the stage of declining death rates and are in the interval of maximum population growth. For them the 'population problem is essentially whether or not [they] will follow Europe and North America in reducing birth rates. . .'[5]

The evidence from some of the smaller, more prosperous LDCs (notably Singapore, Taiwan, Mauritius and Sri Lanka) is that they can reduce birth rates—and probably much more quickly—within 20 or 30 years. Contraceptives are becoming available at little or no cost to users in the Third World, and birth control information is widespread. However, for family planning to be rapidly introduced, people must consciously want fewer children and for this to happen there are certain preconditions. That one of these is a reduction in infant mortality we have already noted. Others revolve around a reduction in the economic attractiveness of large families, both as sources of labour and as old-age insurance, and the availability of opportunities for life styles involving more than just growing food and raising children. Expressed more positively, the preconditions imply access to health facilities, social security and education—all of which we tend to equate with 'improved living levels', 'urbanization' and 'development'.

Hence the quandary faced by the LDCs is best visualized not, as the doomsayers have it, in the sterile terms of race in which food and population push relentlessly toward some hypothetical saturation point. Rather it is a very malleable competition between population growth and economic participation on the one hand, and between economic participation and food on the other.

Notes

1. T.R. Malthus, *An Essay on the Principle of Population* (Parallel chapters from the 1st and 2nd eds.; London: 1906), p.6.
2. Malthus, op. cit., pp.6–8.
3. R. Oliver and J.D. Fage, *A Short History of Africa* (London: 1968), p.26.
4. E.S. Deevey, 'The human population', *Scientific American* (September 1960), p.198.
5. Dudley Kirk, 'Natality in the developing countries: recent trends and prospects', in S.J. Behrman, L. Corsa, and R. Freedman, eds., *Fertility and Family Planning: A World View* (Ann Arbor: 1969), p. 76.

8

Marx, Malthus, and the Concept of Natural Resource Scarcity
(excerpts)
Michael Perelman

Economist Michael Perelman provides further insights on the impetus for Malthus' writings, particularly his *Essay on Population* (Fifth edition, London: Johnson. 1817). As Poleman has suggested in Chapter 7, Malthus' arguments were not based upon extensive data-gathering and interpretation of statistics. Rather, Malthus' ideas were based on the ideology of the ruling class. This also explains in part why Malthus did not advocate "strict population control": a reserve labor force was needed in accordance with the "immediate needs of capital."

In Malthus' age, the concept of scarcity was painfully simple; it was synonymous with a shortage of food (see, e.g., Burke 1795). Malthus proposed that food increases according to an arithmetical progression while population increases geometrically. The empirical basis of his theory was slim indeed, consisting mainly, as Wesley Mitchell has noted, of a "rapid increase of population in several countries" (Mitchell, 1967, p.243n). Although he tried to shore up his argument with more data in subsequent editions, his main interest was not factual but ideological.

Malthus was writing when almost all of well-to-do England lived in constant horror of the egalitarian principles of the French Revolution. One of the solitary exceptions was William Godwin.[1] Malthus' father a close friend of both Hume and Rousseau, was one of the few who supported Godwin's belief in the perfectibility of individuals as well as societies. Malthus's response to his father was the pamphlet on populations, published in 1798. Its intellectual content was not novel, however. For example, thirty-seven years earlier, Adam Smith's friend the Reverend Robert Wallace published *Various Prospects of Mankind, Nature and Providence*, in which he asked whether communism might not benefit society; he concluded that such a society would create a rate of population growth excessive enough that all would be dragged down into grinding poverty. Godwin subsequently answered the arguments of Wallace with a description of the vast expanses of scarcely populated lands and predictions of a more developed rationality which could guide society in regulating its numbers.[2]

Reprinted with permission from *Antipode* II (2): 80–91, 1979.

The success of Malthus' pamphlet was enormous. Even Godwin himself had to admit that it converted his supporters—who were few enough to begin with—by the hundreds (Mitchell, 1967, p.253). Only two years before the pamphlet appeared, the Prime Minister of England, William Pitt, had proposed making welfare payments proportional to family size in order to stimulate population growth (Mitchell, 1967, p. 253). Such ideas often appear during wars when large families promise more soldiers in the future.[3] Yet once Malthus' work became known, Pitt withdrew his scheme in deference to him. Others drew more extreme conclusions. For example, an anonymous pamphleteer, writing under the name Marcus, called for the painless killing of all working class children born to families that had already burdened the world with two offspring (Engels, 1844, pp. 218-219). Malthus' pious disciple, Reverend Thomas Chalmers, proposed that all funds currently intended for relief of the poor be redirected to the building of churches.

In reality, Malthus' ideas prevailed neither by virtue of their merit nor of their originality, but rather by their timeliness. The revolutionary changes in English agriculture and industry were eliminating traditional forms of employment faster than new industries could create alternative employment, producing an apparent "population surplus" and attendant poverty (see, for example, Cowherd, 1977, p. xi). At the same time, the relative surplus population created a huge burden of poor relief. Because relief only seemed an unnecessary expense to the bourgeoisie and also appeared to reduce the necessity to accept employment in the "dark satanic mills" of the industrial revolution, the Poor Laws came in for considerable criticism. In the process, ". . .the Malthusian controversy, which had begun as an abstract discussion as to the possibility of a successful communism, more and more degenerated into a wrangle about Poor Law administration" (Buer, 1927, p. 148).

The concept of scarcity as it appeared in the ideological struggle about the poor laws was very crude, so Malthus' simplistic formulation served admirably as a political weapon. Malthus proved to the satisfaction of the ruling classes that they had no responsibility for the existing state of affairs. They were not about to raise questions about subjects such as the effect of private property on the availability of resources; it was enough for them that Malthus showed that ". . .the real cause of the continued depression and poverty of the lower classes of society was the growth of population" (Malthus, 1800, p. 25). Who among the ruling classes would question the doctrine that the road to salvation lay not in furthering the struggle between classes but in eliminating the lust between sexes? The Reverend Malthus conveniently absolved all members of the parish of capital. The poor are, Malthus told his contemporaries, "the arbiters of their own destiny; and what others can do for them is like dust in the balance compared to what they can do for themselves" (Malthus, 1820, p. 262). Subsequent to Malthus, all plans for improving the status of the poor were judged according to their likely effect on population growth.[4]

Malthus actually never went quite as far as others in his fanaticism. In fact, his work had an air of cynical practicality about it. Unlike his contemporary disciples, Malthus never accepted the limitations of population as an end in itself. The actual position Malthus settled upon in his successive writings was that an appropriate rate of population growth was one consistent with the needs of capital. As early as the first edition of the *Essay* Malthus showed doubts in strict population control by his implicit opposition to contraception in his comments on Condorcet. By the fifth edition, he had become much more straightforward. He condemned "artificial and unnatural modes of checking population," not only on the grounds of their "immorality," but also on "their tendency to remove a necessary stimulus to industry" (Malthus, 1817, iii, p. 393). By the sixth edition, the good parson was so emphatic on this point that he even seemed to prefer prostitution to birth control (Malthus, 1826, p.294; see also Winch, 1965, p. 59).

In other words, Malthus recognized that poverty made the working class more willing to submit to wage labor (see Glass, 1953). Abstract principles allowed him to adopt a cover of scientific objectivity while his actual policy recommendations were tailored to the more immediate needs of capital. Later, in his *Principles of Political Economy*, Malthus was quite clear on the economic impact of population control: "prudential habits, among the labouring classes of a country mainly depending upon manufactures and commerce, might ruin it" (Malthus, 1820, p.221). Only the purist J.B. Say seemed to notice the anomaly between this and the principle of population as originally enunciated (Say, 1821, p. 30).

Notes

1. Godwin's remarkable family included Mary Wollstonecraft (his wife), Mary Shelly (his daughter and author of *Frankenstein*), and the poet Shelly (his son-in-law).
2. This paragraph very closely follows the argument of Wesley Mitchell, 1967, pp.239-41. See also Glacken, 1967.
3. Indeed, the Whigs were busy censuring the Tories for daring to engage in war with a country as populous as France (Cowherd, 1977, p. 19).
4. The Law of Population had the additional merit of proving that Poor Relief only compounded the problem of overpopulation and should be safely restricted for this reason.

References

Buer, Mabel C. 1927. "The Historical Setting of the Malthusian Controversy," T.E. Gregory and Hugh Dalton, eds. *London Essays in Economics: In Honor of Edwin Cannan* (London: George Rutledge and Sons): pp. 136–56.
Burke, Edmund. 1795. "Thoughts and Details on Scarcity," in John R. McCulloch, *A Select Collection of Scarce and Valuable Economical Tracts* (New York: Kelly Reprints, 1966).
Cowherd, Raymond. 1977. *Political Economists and the English Poor Laws* (Athens: Ohio University Press).
Engels, Frederick. 1844. "Outlines of a Critique of Political Economy," in K. Marx, *Economic and Philosophic Manuscripts of 1844* (New York: International Publishers, 1964).
Glacken, Clarence J. 1967. *Traces on the Rhodian Shore* (Berkeley: University of California Press).
Glass, D.V. 1953. "Malthus and the Limitation of Population Growth," in D.V. Glass, *Introduction to Malthus* (London: Watt & Co.): pp. 25–54.
Malthus, Thomas Robert. 1826. *Essay on Population*, 6th edition (London: John Murray).
_____. 1820. *Principles of Political Economy, Considered with a View to their Practical Application* (London: John Murray), reprinted in part in David Ricardo, *Notes on Malthus* Volume 2. *The Works and Correspondence of David Ricardo*, ed. Piero Sraffa (Cambridge, Eng.: Cambridge University Press, 1951).
_____. 1817. *Essay on Population*, 5th edition (London: Johnson).
_____. 1800. "The Present High Price of Provision," reprinted in *The Pamphlets of Thomas Malthus* (New York: Kelly, 1961).
Mitchell, Wesley Clair. 1967. *Types of Economic Theory*, 2 volumes (New York: Augustus M. Kelly).
Say, J.B. 1821. *Letters to Malthus on Several Subjects of Political Economy and on the Cause of Stagnation of Commerce*, tr. John Richter (New York: Kelly Reprints, 1967).
Winch, Donald. 1965. *Classical Political Economy and Colonies* (Cambridge, MA: Harvard University Press).

9

How Poverty Breeds Overpopulation (and not the other way around)

Barry Commoner

The focus of environmentalist Barry Commoner's article is the elucidation of the factors that affect fertility. As is typical of environmental writings, Commoner begins his discourse with a statement of the popular Malthusian syllogism. What is atypical (for example, compare his discourse with Garrett Hardin's (Chapter 18)) is his thoughtful analysis (written in 1974 at the height of "food crisis" hysteria and the relentless ticking away of the "population bomb") of the cause for the discrepency between population numbers and resource availability. Like Poleman (Chapter 7), Commoner discusses the demographic transition characteristic of western countries. Commoner also discusses the colonial legacy and the disruption in the demographic transition that results from colonization. Also included is a description of a field study of birth control in India, conducted by Harvard researchers, that failed miserably. (For a detailed discussion of the study, and why it failed so dramatically, see the classic work of Mahmood Mamdani, *The Myth of Population Control: Family, Caste and Class in an Indian Village* [New York: Monthly Review Press. 1972].)

The world population problem is a bewildering mixture of the simple and the complex, the clear and the confused.

What is relatively simple and clear is that the population of the world is getting larger, and that this process cannot go on indefinitely because there are, after all, limits to the resources, such as food, that are needed to sustain human life. Like all living things, people have an inherent tendency to multiply geometrically—that is, the more people there are the more people they tend to produce. In contrast, the supply of food rises more slowly, for unlike people it does not increase in proportion to the existing rate of food production. This is, of course, the familiar Malthusian relationship and leads to the conclusion that the population is certain eventually to outgrow the food supply (and other needed resources), leading to famine and mass death unless some other countervailing force intervenes to limit population growth. One can argue about the details, but taken as a general summary of the population problem, the foregoing statement is one which no environmentalist can successfully dispute.

When we turn from merely stating the problem to analyzing and attempting to solve it, the issue becomes much more complex. The simple statement that there is a limit to the growth of the human population, imposed on it by the inherent limits of the earth's resources, is a useful but abstract idea. In order to reduce it to the level of reality in which the problem must be solved, what is required is that we find the *cause* of the discrepancy between population growth and the available resources. Current views on this question are neither simple nor unanimous.

One view is that the cause of the population problem is uncontrolled fertility, the countervailing force—the death rate—having been weakened by medical advances. According to this view, given the freedom to do so people will inevitably produce children faster than the goods needed to support them. It follows, then, that the birthrate must be deliberately reduced to the point of "zero population growth."

The methods that have been proposed to achieve this kind of direct reduction in birthrate vary considerably. Among the ones advanced in the past are: (a) providing people with effective contraception and access to abortion facilities and with education about the value of using them (i.e., family planning); (b) enforcing legal means to prevent couples from producing more than some standard number of children ("coercion"); (c) withholding of food from the people of starving developing countries which, having failed to limit their birthrate sufficiently, are deemed to be too far gone or too unworthy to be saved (the so-called "lifeboat ethic").

It is appropriate here to illustrate these diverse approaches with examples. The family planning approach is so well known as to need no further exemplification. As to the second of these approaches, one might cite the following description of it by Kingsley Davis, a prominent demographer, which is quoted approvingly in a recent statement by "The Environmental Fund" that is directed against the family planning position: "If people want to control population, it can be done with knowledge already available . . . For instance, a nation seeking to stabilize its population could shut off immigration and permit each couple a maximum of two children, with possible license for a third. Accidental pregnancies beyond the limit would be interrupted by abortion. If a third child were born without a license, or a fourth, the mother would be sterilized." (Quoted from the Environmental Fund's Statement "Declaration on Population and Food"; original in Daedalus, Fall, 1973).

The author of the "lifeboat ethic" is Garrett Hardin, who stated in a recent paper (presented in San Francisco at the 1974 annual meeting of the American Association for the Advancement of Science) that: "So long as nations multiply at different rates, survival requires that we adopt the ethic of the lifeboat. A lifeboat can hold only so many people. There are more than two billion wretched people in the world—ten times as many as in the United States. It is literally beyond our ability to save them all . . . Both international granaries and lax immigration policies must be rejected if we are to save something for our grandchildren."

Actually, this recent statement only cloaks, in the rubric of an "ethic," a more frankly political position taken earlier by Hardin: "Every day we (i.e., Americans) are a smaller minority. We are increasing at only one percent a year; the rest of the world increases twice as fast. By the year 2000, one person in 24 will be an American; in one hundred years only one in 46 . . . If the world is one great commons, in which all food is shared equally, then we are lost. Those who breed faster will replace the rest . . . In the absence of breeding control a policy of 'one mouth one meal' ultimately produces one totally miserable world. In a less than perfect world, the allocation of rights based on territory must be defended if a ruinous breeding race is to be avoided. It is unlikely that civilization and dignity can survive everywhere; but better in a few places than in none. Fortunate minorities must act as the trustees of a civilization that is threatened by uninformed good intentions." (*Science*, Vol. 172, p. 1297; 1971).

The Quality of Life

But there is another view of population which is much more complex. It is based on the evidence, amassed by demographers, that the birthrate is not only affected by biological factors, such as fertility and contraception, but by equally powerful *social* factors.

Demographers have delineated a complex network of interactions among these social factors. This shows that population growth is not the consequence of a simple arithmetic relationship between birthrate and death rate. Instead, there are circular relationships in which, as in an ecological cycle, every step is connected to several others.

Thus, while a reduced death rate does, of course, increase the rate of population growth, it can also have the opposite effect—since families usually respond to a reduced rate of infant mortality by opting for fewer children. This negative feedback modulates the effect of a decreased death rate on population size. Similarly, although a rising population increases the demand on resources and thereby worsens the population problem, it also stimulates economic activity. This, in turn, improves educational levels. As a result the average age at marriage tends to increase, culminating in a reduced birthrate—which mitigates the pressure on resources.

In these processes, there is a powerful social force which, paradoxically, both reduces the death rate (and thereby stimulates population growth) and also leads people voluntarily to restrict the production of children (and thereby reduces population growth). That force, simply stated, is the quality of life—a high standard of living, a sense of well-being and of security in the future. When and how the two opposite effects of this force are felt differs with the stages in a country's economic development. In a pre-modern society, such as England before the industrial revolution or India before the advent of the English, both death rates and birthrates were high. But they were in balance and population size was stable. Then, as agricultural and industrial production began to increase and living conditions improved, the death rate began to fall. With the birthrate remaining high the population rapidly increased in size. However, later, as living standards continued to improve, the decline in death rate persisted but the birthrate began to decline as well, reducing the rate of population growth.

For example, at around 1800, Sweden had a high birthrate (about 33/1000), but since the death rate was equally high, the population was in balance. Then as agriculture and, later, industrial production advanced, the death rate dropped until, by the mid-nineteenth century, it stood at about 20/1000. Since the birthrate remained constant during that period of time, there was a large excess of births over deaths and the population increased rapidly. Then, however, the birthrate began to drop, gradually narrowing the gap until in the mid-twentieth century it reached about 14/1000, when the death rate was about 10/1000.[1] Thus, under the influence of a constantly rising standard of living the population moved, with time, from a position of balance *at a high death rate* to a new position of near-balance *at a low death rate*. But in between the population increased considerably.

This process, *the demographic transition*, is clearly characteristic of all western countries. In most of them, the birthrate does not begin to fall appreciably until the death rate is reduced below about 20/1000. However, then the drop in birthrate is rapid. A similar transition also appears to be under way in countries like India.

Thus in the mid-nineteenth century, India had equally high birth and death rates (about 50/1000) and the population was in approximate balance. Then, as living standards improved, the death rate dropped to its present level of about 15/1000 and the birthrate dropped, at first slowly and recently more rapidly, to its present level of 42/1000. India is at a critical point; now that death rate has reached the turning point of about 20/1000, we can expect the birthrate to fall rapidly—provided that the death rate is further reduced by improved living conditions.

One indicator of the quality of life—infant mortality—is especially decisive in this process. And again there is a critical point—a rate of infant mortality below which birthrate begins to drop sharply and, approaching the death rate, creates the conditions for a balanced population. The reason is that couples are interested in the number of *surviving* children and respond to a low rate of infant mortality by realizing that they no longer need to have more children to replace the ones that die. Birth control is, of course, a necessary adjunct to this process; but it can succeed—barring compulsion—only in the presence of a rising standard of living, which of itself generates the necessary motivation.

This process appears to be just as characteristic of developing countries as of developed ones. This can be seen by plotting the present birthrates against the present rates of infant mortality for all available national data. The highest rates of infant mortality are in African countries; they are in the range of 53-175/1000 live births and birthrates are about 27-52/1000. In those countries where infant mortality has improved somewhat (for example, in a number of Latin American and Asian countries) the drop in birthrate is slight (to about 45/1000) until the infant mortality reaches about 80/1000. Then, as infant mortality drops from 80/1000 to about 25/1000 (the figure characteristic of most developed countries), the birthrate drops sharply from 45 to about 15-18/1000. Thus a rate of infant mortality of 80/1000 is a critical turning point which can lead to a very rapid decline in birthrate in response to a further reduction in infant mortality. The latter, in turn, is always very responsive to improved living conditions, especially with respect to nutrition. Consequently, there is a kind of critical standard of living which, if achieved, can lead to a rapid reduction in birthrate and an approach to a balanced population.

Thus, in human societies, there is a built-in control on population size: If the standard of living, which initiates the rise in population, *continues* to increase, the population eventually begins to level off. This self-regulating process begins with a population in balance, but at a high death rate and low standard of living. It then progresses toward a population which is larger, but once more in balance, at a low death rate and a high standard of living.

Demographic Parasites

The chief reason for the rapid rise in population in developing countries is that this basic condition has not been met. The explanation is a fact about developing countries which is often forgotten—that they were recently, and in the economic sense often still remain, colonies of more developed countries. In the colonial period, western nations introduced improved living conditions (roads, communications, engineering, agricultural and medical services) as part of their campaign to increase the labor force needed to exploit the colony's natural resources. This increase in living standards initiated the first phase of the demographic transition.

But most of the resultant wealth did not remain in the colony. As a result, the second (or population-balancing) phase of the demographic transition could not take place. Instead the wealth produced in the colony was largely diverted to the advanced nation—where it helped *that* country achieve for itself the second phase of the demographic transition. Thus colonialism involves a kind of demographic parasitism: The second, population-balancing phase of the demographic transition in the advanced country is fed by the suppression of that same phase in the colony.

It has long been known that the accelerating curve of wealth and power of Western Europe, and later of the United States and Japan, has been heavily based on exploitation of resources taken from the less powerful nations: colonies, whether governed legally, or—as in the case of the U.S. control of certain Latin American countries—by extra-legal and economic means. The result has been a grossly inequitable rate of development among the nations of the world. As the wealth of the exploited nations was diverted to the more powerful ones, their power, and with it their capacity to exploit, increased. The gap between the wealth of nations grew, as the rich were fed by the poor.

What is evident from the above considerations is that this process of international exploitation has had another very powerful but unanticipated effect: a rapid growth of the population in the former colonies. An analysis by the demographer, Nathan Keyfitz, leads him to conclude that the growth of industrial capitalism in the western nations in the period 1800-1950 resulted in the development of a one-billion excess in the world population, largely in the tropics. Thus the present world population crisis—the rapid growth of population in developing countries (the former colonies)—is the result not so much of policies promulgated by these countries but of a policy, colonial exploitation, forced on them by developed countries.

A Village in India

Given this background, what can be said about the various alternative methods of achieving a balanced world population? In India, there has been an interesting, if partially inadvertent, comparative test of two of the possible approaches: family planning programs and efforts (also on a family basis), to elevate the living standard. The results of this test show that while the family planning effort itself failed to reduce the birthrate, improved living standards succeeded.

In 1954, a Harvard team undertook the first major field study of birth control in India. The population of a number of test villages was provided with contraceptives and suitable educational programs; birthrates, death rates and health status in this population were compared with the comparable values in an equivalent population in control villages. The study covered the six-year period 1954–1960.

A follow-up in 1969 showed that the study was a failure. Although in the test population the crude birthrate dropped from 40 per 1,000 in 1957 to 35 per 1,000 in 1968, a similar reduction also occurred in the control population. The birth control effort had no measurable effect on birthrate.

We now know *why* the study failed, thanks to a remarkable book by Mahmood Mamdani (*The Myth of Population Control*, Monthly Review Press, New York, 1972). He investigated in detail the impact of the study on one of the test villages, Manupur. What Mamdani discovered is a total confirmation of the view that population control in a country like India depends on the economically-motivated desire to limit fertility. Talking with the Manupur villagers he discovered why, despite the study's statistics regarding ready "acceptance" of the offered contraceptives, the birthrate was not affected:

"One such 'acceptance' case was Asa Singh, a sometime land laborer who is now a watchman at the village high school. I questioned him as to whether he used the tablets or not: 'Certainly I did. You can read it in their books—From 1957 to 1960, I never failed.' Asa Singh, however, had a son who had been born sometime in 'late 1958 or 1959.' At our third meeting I pointed this out to him

. . . Finally he looked at me and responded. 'Babuji, someday you'll understand. It is sometimes better to lie. It stops you from hurting people, does no harm, and might even help them.' The next day Asa Singh took me to a friend's house . . . and I saw small rectangular boxes and bottles, one piled on top of the other, all arranged as a tiny sculpture in a corner of the room. This man had made a sculpture of birth control devices. Asa Singh said: 'Most of us threw the tablets away. But my brother here, he makes use of everything.'"

Such stories have been reported before and are often taken to indicate how much "ignorance" has to be overcome before birth control can be effective in countries like India. But Mamdani takes us much further into the problem, by finding out why the villagers preferred not to use the contraceptives. In one interview after another he discovered a simple, decisive fact: that in order to advance their economic condition, to take advantage of the opportunities newly created by the development of independent India, *children were essential.* Mamdani makes this very explicit:

"To begin with, most families have either little or no savings, and they can earn too little to be able to finance the education of *any* children, even through high school. Another source of income must be found, and the only solution is, as one tailor told me, 'to have enough children so that there are at least three or four sons in the family.' Then each son can finish high school by spending part of the afternoon working . . . After high school, one son is sent on to college while the others work to save and pay the necessary fees . . . Once his education is completed, he will use his increased earnings to put his brother through college. He will not marry until the second brother has finished his college education and can carry the burden of educating the third brother . . . What is of interest is that, as the Khanna Study pointed out, it was the rise in the age of marriage—from 17.5 years in 1956 to 20 in 1969—and not the birth control program that was responsible for the decrease in the birthrate in the village from 40 per 1,000 in 1957 to 35 per 1,000 in 1968. While the birth control program was a failure, the net result of the technological and social change in Manupur was to bring down the birth rate."

Here, then, in the simple realities of the village of Manupur are the principles of the demographic transition at work. There *is* a way to control the rapid growth of populations in developing countries. It is to help them develop—and more rapidly achieve the level of welfare that everywhere in the world is the real motivation for a balanced population.

Enough to Go Around

Against this success, the proponents of the "lifeboat ethic" would argue that it is too slow, and they would take steps to *force* developing nations to reduce their birthrate even though the incentive for reduced fertility—the standard of living and its most meaningful index, infant mortality—is still far inferior to the levels which have motivated the demographic transition in the western countries. And where, in their view, it is too late to save a poor, overpopulated country the proponents of this so-called "ethic" would withdraw support (in the manner of the hopelessly wounded in military "triage") and allow it to perish.

This argument is based (at least in the realm of logic) on the view, to quote Hardin, that "It is literally beyond our ability to save them all." Hardin's assertion, if not the resulting "ethic," reflects a commonly held view that there is simply insufficient food and other resources in the world to support the present world population at the standard of living required to motivate the demographic transition. It is commonly pointed out, for example, that the U.S. consumes about one-third of the world's resources to support only six percent of the world's population, the inference being that there are simply not enough resources in the world to permit the rest of the world to achieve the standard of living and low birthrate characteristic of the U.S.

The fault in this reasoning is readily apparent if one examines the actual relationship between the birthrates and living standards of different countries. The only available comparative measure of standard of living is GNP per capita. Neglecting for a moment the faults inherent in GNP as a measure of the quality of life, a plot of birthrate against GNP per capita is very revealing. The poorest countries (GNP per capita less than $500 per year[2]) have the highest birthrates, 40-50 per 1,000 population per year. When GNP per capita per year exceeds $500 the birthrate drops sharply, reaching about 20/1,000 at $750-$1,000. Most of the nations in North America, Oceania, Europe and the USSR have about the same low birthrates—15-18/1,000— but their GNP's per capita per year range all the way from Greece ($941 per capita per year; birthrate 17/1,000) through Japan ($1,626 per capita per year; birthrate 18/1,000) to the richest country of all, the U.S. ($4,538 per capita per year; birthrate 18/1,000). What this means is that in order to bring the birthrates of the poor countries down to the low levels characteristic of the rich ones, the poor countries do not need to become as affluent (at least as measured, poorly, by GNP per capita) as the U.S. Achieving a per capita GNP only, let us say, one-fifth of that of the U.S.—$900 per capita per year—these countries could, according to the above relationship, reach birthrates almost as low as that of the European and North American countries.

The world average value for birthrate is 34/1,000, which is indicative of the overall rate of growth of the world population (the world average crude death rate is about 13/1,000). However, the world average per capita GNP is about $803 per year—a level of affluence which is characteristic of a number of nations with birthrates of 20/1,000. What this discrepancy tells us is that if the wealth of the world (at least as measured by GNP) were in fact evenly distributed among the people of the world, the entire world population should have a low birthrate—about 20/1,000— which would approach that characteristic of most European and North American countries (15-18/1,000).

Simply stated, the world has enough wealth to support the entire world population at a level that appears to convince most people that they need not have excessive numbers of children. The trouble is that the world's wealth is not evenly distributed, but sharply divided among moderately well-off and rich countries on the one hand and a much larger number of people that are very poor. The poor countries have high birthrates because they are extremely poor, and they are extremely poor because other countries are extremely rich.

The Roots of Hunger

In a sense the demographic transition is a means of translating the availability of a decent level of resources, especially food, into a voluntary reduction in birthrate. It is a striking fact that the efficiency with which such resources can be converted into a reduced birthrate is much higher in the developing countries than in the advanced ones. Thus an improvement in GNP per capita per year from let us say $682 (as in Uruguay) to $4,538 (U.S.) reduces birthrate from 22/1,000 to 18/1,000. In contrast, according to the above relationships if the GNP per capita per year characteristic of India (about $88) were increased to only about $750, the Indian birthrate should fall from its actual value of about 42/1,000 to about 20/1,000. To put the matter more simply, the per capita cost of bringing the standard of living of poor countries with rapidly growing populations to the level which—based on the behavior of people all over the world—would motivate voluntary reduction if fertility is very small, compared to the per capita wealth of developed countries.

Food plays a critical role in these relationships. Hunger is widespread in the world and those who believe that the world's resources are already insufficient to support the world population cite this fact as the most powerful evidence that the world is overpopulated. Conversely, those who are concerned with relieving hunger and preventing future famines often assert that the basic solution to that problem is to control the growth of the world population.

Once more it is revealing to examine actual data regarding the incidence of malnutrition. From a detailed study of nutritional levels among various populations in India by Revelle & Frisch (Vol. III, "The World Food Problem," A Report of the President's Science Advisory Committee, Washington, 1967) we learn, for example, that in Madras State more than one-half the population consumes significantly less than the physiologically required number of calories and of protein in their diet. However, the *average* values for all residents of the state represents 99 percent of the calorie requirement and 98 percent of the protein requirement. What this means, of course, is that a significant part of the population receives *more* than the required dietary intake. About one-third of the population receives 106 percent of the required calories and 104 percent of the required protein; about 8 percent of the population receives 122 percent or more of the calorie requirement and 117 percent or more of the protein requirement. These dietary differences are determined by income. The more than one-half of the population that is significantly below the physiologically required diet earn less than $21 per capita per year, as compared with the state-wide average of $33.40.

What these data indicate is that hunger in Madras State, defined simply in terms of a significantly inadequate intake of calories and protein, is not the result of a biological factor—the inadequate production of food. Rather, in the strict sense, it results from the *social* factors that govern the *distribution* of available food among the population.

In the last year, newspaper stories of actual famines in various parts of the world have also supported the view that starvation is usually not caused by the insufficient production of food in the world, but by social factors that prevent the required distribution of food. Thus, in Ethiopia many people suffered from starvation because government officials failed to mobilize readily available supplies of foreign grain. In India, according to a recent New York Times report, inadequate food supplies were due in part from a government policy which "resulted in a booming black market, angry resentment among farmers and traders, and a breakdown in supplies." The report asserts further that "The central problem of India—rooted poverty—remains unchecked and seems to be getting worse. For the third year out of four per capita income is expected to drop. Nearly 80 percent of the children are malnourished . . . The economic torpor seems symptomatic of deeper problems. Cynicism is rampant: the Government's socialist slogans and calls for austerity are mocked in view of bribes and corruption, luxury construction and virtually open illegal contributions by businessmen to the Congress party." (New York Times, Apr. 17, 1974)

Given these observations and the overall fact that the amount of food crop produced in the world at present is sufficient to provide an adequate diet to about eight billion people—more than twice the world population—it appears to me that the present, tragically widespread hunger in the world cannot be regarded as evidence that the size of the world population has outrun the world's capacity to produce food. I have already pointed out that we can regard the rapid growth of population in developing countries and the grinding poverty which engenders it as the distant outcome of colonial exploitation—a policy imposed on the antecedents of the developing countries by the more advanced ones. This policy has forcefully determined both the distribution of the world's wealth and of its different populations, accumulating most of the wealth in the western countries and most of the people in the remaining, largely tropical, ones.

Thus there is a grave imbalance between the world's wealth and the world's people. But the imbalance is not the supposed disparity between the world's *total* wealth and *total* population. Rather, it is due to the gross *distributive* imbalance among the nations of the world. What the problem calls for, I believe, is a process that now figures strongly in the thinking of the peoples of the Third World: a return of some of the world's wealth to the countries whose resources and peoples have borne so much of the burden of producing it—the developing nations.

Wealth Among Nations

There is no denying that this proposal would involve exceedingly difficult economic, social and political problems, especially for the rich countries. But the alternative solutions thus far advanced are at least as difficult and socially stressful.

A major source of confusion is that these diverse proposed solutions to the population problem, which differ so sharply in their moral postulates and their political effects, appear to have a common base in scientific fact. It is, after all, equally true, scientifically, that the birthrate can be reduced by promulgating contraceptive practices (providing they are used), by elevating living standards, or by withholding food from starving nations.

But what I find particularly disturbing is that behind this screen of confusion between scientific fact and political intent there has developed an escalating series of what can be only regarded, in my opinion, as inhumane, abhorrent political schemes put forward in the guise of science. First we had Paddock's "triage" proposal, which would condemn whole nations to death through some species of global "benign neglect." Then we have schemes for coercing people to curtail their fertility, by physical and legal means which are ominously left unspecified. Now we are told (for example, in the statement of "The Environmental Fund") that we must curtail rather than extend our efforts to feed the hungry peoples of the world. Where will it end? Is it conceivable that the proponents of coercive population control will be guided by one of Garrett Hardin's earlier, astonishing proposals: "How can we help a foreign country to escape over-population? Clearly the worst thing we can do is send food . . . Atomic bombs would be kinder. For a few moments the misery would be acute, but it would soon come to an end for most of the people, leaving a very few survivors to suffer thereafter" ("The Immorality of Being Softhearted," *Stanford Alumni Almanac*, Jan. 1969).

There has been a long-standing alliance between psuedo-science and political repression; the Nazis' genetic theories, it will be recalled, were to be tested in the ovens at Dachau. This evil alliance feeds on confusion.

The present confusion can be removed by recognizing *all* of the current population proposals for what they are—not scientific observations but value judgments that reflect sharply differing ethical views and political intentions. The family planning approach, if applied as the exclusive solution to the problem, would put the burden of remedying a fault created by a social and political evil—colonialism—voluntarily on the individual victims of the evil. The so-called "lifeboat ethic" would compound the original evil of colonialism by forcing its victims to forego the humane course toward a balanced population, improvement of living standards, or if they refuse, to abandon them to destruction, or even to thrust them toward it.

My own purely personal conclusion is, like all of these, not scientific but political: that the world population crisis, which is the ultimate outcome of the exploitation of poor nations by rich ones, ought to be remedied by returning to the poor countries enough of the wealth taken from them to give their peoples both the reason and the resources voluntarily to limit their own fertility.

In sum, I believe that if the root cause of the world population crisis is poverty, then to end it we must abolish poverty. And if the cause of poverty is the grossly unequal distribution of world's wealth, then to end poverty, and with it the population crisis, we must redistribute that wealth, among nations and within them.

Notes

1. This and subsequent demographic information is from: Agency for International Development. *Population Program Assistance*, December 1971.

2. These and subsequent values are computed as U.S. 1969 dollars. The data relate to the 1969–70 period.

10

The Paradox of Kerala

Pran Chopra

And what does happen when resources are more equitably distributed in a society? The advice that Barry Commoner leaves us with in Chapter 9 is put into practice in the state of Kerala, India. Pran Chopra, former chief editor of *The Statesman of Calcutta and New Delhi*, describes how, in Kerala, distributive justice and social welfare are not antithetical to economic growth. As Barry Commoner suggested, birthrates can be brought down even in societies with low per capita income. Food deficits are high, protein content of foods is low, per capita consumption of calories is one-half that in Punjab and yet literacy and life expectancy rates are high. Why?

Kerala introduces itself as a many layered contradiction between the mind and the eye. A closer look resolves the contradiction, but the first impressions are of a paradox.

This tiny state of just under 39,000 km², or 1 percent of India, is tucked away in the southwestern corner and reaches down to within eight degrees of the equator. The density of population is more than three times that of the rest of India. Over 26 million people, or nearly 600 per km², are sandwiched between the Arabian Sea and a ridge of small hills. Yet, as you travel through Kerala, what impresses you most are the trees. From the coconut groves on the coast to the rubber plantations in the uplands, trees of one kind or another fringe the roads, border the farms, screen away every house and hamlet, and this is part of the great physical charm of Kerala. You are left asking yourself whether people live underground or whether the population pressure is exaggerated?

The answer is of course that Kerala, as you quickly discover, is just one continuous village, and the proverbial greenery of the countryside in the rain belt of the tropics (the annual rainfall is 300 cm) is scarred here by only a few cities of any size. The population is more diffusely spread out than in any village typical of northern India, where all houses are clustered together in one area and the farmer does not live surrounded by his fields. In Kerala, he does. House and farm alternate with each other, and the result is that you are never out of sight of groups of people and their daily chores.

Reprinted with permission from The Food and Agricultural Organization of the United Nations. *Ceres* (March-April 1981): 42-45.

The people and their houses add two more dimensions to the contrast between what you see in Kerala and what you would expect to see. The growth rate of the state is faster than the all-India average by about one fourth, and twice as fast as neighbouring Tamil Nadu's. But Kerala remains one of the poorer states. Its per caput income is about 85 percent of India's and only a little over half of Punjab's; it is also lower, though by smaller margins, than of the three neighbouring states, Karnataka, Andhra Pradesh and Tamil Nadu, which together with Kerala form what is popularly known as South India. Its domestic product is half that of the latter two states.

No Child Beggars

Yet, there are hardly any beggars. I must have waited at scores of bus stops during my travels through the state—the usual hunting ground of beggary all over India. But I saw very few beggars there, and none of them a child, as there would have been in any other state.

The people give an impression of being in reasonably good health, even though Kerala has a greater food deficit than many other states, and the food it does produce for its own consumption is markedly poor in protein. Looking at crowds in shops or children, it is impossible not to be impressed by the much higher health standards than are visible in any of the neighbouring states, richer though they are. Finally, the third impression is one of great cleanliness, both of person and habitat. Most people are simply but very cleanly dressed; the humblest hamlets are very tidily kept.

These visual contrasts with the rest of the country have made Kerala justly famous throughout India and elsewhere. But there are other contrasts as well, better known and more startling, which make up the basic explanation of the observable paradox.

One of them is literacy. Almost the entire child population now goes to school, and a higher proportion study up to higher grades than in any other state, which must be one reason why there are no child beggars and few idle street urchins. At more than 60 percent, adult literacy is more than twice as high as the all-India average. And Kerala is still pulling ahead: between the 1961 and 1971 censuses, the all-India figure rose by only 5 percent, Kerala's by 13 percent. Kerala's lead in literacy for women is even greater.

Statistics also support the impression of better health. The crude death rate in Kerala is only slightly above half that in India as a whole; the death rate among rural children under five is only a little more than one third that of India. The infant mortality rate, which the demographer Chandrashekhar calls "the most sensitive index of the level of living and sanitary conditions," is less than 44 percent of the all-India rate. Despite Kerala's earlier history of congenital diseases, mortality among children under five is much lower than in India as a whole. Life expectancy is higher by about one third. On the other hand, the birthrate is significantly lower, and has been falling at the rate of one point per year, from 39 in 1961 to 26.5 in 1974; the rural birthrate fell from 37.4 in 1966 to 25 in 1976. However, Kerala has not come anywhere near solving its population problems. The decline in birthrate is significant, but until quite recently it continued to be offset by a still steeper decline in the death rate. Only now has the rate of decline in the birthrate begun to exceed significantly that of the death rate.

Unemployment is still rising, and for a variety of reasons of which population pressure—though perhaps the most important—is not the only one. Economic resources, and therefore the job market, are limited. This, combined with the remarkable spread of education, means a very high pressure of unemployment among the educated; university graduates seek jobs on salaries of US$1 a day. On the other hand, because the poor, especially the rural poor, are better organized than any other state, the prevailing wage rate for semiskilled and unskilled jobs is higher than in most states and much higher than the economy can afford.

Three Mass Benefits

Demand for jobs is not allowed to depress wages because various workers rotate one job among themselves. But it does not lower the wage bill and ultimately leads to shutdowns, a problem that in Kerala has affected even agriculture; farmers have been switching over from paddy farming, which is labour intensive, to tapioca and coconut farming, which is not, so that the job market shrinks. Labour conditions also do not encourage any rapid investment in industry. Dr. K.N. Haj, Director of the Centre for Development Studies in Trivandrum, whose report on poverty in Kerala is perhaps the best published on the subject as yet, says, "Without effective measures to combat mass unemployment most of the gains secured can be gradually eroded." But how these gains have been achieved is a fascinating story of social engineering.

The recent history of population pressure explains why Kerala has become such an interesting case study for demographers and family planning organizations all over the world. Family planning has indeed scored a great success, even though in Kerala it was never accompanied by any of the harsher measures of persuasion applied in certain parts of India recently. The key to this success lies in the whole social milieu that was created in Kerala.

According to the Demographic Centre of the Government of Kerala, the population of the state as well as the density of population nearly doubled in the 30 years from 1941 to 1971, and the rate of increase in the population mounted in each of the three decades; in the last, it was 15 times as fast as in the first decade of this century, 1901 to 1911. The long-term rate of growth in this century has been twice as high as in the country as a whole. This happened mainly because, under a public health programme which had begun a long time ago, the death rate declined at all levels.

However, it would be wrong to say that because this decline occurred after the introduction of family planning, it occurred because of that. Family planning propagated knowledge of the ways of birth control and provided facilities for adopting them. What made it a success was its acceptability, a willingness on the part of the people to be persuaded, and their ability to practise what they learned about it. These factors are partly the result of an educational system and of a public health programme that have aimed at mass welfare rather than serving the privileged classes.

This egalitarianism is not only due to recent politics in Kerala, though the dominant parties of the left have further accentuated the tendency. The first to practise egalitarian policies on a large scale were the royal houses of the states of Travancore and Cochin, which now constitute the central and southern districts of Kerala. The northern districts, once known as Malabar, were under British colonial rule until India became independent, and did not have the benefit of such policies until they were merged in 1956 to form the present state of Kerala.

The rulers of Travancore and Cochin vigorously spread through their states three mass benefits. First, fair distribution of land and protected rights upon it for all cultivators. More than 100 years ago, they converted the state into a broad-based society of peasant proprietorships at a time when, in the vast stretches of India where they held sway, including Malabar, the British were creating a benighted feudalistic system of permanent exploitative rights for rentier landlords.

By the end of the 1960s, rental income from land had been abolished throughout Kerala and all land permanently placed in the hands of those who cultivated it. Even agricultural labourers became permanent owners of the sites of their dwellings and some surrounding margins. This accounts for two of the most delightful sights Kerala offers: intensive cultivation, and the cleanliness of the meanest dwelling, a product of the pride of owning it. It also accounts for the more even distribution of such wealth as there is and for bringing a higher proportion of the people of Kerala closer to acceptable standards of living than in most other states.

This general lifting up also had the important consequence of making the people more responsive to the other measures of public welfare, that of mass literacy and extensive public health measures.

The report of the Indian census of 1941 quotes a Royal Command issued in 1817 by Rani Gwori Parvati of Travancore, directing that "the state shall defray the entire cost of the education of the people." Subsequent rulers continued this policy, helping to make Kerala the most literate state in India.

It is not that Kerala spends more of its budget upon education than other states. But it does spend more of the educational budget upon schools than on elite education, and spends it with an emphasis upon equality in literacy between male and female, rural and urban and rich and poor sections of the population.

Better Sanitation

More widely diffused education has made a higher proportion of people better able to understand the ways of public health and sanitation; more equitable distribution of wealth has made them more able to afford the means. But what has also helped Kerala reach the lowest mortality rates in the country and a life expectancy much higher than most states is a more equitably distributed health system. The foundation of this was also laid by the princely rulers in the past. An 1865 statement by the Maharaja of Travancore says: "It is my ambition to see that good medical aid is placed within the reach of all classes of my subjects."

Kerala does not spend more upon public health than many other states and in fact does not have more doctors, dispensaries or hospital beds. But what it spends and what it has are more evenly distributed, with added emphasis on the rural and poorer areas, while in most other states facilities are disproportionately concentrated for the benefit of the urban and less poor sections. Hence, as statistics in Raj's study show, there is a much higher utilization of public health facilities in Kerala and a much closer proximation of rural to urban and female to male health standards than in any other state, and distinctions between the richer and poorer peoples' health are minimal. Better sanitation and general cleanliness have sharply brought down the incidence of many diseases.

And this despite a much lower level of nourishment. The per caput consumption of calories in rural Kerala is almost half that in Punjab and yet the rural infant mortality rate and rural crude death rate are 50 percent lower. The key to this riddle is also the same: a more equal distribution of what nourishment there is, which is ensured by a double method. Two thirds of the state's population of children in the age group 6 to 10 take a well-composed free meal at school in a programme assisted by CARE. For the adult population, there is a public distribution system of fair price shops, which covers practically every household, rural or urban. There are not many states that can boast of such features. Out of this century-old package of enlightened policies, begun by princes and greatly expanded by the

Marxist government, has come—virtually as a by-product and without any hard family planning drive—a sharper decline in birthrate than any other state in India has achieved.

Later Marriages

Demographers are disagreed on whether high literacy or a high health standard has had more impact. But they are agreed that both have had an influence. Better health has set the classic chain of demographic transition in motion: first, increase in life expectancy; next, decline in general death rates; next, sharper decline in infant mortality; finally, dramatic fall in birthrates as parents find they do not have to have many children to ensure the survival of the minimum desired. More education has meant a keener desire for working careers and therefore later marriages (which also means fewer children), as well as a better grasp of birth control methods. On the whole, the evidence is stronger in favour of education. The rate of literates among the practitioners of family planning is much higher than in the general population, especially among women.

Thus, Kerala has disproved a number of beliefs that are strongly held in the world of conventional wisdom about development. Kerala has shown that distributive justice and social welfare can be combined with economic growth. It has shown that the birthrate can be brought down sharply, even in societies that have very low per caput incomes and little industrialization or urbanization. And that it can be brought down without coercive family planning.

What is needed for these apparently contradictory achievements is continuous practice of policies of social welfare, with a strong emphasis on equality of opportunity for all and equal distribution of the means of developing the opportunity. That is how Kerala has scored the achievements that have made it famous.

11

The Infant Mortality Rate:
Some Questions and Answers
(excerpts)
Joan Holmes

And who will tell us the good news? Hunger Project Executive Director Joan Holmes says that her organization will "cover the facts of hunger; be they 'good' or 'bad.'" Her news in this particular issue of A Shift in the Wind is good. The Infant Mortality Rate (IMR), one of the most important indicators of world hunger and preconditions to fertility decline, is decreasing. (See World Development Report 1984. New York: Oxford University Press. 1984. pp. 262–263; this volume compiled by the World Bank provides further data on decline in IMRs.) Questions concerning the IMR, including the relationship between the IMR and "population explosion," are discussed below.

Q: What is the IMR?
A: The Infant Mortality Rate (IMR) is a statistic that represents the number of infants, out of every 1,000 live births, who die before they are one year old. For example, in Afghanistan, a country with an IMR of 205, one infant in every five born in a given year does not survive to see his or her first birthday.

Q: What does the IMR mean? What does it show?
A: According to Kathleen Newland of the Worldwatch Institute, a Washington, D.C.-based research organization, "No cold statistic expresses more eloquently the difference between a society of sufficiency and a society of deprivation than the infant mortality rate. . . . The number of children who die before they are one year old is closely related to the overall level of well-being in a country or region—so closely, in fact, that it is regarded as one of the most revealing measures of how well a society is meeting the needs of its people."

Q: Why focus on infant deaths?
A: Children under the age of one year are especially vulnerable to conditions in their environment. Their chances for survival depend to a great extent on external forces. Thus, the number of children who die in a particular environment is a good indicator of the possibilities for survival and well-being in that region.

Reprinted with permission from A Shift in the Wind #18. San Francisco: The Hunger Project.

Q: How long has the IMR been in use as a measurement?

A: The IMR is a form of measurement that has been in widespread use for a comparatively short time. Precise levels of infant mortality have been widely available only in the twentieth century. In the United States, for example, death registration was not initiated until 1900, followed by birth registration in 1915, and those two systems included every state only after 1933. In 1900, the IMR of the U.S. was estimated at 120; in 1940, at 48. Today, it has reached 11.4 and is still falling.

Sweden—the country with the world's lowest IMR—has, interestingly, one of the longest series of infant mortality data. Its records begin in 1748, when parish registers maintained by the state church became the basis of official statistics. Today, Sweden's IMR is 7, with most of these few deaths occurring in the first week of life.

The IMR in various countries now ranges from 7 in Sweden to a high of 210 in Upper Volta, where hunger is a day-to-day issue in the lives of the vast majority of people.

Q: How is hunger related to the IMR?

A: Hunger seldom appears on official records as the cause of an infant's death. However, under-nutrition is the most common factor that turns common illnesses into fatal diseases for a child. A child's ability to withstand the effect of common ailments depends on the child's resistance to infection and on his or her ability to regain strength following illness. Where nutrition is inadequate, the child has little protection against disease and few resources available to recover strength once illness strikes. The fatality rate for measles, for example, can be 400 to 500 times higher for undernourished children than for those who are well-fed.

Diarrhea is the leading killer of young children in developing countries and causes an estimated 5 million child deaths each year. While diarrhea is caused by contact with contaminated food and water, a well-nourished child could easily resist digestive problems that will kill a badly nourished child.

Q: What does the IMR tell us about the persistence of hunger in a country or region?

A: Many authorities—including the World Health Organization, UNICEF and the Overseas Development Council—have agreed that, when a country has brought its IMR to a level of 50 or below, it could be said that hunger as a basic society-wide issue has ended.

In no country where the IMR has dropped below 50—and indeed in the vast majority of such countries, the IMR has continued to decrease to the 30s and lower—has hunger continued to be a basic issue of day-to-day life for the population at large.

This is not, of course, to say that there are no hungry people in countries with low IMRs. In the United States, for example, there are segments of the population for whom hunger remains a very real issue. An IMR of 50 or below means that hunger has ended as an issue affecting the lives of the vast majority of the people.

Q: Using this measurement, where do we stand in ending hunger in the world today?

A: In 1900, no country had an IMR below 50. Since then, 73 countries have brought their IMRs to 50 or below. They have ended hunger as a basic, society-wide issue. In 39 of these countries, this has been accomplished since 1960.

These countries are to be found in North America, Europe and parts of Asia and Latin America. No country on the continent of Africa has yet achieved an IMR of 50 or below.

Q: How does a mother's health and nutrition affect her child's chances of survival?
A: In each of three key factors associated with infant deaths—low birth weight, lack of breast-feeding and too closely spaced births—the mother's health plays a crucial role.
* Low weight at birth—below 5 1/2 pounds (2.5 kilograms)—is the biggest single factor linked to infant mortality. The infant's birth weight is affected by the length of time the child is carried, by the mother's age and, especially, by her nutritional status and overall health care. In developing areas, where nutrition is often inadequate and health care irregular, low-birth-weight babies are a large number of those born in any given year.
* Mother's milk is the most complete form of nutrition available to an infant. The mother's nutrition is a key to ensuring a sufficient supply of breast milk with an appropriate nutritional balance for her child. In societies where women have an inferior role, receive less food, do more strenuous labor and have poorer medical care, mothers may find themselves unable to provide sufficient breast milk to meet their children's needs.
* A child whose mother has borne more than four children is likely to be smaller, weaker and twice as likely to die as a first or second child. Longer intervals between children, with good nourishment for the mother during those times, are critical not only to the mother's well-being but also to the survival of future babies.

Q: How does a family's income level affect the mortality rate of its children?
A: The income level of the family does not of itself affect a child's chances of survival—pound for pound, poor babies do as well as rich ones. However, poor families often cannot afford the nutrition (both for mother and child) that puts on those pounds. Moreover, the parents' income may affect other elements that have a strong impact on the child's survival. For example: . . .

Availability of water and sanitation
Infant deaths are most likely to occur where there is no access to safe water, sanitation systems or regular pest control. Such poor hygienic conditions are most often found in overcrowded cities or in the poorest rural areas.

Level of mother's education
The educational level of mothers is a key influence on the IMR. Education provides access to new information and technologies in nutrition, hygiene and health care. Educated mothers are more likely to detect serious health problems quickly and are then more ready to seek appropriate medical care.

Q: How are births and deaths defined and reported? Are we comparing similar data among nations?
A: The definition of a live birth may vary from one nation to the next. Some countries consider breathing or heartbeat or voluntary movement a sign of life; others require all three. Still others do not register a birth as "live" until the child has survived for one week.
In some nations, births and deaths are reported by medical personnel attending the events; in others, by the families. In other areas, town watchmen who may be uneducated or unpaid must gather and report all vital statistics. These irregularities make the raw IMR data widely variable among the countries in which the IMR is measured.
On the other hand, groups such as the United Nations and the Population Reference Bureau which work with the IMR data have a variety of means for

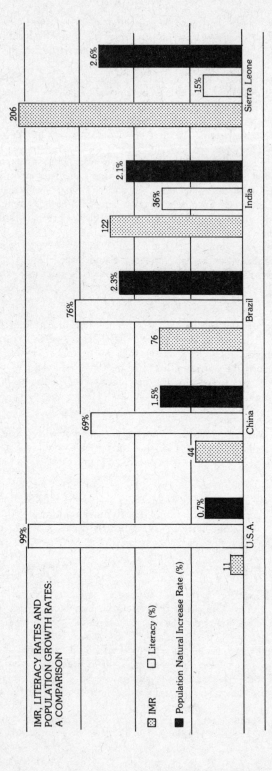

IMR, LITERACY RATES AND
POPULATION GROWTH RATES:
A COMPARISON

IMR   Literacy (%)

Population Natural Increase Rate (%)

U.S.A.   China   Brazil   India   Sierra Leone

99%   0.7%   44   69%   1.5%   76   2.3%   76%   122   36%   2.1%   206   15%   2.6%   11

Figure 11.1. IMR, literacy rates and population growth rates: a comparison. The chart compares IMR with literacy and natural increase of population rates for five countries in the 1980s. As these numbers show, a low IMR is generally accompanied by high literacy rates and by low population growth rates.

adjusting to take individual reported differences into account, and also utilize figures based on specific samples or surveys.

Overall, infant mortality is the single measurable and available factor most consistently related to hunger.

Q: Won't a decline in the IMR lead to a population explosion?

A: No, quite the reverse. Virtually every country has seen a sustained reduction in its population growth rate following the lowering of its IMR. Immediately after a rapid drop in the IMR, national population growth rates are likely to rise, but birth rates soon decline substantially as parents see that their children will survive.

The time lag between a sharp decline in IMR and a parallel drop in birth rates has typically been around a decade in developing countries. The more rapid the drop in the IMR, the faster the birth rates are generally seen to fall.

Q: What can be done to hasten the decline in the IMR?

A: Reductions in IMR are achieved when the nutritional levels of both mothers and children are improved and sustained throughout child-bearing years. Programs designed to achieve these goals are accompanied by dramatic drops in the IMR.

However, the infant mortality rate is not a target or a score. Its value lies in its accurate reflection of the conditions present in a society. The best use of the IMR is as a signpost, to direct us to discover and to provide those conditions in which infants, and all people, can survive, flourish and express their full potential.

The job we face is to create and fulfill the possibility that is reborn with the arrival of each newborn child. The job can and will be done when the public commitment exists to identify those conditions that limit humanity and to transform them throughout the world.

12

Recent Trends in Fertility in Less Developed Countries
(excerpts)
Ansley J. Coale

An earlier work co-authored by Ansley Coale, *Population Growth and Economic Development in Low-Income Countries* (with E.M. Hoover. Princeton: Princeton University Press. 1958), is mentioned in Julian Simon's work (Chapter 6). In Coale's 1983 article, the author notes that in the 1960s, the world birthrate began to decline more rapidly than the death rate, and that from a historical perspective, the peak rate in population growth previously observed will be of short-lived concern. The rapid decrease of fertility in China is of particular note (the decrease may be remarkable although the methods used to achieve this have been questionable). How developing countries have achieved at least a 50 percent reduction of fertility in a very short time period deserves more scientific study as well as legal scrutiny.

Projecting LDC Trends

The period of rapid growth (Fig. 12.1) from 1930 to 2030 (as projected) will surely prove to have been a relatively short one when viewed in a long historical perspective. If the peak rate of increase of 2.5 percent were to persist, the population of the LDC's would reach 33 billion (from the current 3.3 billion) by 2100 and 330 billion about a century later. If the projected decline of the rate of increase to zero by the end of the next century is realized, their total population will increase to about 10 billion.

The rate of increase in the LDC's has already turned down. In the 1960's the birth rate, which had begun to fall a little earlier, began to fall more rapidly than the death rate. According to the median projections of the United Nations made in 1980, the birth rate of the LDC's will decline to 18.7 per thousand in 2025; the projected decline is here extended beyond 2025 in such a way as to bring the rate of increase to zero in 2100. Note that the projected death rate rises during most of the next century. This increase occurs because the projected population contains a progressively larger proportion of old persons as low fertility progressively reduces

Reprinted with permission from *Science* 221 (4613): 828–832 (26 August 1983). Copyright 1983 by the AAAS.

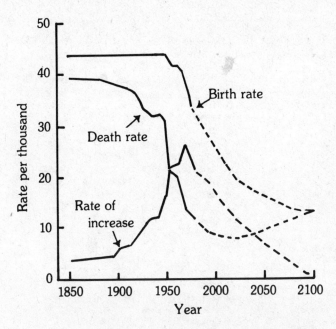

Figure 12.1. Birth rate, death rate, and rate of population increase in less developed countries, 1850 to 2100.

the fraction of younger ones. Mortality rates at each age in the LDC's are in fact assumed to become as favorable as any in the world today.

In Table 12.1 the reduction in the total fertility rate for a list of LDC's in which there has been a large recent decrease is shown. Some of the populations at the top of the list have reduced fertility to levels typical of more developed countries. The first eight have had a reduction of at least 50 percent in a very short period; in all eight the total fertility rate is lower than in the United States only 20 years ago, and in six of the eight fertility is no higher than in Europe as a whole in the early 1960's.

Note that the first five populations in Table 12.1 all have a culture of Chinese origin, and that six of the first ten, and ten of the list of 26; inhabit islands. The total population of the LDC's with a large recent decline is about 2.4 billion. There has been no significant decline, and in some instances a recent increase, in Africa, except for Egypt, Tunisia, and South Africa (total population about 400 million); in Haiti, Honduras, Nicaragua, and Bolivia (total population about 20 million); in Burma, Laos, and Vietnam (total population about 90 million); in Nepal, Bangladesh, Pakistan, Iran, and other populations in South Central Asia (total population 250 million); and in Arab countries (total population about 50 million). The grand total population of LDC's with no significant recent decline in fertility is about 800 million. In the remainder of the LDC's, with a total population of about 100 million, there has been at most a slight decrease in the rate of childbearing.

Of the total population of some 2.4 billion in LDC's with a substantial recent fall in fertility, about 42 percent is in China and 29 percent is in India. The importance of China in the recent decline of the birth rate is seen in Fig. 12.2. In the past 2 or 3 years in various Chinese publications data have appeared from which a series of annual birth rates can be derived (1). Two remarkable features of the

TABLE 12.1. Recent Reduction in Fertility (total fertility rate)
in Selected Less Developed Countries (2)

Country	Total Fertility Rate		Reduction
	Earlier	Later	(%)
Singapore	6.3 (1959)	1.9 (1977)	70
Taiwan	6.5 (1956)	2.5 (1980)	61
China	5.5 (1953)	2.4 (1978)	56
Hong Kong	5.1 (1960)	2.4 (1977)	53
South Korea	6.0 (1960)	2.9 (1976-80)	52
Cuba	4.7 (1960-64)	2.3 (1977)	52
Mauritius	6.4 (1952)	3.1 (1977)	52
Puerto Rico	5.0 (1950-54)	2.4 (1975-79)	51
Costa Rica	7.4 (1960)	3.8 (1976)	49
Thailand	6.6 (1965)	3.9 (1979)	41
Chile	5.3 (1955-59)	3.1 (1975-79)	41
Colombia	6.8 (1964)	4.2 (1978)	38
Malaysia	6.9 (1957)	4.3 (1976)	38
Sri Lanka	5.9 (1950-54)	3.7 (1970-74)	37
Mexico	7.2 (1965)	4.7 (1979)	35
Brazil	6.2 (1945-49)	4.3 (1975-79)	31
Venezuela	6.8 (1960-64)	4.8 (1975-79)	30
Turkey	6.8 (1945-49)	5.1 (1970-74)	25
Philippines	6.6 (1960)	5.1 (1976)	23
Dominican Republic	6.7 (1960-64)	5.3 (1975-79)	23
India	6.2 (1951-60)	4.9 (1979)	21
Tunisia	7.3 (1965-66)	5.9 (1974-75)	19
Panama	5.9 (1960-64)	4.8 (1975)	19
Egypt	6.7 (1959-60)	5.5 (1975-76)	18
Peru	6.6 (1964)	5.5 (1974)	17
Indonesia	5.5 (1968)	5.0 (1977)	10

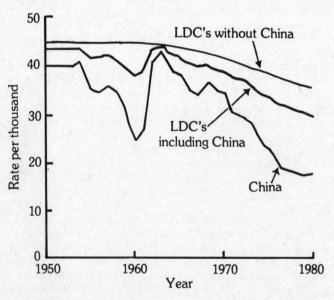

Figure 12.2. Birth rates in less developed countries as a whole,
in China, and in less developed countries, not including China.

birth rate in China since 1950 are the large dip in 1958 to 1961 during the Great Leap Forward and the ensuing economic crisis, and the very large decline from 1963 to 1980, after recovery from the low birth rates around 1960. The population of China is so large (nearly one-third of the total LDC population during the past three decades) and its birth rate has been so variable that much of the variation in the overall LDC birth rate since 1950 is contributed by China. In particular, the impressive overall decline from a birth rate of 44 per thousand in 1963 to about 30 per thousand in 1980 would have been much smaller without the remarkable fall of fertility in China.

Notes

1. J. Aird, *Popul. Dev. Rev.* 8, 267 (1982).
2. The choice of the earlier date was determined by the availability of a valid estimate of the total fertility rate and by the likelihood that fertility at that date had not yet begun a sustained decline. Because of differences in the availability of data, and the date of the initiation of the reduction in fertility, the ordering of populations by the size of the proportionate decline in fertility is not an ordering by the rate of decline. Moreover, in some populations listed (Hong Kong, Cuba, Chile, and Indonesia), the total fertility rate in the not very distant past was higher than at the earlier date shown; also, there are in several instances indications of a further decline after the later date. The sources for Table 12.1 are as follows: United Nations, *Demographic Yearbook, Historical Supplement* (United Nations Publications, New York, 1979). Costa Rica, Hong Kong, Mauritius, Singapore; *World Population Prospects as Assessed in 1980* (United Nations Publications, New York, 1981), Chile, Puerto Rico; Republic of China, *Statistical Year Book, 1981*, Taiwan; National Research Council, Committee on Population and Demography, reports on Brazil, Colombia, Egypt, India, Indonesia, Korea, Thailand, and Turkey (National Academy Press, Washington, D.C., 1980, 1981, 1982, and forthcoming); J. Knodel *et al., Int. Fam. Plann. Perspect.* 6, No. 3 (1980), Thailand; A. Coale, *Popul. Dev. Rev.* 7, 512 (1981), China; R. Rutherford *et al.*, "Estimates of current fertility derived from the 1980 census of Korea" (East-West Population Institute, Honolulu unpublished); N. Goldman and J. Hobcraft, *Birth Histories, Comp. Stud. No. 17* (World Fertility Survey, London, 1982), Panama, Peru, Philippines, Sri Lanka; J. Hobcraft and G. Rodriguez, *The Analysis of Repeat Surveys, Scientific Studies No.29* (World Fertility Survey, London, 1980), Dominican Republic; S. Diaz-Briquets and L. Perez, *Popul. Ref. Bur. Bull.* 36, 1 (1981), Cuba; D. Tabutin, in *Nuptiality and Fertility*, L. Ruzicka, Ed. (Ordina, Liege, Belgium, 1981), Tunisia.

13

The Depo-Provera Debate

Matt Clark with Mary Lord, Timothy Nater and Deborah Witherspoon

When Depo-Provera was introduced in the 1960s, it appeared to be the perfect contraceptive. Not only was the drug nearly 100 percent effective, but it needed to be taken only four times per year. Depo-Provera has been used by millions of women since its introduction. Yet scientists are concerned about its safety.

Banned in the U.S. since 1978 for use as a contraceptive, it is still used in population control programs in developing countries. (For further information on this double standard, see the November, 1979 issue of *Mother Jones*.) Part of the debate over the safety of Depo concerns the validity of animal studies. Although we may have doubts concerning extrapolation of results to human populations, the alternatives (longer-term experiments which are costly, use of human subjects) seem either financially prohibitive or ethically unacceptable.

Depending on whom you listen to, Depo-Provera is either the ideal contraceptive or a serious health hazard. A single injection of the drug prevents pregnancy for three months, but there is some evidence that it may cause cancer and other problems. Although Depo has been taken by more than 11 million women in 80 countries during the last two decades, its critics have kept it off the market as a contraceptive in the United States. Last week the U.S. Food and Drug Administration convened an unusual "board of inquiry" to listen to arguments on both sides and decide whether the drug should become a birth-control option for American women.

The three-member panel faces the classic question in medicine: do the benefits of a drug outweigh the risks? The issue has cropped up frequently in the field of birth control. "All currently available techniques, from oral contraceptives to intrauterine devices, barrier methods and injectables like Depo-Provera, have advantages and disadvantages," points out Dr. Pramilla Senanayake of the International Planned Parenthood Federation. The active ingredient in Depo is a synthetic progestogen hormone that suppresses the pituitary hormones that normally bring about ovulation. The drug is approved for the treatment of certain kinds of kidney and uterine cancer. In the 1960s it was introduced as a long-acting injectable contraceptive, and proponents claim it is more effective than either the Pill or IUD's, especially in

Third World countries where women often use the more established birth-control methods improperly.

The FDA banned the use of Depo as a contraceptive in the United States in 1978 because of animal experiments suggesting it might cause cancer. In one study, beagles developed breast tumors when given 25 times the human dose of the drug. Cancer of the lining of the uterus occurred in some rhesus monkeys getting huge doses of the drug in another trial.

The Upjohn Co., manufacturers of Depo, is pressing hard to lift the ban. The firm expects that up to 4 million American women would use the drug. The market would expand even further because countries like India and Egypt, which usually use FDA decisions to guide their own drug policies, would probably approve Depo.

Coalition: An impressive array of health organizations favor approval, including the World Health Organization, International Planned Parenthood and the American College of Obstetrics and Gynecology. "There is a clear need for this agent, and I think it should be made available," says Dr. Elizabeth Connell of Emory University School of Medicine. But a coalition of consumer and feminist groups, such as Ralph Nader's Health Research Group and the National Women's Health Network, as well as many government scientists, vehemently support the ban. The long-acting advantage of Depo, contends Dr. Sidney Wolfe of the HRG, does not "justify exposing healthy women to a dangerous drug."

Part of the debate concerns the significance of the animal studies. The pro-Depo faction points out that beagles are especially prone to breast tumors and are therefore inappropriate for testing such drugs. As for the monkey study, they note that monkeys and humans respond quite differently to progestogens. The Depo defense rests its case on the fact that surveys of women who have taken the drug around the world have showed no evidence of an increased risk of cancer or, as has also been charged, birth defects. "You don't get the impression that Depo is any more harmful than any of the other contraceptives we're using," says Dr. Howard Ory of the U.S. Centers for Disease Control.

Critics contend, however, that the drug hasn't been used long enough to really tell how risky it is for humans, given the latent period for the development of many types of cancer. "There is a considerable amount of evidence that if a compound is carcinogenic in one species, it is carcinogenic in another," says Dr. T.C. Jones, a research pathologist.

The debate points up the fact that there is no truly ideal contraceptive, and it may spur research toward the development of safer, more effective methods:

* Family-planning experts in several countries are testing RU-486, a pill taken only two or three times a month that induces menstruation and terminates pregnancy if it has occurred. The drug blocks the action of the hormone progesterone, which normally thickens the lining of the uterus permitting implantation of the fertilized egg. The major advantage of RU-486 is that it doesn't affect the pituitary, the master endocrine gland.

* The National Institutes of Health is developing a capsule containing a progestogen similar to Depo that would be implanted under the skin and provide contraception for up to six months. The capsule releases the drug slowly and evenly and doesn't expose the user to a surge of hormone as a Depo injection does.

Within a few months, the FDA is expected to approve a contraceptive sponge permeated with a spermicide and intended to be inserted prior to intercourse. Another barrier contraceptive under trial is a molded rubber cap to be fitted over the cervix. One model can be worn for months at a time because it has a valve to permit menstrual flow.

* Male contraceptives aren't quite so close to practical use. Gossypol, derived from cottonseed oil, has been tried on more than 4,000 men in China and seems to block sperm production. But the safety of the drug hasn't been established. The hormone LHRH, produced by the hypothalamus in the brain, also suppresses sperm development if given in sufficiently high doses. But it could prove useless as a contraceptive because of overkill: such doses undermine sexual performance.

The board of inquiry on Depo will take its time before making a recommendation. It will then be up to FDA Commissioner Dr. Arthur Hull Hayes to decide whether to approve its use. Some observers believe the agency may compromise, permitting the drug's sale but ordering Upjohn to do careful follow-ups on women who take it.

14

Sterilization Regulations: Debate Not Quelled by HEW Document

Judith Coburn

Sterilization abuse and use of unsafe contraceptive drugs and mechanical devices have been a problem particularly in India where between 1969 and 1972 the population control budget expressed as a percentage of the health budget exceeded 140 percent (see "Population Control Programs: Basic Data 1968–1973 for Selected Countries" by Pierre Borgoltz, Department of Agricultural Economics, Cornell University, Ithaca. 1975). Population control zeal is not limited to developing countries, as is discussed in this article that appeared in *Science* in 1974. *Time* and *Newsweek* also reported (see "Sterilization Bibliography—Periodicals" by Janis Boettinger, Department of Natural Resources, Cornell University, Ithaca. 1983) on sterilization abuse and the concomitant issues of informed consent and free choice.

The release of regulations on sterilization of minors and mental incompetents by the Department of Health, Education, and Welfare has not resolved the controversy surrounding the practice. Since last summer's disclosure of the sterilization of two Alabama teenagers, the argument has extended beyond the immediate issues into a full dress debate over informed consent, medical ethics, and the rights of patients. The charge that Minnie and Mary Alice Relf, ages 14 and 12, had been sterilized without their own or their parents' understanding thrust the special issue of the sterilization of minors and the mentally retarded, long controversial with civil libertarians, onto the front pages of the nation's newspapers. Senator Edward Kennedy (D-Mass.) immediately called the Relf family to testify as part of his health subcommittee's ongoing investigation of the ethics of medical experimentation. After the hearings, Kennedy deplored the lack of any guarantee that patients are fully informed about medical procedures to be used upon them.

Meanwhile, HEW, faced with criticism from public interest groups and a law suit from the Relfs' attorneys, has temporarily suspended until 8 March the regulations which it brought forth for public view on 6 February.

Since the disclosures about the Relf case, a score of other cases of uninformed sterilization have been discovered, most of them involving operations on black teenagers or women on welfare performed by doctors in the South. The Relf family has sued the local family planning officials and federal health officials for $5 million and American Civil Liberties Union (ACLU) lawyers on the national and local level have entered a number of cases. Statistics on sterilizations are incomplete. HEW says that 25,000 adults were sterilized in federally aided birth control clinics from mid-1972 to mid-1973. The North Carolina State Eugenics Board reports that between 1960 and 1968 1620 persons (1583 were women, 1023 black) were sterilized in North Carolina; 55.9 percent were under 20 years old. Twenty-six states have eugenics statutes permitting the sterilizations of minors or mental incompetents, or both, but they vary widely.

On 6 February, in response to the growing controversy, HEW issued a set of regulations that would permit federal funds to be used for nontherapeutic sterilizations of minors and mental incompetents only if certain protective procedures prescribed in the regulations are followed. These procedures must be followed even if parental consent is granted. Sterilizations in these cases will have to be approved by a review committee of at least five members appointed by "responsible authorities of the program or project"; two of the members must be representatives of the population served by the project. The regulations require that "no member of the Review Committee be an officer, employee, or other representative of the program under which the procedure is proposed." According to the regulations, both sexes would have to be represented on the committees. Besides committee approval of the sterilization of a minor or mental incompetent, a court must determine that the operation is "in the best interest of the patient." An amendment to the Social Security Act will also make the regulations apply to any sterilization financed by Medicaid or Social Security.

For HEW's critics, the new regulations seem to raise more problems than they have resolved. Criticism of the regulations ranges from opposition to any federal aid at all for sterilization to technical points about the review committees and how they are chosen. The regulations are being issued at a time when debate about state regulation of reproduction and contraception is at a fever pitch. Roman Catholic and "right-to-life" groups, hard at work trying to reverse the recent pro-abortion trend, oppose any state or federal aid for sterilizations. At the other extreme is an increasingly growing minority, some of them state legislators, who ask the review committees and the courts to approve sterilizations of minors and mental incompetents even if the parents or guardians do not consent.

In response to criticism of an earlier draft of the regulations, HEW strengthened the requirements for informed consent in all federally aided sterilizations, including those performed on adults. The requirements for informed consent in sterilizations follow the new procedures developed by HEW for human experimentation. These specify that the consent form show that the patient understands the operation, its effects, and alternatives as well as giving consent. Officials of HEW hope that this requirement will prevent the sort of thing that happened in the Relf case—when Mrs. Relf signed a consent form for her daughters' sterilization, but thought that it was for "shots." The new regulations also require a 72-hour waiting period between the signing of the consent form and the operation.

In a number of the lawsuits involving sterilization, critics have raised the question of whether a signed consent form means that the consent is voluntary. A recent study by the Health Research Group found that pressuring poor and black women to consent to sterilization is a widespread practice in American hospitals. In Ruth Nial Cox's case, and in a number of other cases that have been discovered in the South, welfare recipients were told they would be cut off unless they agreed to be sterilized. The four black women representatives in Congress sent a letter last summer to HEW Secretary Caspar Weinberger asking for clarification of federal policy on sterilizations. The proposals "raise serious questions about the government's ability to prevent involuntary sterilization of poor people and minorities," the letter said. The ACLU has suggested that, to avert "institutional pressures" on welfare recipients, each patient to be sterilized be assigned an "advocate," much in the way legal services programs provide free legal counsel for the poor. But HEW specifically rejected this approach in announcing the regulations.

With civil libertarians dissatisfied with the regulations and HEW firmly behind them, the controversy seems headed for resolution in the courts. Lower court decisions have given both sides some encouragement. In Montgomery, Alabama, recently, a federal judge issued a stringent set of guidelines that must be followed before the mentally retarded in state institutions can be sterilized; these guidelines parallel the new regulations. On the other hand, there is the landmark Michigan decision, which held that an involuntarily detained mental patient is not capable of giving voluntary consent to psychosurgery and that the consent of his parents and approval of the project's review committee are not sufficient. In the Relf case and the Cox cases, ACLU lawyers are making a series of constitutional arguments that they hope will lead the Supreme Court to strike down many of the states' eugenics statutes and the new HEW guidelines.

There is probably no mechanism that can completely protect each and every patient from an overzealous or venal public official or doctor. Even the critics agree with HEW on that. But in this situation, the civil libertarians prefer to err on the side of overprotection, while HEW appears most worried about limits on patients' access to sterilization. Until a Supreme Court decision (and perhaps after), the fact is, as Kennedy put it at his hearings last summer, "Time after time we have seen that the patient's only remedy is malpractice litigation—after the fact."

15

Controlling Births or Controlling the Population?
(excerpts from *Food First*)
Frances Moore Lappé and
Joseph Collins

The question remains, what are the essential components of a nonabusive and readily accepted population control program. Given that high population growth rates, although not a cause of hunger, may slow the development process (Julian Simon might disagree, see Chapter 6), how can birth control programs be effective? It seems that contraceptive inundation alone is not the answer. Frances Moore Lappé and Joseph Collins pose their own question on population control and offer their response below.

Question: Certainly basic security through economic justice appears to be the prerequisite for bringing down growth rates. But isn't this only half the story? Even if the economic prerequisites exist that make it in the people's interest to choose smaller families, aren't birth control programs needed? You are not saying, are you, that when there is more equitable distribution of control over resources, the problem of rapid population growth will automatically take care of itself?

Our Response: The questioner is right. Reconstruction of the social order, providing all the people with basic material security, is necessary to make birth control a *rational* option. Then, birth control programs are essential to make having fewer children a *feasible* option as well.

But birth control programs that simply aim to shower rural areas with contraceptives will never work. Moreover, they run the risk of actually harming the poor. Without regular supervision by trained health care personnel, women can suffer both physical and psychological damage. Reports from Bangladesh stress that symptoms caused by irregular supply of oral contraceptives and bleeding from IUD's have caused severe personal suffering. In the Moslem cultures a woman too weak to do her household tasks can simply be rejected in favor of another wife.

Moreover, without improved health care having already reduced child mortality rates, families run the risk of severe loss. Sterilization programs are becoming a major part of birth control programs in the underdeveloped countries. But if child mortality rates are still high, parents who become sterilized run the risk of great economic loss if their children die and they are unable to replace them.

Thus birth control programs can only be effective and serve the interests of the poor when they

—are integrated into a total health care system that reduces child mortality rates.

—include both men and women.

—are village-based, training people from the village in which they will serve. (Dacca-based health workers in fine silk saris were perceived by the rural Bangladesh women as Americans.)

—can become self-supporting and therefore permanent through, for example, a health insurance program. (One such effort in rural Bangladesh requires 13 [cents] a month per family.)

—are part of an educational program in which people become conscious of the economic forces limiting their lives. Without this, the poor are unable to build effective organizations to protect their own interests, so necessary when the village elite tries to sabotage their efforts. . . .

Clearly we support the goals of lowered population growth rates and a stabilized global population. And we do not underestimate the need for positive action in providing family planning programs once the social prerequisites are being met. We stand firmly against, however, family planning programs that *purport to alleviate the problem of hunger.* They carry the message that the poor themselves are to blame for their own hunger, masking the true economic and political roots of their suffering.

Part III

TRIAGE AND LIFEBOAT ETHICS

16

Triage Applied to the Time of Famines
(excerpts from *Famine, 1975*)
William and Paul Paddock

It was William and Paul Paddock who, in 1967, wrote *Famine, 1975* and popularized the idea of triage. They borrowed the concept from the battlefields of wars in which medical supplies were scarce and had to be allocated according to some criteria. The Paddocks, one an agronomist and the other a retired career officer of the Foreign Service, argue that food supplies are scarce (where have we heard that before? See readings in Part I) and thus must be allocated according to the criteria outlined below. The reader of *Famine, 1975* is then invited to do some triage reckoning in later chapters (the example for Haiti is given below).

President Johnson has proposed "that the United States lead the world in a war against hunger."[1] On the battlefields of this forthcoming war the practice of triage will be vital because choices must be made as to which wounded countries will receive our food.

The leadership in Washington comprises the medical staff. The stricken ones in need of medical attention (American food aid) are the hungry nations. To provide maximum effective treatment the medical staff must divide them into the three classifications of triage:

(1) Nations in which the population growth trend has already passed the agricultural potential. This combined with inadequate leadership and other devisive factors make catastrophic disasters inevitable. These nations form the "can't-be-saved" group. To send food to them is to throw sand in the ocean.

(2) Nations which have the necessary agricultural resources and/or foreign exchange for the purchase of food from abroad and which therefore will be able to cope with their population growth. They will be only moderately affected by the shortage of food. They are the "walking wounded" and do not require *food* aid in order to survive.

(3) Nations in which the imbalance between food and population is great but the *degree* of the imbalance is manageable. Rather, it is manageable in the sense that

it can give enough time to allow the local officials to initiate effective birth control practices and to carry forward agricultural research and other forms of development. These countries will have a chance to come through their crisis provided careful medical treatment is given, that is, receipt of enough American food and also of other types of assistance.

The stocks of American food will be limited. Therefore, the extent of aid to the nations in the third group must be limited proportionately.

Call it a sieve. Adjust the size of the openings to the amount of food available to be shipped. The smaller the openings (of food), the fewer can be treated.

Unfortunately, it is not that simple. The size of a nation can itself be the determining factor against it or for it. If the available food is sent to the few big, politically important nations, then nothing will be left over for the smaller ones. Or vice versa. Thus, strictly on the basis of size and without regard to any other factors the decision might be to send food to:

Brazil but not to Central America
Central America but not Brazil
Nigeria but not the rest of West Africa
India but not Africa and Latin America

Decisions that take into account all the assorted, highly complex factors affecting differently each nation cannot be made within a vacuum. Political, economic and psychological factors must be considered. This calls for the careful analysis by experts studying the actual food capacity of the United States as set against the food needs and *survival capabilities* of the individual nations.

One delusion must be fought. Because each of these nations is hungry it is easy to jump to the conclusion that all internal problems can be solved by sending in enough food. Unfortunately, the affected nations have an assortment of wounds from an assortment of causes in addition to the food shortage. Ceylon has its language division. Sudan has its racial conflict. Bolivia has its class schism. Many have stifling corruption and graft.

In certain cases no amount of food can prevent political and social upheavals and continued, steady degeneration. Food sent to these will by itself not heal the wounds, wounds already festered. Nor can the national interests of the United States be excluded, whether political, military or economic. American officials when applying triage decisions and shipping out *American* food are surely justified in thinking beyond only the food requirements of the individual hungry nations. They are justified, it seems to me, to consider whether the survival of a specific nation will:

(a) help maintain the economic viability and relative prosperity of the United States during the Time of Famines.
(b) help maintain the economic stability of the world as a whole.
(c) help create a "better" world after the troubles of the Time of Famines have ended.

No nation lives on an island all alone. Each is a part of the whole. Thus, if two nations are equal in their need for American food to increase their chances for eventual self-sufficiency but there is not enough food to send to both, then, assuredly, the one must be chosen which is better able to contribute to the foregoing three goals.

And when overall demand for food in the hungry world catches up with the American capacity to produce food (to repeat from Chapter 5: the Department of Agriculture officially forecasts this will be by 1984 and I maintain it will occur by 1975), then America's own consumption of food will have to be curtailed or altered in order to maintain the same level of food aid. For instance, curtailment of meat. Every pound of grain-fed meat that a person eats takes four to twelve pounds of feed grain. "How much grain-fed meat will the heavy meat eaters in the United States and Europe be willing to forgo in order to feed hungry people thousands of miles away?"[2]

Now is the time to recognize the implications of this. For when such shortages and/or high prices do force the American public to change their diet, it is certain that our citizens will become dead serious about this food, food which they will forgo in order to feed distant foreigners. When this happens, I take for granted that American public opinion will demand that this food be distributed in a manner which will give them their "money's worth." But unless we begin *now* to concentrate our food aid on those who can be saved during the Time of Famines, our future efforts may be ineffective. By the next decade today's savable nations may have passed beyond the point of help.

What will Americans, ten years from now, consider to be their "money's worth"? What will be a legitimate return on the food they are sending to others?

The ultimate answer, I am sure, will be stated in terms of American economic and political aims. Some can criticize this as selfish, as unhumanitarian and as unchristian. Yet the continued stability and relative prosperity of the United States during the coming decades are, surely, the single most important guarantee to insure:

—*that the world as a whole, and especially the selected hungry nations themselves, will survive the Time of Famines without sinking into chaos, and*
—*that the world will evolve into that "better" life which we hope will come to all peoples afterwards; a "better" life (both spiritual and material) is difficult to visualize as coming to fruition without the support of American capital goods which today nearly equal all those possessed by the rest of mankind.*

Therefore, I emphasize the following pertinent aspects which American officials must consider when they make their decisions as to which countries will receive our food:

(1) *Ignore the prospect that if food is withheld from a country it will "go communist."*
(2) *Ignore the short-range political changes in these countries.*
(3) *Take into consideration the quality of local leadership.*
(4) *Give maximum NON-FOOD aid to those nations where we wish short-range political advantages.*
(5) *Favor nations which have raw materials required by the American and the world economy.*
(6) *Favor nations which have military value to the United States.*

Examples of How to Apply Triage

The clearest way to understand a theory is, of course, to apply it to specific examples. So now I present certain nations most of whom, I am sure, will make strident calls during the coming decade for American food and assistance above the levels they may already be receiving.

To bring home the painful responsibility of the official when he must himself sign the paper that will give one applicant nation priority over another, I provide a blank space where the reader can insert his own considered view of what the decision should be.

Afterwards, I give my own opinion and I recognize that my presentation of each "case" is colored by that opinion. Nevertheless, the adverse facts I state must be faced up to by the American official judging the case; and the local officials anxious to present only their country's good points must refute these same adverse facts.

Haiti

Its population long ago exploded beyond the level of what the nation's resources can provide for a viable economy. There is nothing whatever in sight that can lift up the nation, that can alter the course of anarchy already in force for a century. At one time Haiti was one of the most agriculturally productive regions in the world, but now its fecundity has outstripped the country's resources (432 persons per square mile).[3] Now it is too late for an energetic, nationwide birth control program. (The nation is 90 percent illiterate and has only one doctor for each 11,000 persons).[4] It is too late for intensive agricultural research efforts. The people are sunk in ignorance and indifference, and the government is entrapped in the tradition of violence.

Can't-be-saved _____
Walking Wounded _____
Should Receive Food _____

Notes

1. President Lyndon B. Johnson, message to the 89th Cong., Feb 10, 1966.
2. Karl Hobson, "The Wheat Shortage is Here," *Farm Journal*, Aug. 1966, p. 47.
3. *Selected Economic Data for Less Developed Countries*, Statistics and Reports Division, Agency for International Development, Washington, D.C., June 1965.
4. *Ibid.*

17

Merchants of Grain
(excerpts)
Dan Morgan

In 1968, Paul Ehrlich wrote *The Population Bomb* (New York: Ballantine Books. 1968) which referred to the idea of "triage" popularized earlier by William and Paul Paddock (see Chapter 16). In that same year, ecologist-biologist Garrett Hardin wrote "The Tragedy of the Commons" (*Science* 162: 1243–1248 [13 December 1968]) which was readily accepted as dogma by environmental scientists everywhere. Hardin wrote about food as a commons; food (in particular the World Food Bank) is a resource held in common that is subject to inevitable "mutual ruin" since "there are no controls." He compares the World Food Bank to the Food for Peace Program, or PL 480, that "moved billions of dollars worth of U.S. surplus grains to food-short, population-long countries during the past two decades." Indeed. Dan Morgan, in *Merchants of Grain*, discusses the economic and political purposes of PL 480 with specific examples (e.g., Chile) lest we see it as a gesture of humanitarianism as Garrett Hardin, whose Lifeboat Ethics article immediately follows, would have us believe.

[It] was Public Law 480, passed by Congress in 1954, which gave the U.S. government a perfectly designed tool for disposing of [food] surplus. PL 480 organized dribs and drabs of food aid into a permanent fixture of farm policy and of foreign policy as well. It became one of the most durable pieces of legislation ever passed by Congress.

PL 480 is now such an accepted part of the agricultural and diplomatic landscape of the United States that it takes an effort of imagination to recall that there was some opposition when it was first proposed. Shipping American food abroad to help war-torn nations or to prevent famines was one thing. A permanent welfare program for the world was something else. Many conservatives and southern Democrats were philosophically opposed to foreign aid. Corn and cotton congressmen were worried that if U.S. food were too readily available, farmers abroad might shift their own production out of food grains into exportable crops that might compete for foreign markets against *American* commodities.

But a permanent food aid program had appeal that far outweighed the reservations. It appealed, of course, to most of the farm bloc, which realized that the program would enable farmers to keep getting paid for growing surpluses. Senator Hubert H. Humphrey saw a mixture of humanitarian and ideological (not to mention agricultural) benefits. It would, he felt, add a "new, positive, humanitarian force into the world ideological struggle." It would be a "simple, Christian, humanitarian approach to better world understanding." Foreign-policy hawks also were attracted. Secretary of State John Foster Dulles was an outspoken advocate of food aid to drought-threatened Pakistan in 1953: He was impressed with the "martial spirit of the people" and with what he believed was their strong anticommunism. He reminded Congress that Pakistan controlled access to the Khyber Pass—which guarded the route from the Soviet Union to South Asia. Food to Pakistan made foreign-policy sense.

The P.L. 480 finally passed by Congress in 1954 was worded broadly enough to satisfy all the various supporters of food aid. The aid was to promote the foreign policy of the United States, combat hunger, and dispose of surpluses. But in its early years the last provision was the main rationale for the program.[1]

In the first years, an average of one bushel of wheat in four and one bushel of rice in five ended up going abroad with P.L. 480 financing. In 1959, a particularly bleak year for the grain trade, four out of five dollars' worth of wheat exports and nine out of ten dollars' worth of soybean oil exports were so financed.

P.L. 480 was advertised as an aid program for foreign countries, but above all it provided assistance to American farmers and the grain trade. Foreign governments received authorizations from the U.S. government to purchase, with American loans, certain quantities of American farm commodities; and the foreigners handled the actual transactions, contracting with private exporters to obtain the goods. But payment for these goods actually went straight from the U.S. Treasury to commercial banks in the United States and then to the private exporters—as soon as they presented documents certifying that the commodities were loaded aboard ship. The foreign governments had the obligation to repay the loans, but the terms provided grace periods and long maturities.[2] Essentially, the system was that agricultural commodities left the country, but the money stayed home. . . .

America's postwar food relief always had a political component. Subsidized U.S. food supported Marshal Tito's drive for independence from Soviet influence after Yugoslavia refused to join the Cominform in 1948. And the lion's share of P.L. 480 food aid went to foreign countries in which the United States had a political, economic, or military interest. Military clients such as Pakistan, South Korea, Israel, and Turkey all received substantial amounts of this food assistance. So did Yugoslavia and Poland, the two most independent Communist countries in Eastern Europe. Brazil and Indonesia, the sources of enormous reserves of raw materials, were also beneficiaries of subsidized American wheat, rice, and cotton. A State Department official justified the cotton and rice shipments to Indonesia succinctly: "They have the oil, we have the food." And the P.L. 480 leverage could also be used in reverse. When Egypt went to war against Israel in 1967, P.L. 480 stopped.

Food's function in diplomacy was extended and broadened under President Nixon and President Ford, and the food-aid programs were politicized as never before. In 1972 and 1973, 70 per cent of all the P.L. 480 dollars purchased food for the war economies of South Vietnam and Cambodia. In the final stages of that war, Food for Peace was cynically nicknamed Food for War by critics in Congress who maintained that the assistance was only helping to prolong suffering and postpone the inevitable. Elsewhere, the granting or withholding of food aid was used alternately as carrot and stick in nations whose economies and populations had become dependent on imported food. The food-buying credits of P.L. 480 went to South Korea in 1971 in return for that government's secret promise to reduce textile exports to the United States; to Portugal the same year in return for the continuation of American base rights in the Azores; and to Bangladesh in 1974 only after that country agreed to halt its exports of jute to Cuba.

Chile provides the best example of a country where the American food tap was turned off and on again in response to political developments. Subsidized food shipments to Chile were stopped after the Marxist Salvador Allende was elected president in 1970,[3] and it was one of the first forms of aid to resume after he was overthrown on September 11, 1973. This was part of the covert tactics of "destabilization" adopted by the Nixon administration against Allende.

Chile had imported large volumes of wheat before Allende became president— between 380,000 and 600,000 tons a year—covering a quarter to a third of the country's requirements. Most came from Australia, Argentina, or Uruguay, but as much as 200,000 tons was shipped from the United States. When the American government credit for food buying stopped, imports of U.S. wheat dropped to the tiny amount of 8,000 tons in 1971-72.

There is no doubt that trouble in the food and agricultural sectors helped to bring about Allende's eventual downfall. But these difficulties certainly were not exclusively the result of his administration's mismanagement. New and untried governments dedicated to reform and experiment usually make mistakes at the beginning, but Allende's problems were compounded by external pressures beyond his control. As the government followed through on its promises to redistribute wealth and guarantee milk to Chileans every day, demand for food products increased faster than food production. Chilean wheat production actually *increased* by 5 per cent in the 1970-71 crop year, but wheat imports were nonetheless essential. By 1972, the Nixon administration not only had stopped P.L. 480 and other U.S. assistance, but also had succeeded in blocking some loans from international organizations. So, the Chilean government dipped into its limited foreign exchange reserves to pay for 700,000 tons of imported wheat—this at a time when world grain prices were undergoing their steepest increases since World War II. (Wheat had tripled in price between mid-1972 and late 1973—partly because of the purchases by Russia, the country that, ironically, Allende now looked to for support.)

By the summer of 1973, Chile's food sector was in desperate straits. Agricultural production had declined[4] and food consumption had increased. There were breadlines, and meat products were in unusually short supply owing to shortages of feed grain. The government made arrangements with the Australian Wheat Board to import 250,000-500,000 tons of wheat after January 1974—presumably in hopes of obtaining credits from some source by that time. To help tide the country over, it counted on 100,000 tons of Soviet-financed wheat from Bulgaria, East Germany, and Australia. But as the global shortages worsened, the difficulties of trying to get by without American wheat became more and more acute. In August, agents of the government grain board went to the United States and arranged to buy American grain with the aid of financing from France and Mexico. Cook and Andre's American associate, Garnac, filled orders for 300,000 tons.

When Chilean military leaders launched their coup against Allende on the morning of September 11, 1973, about 100,000 tons of wheat financed or shipped by socialist countries was en route to Valparaiso. The U.S. Department of Agriculture reported that the shipments were diverted. The wheat never reached Chile, though where it did end up is uncertain. Probably the Cubans received some of it.

Grain, in any case, was a crucial priority for the new military rulers who had overthrown Allende's elected government, and on September 26, the government ordered 120,000 tons of American wheat from Continental, Bunge, Dreyfus, and

Garnac. Since the regime had no money to pay for it, the purchases were conditioned on approval of a $24-million American government line of credit.

In Washington, there were two major problems in this Chilean request for aid. One was that American grain was becoming increasingly scarce and high-priced in the United States itself. New food-buying credits for other nations had been frozen for several months. The other difficulty was Chile's questionable credit-worthiness. It had $450 million in foreign debts, and the "destabilized" Chilean economy was on the rocks. But on October 4, the National Advisory Council on International Monetary and Financial Policies, acting on a "strong recommendation" from the State Department, granted the credit line. The NAC justified the loan under a provision of the law allowing such financial aid "for overriding foreign policy considerations." The loading of U.S wheat for Chile began at the Gulf of Mexico that very weekend.

On November 13, NAC authorized a second line of credit—$28 million for corn purchases. The justification, which could just as easily have applied during the Allende period, was that Chile "is faced with a critical supply situation for protein products such as beef, pork and poultry." In 1974, Chile was put back on the list of countries eligible for the special "soft" loans of P.L. 480. The next year the United States shipped about 600,000 tons of wheat to Chile—about five times the volume immediately before Allende came to power. Chile's dependence on American wheat continued long after the new regime had seized power. The country joined Iran and Southeast Asia as a "grain protectorate" of the United States.

A year later, Kissinger directed that the food-aid "carrot" be similarly used in the Middle East. In September 1974, the United States pledged 100,000 tons of wheat aid to Egypt. It was an extremely significant step—the first such assistance since relations between the two countries had been ruptured in the Six-Day War of 1967. Kissinger said this assistance was the ultimate in "humanitarian" aid, in that it might prevent war. As this suggested, the food deliveries were conditional upon Egypt's readiness to cooperate and participate in the peace plan Kissinger was then drafting.

The food incentive was a powerful one indeed. As Egyptians' memories of their glorious military deeds in the 1973 war faded, President Anwar Sadat was left to deal with the mundane realities of everyday life. His country was rapidly sinking into an economic quagmire. Cairo was one of the world's most overcrowded cities. Squatters camped in cemeteries on the urban outskirts, and camels, busses, and humans vied for space on the downtown streets. Basic food staples were heavily subsidized, and the food imports required by Egypt were a drain on its dwindling foreign-currency reserves. Food, in short, was essential to President Sadat's political survival. It was against this background that Kissinger directed that the flow of American food aid, halted for seven years, be resumed.[5]

The United States thus obtained political and economic benefits from the food it dispensed to Egypt, Chile, and other countries through the P.L. 480 aid program. But these were nations at the periphery of American diplomacy, and the subsidized food shipments were like any other foreign aid: an effective weapon in foreign policy only because the nations receiving it were weak, poor, or lacking in the foreign exchange needed to pay for food in world markets.

Notes

1. Later, Secretary of Agriculture Freeman was to stress market development and combating hunger. Under Jimmy Carter, the program was nudged toward supporting agricultural development abroad.

2. Initially, foreign governments could repay these "loans" with their local currencies. The United States accummulated vast accounts of such currencies as Indian rupees and eventually wrote all or some of the money off. The problem of how to get rid of the money occupied officials in Washington in the 1950s and 1960s.

3. Except for one $3.2 million credit in 1971.

4. Bad weather and a truck drivers' strike, partly financed by the CIA, hindered distribution of seed and fertilizer in 1972 and 1973.

5. By 1978, Egypt was the largest recipient of P.L. 480 assistance. It received more than 1 million tons of subsidized wheat a year.

18

Lifeboat Ethics:
The Case Against Helping the Poor
Garrett Hardin

Hardin presents an ethics of survival justified by the precarious resource situation in which we find our "spaceship earth."

Environmentalists use the metaphor of the earth as a "spaceship" in trying to persuade countries, industries and people to stop wasting and polluting our natural resources. Since we all share life on this planet, they argue, no single person or institution has the right to destroy, waste, or use more than a fair share of its resources.

But does everyone on earth have an equal right to an equal share of its resources? The spaceship metaphor can be dangerous when used by misguided idealists to justify suicidal policies for sharing our resources through uncontrolled immigration and foreign aid. In their enthusiastic but unrealistic generosity, they confuse the ethics of a spaceship with those of a lifeboat.

A true spaceship would have to be under the control of a captain, since no ship could possibly survive if its course were determined by committee. Spaceship Earth certainly has no captain; the United Nations is merely a toothless tiger, with little power to enforce any policy upon its bickering members.

If we divide the world crudely into rich nations and poor nations, two thirds of them are desperately poor, and only one third comparatively rich, with the United States the wealthiest of all. Metaphorically each rich nation can be seen as a lifeboat full of comparatively rich people. In the ocean outside each lifeboat swim the poor of the world, who would like to get in, or at least to share some of the wealth. What should the lifeboat passengers do?

First, we must recognize the limited capacity of any lifeboat. For example, a nation's land has a limited capacity to support a population and as the current energy crisis has shown us, in some ways we have already exceeded the carrying capacity of our land.

Reprinted with permission from Psychology Today (Magazine): 38-40+ (September, 1974). Copyright (c) 1974 American Psychological Association.

Adrift in a Moral Sea

So here we sit, say 50 people in our lifeboat. To be generous, let us assume it has room for 10 more, making a total capacity of 60. Suppose the 50 of us in the lifeboat see 100 others swimming in the water outside, begging for admission to our boat or for handouts. We have several options: we may be tempted to try to live by the Christian ideal of being "our brother's keeper," or by the Marxist ideal of "to each according to his needs." Since the needs of all in the water are the same, and since they can all be seen as "our brothers," we could take them all into our boat, making a total of 150 in a boat designed for 60. The boat swamps, everyone drowns. Complete justice, complete catastrophe.

Since the boat has an unused excess capacity of 10 more passengers, we could admit just 10 more to it. But which 10 do we let in? How do we choose? Do we pick the best 10, the neediest 10, "first come, first served"? And what do we say to the 90 we exclude? If we do let an extra 10 in our lifeboat, we will have lost our "safety factor," an engineering principle of critical importance. For example, if we don't leave room for excess capacity as a safety factor in our country's agriculture, a new plant disease or a bad change in the weather could have disastrous consequences.

Suppose we decide to preserve our small safety factor and admit no more to the lifeboat. Our survival is then possible, although we shall have to be constantly on guard against boarding parties.

While this last solution clearly offers the only means of our survival, it is morally abhorrent to many people. Some say they feel guilty about their good luck. My reply is simple: "Get out and yield your place to others." This may solve the problem of the guilt-ridden person's conscience, but it does not change the ethics of the lifeboat. The needy person to whom the guilt-ridden person yields his place will not himself feel guilty about his good luck. If he did, he would not climb aboard. The net result of conscience-stricken people giving up their unjustly held seats is the elimination of that sort of conscience from the lifeboat.

This is the basic metaphor within which we must work out our solutions. Let us now enrich the image, step by step, with substantive additions from the real world, a world that must solve real and pressing problems of overpopulation and hunger.

The harsh ethics of the lifeboat become even harsher when we consider the reproductive differences between the rich nations and the poor nations. The people inside the lifeboats are doubling in numbers every 87 years; those swimming around outside are doubling, on the average, every 35 years, more than twice as fast as the rich. And since the world's resources are dwindling, the difference in prosperity between the rich and the poor can only increase.

As of 1973, the U.S. had a population of 210 million people, who were increasing by 0.8 percent per year. Outside our lifeboat, let us imagine another 210 million people, (say the combined populations of Colombia, Ecuador, Venezuela, Morocco, Pakistan, Thailand and the Philippines) who are increasing at a rate of 3.3 percent per year. Put differently, the doubling time for this aggregate population is 21 years, compared to 87 years for the U.S.

Multiplying the Rich and the Poor

Now suppose the U.S. agreed to pool its resources with those seven countries, with everyone receiving an equal share. Initially the ratio of Americans to non-Americans in this model would be one-to-one. But consider what the ratio would be after 87 years, by which time the Americans would have doubled to a population of 420 million. By then, doubling every 21 years, the other group would have swollen to 354 billion. Each American would have to share the available resources with more than eight people.

But, one could argue, this discussion assumes that current population trends will continue, and they may not. Quite so. Most likely the rate of population increase will decline much faster in the U.S. than it will in the other countries, and there does not seem to be much we can do about it. In sharing with "each according to his needs," we must recognize that needs are determined by population size, which is determined by the rate of reproduction, which at present is regarded as a sovereign right of every nation, poor or not. This being so, the philanthropic load created by the sharing ethic of the spaceship can only increase.

The Tragedy of the Commons

The fundamental error of spaceship ethics, and the sharing it requires, is that it leads to what I call "the tragedy of the commons." Under a system of private property, the men who own property recognize their responsibility to care for it, for if they don't they will eventually suffer. A farmer, for instance, will allow no more cattle in a pasture than its carrying capacity justifies. If he overloads it, erosion sets in, weeds take over, and he loses the use of the pasture.

If a pasture becomes a commons open to all, the right of each to use it may not be matched by a corresponding responsibility to protect it. Asking everyone to use it with discretion will hardly do, for the considerate herdsman who refrains from overloading the commons suffers more than a selfish one who says his needs are greater. If everyone would restrain himself, all would be well; but it takes only one less than everyone to ruin a system of voluntary restraint. In a crowded world of less than perfect human beings, mutual ruin is inevitable if there are no controls. This is the tragedy of the commons.

One of the major tasks of education today should be the creation of such an acute awareness of the dangers of the commons that people will recognize its many varieties. For example, the air and water have become polluted because they are treated as commons. Further growth in the population or per-capita conversion of natural resources into pollutants will only make the problem worse. The same holds true for the fish of the oceans. Fishing fleets have nearly disappeared in many parts of the world, technological improvements in the art of fishing are hastening the day of complete ruin. Only the replacement of the system of the commons with a responsible system of control will save the land, air, water and oceanic fisheries.

The World Food Bank

In recent years there has been a push to create a new commons called a World Food Bank, an international depository of food reserves to which nations would contribute according to their abilities and from which they would draw according to their needs. This humanitarian proposal has received support from many liberal international groups, and from such prominent citizens as Margaret Mead, U.N. Secretary General Kurt Waldheim, and Senators Edward Kennedy and George McGovern.

A world food bank appeals powerfully to our humanitarian impulses. But before we rush ahead with such a plan, let us recognize where the greatest political push comes from, lest we be disillusioned later. Our experience with the "Food for Peace program," or Public Law 480, gives us the answer. This program moved billions of dollars worth of U.S. surplus grain to food-short, population-long countries during the past two decades. But when P.L. 480 first became law, a headline in the business magazine *Forbes* revealed the real power behind it: "Feeding the World's Hungry Millions: How It Will Mean Billions for U.S. Business."

And indeed it did. In the years 1960 to 1970, U.S. taxpayers spent a total of $7.9 billion on the Food for Peace program. Between 1948 and 1970, they also paid an additional $50 billion for other economic-aid programs, some of which went for food and food-producing machinery and technology. Though all U.S. taxpayers were forced to contribute to the cost of P.L. 480, certain special interest groups gained handsomely under the program. Farmers did not have to contribute the grain; the Government, or rather the taxpayers, bought it from them at full market prices. The increased demand raised prices of farm products generally. The manufacturers of farm machinery, fertilizers and pesticides benefited by the farmers' extra efforts to grow more food. Grain elevators profited from storing the surplus until it could be shipped. Railroads made money hauling it to ports, and shipping lines profited from carrying it overseas. The implementation of P.L. 480 required the creation of a vast Government bureaucracy, which then acquired its own vested interest in continuing the program regardless of its merits.

Extracting Dollars

Those who proposed and defended the Food for Peace program in public rarely mentioned its importance to any of these special interests. The public emphasis was always on its humanitarian effects. The combination of silent selfish interests and highly vocal humanitarian apologists made a powerful and successful lobby for extracting money from taxpayers. We can expect the same lobby to push now for the creation of a World Food Bank.

However great the potential benefit to selfish interests, it should not be a decisive argument against a truly humanitarian program. We must ask if such a program would actually do more good than harm, not only momentarily but also in the long run. Those who propose the food bank usually refer to a current "emergency" or "crisis" in terms of world food supply. But what is an emergency? Although they may be infrequent and sudden, everyone knows that emergencies will occur from time to time. A well-run family, company, organization or country prepares for the likelihood of accidents and emergencies. It expects them, it budgets for them, it saves for them.

Learning the Hard Way

What happens if some organizations or countries budget for accidents and others do not? If each country is solely responsible for its own well-being, poorly managed ones will suffer. But they can learn from experience. They may mend their ways, and learn to budget for infrequent but certain emergencies. For example, the weather varies from year to year, and periodic crop failures are certain. A wise and competent government saves out of the production of the good years in anticipation of bad years to come. Joseph taught this policy to Pharaoh in Egypt more than 2,000 years ago. Yet the great majority of the governments in the world today do not follow such a policy. They lack either the wisdom or the competence, or both. Should those nations that do manage to put something aside be forced to come to the rescue each time an emergency occurs among the poor nations?

"But it isn't their fault!" Some kind-hearted liberals argue. "How can we blame the poor people who are caught in an emergency? Why must they suffer for the sins of their governments?" The concept of blame is simply not relevant here. The real question is, what are the operational consequences of establishing a world food bank? If it is open to every country everytime a need develops, slovenly rulers will not be motivated to take Joseph's advice. Someone will always come to their aid. Some countries will deposit food in the world food bank, and others will withdraw it. There will be almost no overlap. As a result of such solutions to food shortage emergencies, the poor countries will not learn to mend their ways, and will suffer progressively greater emergencies as their populations grow.

Population Control the Crude Way

On the average, poor countries undergo a 2.5 percent increase in population each year; rich countries, about 0.8 percent. Only rich countries have anything in the way of food reserves set aside, and even they do not have as much as they should. Poor countries have none. If poor countries received no food from the outside, the rate of their population growth would be periodically checked by crop failures and famines. But if they can always draw on a world food bank in time of need, their population can continue to grow unchecked, and so will their "need" for aid. In the short run, a world food bank may diminish that need, but in the long run it actually increases the need without limit.

Without some system of world wide food sharing, the proportion of people in the rich and poor nations might eventually stabilize. The overpopulated poor countries would decrease in numbers, while the rich countries that had room for more people would increase. But with a well-meaning system of sharing, such as a world food bank, the growth differential between the rich and the poor countries will not only persist, it will increase. Because of the higher rate of population growth in the poor countries of the world, 88 percent of today's children are born poor, and only 12 percent rich. Year by year the ratio becomes worse, as the fast-reproducing poor outnumber the slow-reproducing rich.

A world food bank is thus a commons in disguise. People will have more motivation to draw from it than to add to any common store. The less provident and less able will multiply at the expense of the abler and more provident, bringing eventual ruin upon all who share in the commons. Besides, any system of "sharing" that amounts to foreign aid from the rich nations to the poor nations will carry the taint of charity, which will contribute little to the world peace so devoutly desired by those who support the idea of a world food bank.

As past U.S. foreign-aid programs have amply and depressingly demonstrated, international charity frequently inspires mistrust and antagonism rather than gratitude on the part of the recipient nation [see "What Other Nations Hear When the Eagle Screams," by Kenneth J. and Mary M. Gergen, PT, June].

Chinese Fish and Miracle Rice

The modern approach to foreign aid stresses the export of technology and advice, rather than money and food. As an ancient Chinese proverb goes: "Give a man a fish and he will eat for a day; teach him how to fish and he will eat for the rest of his days." Acting on this advice the Rockefeller and Ford Foundations have financed a number of programs for improving agriculture in the hungry nations. Known as the "Green Revolution," these programs have led to the development of "miracle rice" and "miracle wheat," new strains that offer bigger harvests and greater resistance to crop damage. Norman Borlaug, the Nobel Prize winning agronomist who, supported by the Rockefeller Foundation, developed "miracle wheat," is one of the most prominent advocates of a world food bank.

Whether or not the Green Revolution can increase food production as much as its champions claim is a debatable but possibly irrelevant point. Those who support this well-intended humanitarian effort should first consider some of the fundamentals of human ecology. Ironically, one man who did was the late Alan Gregg, a vice president of the Rockefeller Foundation. Two decades ago he expressed strong doubts about the wisdom of such attempts to increase food production. He likened the growth and spread of humanity over the surface of the earth to the spread of cancer in the human body, remarking that "cancerous growths demand food; but, as far as I know, they have never been cured by getting it."

Overloading the Environment

Every human born constitutes a draft on all aspects of the environment: food, air, water, forests, beaches, wildlife, scenery and solitude. Food can, perhaps, be significantly increased to meet a growing demand. But what about clean beaches, unspoiled forests, and solitude? If we satisfy a growing population's need for food, we necessarily decrease its per capita supply of the other resources needed by men.

India, for example, now has a population of 600 million, which increases by 15 million each year. This population already puts a huge load on a relatively impoverished environment. The country's forests are now only a small fraction of what they were three centuries ago, and floods and erosion continually destroy the insufficient farmland that remains. Every one of the 15 million new lives added to India's population puts an additional burden on the environment, and increases the economic and social costs of crowding. However humanitarian our intent, every Indian life saved through medical or nutritional assistance from abroad diminishes the quality of life for those who remain, and for subsequent generations. If rich countries make it possible, through foreign aid, for 600 million Indians to swell to 1.2 billion in a mere 28 years, as their current growth rate threatens, will future generations of Indians thank us for hastening the destruction of their environment? Will our good intentions be sufficient excuse for the consequences of our actions?

My final example of a commons in action is one for which the public has the least desire for rational discussion—immigration. Anyone who publicly questions the wisdom of current U.S. immigration policy is promptly charged with bigotry, prejudice, ethnocentrism, chauvinism, isolationism or selfishness. Rather than encounter such accusations, one would rather talk about other matters, leaving immigration policy to wallow in the crosscurrents of special interests that take no account of the good of the whole, or the interests of posterity.

Perhaps we still feel guilty about things we said in the past. Two generations ago the popular press frequently referred to Dagos, Wops, Polacks, Chinks and Krauts, in articles about how America was being "overrun" by foreigners of supposedly inferior genetic stock [see "The Politics of Genetic Engineering: Who Decides Who's Defective?" PT. June]. But because the implied inferiority of foreigners was used then as justification for keeping them out, people now assume that restrictive policies could only be based on such misguided notions. There are other grounds.

A Nation of Immigrants

Just consider the numbers involved. Our Government acknowledges a net inflow of 400,000 immigrants a year. While we have no hard data on the extent of illegal entries, educated guesses put the figure at about 600,000 a year. Since the natural increase (excess of births over deaths) of the resident population now runs about 1.7 million per year, the yearly gain from immigration amounts to at least 19 percent of the total annual increase, and may be as much as 37 percent if we include the estimate for illegal immigrants. Considering the growing use of birth-control devices, the potential effect of educational campaigns by such organizations as Planned Parenthood Federation of America and Zero Population Growth, and the influence of inflation and the housing shortage, the fertility rate of American women may decline so much that immigration could account for all the yearly increase in population. Should we not at least ask if that is what we want?

For the sake of those who worry about whether the "quality" of the average immigrant compares favorably with the quality of the average resident, let us assume that immigrants and nativeborn citizens are of exactly equal quality, however one defines that term. We will focus here only on quantity; and since our conclusions will depend on nothing else, all charges of bigotry and chauvinism become irrelevant.

Immigration Vs. Food Supply

World food banks *move food to the people*, hastening the exhaustion of the environment of the poor countries. Unrestricted immigration, on the other hand, *moves people to the food*, thus speeding up the destruction of the environment of the rich countries. We can easily understand why poor people should want to make this latter transfer, but why should rich hosts encourage it?

As in the case of foreign-aid programs, immigration receives support from selfish interests and humanitarian impulses. The primary selfish interest in unimpeded immigration is the desire of employers for cheap labor, particularly in industries and trades that offer degrading work. In the past, one wave of foreigners after another was brought into the U.S. to work at wretched jobs for wretched wages. In recent years the Cubans, Puerto Ricans and Mexicans have had this dubious honor. The interests of the employers of cheap labor mesh well with the guilty silence of the country's liberal intelligentsia. White Anglo-Saxon Protestants are particularly reluctant to call for a closing of the doors to immigration for fear of being called bigots.

But not all countries have such reluctant leadership. Most educated Hawaiians, for example, are keenly aware of the limits of their environment, particularly in terms of population growth. There is only so much room on the islands, and the islanders know it. To Hawaiians, immigrants from the other 49 states present as great a threat as those from other nations. At a recent meeting of Hawaiian government officials in Honolulu, I had the ironic delight of hearing a speaker, who like most of his audience was of Japanese ancestry, ask how the country might practically and constitutionally close its doors to further immigration. One member of the audience countered: "How can we shut the doors now? We have many friends and relatives in Japan that we'd like to bring here some day so that they can enjoy Hawaii too." The Japanese-American speaker smiled sympathetically and answered: "Yes, but we have children now, and someday we'll have grandchildren too. We can bring more people here from Japan only by giving away some of the land that we hope to pass on to our grandchildren some day. What right do we have to do that?"

At this point, I can hear U.S. liberals asking: "How can you justify slamming the door once you're inside? You say that immigrants should be kept out. But aren't we all immigrants, or the descendants of immigrants? If we insist on staying, must we not admit all others?" Our craving for intellectual order leads us to seek and prefer symmetrical rules and morals: a single rule for me and everybody else; the same rule yesterday, today and tomorrow. Justice, we feel, should not change with time and place.

We Americans of non-Indian ancestry can look upon ourselves as the decendants of thieves who are guilty morally, if not legally, of stealing this land from its Indian owners. Should we then give back the land to the now living American descendants of those Indians? However morally or logically sound this proposal may be, I, for one, am unwilling to live by it and I know no one else who is. Besides, the logical consequence would be absurd. Suppose that, intoxicated with a sense of pure justice, we should decide to turn our land over to the Indians. Since all our other wealth has also been derived from the land, wouldn't we be morally obliged to give that back to the Indians too?

Pure Justice Vs. Reality

Clearly, the concept of pure justice produces an infinite regression to absurdity. Centuries ago, wise men invented statutes of limitations to justify the rejection of such pure justice, in the interests of preventing continual disorder. The law zealously defends property rights, but only relatively recent property rights. Drawing a line after an arbitrary time has elapsed may be unjust, but the alternatives are worse.

We are all the descendants of thieves, and the world's resources are inequitably distributed. But we must begin the journey to tomorrow from the point where we are today. We cannot remake the past. We cannot safely divide the wealth equitably among all peoples so long as people reproduce at different rates. To do so would guarantee that our grandchildren, and everyone else's grandchildren, would have only a ruined world to inhabit.

To be generous with one's own possessions is quite different from being generous with those of posterity. We should call this point to the attention of those who, from a commendable love of justice and equality, would institute a system of the commons, either in the form of a world food bank, or of unrestricted immigration. We must convince them if we wish to save at least some parts of the world from environmental ruin.

Without a true government to control reproduction and the use of available resources, the sharing ethic of the spaceship is impossible. For the foreseeable future, our survival demands that we govern our actions by the ethics of a lifeboat, harsh though they may be. Posterity will be satisfied with nothing less.

19

Population and Food:
Metaphors and the Reality
William W. Murdoch and
Allan Oaten

Garrett Hardin's argument (Chapter 18) emphasizes metaphors and is simplistic and thus appealing. William Murdoch and Allan Oaten, Hardin's colleagues at the University of California, Santa Barbara, provide one of the most cogent and effective critiques that have been published to date. (When the article was published in *Psychology Today* the mail had been running about 95 percent against Hardin's doctrine according to Wade Green in "Triage. Who Shall Be Fed? Who Shall Starve?" (*The New York Times Magazine*, 5 January 1975)).

Should rich countries provide food, fertilizers, technical assistance, and other aid to poor countries? The obvious answer is "yes." It is natural to want to fight poverty, starvation, and disease, to help raise living standards and eliminate suffering.

Yet, after 25 years of aid, diets and living standards in many poor countries have improved little, owing partly to the population explosion that occurred during these same years. Death rates in poor countries dropped sharply in the 1940's and 1950's, to around 14/1,000 at present, while their birth rates declined very little, remaining near 40/1,000. Some populations are now growing faster than their food supply.

As a result an apparently powerful argument against aid is increasingly heard. Its premise is simply stated. "More food means more babies" (Hardin 1969). Our benevolence leads to a spiral that can result only in disaster: aid leads to increased populations, which require more aid, which leads . . . This premise mandates a radically new policy: rich countries can perhaps provide contraceptives to poor countries, but they should not provide food, help increase food production, or help combat poverty or disease.

This policy would result in the agonizing deaths, by starvation and disease, of millions of people. Consequently, one expects its advocates to have arrived at it reluctantly, forced to suppress their humanitarian feelings by inexorable logic and the sheer weight of evidence. Its apparent brutality seems a sure guarantee of its realism and rationality.

We believe that this allegedly realistic "nonhelp" policy is in fact mistaken as well as callous; that the premise on which it is based is at best a half-truth; and that the arguments adduced in its support are not only erroneous, but often exhibit indifference to both the complexities of the problem and much of the available data. We also believe that the evidence shows better living standards and lower population growth rates to be complementary, not contradictory; that aid programs carefully designed to benefit the poorest people can help to achieve both of these ends; and that such programs, though difficult to devise and carry out, are not beyond either the resources or the ingenuity of the rich countries.

In the next two sections, we analyze some of the standard arguments in support of nonhelp policies, by focusing first on the article "Living on a Lifeboat" (Hardin 1974) and then on "The Tragedy of the Commons" (Hardin 1968). We will consider the long-term effects of nonhelp policies and some possible reasons for their widespread appeal. Then we will summarize some of the evidence about birth rates that is available and seems relevant. This evidence suggests that if we are serious about halting the food-population spiral and minimizing deaths from starvation and disease (in the long-term as well as the short), then it may be more rational to help than to stand back and watch. Finally, we will estimate the costs of some aid and discuss some difficulties in achieving reduced birth rates.

Misleading Metaphors

The "lifeboat" article actually has two messages. The first is that our immigration policy is too generous. This will not concern us here. The second, and more important, is that by helping poor nations we will bring disaster to rich and poor alike:

Metaphorically, each rich nation amounts to a lifeboat full of comparatively rich people. The poor of the world are in other, much more crowded lifeboats. Continuously, so to speak, the poor fall out of their lifeboats and swim for a while in the water outside, hoping to be admitted to a rich lifeboat, or in some other way to benefit from the "goodies" on board. What should the passengers on a rich lifeboat do? This is the central problem of "the ethics of a lifeboat." (Hardin 1974, p. 561)

Among these so-called "goodies" are food supplies and technical aid such as that which led to the Green Revolution. Hardin argues that we should withhold such resources from poor nations on the grounds that they help to maintain high rates of population increase, thereby making the problem worse. He foresees the continued supplying and increasing production of food as a process that will be "brought to an end only by the total collapse of the whole system, producing a catastrophe of scarcely imaginable proportions" (p. 564).

Turning to one particular mechanism for distributing these resources, Hardin claims that [with] a world food bank—a commons—people have more motivation to draw from it than to add to it; it will have a ratchet or escalator effect on population because inputs from it will prevent population declines in overpopulated countries. Thus "wealth can be steadily moved in one direction only, from the slowly-breeding rich to the rapidly-breeding poor, the process finally coming to a halt only when all countries are equally and miserably poor" (p. 565). Thus our help will not only bring ultimate disaster to poor countries, but it will also be suicidal for us.

As for the "benign demographic transition" to low birth rates, which some aid supporters have predicted, Hardin states flatly that the weight of evidence is against this possibility.

Finally, Hardin claims that the plight of poor nations is partly their own fault: "wise sovereigns seem not to exist in the poor world today. The most anguishing problems are created by poor countries that are governed by rulers insufficiently wise and powerful." Establishing a world food bank will exacerbate this problem: "slovenly rulers" will escape the consequences of their incompetence—"Others will bail them out whenever they are in trouble"; "Far more difficult than the transfer of wealth from one country to another is the transfer of wisdom between sovereign powers or between generations" (p. 563).

What arguments does Hardin present in support of these opinions? Many involve metaphors: lifeboat, commons, and ratchet or escalator. These metaphors are crucial to his thesis, and it is, therefore, important for us to examine them critically.

The lifeboat is the major metaphor. It seems attractively simple, but it is in fact simplistic and obscures important issues. As soon as we try to use it to compare various policies, we find that most relevant details of the actual situation are either missing or distorted in the lifeboat metaphor. Let us list some of these details.

* Most important, perhaps, Hardin's lifeboats barely interact. The rich lifeboats may drop some handouts over the side and perhaps repel a boarding party now and then, but generally they live their own lives. In the real world, nations interact a great deal, in ways that affect food supply and population size and growth, and the effect of rich nations on poor nations has been strong and not always benevolent.

First, by colonization and actual wars of commerce, and through the international marketplace, rich nations have arranged an exchange of goods that has maintained and even increased the economic imbalance between rich and poor nations. Until recently we have taken or otherwise obtained cheap raw material from poor nations and sold them expensive manufactured goods that they cannot make themselves. In the United States, the structure of tariffs and internal subsidies discriminates selectively against poor nations. In poor countries, the concentration on cash crops rather than on food crops, a legacy of colonial times, is now actively encouraged by western multinational corporations (Barraclough 1975). Indeed, it is claimed that in famine-stricken Sahelian Africa, multinational agribusiness has recently taken land out of food production for cash crops (Transnational Institute 1974). Although we often self-righteously take the "blame" for lowering the death rates of poor nations during the 1940's and 1950's, we are less inclined to accept responsibility for the effects of actions that help maintain poverty and hunger. Yet poverty directly contributes to the high birth rates that Hardin views with such alarm.

Second, U.S. foreign policy, including foreign aid programs, has favored "pro-Western" regimes, many of which govern in the interests of a wealthy elite and some of which are savagely repressive. Thus, it has often subsidized a gross maldistribution of income and has supported political leaders who have opposed most of the social changes that can lead to reduced birth rates. In this light, Hardin's pronouncements on the alleged wisdom gap between poor leaders and our own, and the difficulty of filling it, appear as a grim joke: our response to leaders with the power and wisdom Hardin yearns for has often been to try to replace them or their policies as soon as possible. Selective giving and withholding of both military and nonmilitary aid has been an important ingredient of our efforts to maintain political leaders we like and to remove those we do not. Brown (1974b), after noting that the withholding of U.S. food aid in 1973 contributed to the downfall of the Allende government in Chile, comments that "although Americans decry the use of petroleum as a 'political blackmail,' the United States has been using food aid for political purposes for twenty years—and describing this as 'enlightened diplomacy.'"

* Both the quantity and the nature of the supplies on a lifeboat are fixed. In the real world, the quantity has strict limits, but these are far from having been reached (University of California Food Task Force 1974). Nor are we forced to devote fixed proportions of our efforts and energy to automobile travel, pet food, packaging, advertising, corn-fed beef, "defense," and other diversions, many of which cost far more than foreign aid does. The fact is that enough food is now produced to feed the world's population adequately. That people are malnourished is due to distribution and to economics, not to agricultural limits (United Nations Economic and Social Council 1974).

* Hardin's lifeboats are divided merely into rich and poor, and it is difficult to talk about birth rates on either. In the real world, however, there are striking differences among the birth rates of the poor countries and even among the birth rates of different parts of single countries. These differences appear to be related to social conditions (also absent from lifeboats) and may guide us to effective aid policies.

* Hardin's lifeboat metaphor not only conceals facts, but misleads about the effects of his proposals. The rich lifeboat can raise the ladder and sail away. But in real life, the problem will not necessarily go away just because it is ignored. In the real world, there are armies, raw materials in poor nations, and even outraged domestic dissidents prepared to sacrifice their own and others' lives to oppose policies they regard as immoral.

No doubt there are other objections. But even this list shows the lifeboat metaphor to be dangerously inappropriate for serious policy making because it obscures far more than it reveals. Lifeboats and "lifeboat ethics" may be useful topics for those who are shipwrecked; we believe they are worthless—indeed detrimental—in discussions of food-population questions.

The ratchet metaphor is equally flawed. It, too, ignores complex interactions between birth rates and social conditions (including diets), implying as it does that more food will simply mean more babies. Also, it obscures the fact that the decrease in death rates has been caused at least as much by developments such as DDT, improved sanitation, and medical advances, as by increased food supplies, so that cutting out food aid will not necessarily lead to population declines.

The lifeboat article is strangely inadequate in other ways. For example, it shows an astonishing disregard for recent literature. The claim that we can expect no "benign demographic transition" is based on a review written more than a decade ago (Davis 1963). Yet, events and attitudes are changing rapidly in poor countries: for the first time in history, most poor people live in countries with birth control programs; with few exceptions, poor nations are somewhere on the demographic transition to lower birth rates (Demeny 1974); the population-food squeeze is now widely recognized, and governments of poor nations are aware of the relationship. Again, there is a considerable amount of evidence that birth rates can fall rapidly in poor countries given the proper social conditions (as we will discuss later); consequently, crude projections of current population growth rates are quite inadequate for policy making.

The Tragedy of the Commons

Throughout the lifeboat article, Hardin bolsters his assertions by reference to the "commons" (Hardin 1968). The thesis of the commons, therefore needs critical evaluation.

Suppose several privately owned flocks, comprising 100 sheep altogether, are grazing on a public commons. They bring in an annual income of $1.00 per sheep. Fred, a herdsman, owns only one sheep. He decides to add another. But 101 is too many: the commons is overgrazed and produces less food. The sheep lose quality and income drops to 90 [cents] per sheep. Total income is now $90.90 instead of $100.00. Adding the sheep has brought an overall loss. But Fred has gained: *his* income is $1.80 instead of $1.00. The gain from the additional sheep, which is his alone, outweighs the loss from overgrazing, which he shares. Thus he promotes his interest at the expense of the community.

This is the problem of the commons, which seems on the way to becoming an archetype. Hardin, in particular, is not inclined to underrate its importance: "One of the major tasks of education today is to create such an awareness of the dangers of the commons that people will be able to recognize its many varieties, however disguised" (Hardin 1974, p. 562) and "All this is terribly obvious once we are acutely aware of the pervasiveness and danger of the commons. But many people still lack this awareness. . ." (p. 565).

The "commons" affords a handy way of classifying problems: the lifeboat article reveals that sharing, a generous immigration policy, world food banks, air, water, the fish populations of the ocean, and the western range lands are, or produce, a commons. It is also handy to be able to dispose of policies one does not like as "only a particular instance of a class of policies that are in error because they lead to the tragedy of the commons" (p. 561).

But no metaphor, even one as useful as this, should be treated with such awe. Such shorthand can be useful, but it can also mislead by discouraging thought and obscuring important detail. To dismiss a proposal by suggesting that "all you need to know about this proposal is that it institutes a commons and is, therefore, bad" is to assert that the proposed commons is worse than the original problem. This might be so if the problem of the commons were, indeed, a tragedy—that is, if it were insoluble. But it is not.

Hardin favors private ownership as the solution (either through private property or the selling of pollution rights). But, of course, there are solutions other than private ownership; and private ownership itself is no guarantee of carefully husbanded resources.

One alternative to private ownership of the commons is communal ownership of the sheep—or, in general, of the mechanisms and industries that exploit the resource—combined with communal planning for management. (Note, again, how the metaphor favors one solution: perhaps the "tragedy" lay not in the commons but in the sheep. "The Tragedy of the Privately Owned Sheep" lacks zing, unfortunately.) Public ownership of a commons has been tried in Peru to the benefit of the previously privately owned anchoveta fishery (Gulland 1975). The communally owned agriculture of China does not seem to have suffered any greater over-exploitation than that of other Asian nations.

Another alternative is cooperation combined with regulation. For example, Gulland (1975) has shown that Antarctic whale stocks (perhaps the epitome of a commons since they are internationally exploited and no one owns them) are now being properly managed, and stocks are increasing. This has been achieved through cooperation in the International Whaling Commission, which has by agreement set limits to the catch of each nation.

In passing, Hardin's private ownership argument is not generally applicable to nonrenewable resources. Given discount rates, technology substitutes, and no more than an average regard for posterity, privately owned nonrenewable resources, like oil, coal and minerals are mined at rates that produce maximum profits, rather than at those rates that preserve them for future generations.

Thus, we must reject the temptation to use the commons metaphor as a substitute for analysis. Not all commons are the same: they differ in their origin, their nature, the type and seriousness of the problems they cause, the solutions that are appropriate for them, and the difficulty of implementing those solutions. In particular, we cannot rule out a proposal just because someone calls it a commons; a "solved" or benign commons may be the correct approach to some problems.

On Malign Neglect

Hardin implies that nonhelp policies offer a solution to the world population-food problem. But what sort of solution would in fact occur?

Nonhelp policies would have several effects not clearly described in "Lifeboat" (Hardin 1974). First, it is not true that people in poor countries "convert extra food into extra babies" (p. 564). They convert it into longer lives. Denying them food will not lower birth rates; it will increase death rates.

These increases might not take effect immediately after the withdrawal of aid.. Increases in local food production and improvements in sanitation and medicine would probably allow populations to continue growing for some time. (Death rates would need to increase almost three-fold to stabilize them.) Thus, in the future we could expect much larger populations in poor countries, living in greater misery than today. The negative relation between well-being and family size could easily lead to even higher birth rates. A "solution" that puts us back to prewar birth and death rates, at even higher population levels, is certainly not a satisfactory permanent solution.

Second, the rich countries cannot remain indifferent to events in poor countries. A poor country or a group of poor countries that controls supplies of a vital raw material, for example, may well want to use this leverage to its advantage; it may be very uncompromising about it, especially if its need is desperate and its attitude resentful, as would be likely. Just how intolerable this situation would be to the rich countries can be guessed at by recent hints of war being an acceptable means for the United States to ensure itself adequate supplies of oil at a "reasonable" price.

War is an option open to poor countries, too. China and India have nuclear weapons; others can be expected to follow. With Hardin's policies, they may feel they have little to lose, and the rich have a great deal to lose.

Thus we could look forward to continuing, and probably increasing, interference in and manipulation of the increasingly miserable poor countries by the rich countries. We do not believe this is a stable situation. One or more poor countries will surely want to disrupt it; recent events show that our ability to prevent this is limited. Alternatively, in the future, one or more of the rich countries may decide to help poor countries reduce their birth rates, but will then be faced with an even greater problem than we face today. In sum, malign neglect of poor nations is not likely to cause the problem to go away.

If Hardin's proposals are so defective, why are they attractive to so many people? We have already discussed Hardin's use of oversimplified metaphors, but there are other temptations.

An obvious one is the presentation of false choices: either we continue what we are doing, or we do nothing. Aid is either effective or ineffective; much of our aid has been ineffective, so all aid is, and it always will be. Such absolute positions are tempting because they save thought, justify inaction, never need reconsideration,

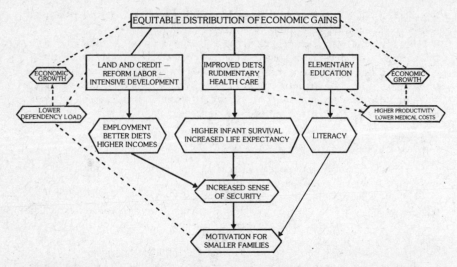

Figure 19.1. The factors affecting birth rates. Positive feedback upon economic growth is indicated by dashed lines and smaller boxes.

and convey an impression of sophisticated cynicism. But they do not conform to the facts. Intelligent and effective aid, though difficult, is possible.

The apparent callousness of Hardin's proposals is itself a temptation. There is an implication that these policies are so brutal that they would not be proposed without good reasons. Conversely, those who argue for increased aid can be dismissed as "highly vocal humanitarian apologists" or "guilt addicts" (Hardin 1974, pp. 563 and 562). The implication is that these views *could* arise from unreasoning emotion, so therefore they *must* arise this way. Proposals for increased aid are then "plaintive cries" produced by guilt, bad conscience, anxiety, and misplaced Christian or Marxist idealism. But such argument by association is plainly misleading. Benign policies can also be the most rational; callous policies can be foolish.

Birth Rates: An Alternative View

Is the food-population spiral inevitable? A more optimistic, if less comfortable, hypothesis, presented by Rich (1973) and Brown (1974a), is increasingly tenable: contrary to the "ratchet" projection, population growth rates are affected by many complex conditions beside food supply. In particular, a set of socioeconomic conditions can be identified that motivate parents to have fewer children; under these conditions, birth rates can fall quite rapidly, sometimes even before birth control technology is available. Thus, population growth can be controlled more effectively by intelligent human intervention that sets up the appropriate conditions than by doing nothing and trusting to "natural population cycles."

These conditions are: parental confidence about the future, an improved status of women, and literacy. They require low infant mortality rates, widely available rudimentary health care, increased income and employment, and an adequate diet above subsistence levels (Fig. 19.1). Expenditure on schools (especially elementary schools), appropriate health services (especially rural paramedical services), and agricultural reform (especially aid to small farmers) will be needed, and foreign aid can help here. It is essential that these improvements be spread across the population;

aid can help here, too, by concentrating on the poor nations' poorest people, encouraging necessary institutional and social reforms, and making it easier for poor nations to use their own resources and initiative to help themselves. It is not necessary that per capita GNP be very high, certainly not as high as that of the rich countries during their gradual demographic transition. In other words, low birth rates in poor countries are achievable long before the conditions exist that were present in the rich countries in the late 19th and early 20th centuries.

Twenty or thirty years is not long to discover and assess the factors affecting birth rates, but a body of evidence is now accumulating in favor of this hypothesis. Rich (1973) and Brown (1974a) show that at least 10 developing countries have managed to reduce their birth rates by an average of more than one birth per 1,000 population per year for periods of 5 to 16 years. A reduction of one birth per 1,000 per year would bring birth rates in poor countries to a rough replacement level of about 16/1,000 by the turn of the century, though age distribution effects would prevent a smooth population decline. We have listed these countries in Table 19.1, together with three other nations, including China, that are poor and yet have brought their birth rates down to 30 or less, presumably from rates of over 40 a decade or so ago.

These data show that rapid reduction in birth rates is possible in the developing world. No doubt it can be argued that each of these cases is in some way special. Hong Kong and Singapore are relatively rich; they, Barbados, and Mauritius are also tiny. China is able to exert great social pressure on its citizens; but China is particularly significant. It is enormous; its per capita GNP is almost as low as India's; and it started out in 1949 with a terrible health system. Also, Egypt, Chile, Taiwan, Cuba, South Korea, and Sri Lanka are quite large, and they are poor or very poor (Table 19.1). In fact, these examples represent an enormous range of religion, political systems, and geography and suggest that such rates of decline in the birth rate can be achieved whenever the appropriate conditions are met. "The common factor in these countries is that the *majority* of the population has shared in the economic and social benefits of significant national progress. . . . [M]aking health, education and jobs more broadly available to lower income groups in poor countries contribute[s] significantly toward the motivation for smaller families that is the prerequisite of a major reduction in birth rates" (Rich 1973).

The converse is also true. In Latin America, Cuba (annual per capita income $530), Chile ($720), Uruguay ($820), and Argentina ($1,160) have moderate to truly equitable distribution of goods and services and relatively low birth rates (27, 26, 23 and 22, respectively). In contrast, Brazil ($420), Mexico ($670), and Venezuela ($980) have very unequal distribution of goods and services and high birth rates (38, 42, and 41, respectively). Fertility rates in poor and relatively poor nations seem unlikely to fall as long as the bulk of the population does not share in increased benefits.

We have tried briefly to bring the major evidence before the reader. However, there is a large literature, well summarized by Rich, and the details of the evidence are well worth reading in their entirety.

This evidence is certainly not overwhelming. Its accuracy varies. There are many unmeasured variables. Some measured variables, like income and literacy, are highly interrelated. We have no evidence that we can extrapolate to other countries or to still lower birth rates. By the standards of scientific experiment, these data are not conclusive. But policy decisions such as those discussed here are always based on uncertainty, and this evidence is at least as convincing as simple projections of average birth and death rates now prevailing in poor nations. Certainly the evidence

TABLE 19.1.   Declining Birth Rates and Per Capita Income in Selected
Developing Countries   (These are crude birth rates,
uncorrected for age distribution)

Births/1,000/year

Country	Time Span	Average annual Decline in Crude Birth Rate	Crude Birth Rate 1972	$ per capita per Year 1973
Barbados	1960-69	1.5	22	570
Taiwan	1955-71	1.2	24	390
Tunisia	1966-71	1.8	35	250
Mauritius	1961-71	1.5	25	240
Hong Kong	1960-72	1.4	19	970
Singapore	1955-72	1.2	23	920
Costa Rica	1963-72	1.5	32	560
South Korea	1960-70	1.2	29	250
Egypt	1966-70	1.7	37	210
Chile	1963-70	1.2	25	720
China			30	160
Cuba			27	530
Sri Lanka			30	110

is good enough that we need to treat the reduction of birth rates as a viable alternative to nonhelp.

A useful evaluation of the demographic transition hypothesis is provided by Beaver (1975), whose book became available only after we had completed the final revision of this article. Beaver restates the hypothesis as a set of assumptions, yielding specific predictions that can be tested against recent population data. These assumptions are similar to those given here, with some additional details and emphases. In particular, Beaver stresses the importance of a time lag of about 10 to 15 years before factors which tend to reduce birth rates can take effect. For example, both mortality decline and economic development reduce birth rates in the long run by raising expectations and confidence in the future, but both can increase birth rates in the short run by simply making it possible, physically and economically, for parents to have more children. The demographic transition hypothesis receives "strong empirical support" from a variety of statistical tests using recent Latin American data. Furthermore, the recent declines in natality in Latin America have been much more rapid than the declines in Europe during its demographic transition (See also Teitelbaum 1975).

Costs, Gains and Difficulties

We have neither the space nor the expertise to propose detailed food population policies. Our main concern has been to help set the stage for serious discussion by disposing of simplistic proposals and irrelevant arguments, outlining some of the complexities of the problem, and indicating the existence of a large quantity of available data.

However, some kind of positive statement seems called for, if only to provide a target for others. We approach this task with trepidation. A full discussion of aid possibilities would require detailed consideration of political, social, and cultural complexities in a wide variety of recipient and donor countries. A thorough cost accounting would require detailed, quantitative knowledge about the relation between social conditions and the motivation for smaller families. Here we merely list some forms of aid, crudely estimate their costs, indicate some of their benefits and briefly discuss their feasibility.

Brown (1974a) estimates that $5 billion per year could provide:

* family planning services to the poor nations (excluding China, which already provides them); the cost includes training personnel and providing transportation facilities and contraceptives;
* literacy for all adults and children (a five-year program); and
* a health care program for mothers and infants (again excluding China).

To this we could add the following:
* 10 million metric tons of grain at an annual cost of $2 billion;
* 1.5 million metric tons of fertilizer, which is the estimated amount of the "shortfall" last year in the poor countries (U.N. 1974); the cost including transportation, is roughly $1 billion; and
* half of the estimated annual cost of providing "adequate" increases in the area of irrigated and cultivated land in the poor countries (U.N. 1974), about $2 billion.

These costs may well be too low, although, according to Abelson (1975), the annual cost of an "effective" global food reserve is only $550 million to $800 million, compared with the $2 billion cited above. The estimates do suggest that aid on this scale, *properly designed and properly used in the recipient nations,* could make a sizeable improvement in social well-being.

The total cost is $10 billion. Still, these estimates are very crude. Let us suppose the real cost is $20 billion. Other wealthy countries could (and should) provide at least half of this. This leaves about $10 billion to be provided by the United States. Can the United States afford it?

In the past, U.S. aid has not normally been free. Indeed, India is now a net exporter of capital to the United States because it pays back more interest and principal on previous aid loans than it receives in aid. However, even giving away $10 billion is likely to have only minor effects on the U.S. economy and standard of living. It is about 1% of the GNP, about 10% of current military expenditure. It would decrease present and future consumption of goods and services in the United States by slightly more than 1% (because the cost of government accounts for about 25% of the GNP). It could result in a slight lowering of the value of the dollar abroad, unless other rich nations were also contributing proportionately. The most noticeable effects within the United States would be on the relative prices of goods and services and, as a consequence, on the poor in this country. Those items most in demand by poor countries would increase in price relative to "luxury" goods, so that the poor in the United States would be hurt more than the rich unless counter-measures were taken.

In short, although we must take care that the burden is equitably borne, the additional aid could be provided with only minor effects on the well-being of the U.S. population. Such a reduction in living standard is hardly "suicidal" or a matter of "human survival" in the United States, to use Hardin's terms. It is not a question

TABLE 19.2. Projected Annual Growth in Food Supply and
Population until 1985 in Selected Areas
(U.N. 1974)

Area	Food	Population
Rich countries	2.8	0.9
Poor countries	2.6	2.7
(excluding communist Asia)		
Africa	2.5	2.9
Asia	2.4	2.6
Latin America	2.9	3.1
Near East	3.1	2.9
Communist Asia	2.6	1.6
World	2.7	2.0

of "them or us," as the lifeboat metaphor implies. This simple-minded dichotomy may account for the appeal of Hardin's views, but it bears no relation to reality.

The six measures suggested above should encourage economic growth as well as lower birth rates in poor countries (see Fig. 19.1). Adequate diet and health care improve work performance and reduce medical costs and lost work days. There is evidence (Owens and Shaw 1972) that agricultural improvements made available to small farmers can lead not only to improved diets and increased employment but also to greater productivity per hectare than occurs on large, capital intensive farms, and that the poor can save at very high rates provided they own or rent their economic facilities (e.g., farms) and are integrated into the national economy through a network of financial institutions. Since small farms are labor-intensive, agricultural improvements that concentrate on them are not only well suited to poor countries but make them less vulnerable to fluctuations in energy supplies and costs.

Improved living conditions probably would first decrease the death rate. Does this mean that the decrease in the birth rate must be very great just to compensate? Infant mortality is the major part of the death rate that can still be decreased easily in poor countries. Suppose a poor country has a birth rate of 40/1,000 per population and an infant mortality rate of 150/1,000 live births; India is close to this. These six dead infants (15% of 40) help motivate parents to have many babies. Suppose, in the next decade, conditions improve so much that infant mortality drops to zero—a ludicrous hope. This decrease would be exactly balanced if the birth rate dropped from 40/1,000 to 34/1,000. All 10 of the countries in Table 19.1 dropped this many points (and greater percentages) in five years or less. Further, once mortality rates are very low, every reduction in the birth rate reduces population growth. These calculations are over simplified, but they illustrate that even a great decrease in poverty-related deaths can be balanced by a modest decrease in births.

We can gauge the effect of lowered birth rates upon the food-population ratio. Table 19.2 shows currently projected rates of population growth and food production for the major areas of the world (U.N. 1974). These projections assume continued improvement in food production at previous rates; they do not assume increased success in programs against high birth rates. For the next decade, the annual percentage increase of population would be 0.2 to 0.4 greater than that of food supply in Africa, noncommunist Asia, and Latin America (although for the world in general food grows faster than population). A successful program that reduced births by 0.5/1,000 or more per year would quickly remove the projected imbalance between food and population, even allowing for increased survival. This effect would accelerate as gains in survival gradually declined, thus vastly reducing the amount of aid that would be needed.

Will the aid in fact be used in ways that help reduce birth rates? As a disillusioning quarter-century of aid giving has shown, the obstacles to getting aid to those segments of the population most in need of it are enormous. Aid has typically benefitted a small rich segment of society, partly because of the way aid programs have been designed but also because of human and institutional factors in the poor nations themselves (Owens and Shaw 1972). With some notable exceptions, the distribution of income and services in poor nations is extremely skewed—much more uneven than in rich countries. Indeed, much of the population is essentially outside the economic system. Breaking this pattern will be extremely difficult. It will require not only aid that is designed specifically to benefit the rural poor, but also important institutional changes such as decentralization of decision making and the development of greater autonomy and stronger links to regional and national markets for local groups and industries, such as cooperative farms.

Thus, two things are being asked of rich nations and of the United States in particular: to increase nonmilitary foreign aid, including food aid, and to give it in ways, and to governments, that will deliver it to the poorest people and will improve their access to national economic institutions. These are not easy tasks, particularly the second, and there is no guarantee that birth rates will come down quickly in all countries. Still, many poor countries have, in varying degrees, begun the process of reform, and recent evidence suggests that aid and reform together can do much to solve the twin problems of high birth rates and economic underdevelopment. The tasks are far from impossible. Based on the evidence, the policies dictated by a sense of decency are also the most realistic and rational.

Acknowledgments

Joe Connell, William Felstiner, Elvin Hatch, Patrick McNulty, John Pippinger, and David Simonett read early drafts of this article and gave liberally of their time in discussion.

References

Abelson, P.H. 1975. The world's disparate food supplies. *Science* 187: 218.
Barraclough, G. 1975. The great world crisis I. *The N.Y. Rev. Books* 21: 20–29.
Beaver, S.E. 1975. Demographic Transition Theory Reinterpreted. Lexington Books, Lexington, Mass. 177 pp.
Brown, L.R. 1974a. *In the Human Interest.* W.W. Norton & Co., Inc., New York. 190 pp.
———. 1974b. *By Bread Alone.* Praeger, New York. 272 pp.
Davis, K. 1963. Population. *Sci. Amer.* 209(3): 62–71.
Demeny, P. 1974. The populations of the underdeveloped countries. *Sci. Amer.* 231(3): 149–159.
Gulland, J. 1975. The harvest of the sea. Pages 167–189 in W.W. Murdoch, ed. *Environment: Resources, Pollution and Society,* 2nd ed. Sinauer Assoc., Sunderland, Mass.
Hardin, G. 1968. The tragedy of the commons. *Science* 162: 1243–1248.
———. 1969. Not peace, but ecology. In Diversity and Stability in Ecological Systems. *Brookhaven Symp. Biol.* 22: 151–161.
———. 1974. Living on a lifeboat. *BioScience* 24(10): 561–568.
Owens, E., and R. Shaw. 1972. Development Reconsidered. D.C. Heath & Co., Lexington, Mass. 190 pp.

Rich, W. 1973. Smaller families through social and economic progress. Overseas Development Council, Monograph #7, Washington, D.C. 73 pp.

Teitelbaum, M.S. 1975. Relevance of demographic transition theory for developing countries. *Science* 188: 420–425.

Transnational Institute. 1974. World Hunger: Causes and Remedies. Institute for Policy Studies, 1520 New Hampshire Ave., NW, Washington, D.C.

United Nations Economic and Social Council. 1974. Assessment [of the] present food situation and dimensions and causes of hunger and malnutrition in the world. E/Conf. 65/Prep/6, 8 May 1974.

University of California Food Task Force. 1974. A hungry world: the challenge to agriculture. University of California, Division of Agricultural Sciences. 303 pp.

Part IV

AGRICULTURE IN THE UNITED STATES

20

Food Production and the Energy Crisis
(excerpts)

David Pimentel, L.F. Hurd,
A.C. Bellotti, M.J. Forster, I.N. Oka,
O.D. Sholes and R.J. Whitman

The first essay appearing in this section was one of the first to document the inefficient use of fossil energy in American agriculture. (Chapter 28, "Biotechnology, Seeds and the Restructuring of Agriculture," will document a different impending crisis, with far-reaching implications for the structure of agriculture in the United States.) Other researchers who published similar research findings in the early 1970s included Michael Perelman ("Mechanization and the Division of Labor." *The American Journal of Agriculture Economics* 55:523–526 (August 1973) and John and Carol Steinhart ("Energy Use in the U.S. Food System." *Science* 184: 307–316 [19 April 1974]).

David Pimentel and his colleagues documented the increase in average energy inputs in corn (which, according to the authors, typifies the energy inputs for crops in general) from 1945 to 1970. Process analysis, a type of energy accounting, is used to determine the fossil energy equivalents of crop inputs. Although energy accounting is considered a useful tool in evaluating the efficiency of various agricultural processes (since energy values are based upon physical laws and are not subject to change), critics of energy accounting argue that "efficiency comparisons that exclude price relationships ignore the primary function of a market—to allocate scarce resources to their most valuable uses" ("Economics of Agricultural Energy Use" by L. Hill and S. Erickson in *Agworld* 2[3]:2 [April 1978]). Thus, care must be exercised in evaluating input/output ratios for crops and livestock because most products are raised for more than their food energy.

As [the world population] continues to grow, there is increasing concern about ways to prevent wholesale starvation (1). . . . As agriculturalists, we feel that a careful analysis is needed to measure energy inputs in U.S. and green revolution style crop production techniques. Our approach is to select a single crop, corn (maize), which typifies the energy inputs for crops in general, and to make a detailed analysis of

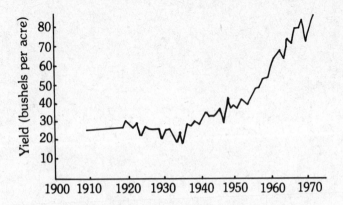

Figure 20.1. Corn production (bushels per acre) in the United States from 1909 to 1971 (23, 26, 27).

its production energy inputs. With the data on input and output for corn as a model, an examination is then made of energy needs for a world food supply that depends on modern energy intensive agriculture. Using corn as an example, we consider alternatives in crop production technology which might reduce energy inputs in food production. Other than recognizing the high costs of U.S. energy intensive agriculture, we make no effort to examine any of the projected economic, sociological, or political "trade-offs" in the United States or other countries when the energy crisis upsets the world community (4). . . .

Corn Production and Energy Inputs

To investigate the relationship of energy inputs to crop production, we selected corn for the following reasons. (i) Corn generally typifies the energy inputs in U.S. crop production for it is intermediate in energy inputs between the extremes of high energy-demand fruit production and low energy-demand tame hay and small grain production. (ii) Corn is one of the leading grain crops in the United States and the world. (iii) More data are available on corn than on other crops. Concerning corn data, we have had to rely heavily on Department of Agriculture survey data and estimates provided by various other studies. Although the best available, some of these data have inherent limitations. Despite these shortcomings, this analysis provides a valuable perspective concerning the large energy inputs in U.S. agriculture.

Corn, the most important grain crop grown in the United States, ranks third in world production of food crops (5). In terms of world cereal grains, it ranks second to wheat. During 1971, world corn production on 279 million acres was 308 million metric tons (6). Corn yield per acre (1 acre = 0.405 hectare) in the United States has increased significantly from 1909 to 1971 (Fig. 20.1). During 1909, the corn yield averaged 26 bushels per acre, and during 1971 it averaged 87 bushels per acre. A sharp rise in production per acre started about 1950—a time when many changes, including the planting of hybrid corn, were taking place in corn culture (7-9). The planting of hybrid corn probably accounts for 20 to 40 percent of the increased corn yields since the 1940's with energy resource inputs accounting for 60 to 80 percent (7, 10, 11). Hybrid corn and energy inputs toward increased yields overlap because corn plants are often selected for characteristics that make the plant perform well under specific environmental conditions as, for example, with high fertilizer inputs. Without the appropriate genetic background, the corn plant

TABLE 20.1. Average Energy Inputs in Corn Production During Different
           Years (all figures per acre)

Inputs	1945	1950	1954	1959	1964	1970
Labor*	23	18	17	14	11	9
Machinery (kcal x 10^3)!	180	250	300	350	420	420
Gasoline (gallons)@	15	17	19	20	21	22
Nitrogen (pounds)#	7	15	27	41	58	112
Phosphorus (pounds)#	7	10	12	16	18	31
Potassium (pounds)#	5	10	18	30	29	60
Seeds for planting (bushels)/	0.17	0.20	0.25	0.30	0.33	0.33
Irrigation (kcal x 10^3)¢	19	23	27	31	34	34
Insecticides (pounds)&	0	0.10	0.30	0.70	1.00	1.00
Herbicides (pounds)**	0	0.05	0.10	0.25	0.38	1.00
Drying (kcal x 10^3)!!	10	30	60	100	120	120
Electricity (kcal x 10^3)@@	32	54	100	140	203	310
Transportation (kcal x 10^3)##	20	30	45	60	70	70
Corn Yields (bushel)//	34	38	41	54	68	81

*Mean hours of labor per crop acre in United States (3, 14).

!An estimate of the energy inputs for the construction and repair of
tractors, trucks, and other farm machinery was obtained from the data of
Berry and Fels (30), who calculated that about 31,968,000 kcal of energy was
necessary to construct an average automobile weighing about 3400 pounds. In
our calculations we assumed that 244,555,000 kcal (an equivalent of 13 tons
of machinery) were used for the production of all machinery (tractors,
trucks, and miscellaneous) to farm 62 acres of corn. This machinery was
assumed to function for 10 years. Repairs were assumed to be 6 percent of
total machinery production or about 15,000,000 kcal. Hence, a conservative
estimate for the production and repair of farm machinery per corn acre per
year for 1970 was 420,000 kcal. A high for the number of tractors and other
farm machinery on farms was reached in 1964 and continues (31, 32). The
number of tractors and other types of machinery in 1945 were about half what
they are now.

@DeGraff and Washbon (33) reported that corn production required about 15
gallons of fuel per acre for tractor use--intermediate between fruit and
small grain production. Because corn appeared to be intermediate, the
estimated mean fuel (gallons) burned in farm machinery per harvested acre
was based on U.S. Department of Agriculture (12, 31) and U.S. Bureau of the
Census (32) data.

#Fertilizers (N, P, K) applied to corn are based on USDA (14, 15, 28, 29)
estimates.

/During 1970, relatively dense corn planting required about one-third of
a bushel of corn (25,000 kernels or 34,000 kcal) per acre; the less dense
plantings in 1945 were estimated to use about one-sixth of a bushel of
seed. Because hybrid seed has to be produced with special care, the input
for 1970 was estimated to be 68,000 kcal.

¢Only about 3.8 percent of the corn grain acres in the United States were
irrigated in 1964 (34), and this is not expected to change much in the near
future (35). Although a small percentage, irrigation is costly in terms of
energy demand. On the basis of the data of Epp (36) and Thorfinnson et al.
(37), an estimated 905,600 kcal is required to irrigate an acre of corn with
an acre-foot of water for one season. Higher energy costs for irrigation
water are given by The Report on the World Food Problem (1). Since only 3.8
percent of the corn acres are irrigated (1964-1970), it was estimated that
only 34,000 kcal were used per acre for corn irrigation. The percentage of
acres irrigated in 1945 was based on trends in irrigated acres in agriculture
(23, 34).

&Estimates of insecticides applied per acre of corn are based on the fact
that little or no insecticide was used on corn in 1945, and this reached a
high in 1964 (17, 22).

**Estimates of herbicides applied per acre of corn are based on the fact
that little or no herbicides were used on corn in 1945 and that this use
continues to increase (17, 22).

!!When it is dried for storage to reduce the moisture from about 26.5
percent to 13 percent, about 408,204 kcal are needed to dry bushels (38).
About 30 percent of the corn was estimated to have been dried in 1970 as
compared to an estimated 10 percent in 1945.

@@Agriculture consumed about 2.5 percent of all electricity produced in
1970 (13) and an estimated 424.2 trillion British thermal units of fossil fuel
were used to produce this power (39); on croplands this divides to 310,000
kcal per acre for 1970 (3, 22). The fuel used to produce the electrical
energy for earlier periods was estimated from data reported in Statistical
Abstracts (40).

##Estimates of the number of calories burned to transport machinery and
supplies to corn acres and to transport corn to the site of use is based on
data from U.S. Department of Commerce (41). U.S. Bureau of the Census (32,
34, 39), Interstate Commerce Commission (42), and U.S. Department of
Transportation (43). For 1964 and 1970 this was estimated to be about 70,000
kcal per acre, it was about 20,000 kcal per acre in 1945.

//Corn yield is expressed as a mean of 3 years, 1 year previous and 1 year
past (23, 26, 27).

---

will not respond to the fertilizer inputs and, of course, the corn plant cannot
respond if fertilizer is absent.

While corn yields increased about 240 percent from 1945 to 1970, the labor
input per acre decreased more than 60 percent (Table 20.1). Intense mechanization
reduced the labor input and, in part, made possible the increased corn yield.

Machinery in agriculture has increased significantly during the past 20 years; the
mean rate of horsepower per farm worker has increased from 10 in 1950 to 47 in
1971 (2). The number of tractors increased (88 percent) from 2.4 million in 1945
to 4.5 million in 1972 (3, 12). Concurrently, the rated horsepower of these tractors
increased 2.6-fold from 18.0 to 46.6 horsepower (3, 12). The mean number of acres
farmed per tractor was 62 in 1963 (12). In our estimates we assumed that tractors
and other machinery were used to farm 62 acres and assumed to function for 10
years (Table 20.1).

Fuel consumption for all farm machinery rose from slightly more than 3.3 billion
gallons (1 gallon = 3.8 liters) in 1940 to about 7.6 billion gallons in 1969 (12, 30).
For total U.S. corn production, fuel consumption for all machinery rose from an

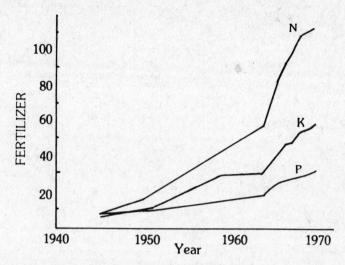

Figure 20.2. Fertilizer (nitrogen, phosphorus, and potassium) applied per acre in corn production (14, 15, 28, 29).

estimated 15 gallons per acre in 1945 to about 22 gallons per acre in 1970 (Table 20.1). Indeed, farming uses more petroleum than any other single industry (13).

The use of fertilizer in corn production has been rising steadily since 1945 (Fig. 20.2). An estimated 7 pounds (1 pound = 0.4 kilogram) of nitrogen, 7 pounds of phosphorus, and 5 pounds of potassium were applied per acre to the acres fertilized in 1945 (14). By 1970 the application of fertilizers had risen to 112 pounds of nitrogen, 31 pounds of phosphorus, and 60 pounds of potassium per acre (15). The increase in nitrogen alone has been about 16-fold.

Other inputs in corn production include seeds, irrigation, and pesticides (Table 20.1). The use of pesticides in corn has been increasing rapidly during the past 20 years and this parallels the general increase in pesticide use in the United States (16) (Table 20.1). About 41 percent of all herbicides and 17 percent of all insecticides used in agriculture are applied to corn (17).

Hybrid corn that is currently harvested has a higher moisture content because the newer varieties have growing seasons which extend further into the fall when drying conditions are poor (9). Moisture content above 13 percent (the maximum suitable for long-term storage) causes spoilage, and a drying process is used to reduce moisture (Table 20.1).

Agriculture consumed about 2.5 percent of all electricity produced (Table 20.1). The energy input for transportation is an important feature of modern intensive agriculture (Table 20.1). Machinery, pesticides, seeds, gasoline, and other supplies must be transported to the farm. Then the corn harvest must be transported to the place of use for animal feed or processing.

To gain an idea of the changes occurring over a period of time in corn production energy inputs, the years 1945, 1950, 1954, 1959, 1964, and 1970 were selected for a detailed analysis (Table 20.1 and Table 20.2). Exact 5-year intervals were not selected because more complete data were available on these specific years than on others.

In 1970 about 2.9 million kcal was used by farmers to raise an acre of corn (equivalent to 80 gallons of gasoline) (Table 20.2). From 1945 to 1970, mean corn

TABLE 20.2. Energy Inputs (kilocalories) in Corn Production

Input	1945	1950	1954	1959	1964	1970
Labor*	12,500	9,800	9,300	7,600	6,000	4,900
Machinery!	180,000	250,000	300,000	350,000	420,000	420,000
Gasoline@	543,400	615,800	688,300	724,500	760,700	797,000
Nitrogen#	58,800	126,000	226,800	344,400	487,200	940,800
Phosphorus$	10,600	15,200	18,200	24,300	27,400	47,100
Potassium%	5,200	10,500	50,400	60,400	68,000	68,000
Seeds for planting¢	34,000	40,400	18,900	36,500	30,400	63,000
Irrigation!	19,000	23,000	27,000	31,000	34,000	34,000
Insecticides**	0	1,100	3,300	7,700	11,000	11,000
Herbicides!	0	600	1,100	2,800	4,200	11,000
Drying!	10,000	30,000	60,000	100,000	120,000	120,000
Electricity!	32,000	54,000	100,000	140,000	203,000	310,000
Transportation!	20,000	30,000	45,000	60,000	70,000	70,000
Total Inputs	925,500	1,206,400	1,548,300	1,889,200	2,241,900	2,896,800
Corn Yield (output)//	3,427,200	3,830,400	4,132,800	5,443,200	6,854,400	8,164,000
kcal Return/Input kcal	3.70	3.18	2.67	2.88	3.06	2.82

*It is assumed that a farm laborer consumes 21,770 kcal per week and works a 40-hour week.
For 1970: (9 hours/40 hours) x 21,770 kcal = 4,980 kcal.
!See Table 20.1.
@Gasoline, 1 gallon = 36,225 kcal (44).
#Nitrogen, 1 pound = 8,400 kcal, including production and processing (45).
$Phosphorus, 1 pound = 1,520 kcal, including mining and processing (44).
%Potassium, 1 pound = 1,050 kcal, including mining and processing (46).
¢Corn seed, 1 pound = 1,800 kcal (21). This energy input was doubled because of the effort employed in producing hybrid seed corn.
**Insecticides, 1 pound = 11,000 kcal including production and processing (similar to herbicide, see !!).
!!Herbicides, 1 pound = 11,000 kcal including production and processing (20).
//Each pound of corn was assumed to contain 1,800 kcal (21) and a bushel of corn was considered to be 56 pounds.

yields increased from about 34 bushels per acre to 81 bushels per acre (2.4-fold); however, mean energy inputs increased from 0.9 million kcal to 2.9 million kcal (3.1-fold) (Table 20.2). Hence, the yield in corn calories decreased from 3.7 kcal per one fuel kilocalorie input in 1945 to a yield of about 2.8 kcal from the period of 1954 to 1970, a 24 percent decrease.

The 2.9 million kcal input of fossil fuel represents a small portion of the energy input when compared with the solar energy input. During the growing season, about 2043 million kcal reaches a 1-acre cornfield; about 1.26 percent of this is converted into corn and about 0.4 percent in corn grain (at 100 bushels per acre) itself (18). The 1.26 percent represents about 26.6 million kcal. Hence, when solar energy input is included, man's 2.9-million-kcal fossil fuel input represents about 11 percent of the total energy input in corn production. The important point is that the supply of solar energy is unlimited in time, whereas fossil fuel supply is finite.

The trends in energy inputs and corn yields confirm several agricultural evaluations which conclude that the impressive agricultural production in the United States has been gained through large inputs of fossil energy (18, 19). . . .

Conclusions

The principal raw material of modern U.S. agriculture is fossil fuel, whereas the labor input is relatively small (about 9 hours per crop acre). As agriculture is dependent upon fossil energy, crop production costs will also soar when fuel costs increase two- to fivefold. A return of 2.8 kcal of corn per 1 kcal of fuel input may then be uneconomical.

Green revolution agriculture also uses high energy crop production technology, especially with respect to fertilizers and pesticides. While one may not doubt the sincerity of the U.S. effort to share its agricultural technology so that the rest of the world can live and eat as it does, one must be realistic about the resources available to accomplish this mission. In the United States we are currently using an equivalent of 80 gallons of gasoline to produce an acre of corn. With fuel shortages and high prices to come, we wonder if many developing nations will be able to afford the technology of U.S. agriculture.

Problems have already occurred with green revolution crops, particularly problems related to pests (24). More critical problems are expected when there is a world energy crisis. A careful assessment should be made of the benefits, costs, and risks of high energy-demand green revolution agriculture in order to be certain that this program will not aggravate the already serious world food situation (25).

To reduce energy inputs, green revolution and U.S. agriculture might employ such alternatives as rotations and green manures to reduce the high energy demand of chemical fertilizers and pesticides. U.S. agriculture might also reduce energy expenditures by substituting some manpower currently displaced by mechanization.

While no one knows for certain what changes will have to be made, we can be sure that when conventional energy resources become scarce and expensive, the impact on agriculture as an industry and a way of life will be significant. This analysis is but a preliminary investigation of a significant agricultural problem that deserves careful attention and greater study before the energy situation becomes more critical.

Acknowledgments

We thank the following specialists for reading an earlier draft of the manuscript and for their many helpful suggestions: Georg Borgstrom, Department of Food Science and Geography, Michigan State University; Harrison Brown, Foreign Secretary, National Academy of Sciences; Gordon Harrison, Ford Foundation; Gerald Leach, Science Policy Research Unit, University of Sussex; Roger Revelle, Center for Population Studies, Harvard University; Malcolm Slesser, Department of Pure and Applied Chemistry, University of Strathclyde; and, at Cornell University: R.C. Loehr, Department of Agricultural Engineering; W.R. Lynn and C.A. Shoemaker, Department of Environmental Engineering; K.L. Robinson, Department of Agricultural Economics; C.O. Grogan, Department of Plant Breeding; R.S. Morison, Program of Science, Technology and Society; N.C. Brady and W.K. Kennedy, Department of Agronomy; and L.C. Cole and S.A. Levin, Section of Ecology and Systematics. Any errors or omissions are the authors' responsibility. This study was supported in part by grants from the Ford Foundation and NSF (GZ 1371 and GB 19239).

Notes

1. President's Science Advisory Committee, *Report of the Panel on the World Food Supply*, I-III (The White House, Washington, D.C., 1967).
2. U.S. Department of Agriculture, *Misc. Publ.* No. 1063 (1972).
3. ———. *Stat. Bull.* No. 233 (1972).
4. L. Rocks and R.P. Runyon. *The Energy Crisis* (Crown, New York, 1972), pp.12 and 131.

5. Food and Agriculture Organization of the United Nations, *Production Yearbook* 25, 35 (1972).
6. ———. *Monthly Bull. Agr. Econ. Stat.* No. 20 (1971).
7. C.V. Griliches, *Econometrica* 25, 501 (1957).
8. R.W. Allard, *Principles of Plant Breeding* (Wiley, New York, 1960), p.265.
9. S.R. Aldrich and E.R. Leng, "Modern corn production." *Farm Quarterly* (1966), p. 296 and figure 150.
10. C. Grogan, personal communication.
11. H.L. Everett, personal communication.
12. U.S. Department of Agriculture, *Stat. Bull.* No.344 (1964).
13. Committee on Agriculture, *House of Representatives* (92nd Congress, 1971), p. 20.
14. U.S. Department of Agriculture, *Changes in Farm Production and Efficiency* (Agricultural Research Service, Washington, D.C., 1954).
15. ———, *Fertilizer Situation* (Economics Research Service, FS-1, 1971).
16. ———, *The Pesticide Review 1970* (Agricultural Stabilization and Conservation Service, Washington, D.C., 1971).
17. ———, *Agricultural Economics Report* No. 179 (Economics Research Service, 1970).
18. E.N. Transeau, *Ohio J. Sci.* 26, 1 (1926).
19. P. Handler, *Biology and the Future of Man* (Oxford Univ. Press, New York, 1970), p. 462; H.T. Odum, *Environment, Power, and Society* (Wiley, New York, 1971), p. 115; R.A. Rappaport, *Sci. Amer.* 225, 117 (1971); G. Borgstrom, *Hungry Planet* (Macmillan, New York, 1972), p. 513; K.E.F. Watt, *Principles of Environmental Science* (McGraw-Hill, New York, 1973), p. 216.
20. D. Pimentel, H. Mooney, L. Stickel, *Panel Report for Environmental Protection Agency*, in preparation.
21. F.B. Morrison, *Feeds and Feeding* (Morrison, Ithaca, N.Y. 1946), pp. 50 and 429.
22. U.S. Department of Agriculture, *Agr. Econ. Rep.* No. 147 (1968).
23. U.S. Department of Agriculture, *Agricultural Statistics 1970* (Government Printing Office, Washington, D.C., 1970), pp. 28 and 430.
24. G.R. Conway, *Environment, Resources, Pollution, and Society* (Sineurer Associates, Inc., Stamford, 1971), pp. 302–325; S. Pradhan, *World Sci. News* 8, 41 (1971).
25. J.N. Black, *Ann. Appl. Biol.* 67, 272 (1971).
26. U.S. Department of Agriculture, *Agricultural Statistics 1967* (Government Printing Office, Washington, D.C. 1967), pp. 34–35.
27. ———, *Crop Production, 1971 Annual Summary* (State Report Service, 1972).
28. ———, *Agr. Res. Ser. Stat. Bull.* No. 216 (1957).
29. ———, *Stat. Rep. Serv. Bull.* No. 408 (1967).
30. R.S. Berry and M.F. Fels. *The Production and Consumption of Automobiles. An Energy Analysis of the Manufacture, Discard, and Reuse of the Automobile and its Component Materials* (Univ. of Chicago, Chicago, 1973).
31. U.S. Department of Agriculture, *Bur. Agron. Econ. Bull.* No. FM 101 (1953).
32. U.S. Bureau of the Census, *Statistical Abstract of the U.S. 93rd Edition* (Government Printing Office, Washington, D.C., 1972), pp. 600–601.
33. H.F. DeGraff and W.E. Washbon, *Agr. Econ.* No. 449 (1943).
34. U.S. Bureau of the Census, *Census of Agriculture 1964* II (1968), pp. 909–955.
35. E.O. Heady, H.C. Madsen, K.J. Nicol, S.H. Hargrove, *Report of the Center for Agriculture and Rural Development*, prepared at Iowa State University, for the National Water Commission (NTIS, Springfield, Va., 1972).
36. A.W. Epp, *Nebr. Exp. Sta. Bull.* No.426 (1954).
37. T.S. Thorfinnson, M. Hunt, A.W. Epp, *Nebr. Exp. Sta. Bull.* No. 432 (1955).
38. *Corn Grower's Guide* (W.R. Grace and Co., Aurora, Ill., 1968), p. 113.
39. U.S. Bureau of the Census, *Statistical Abstract for the United States, 92nd Edition* (Government Printing Office, Washington, D.C., 1971), p. 496.
40. ———, *Statistical Abstract of the United States, 96th Edition* (Government Printing Office, Washington, D.C. 1965), p. 538.
41. U.S. Department of Commerce, *Census of Transportation,* III (3) (Government Printing Office, Washington, D.C., 1967), pp. 102–105.
42. Interstate Commerce Commission, *Freight Commodity Statistics, Class I Motor Carriers of Property in Intercity* (Government Printing Office, Washington, D.C., 1968), p. 97;

———, *Freight and Commodity Statistics Class I Railroads* (Government Printing Office, Washington, D.C., 1968);

———, *Transportation Statistics* I, V, VII (Government Printing Office, Washington, D.C., 1968).

43. U.S. Department of Transportation, *Highway Statistics* (Government Printing Office, Washington, D.C., 1970), p.5.

44. *Handbook of Chemistry and Physics* (Chemical Rubber Company, Cleveland, 1972), Table D-230.

45. A.J. Payne and J.A. Canner, *Chem. Process Eng.* 50, 81 (1969).

46. G. Leach and M. Slesser, *Energy Equivalents of Network Inputs to Food Producing Processes* (Univ. of Strathclyde, Glasgow, 1973).

21

World Champions:
A Survey of American Farming
(the revolution is not yet over)
An Anonymous Author

The Economist discusses the mechanical/chemical revolution that has occurred in American agriculture and warns of yet another upheaval—the heavy reliance on an expanding world market to bolster farm income. Also discussed are some socio-economic phenomena, e.g. labor displacement, associated with the "revolution."

Nothing is more misleading than the common use of the word "conservative" to describe the American farmer. For if conservative is supposed to mean an abiding respect for the traditional way of doing things then the American farmer is an extreme radical, keener even on buying new gadgetry than affluent Californians. If it is supposed to mean a firm commitment to free enterprise the label is equally misleading. The American farmer is as two-faced as anybody else about the joys of the free market: determined to keep the government's nose out of his business when the prices are high, gung-ho for government intervention when prices are low.

Extraordinary adaptability is his real strength. In just over a century American farming has gone through two revolutions. The first, starting around the time of the Civil War, was the move from manpower to horsepower; the second was the move from horse to mechanical power (the number of tractors exceeded the number of horses and mules for the first time in 1955) together with the introduction of better seeds, better breeding, the exact application of fertiliser and the increasingly sophisticated use of chemicals as weed and insect killers.

These two revolutions have drastically changed both the face and the character of American agriculture. Travel through the cottonbelt of the South (which now stretches to California), the cornbelt of the Mid-West or the wheatbelt of the Great Plains and the fields are empty. Machines as big as brontosauruses have replaced the horses and people. At the last count the country's 2.7m farms owned 4.4m tractors. The average size of new tractors bought by farmers in 1978 was 105

Reprinted with permission from The Economist : 5-6 (5 January 1980).

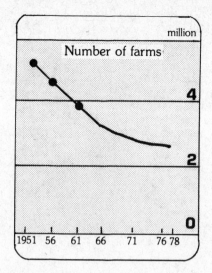

Figure 21.1. Number of farms. [Source: USDA]

horsepower, a figure set to become mightier. Several companies manufacture tractors in the 350 horsepower range; one markets a 525 horsepower monster.

Animals, too, have left the fields. Chickens and increasingly pigs are raised indoors. Cattle are fattened on feedlots. Many of the grain farmers of the Mid-West have no animals at all apart from pet cats and dogs. They used to feed part of their crop to their own livestock. Now they concentrate instead on raising grain to sell to feed animals in Russia, Europe and Japan.

In the Mississippi Delta the absence of both animals and people on the plantations is almost eerie. After all, it does not take a long memory to recall seeing 50 or 60 black cotton-pickers in a field, or the multitude of small farms of the 40 acres-and-a-mule sort where poor black and white cotton growers eked out a living. Mechanical cotton pickers, and associated inventions like desiccants and defoliants, have sent them packing. Their little dog-trot and shotgun houses have been bulldozed away for the expansion of a cotton field—or more likely for soyabeans, which have dethroned King Cotton in parts of the South. Or even perhaps to make room for a dam where catfish, an even more efficient converter of feed into meat than chickens, can be farmed in much the same way as trout are farmed in less sultry places.

The mechanical/chemical revolution set off one of the greatest, only semi-voluntary, migrations in history. Mr Calvin Beale, a demographer at the agriculture department, calculates that from 1940 to 1960 a net of 21.5m people left farming, an average of more than a million a year. As this far exceeded the excess of births over deaths among farm people, and as the drift has continued since, albeit at a more sedate pace, the farm population has declined rapidly, from 30.5m people in 1940 to less than one third of that now.

The farms have got larger as the farm labour force has got smaller. In 1950 there were 5.6m farms with an average size of 214 acres; in 1960 4m farms with an average size of 297 acres; in 1970 2.9m farms with an average size of 374 acres; and in 1978 2.7m farms with an average size of 400 acres. Small farms, officially defined as farms with sales of less than $20,000 a year, still make up 70% of the

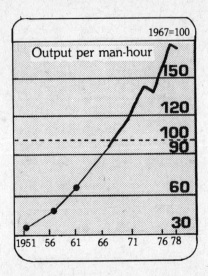

Figure 21.2. Output per man hour. [Source: USDA]

total, but they account for only one tenth of total farm sales and their operators earn 85% of their income away from the farm.

The revolution is not yet over. About 6% of all farms (162,000 farms with sales over $100,000 a year) account for over half of total farm receipts and the farm labour force is sure to contract further as the bigger farms continue to absorb smaller ones and as mechanical harvesting becomes as efficient and entrenched in vegetable and fruit farming as it already is in grains, cotton and soyabeans.

Tomato growing is a pointer. University researchers opened the way for mechanical harvesting by developing a tomato plant on which most of the fruit ripens at about the same time and has a hard skin that resists bruising. Critics say it tastes awful. They have also lambasted agricultural scientists for wasting time and money by working on a green cauliflower through crossing broccoli with a standard white cauliflower and by striving to develop a seedless cucumber.

Scientists and the farmers who profit from their inventions are undeterred. California grows 80% of the processing tomatoes grown in the United States and virtually all of these are already harvested by a machine that severs the vine and shakes the fruit loose. About three quarters of these tomatoes are then sorted not by hand but by a smart machine that rejects the rotten, green or blemished tomatoes and gets rid of the dirt.

The labour savings are immense. Mr Robert Curley, an agricultural engineer at the University of California reports:

A typical harvester without electronic sorting requires a sorting crew of 16 to 22 people. With electronic sorters the hand sorting crew is reduced to three to five persons per machine. A modern tomato harvest with electronic sorting and a crew of five people can harvest 25 to 35 tons per hour.

Mechanical harvesting is also used for California's prunes: the "shake and catch" system that employs mechanical tree-shakers and a padded catching frame. Wine grapes are harvested by trunk shakers. A spooky machine with grasping steel fingers that can tell the difference between ripe and unripe fruit is being tested as a picker of Valencia oranges in California. Research is in train, too, for mechanical harvesting of lettuces (one experimental machine uses a gamma ray sensor to determine bulk density or maturity), broccoli, cauliflowers, onions and peppers.

All this surely means that the vegetable pickers, many of them Mexican-Americans, will be forced off the farms on to the unemployment and welfare rolls, just as the Okies of John Steinbeck's "The Grapes of Wrath" were when the dust bowl drought churned their farms into red flour and as the blacks of the Deep South were when mechanical cotton pickers made them redundant.

For farmers the continuing mechanical/chemical revolution has been economic Darwinism at its most gory. Those who have not gone boisterously, even recklessly, into debt to buy new machines, not sown the new hybrid seeds, not learnt to adapt their marketing to bouncing prices on the Chicago exchanges and not bought or leased neighbouring land to reap the economies of scale have either had to get out of farming altogether or to become "sundown farmers" who commute downtown to work for a boss every day.

Yet while still coping with the backwash of the mechanical/chemical revolution the surviving farmers are going into another, still widely misunderstood, upheaval: the heavy reliance on an expanding, but fluctuating, world market for their prosperity. This might yet cause enough commotion to be called the third revolution.

22

Pizzas, Cheese and Surpluses

George F. Will

Unfortunately for U.S. farmers, decreasing crop prices have plagued farmers consistently in the 1980s. George Will speculates on this odd situation, agricultural surplus and low prices amidst worldwide malnutrition, and suggests either cutting price supports for agriculture (a most unpalatable thought for U.S. farm men and women and the Senators and Representatives who are elected by them) or increasing American food aid abroad. It seems that U.S. farm policy is in need of an overhaul.

Washington—The federal government is nibbling at the cheese glut. The Agriculture Department has proposed requiring that frozen pizzas contain a certain minimum amount of cheese and that the use of cheese substitutes be clearly confessed on packages.

The frozen pizza industry regards this proposal as the kind of Leninism that Ronald Reagan was elected to stop. But the cheese glut (which is just a portion of the dairy products surplus, which is just a bit of the agriculture surplus) demands boldness.

Jeffrey Birnbaum, a Wall Street Journal reporter, recently toured a dormant limestone mine in Missouri. There, the government "stores so much surplus cheese, butter and powdered milk that a visitor would be hard pressed to walk past it all in one day." A tour by golf cart reveals canyons of cheddar cheese in 500-pound barrels, towers of frozen butter in 68-pound boxes, endless aisles of 100-pound sacks of dried milk—61 million pounds of dairy products, enough to cover 13 football fields 17 feet deep, or fill a train stretching from Manhattan to Toledo.

This is just two percent of the 2.9 billion pounds of dairy products that taxpayers have bought. In recent years they have paid $3 billion, or $13,000 for every dairy farmer. Taxpayers are currently paying $275,000 an hour to buy more surpluses, and are paying $5 million a month to store the stuff.

Well, now. Perhaps a dozen-trillion pizzas would cut the current cheese glut, but that many pizzas would lead to a terrible pepperoni shortage. We need another idea.

Perhaps we should sell frozen pizzas to the Soviet Union. Moscow might send some of our pizzas, as it sends grain, to Nicaragua, but that is commerce in fungible goods. If Moscow cannot afford the pizzas, we can do what we do regarding grain:

Give them credits and generally fiddle things so that pizzas (like the grain) cost Moscow less than it costs Americans to produce them.

Here is another whimsical idea: We could stop paying farmers to inundate markets and limestone mines with dairy products. Today the government is taxing consumers (everyone) to pay farmers to produce food that is, because of price supports, unnecessarily expensive when taxpayers buy it at supermarkets and is expensive when taxpayers pay to store it.

One study says that a $1-per-hundredweight reduction in the support price would knock nine cents off a gallon of milk and a pound of cheese, and 11 cents off a pound of butter, and $1.2 billion off consumers' food bills in a year. Furthermore, dairy products, being cheaper, would be more exportable, so there would be less to store.

But here is a better idea: Use the food as food. America does not have enough productivity. Government should not pay people, as it today is paying farmers, to produce less—less of something that parts of the world need desperately. Surely it is not beyond the capacity of public policy to make America's agricultural bounty an asset to American policy. Indeed, it is a scandal not to.

Today in 18 black African countries (Morocco and Algeria, too, have desperate needs), 20 million persons face starvation unless 600,000 tons of extra food reach them. Since 1960, Africa's food production has increased less than two percent a year—less than population growth. In nine countries, food production is more than 10 percent below 1960 levels.

The World Bank estimates that nearly 200 million persons—60 percent of all Africans—eat fewer calories daily than the United Nations considers a survival diet.

Drought is only part of the problem. Governments have made Africa unnecessarily vulnerable to such natural phenomena. Urban mobs demand food at artificially low prices, thus discouraging production. Government planners have tried to spur industrialization by holding down food prices in the hope that this would hold down urban wages. If someone could leash Africa's governments and unleash American farmers on Africa, the continent could produce 100 times more food than it does today.

Logistical problems (including problems posed by African bureaucracies) involved in even distributing food are staggering, and there is the danger that American food could produce dependency and further depress African agriculture. But an American attempt to solve these problems is as close as one can come in this world to an absolute moral imperative.

I am staring at a photograph of what looks, at first glance, to be a bald, wizened old man. Actually, it is a child. The child is sucking the withered breast of a woman who could be 19 years old. It is a sight to concentrate the mind on limestone mines full of food.

23

The Peasant Perspective:
Ye Olde Survival Tips
for the Modern Farmer
(excerpts)
Farmer Jones

It seems that a new farm and food policy is in order . . . we have become "too" productive and neither costly government programs nor dubious food aid programs to other countries can offer a long-term solution to our supply management problems. Garrett Hardin, in Chapter 18, worries that America is the world's breadbasket; the American farmer worries that it is not.

It could be argued that the European peasant and the modern farmer have so little in common that any comparisons are meaningless. However, some similarities are worth noting. Both lack political clout and neither commands much attention from the authorities unless there is a lack of production or a threat of a food shortage. Perhaps the overriding difference between an old line peasant and a modern American farmer is the peasant's complete lack of faith in political authority. He harbored no illusions as to where he stood in the economic pecking order. No one could pat him on the head with praise that he represented the country's most productive citizenry and that his role in feeding the world made the balance of payments picture tolerable and that the king and indeed, the whole country, looked up to him as a hard-working fellow. A peasant wouldn't have believed such rubbish for a minute. He acted as if the government were his sworn enemy, a perfectly logical mode of behavior.

American plowjockeys might do well to ponder this peasant cynicism in light of our own experiences of the past fifty years. Is there any reason to suppose that governments, bankers, agribusiness concerns, or consumers have any interest in an agricultural system which might entail chronic shortages and with them inherent profitability for the working farmer? What in the world would Monsanto and Dow do with all that herbicide? Who would buy Farmland Industry's anhydrous ammonia? Poor Deere and Company might have to sell $100,000 combines to the Russians. Who would be paying interest to good old Federal Land Bank? Continental Grain

Reprinted from The Prairie Sentinel: 16 (December 1981).

would be bankrupt, for without mountainous surpluses to control through storage and transportation facilities, its reason for existence would cease. The consumers would, of course, become somewhat irritated at the price of food, but we know what villanous churls they are, so who cares? A true peasant does not grieve over an unhappy consumer, so long as he keeps buying.

24

The Threat of Soil Erosion to Long-Term Crop Production
(excerpts)

W.E. Larson, F.J. Pierce
and R.H. Dowdy

In 1983, W.E. Larson and his colleagues documented the extent of wind- and water-induced erosion in the U.S. as well as predicted erosion-induced losses from potential cropland. Areas of the country with serious erosion problems included the Appalachian states, Great Plains region and Corn Belt. Soil loss translates into crop nutrient loss and thus economic cost. Larson, Pierce and Dowdy suggest that sustained soil loss will result in long-term decreases in crop productivity.

Although soil erosion was of concern to George Washington, Thomas Jefferson, and James Madison (1), it was not until the early 1930's that the problem was brought to the attention of Congress and the nation. A prime mover in this was H.H. Bennett (2), a soil scientist with the U.S. Department of Agriculture (USDA). Bennett was responsible for the establishment of the Soil Conservation Service in 1935.

Since 1928, when the first estimate of the amount of erosion occurring nationally was published (3), there have been many additional estimates (4). The bases of these estimates, however, are obscure, inadequate, and variable. Thus the debate as to whether soil erosion on cropland has increased or decreased since the 1930's cannot be resolved. Instead, we should seek to ascertain the seriousness of current soil erosion with respect to long-term food and fiber production.

Erosion is a group of processes whereby earthy and rock materials are loosened or dissolved and removed from the earth's surface. It includes the processes of weathering, solution, corrasion, and transportation. Before cultivation of crops, erosion was beneficial for the most part, leading as it did to the formation of fertile deltas and valleys. During the period of evolution of the present landscape (Wisconsin to Recent geologic time), erosion may have been cyclic, occurring in a series of cut-and-fill cycles separated by periods of stability (5). It is even possible that erosion

Reprinted with permission from Science 219 (4585): 458–465 (4 February 1983). Copyright 1983 by the AAAS.

rates in the geologic past at times exceeded current rates. The fundamental issue today is the sustained acceleration of erosion resulting from human activities.

The Soil and Water Resources Conservation Act (RCA) of 1977 (6) and the National Agricultural Lands Study (7) have raised serious concern over the degradation of U.S. soil resources. Factors contributing to this concern have been the sharp increase in grain exports during the past decade and the increased area of sloping, marginal, and fragile soils planted in row crops. On the basis of 1977 estimates (6,8), it was concluded in the RCA report that soil erosion is the main conservation problem on about 50 percent of the nation's cultivated cropland. While the RCA study was the most extensive inventory of soil quality and erosion ever completed in the United States, the long-term effects of erosion on crop productivity were not assessed. A recent national workshop sponsored by ten scientific societies cited "sustaining soil productivity" as their first research objective (9). They stated the need for studies "to quantify the relationship between plant growth and those soil attributes affected by erosion."

Research to quantify erosion has been based on the physical principle that soil movement occurs in response to forces generated by the flow of water or wind. For movement of soil particulates to occur, a threshold level of energy must be attained. Similarly, a minimum energy level must be maintained to keep the particulates in motion. The amount of erosion, therefore, is determined by the amount of energy available at the soil surface and the energy requirements for dislodging particulates and maintaining flow. These vary by location (climate), surface configuration, soil type, vegetative cover, and landscape. Erosion control practices have been aimed at either minimizing the energy available or maximizing the energy required to discharge soil particulates. Terracing, contour cultivation, planting of windbreaks, improving the stability of soil aggregates through soil stabilization, crop residue management, and conservation tillage are examples of such practices.

Concern over erosion is universal. There is, however, disagreement as to the extent of erosion, its effects on plant productivity and the environment, and its socioeconomic impacts. This article addresses the threat of erosion to long-term crop productivity.

Soil Layers

Erosion results in both on-site damage to soil and crops and off-site damage in the form of water and air pollution and damage to man-made and natural structures. The degree of damage is determined, to a great extent, by the nature of the soil and its position in the landscape.

The soil is a natural, organized body evolving slowly under the influence of many factors (10). The processes of soil formation include the processes of erosion. A soil survives erosion because it is protected or forms as fast as it is dissipated.

A vertical soil profile (Fig. 24.1) displays layers or horizons with characteristic physical and chemical properties. Soils with similar horizons are grouped into soil series. In a particular landscape, two or more soil series form a soil association. Soil associations are important in determining optimum land-use patterns for agriculture (11).

The profile of a soil provides the key to its vulnerability to erosion. The letters A, B, and C are used to designate soil horizons (Fig. 24.1). The A horizons lie at or near the surface and are characterized by maximum accumulation of organic matter and maximum leaching of clay materials, iron, and aluminum. The B horizons (subsoil) consist of weathered material with maximum accumulation of iron and aluminum oxides and silicate clays. The C horizons are unconsolidated material

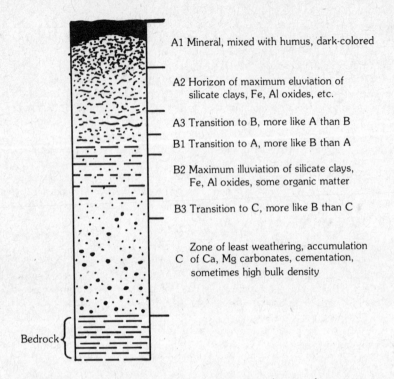

A1 Mineral, mixed with humus, dark-colored

A2 Horizon of maximum eluviation of silicate clays, Fe, Al oxides, etc.

A3 Transition to B, more like A than B

B1 Transition to A, more like B than A

B2 Maximum illuviation of silicate clays, Fe, Al oxides, some organic matter

B3 Transition to C, more like B than C

C Zone of least weathering, accumulation of Ca, Mg carbonates, cementation, sometimes high bulk density

Bedrock

Figure 24.1. Theoretical soil profile showing major horizon designations. [Adapted from (11)]

underlying the A and B horizons, and are affected relatively little by soil-forming processes. Not all horizons are present in all soils, since interactions of the soil-forming processes produce different profiles.

The A horizons of cultivated soils play an important role in controlling water, heat, and gas balances. Plant roots and available nutrients are concentrated in this layer, whose thickness varies from a few centimeters to as many as 50. In many cultivated soils the A horizons have been decreased in thickness or removed by erosion. When tilled, the A horizons may be mixed with the upper B horizons, resulting in a surface soil quite different in texture and other characteristics from that observed in the uneroded condition. This is important since the stability of the soil surface and the rate at which it conducts water affect the amount of erosion that occurs.

Many soils have B horizons that are unfavorable for plant root growth. Among these are horizons with excessive accumulations of clay (argillic), high density and strength (fragic), cement-like qualities (duric), low pH (acidic), salt accumulation (salic), and high aluminum saturation. In addition, water permeability is often controlled by the B horizons. Hence, soils with unfavorable B horizon characteristics pose a double threat by increasing the potential for runoff and erosion and by forming a barrier to root development as erosion brings these horizons closer to the surface.

Landscapes

Most cultivated landscapes fall between two topographic extremes. One has small relief, no major surface outlet, and containment of runoff water and transported sediment in depressional areas (14). In this landscape very little or no sediment may leave the cultivated area. This topography is common in areas of the north-central United States with glacial-derived soils [for example, Major Land Resource Area (MLRA) 103] (13).

The other topographic extreme has distinct slopes and deep incised stream valleys (12). In this landscape erosion may be severe and a relatively large amount of the sediment may leave the cultivated area and be deposited on a floodplain or carried far away. Examples of this landscape are the loess hills bordering the Mississippi and Missouri rivers (MLRA's 107 and 134). . . .

Measurement of Erosion

Quantifying energy flow at the soil surface temporally and spatially is extremely difficult. most attempts to quantify erosion have involved the direct measurement of runoff and soil loss and the empirical relation of these measurements to soil, landscape, and climate.

Two methods for estimating soil erosion have predominated: the Universal Soil Loss Equation (USLE) (15) and the Wind Erosion Equation (WEQ) (16). The 1977 National Resource Inventory (NRI) data base (8) on erosion in the United States was derived from the application of these equations to data on soil, topography, climate, and soil management at specific sample sites.

Both equations were empirically derived. The USLE is statistically based on years of field plot measurements at 49 locations under natural rainfall conditions and additional measurements under simulated rainfall conditions. It calculates soil loss as a product of six factors:

$$A = R\ K\ L\ S\ C\ P$$

where A is estimated soil loss in metric tons per hectare per year, R is rainfall (a function of local rainstorm characteristics), K is soil erodibility (a function of soil properties), L is slope length, S is degree of slope, C is cropping (a function of crop type, residue management, tillage practices, and crop calendar), and P is erosion control (practices such as contouring, strip-cropping, or terracing).

The WEQ is based on soil erosion measurements by sediment traps at or near the soil surface and by wind tunnels in the laboratory or field. Wind erosion is calculated as a function of five factors:

$$E = f\,(I,\ K,\ C,\ L,\ V)$$

where E is the potential annual soil loss, I is the soil erodibility (analogous to K in the USLE). K is ridge roughness (surface roughness and configuration), C is climate (wind speed and duration), L is the field length (unsheltered distance across a field parallel to the prevailing wind direction), and V is vegetative cover.

Both equations were designed to predict long-term (10 years or more) soil loss from fields under specific types of crop and soil management. Although erosion estimates obtained with these equations are, in fact, point measurements (17) and thus are not exact, they do indicate where potential erosion problems are likely to exist. The USLE, however, probably underestimates erosion in areas where rill and gully erosion are important and does not estimate sediment delivery to a stream.

Erosion is extremely variable with time. Most of the erosion of susceptible soils takes place during short intervals of high energy availability and when the soil is

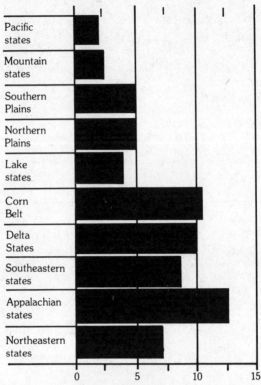

Figure 24.2. Average sheet and
rill erosion by cropland region in
1977 (tons/ha) (7).

not protected by a mulch or crop canopy. For example, Browning *et al.* (18) reported that, annually, 13 percent of the storms causing runoff account for 60 percent of the erosion in southwest Iowa. Over 50 percent of the erosion from land planted in corn occurs in May and June. In the Great Plains, winds whose speeds are above threshold velocities for visibility reduction blow for a total of 400 to 2000 hours annually (19). Projecting long-term erosion, then, has the liability that assumptions must be made about climate and cropping practices.

Universality of Erosion

In 1977 the Soil Conservation Service completed the NRI (8), the most extensive quantitative study yet performed on the occurrence and amount of soil erosion in the United States. About 200,000 primary sampling units were randomly selected. Crop, soil, and topographic features were measured or observed at each unit. The data, along with geographic and other information, were used to estimate water (sheet and rill) erosion and wind erosion by the USLE and WEQ. These data form the basis of the RCA analysis (6) of soil erosion.

The seriousness of erosion must be viewed temporally in the context of maintaining crop production. The USDA has assigned a soil loss tolerance (*T*) value to most of the soils mapped in the United States. The *T* value, as defined by Wischmeier and Smith (15), "denotes the maximum level of soil erosion that will permit a high level of crop productivity to be maintained economically and indefinitely." T values never exceed 11.2 tons per hectare annually. Some are lower, depending on soil quality. (If a metric ton of soil represents about 0.0077 centimeter of soil over an area of 1 ha, a soil eroding at the rate of 13 ton/ha per year will lose about 1 centimeter of soil in 10 years.) T values are used in the RCA (6) to measure the extent and seriousness of erosion.

Average rates of sheet and rill erosion are shown in Fig. 24.2 for the major U.S. cropland regions. In 1977 erosion exceeded T on more than 45.4 million hectares of cropland (27 percent of the total) (Fig. 24.3). Approximately 10 percent of the cropland had erosion rates exceeding 22.4 ton/ha per year—twice the maximum soil loss tolerance (Table 24.1). These estimates do not include wind or gully erosion.

Other factors being constant, sheet erosion and rill erosion increase with steepness of the slope (15). Nationally, 45 percent of the cropland has slopes of 0 to 2 percent, 25 percent has slopes of 2 to 6 percent, 20 percent has slopes of 6 to 12 percent, and 10 percent has slopes over 12 percent.

A factor contributing to increased erosion is the trend toward more production of row crops, chiefly corn and soybeans. Nationally, the area planted in row crops increased 27 percent between 1967 and 1977, close-grown crops increased 4 percent, and rotation hay and pasture decreased 40 percent. About 20 percent of U.S. cropland is now planted in corn and 16 percent is in soybeans. Over 80 percent of the cropland in the central Corn Belt is planted in corn and soybeans. The cultivation of these crops on steeper slopes has increased significantly in recent years. Approximately 50 percent of the land in central Iowa and Illinois with slopes of 6 to 12 percent is planted in these two crops (20).

In 1977 average erosion rates exceeded T for all row crops produced in the Southeast (8). Annual soil loss exceeded 22.4 ton/ha on 32, 19, and 9 percent of the cultivated areas in the Southeast, Northeast, and Corn Belt, respectively. Erosion rates were greater than T on 33 percent of the land planted in corn, 44 percent of the soybean land, 34 percent of the cotton land, and 39 percent of the sorghum land. In general, erosion is greatest on land with row crops, less with close-seeded crops, and least with grass and legume forage crops.

Wind erosion is a serious problem in many areas of the nation, especially the Great Plains. Wind erosion may be expected to occur "whenever the surface soil is finely divided, loose, and dry; the surface is smooth and bare; and the field is unsheltered, wide, and improperly oriented with respect to the prevailing wind direction" (21). Except for a ten-state area of the Great Plains, the extent of wind erosion was not quantified in the RCA because of insufficient data for the WEQ (6). Cropland in Texas, New Mexico, and Colorado has average wind erosion rates exceeding 11.2 ton/ha per year (Fig. 24.4). . . .

Stresses on the Resource Base

The potential impact of erosion on agricultural productivity must be assessed in terms of both the total cropland available and the future needs of the nation. In 1977 the United States had 168 million hectares in crop production and an additional 51 million hectares with high or medium potential for conversion to cropland, for a total base of 219 million hectares (6). The base is subject to noncrop use, damage from erosion and other forms of degradation, and the effects of increases in production per unit of land area. According to a recent USDA study (7), it is likely that the entire U.S. cropland base will be in production by the year 2000. Although it is

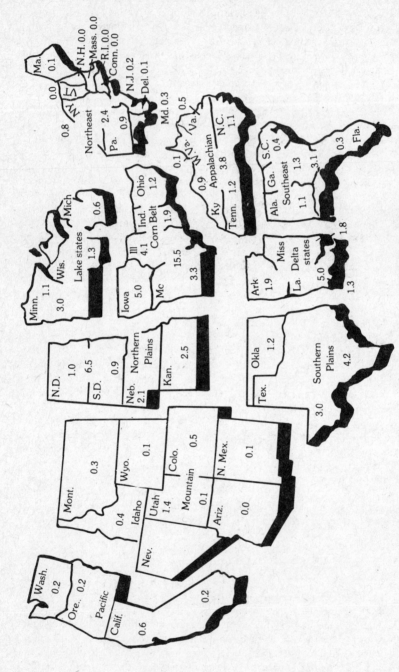

Figure 24.3. Hectares of cropland (millions), by farm production region, on which the rate of sheet and rill erosion exceeded the soil loss tolerance level in 1977. [Adapted from (6)]

TABLE 24.1. Estimated Amount of Sheet and Rill
Erosion on U.S. Cropland in 1977 (6)

Amount Eroded (ton/ha-year)	Percentage of Total Cropland Affected
less than 4.5	48
4.5 to 11.2	28
11.2 to 22.4	14
greater than 22.4	10

not our objective to discuss the adequacy of available cropland resources, it is pertinent to comment on the possible effects of erosion on the cropland base. . . .

If the loss in crop production from erosion on the current 168 million hectares of cropland is 0.1 percent per year, then the equivalent of 4.2, 8.4, and 16.8 million hectares of productive cropland will be lost over the next 25, 50, and 100 years, respectively. These losses loom even larger when the costs of replaceable inputs, poor management of land, and removal of erosion-damaged land from production are considered.

Of the 51 million hectares of potential U.S. cropland, more than half is susceptible to erosion (22). Selectivity in bringing this land into production and improved conservation practices will be needed to safeguard this reserve. Conservatively assuming that erosion-induced losses in crop production on the potential cropland will also be 0.1 percent, the equivalent loss will be 1.3, 2.6, and 5.1 million hectares over the next 25, 50, and 100 years, respectively. Adding the losses from land now under cultivation to those from potential cropland results in losses of 5.5, 11, and 22 million hectares over the period considered. While losses of this magnitude are not catastrophic, they would hasten the time when our total cropland base would be in full production.

While additional land with low potential for use as cropland (101 million hectares) could be converted to cropland, this would require substantial capital expenditures for clearing, draining, and land forming. High annual expenditures for erosion control, fertilization, and other inputs necessary to sustain production would follow. In addition, the environmental consequences of bringing such land into cultivation would be enormous. Development of technology and conservation systems to facilitate the economic use of this land is a major challenge for researchers.

Conclusions

The effects of erosion on cropland soils depend on the characteristics of the soils and the landscapes in which they occur. Further, when considered in the context of long-term productivity, erosion rates alone are not good indicators of soil degradation. Erosion rates should not be the sole criterion in targeting government resources for erosion control. . . .

We have concentrated on losses in irreplaceable soil attributes. The data presented here for two MLRA's indicate that a significant percentage of soils has the potential for serious losses in productivity due to erosion. This percentage would become very large if we became unable to apply the advanced technology needed to optimize

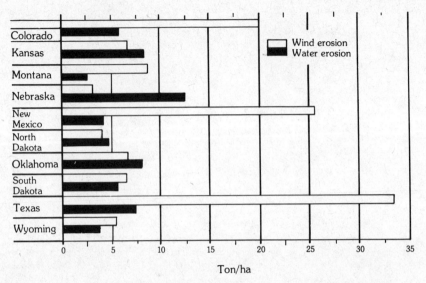

Figure 24.4. Average annual wind and water erosion for the Great Plains states (6).

factors affecting plant growth. When losses in replaceable and irreplaceable soil attributes, damage to plants, gullying, off-site damage from sediment, and contribution of particulates to the air are considered, the seriousness of the erosion threat becomes disturbingly clear. As a national problem, soil erosion deserves attention from scientists, the government, and the public.

Notes

1. R.F. Gustafson, *Soils and Soil Management* (McGraw-Hill, New York, 1948).
2. H.H. Bennett, *Ann. Assoc. Am. Geogr.* 21, 147 (1931).
3._____ and W.R. Chapline, *U.S. Dep. Agric. Cir.* 33 (1928).
4. R.B. Held and M. Clawson, *Soil Conservation in Perspective* (Johns Hopkins Univ. Press, Baltimore, 1965).
5. R.V. Rube, R.B. Daniels, J.G. Cady, *U.S. Dep. Agric. Tech. Bull 1349* (1967).
6. *RCA Appraisal* (Department of Agriculture, Washington D.C., 1981), parts 1 and 2.
7. Department of Agriculture and Council on Environmental Quality, *National Agricultural Lands-Study, Final Report* (Government Printing Office, Washington, D.C., 1981).
8. Soil Conservation Service, National Resource Inventory of 1977 (unpublished). The NRI data base contains information on acreage, ownership, land use, erosion and other pertinent soil resource information for soil mapping units in the United States.
9. W.E. Larson, L.M. Walsh, B.A. Stewart, D.H. Boelter, Eds., *Soil and Water Resources: Research Priorities for the Nation* (Soil Science Society of America, Madison, Wis., 1981).
10. S.W. Buol, F.D. Hole, R.J. McCracken, *Soil Genesis and Classification (Iowa State Univ. Press, Ames. 1973).*
11. N.C. Brady, *The Nature and Properties of Soils* (Macmillan, New York, ed. 8, 1974).
12. G.A. Poch, *Soil Survey of Olmsted County, Minnesota* (Soil Conservation Service, Washington, D.C., 1980), p.6.
13. *U.S. Dep. Agric., Agric. Handb.* 296 (1981). Major land resource areas, usually several thousand hectares in extent, are characterized by particular patterns of soil (including slope and erosion), climate, water resources, land use, and type of farming. These areas consist of geographically associated land resource units. The two MLRA's discussed in this article are 107 and 134. MLRA 107 is rolling to hilly with intricately dissected, loess-mantled plains. The major soil suborder is Udoll and the major soil series are Marshall, Sharpsburg, Monona, and

Ida. MLRA 134 comprises sharply dissected plains with a thick loess mantle, underlain by unconsolidated sands, silts, and clays, mainly of marine origin. Valley sides are hilly to steep. The major soil suborder is Udult and the major soil series are Memphis, Grenada, Loring, Calloway, and Lexington.

14. R.E. Rolling, *Soil Survey of Cottonwood County, Minnesota* (Soil Conservation Service, Washington, D.C. 1979), p. 90.

15. W.H. Wischmeier and D.D. Smith, *U.S. Dep. Agric. Agric.* Handb. 537 (1978).

16. N.P. Woodruff, F.H. Siddoway, D.W. Fryrear, *U.S. Dep. Agric. Agric. Inf. Bull.* 354 (1972).

17. Attempts have been made to develop field-scale, physically based models to predict erosion from specific storms. CREAMS is one example, but has not yet played an important role in defining the national extent of erosion [W.G. Knisel, Jr., Ed., *U.S. Dep. Agric. Sci. Educ. Admin. Conserv. Res. Rep.* 26 (1980); C.A. Onstad and G.R. Foster, *Trans. Am. Soc. Agric. Eng.* 18, 288 (1975)].

18. G.M. Browning, R.A. Norton, A.G. McCall, F.G. Bell, *U.S. Dep. Agric. Tech. Bull.* 959 (1948).

19. L.J. Hagen and E.L. Skidmore, *Trans. Am. Soc. Agric. Eng.* 20, 898 (1977).

20. M.J. Lindstrom, S.C. Gupta, C.A. Onstad, R.F. Holt, W.E. Larson, *U.S. Dep. Agric. Agric. Inf. Bull.* 442 (1981).

21. L. Lyles, *Trans. Am. Soc. Agric. Eng.* 20, 880 (1977).

22. C. Benbrook and A.R. Hidlebaugh, *Nat. Agric. Lands Tech. Pap.* 14 (1981).

25

Organic Farming in the Corn Belt

William Lockeretz, Georgia Shearer
and Daniel H. Kohl

It would appear that organic farming might provide the solution for the agricultural problems discussed earlier in Part IV. Both yields and operating costs averaged lower (in general, this is true during the transition period from conventional to organic practices) than for conventional farmers. Assuming no serious reductions in yield, the organic matter content of the soil should be relatively high on organic farms; thus helping to reduce the rate of soil erosion.

Between 1974 and 1978, one of the first major studies of organic farming in the U.S. was conducted by William Lockeretz and his colleagues at the Center for the Biology of Natural Systems in St. Louis, Missouri. Support was provided by the National Science Foundation. The purpose of the study was to determine the economic profitability and energy use, crop yields and crop quality for conventional and organic agriculture, as well as determine the organic farmers' motivations and social relations. The authors dispel popularly held conceptions of organic farmers and discuss both types of farmers' cultivation practices, pest control methods, rotations, crop mix, soil fertility and labor requirements.

Widespread use of chemicals—manufactured fertilizers, as well as synthetic herbicides, insecticides, and other pesticides—is one of the most characteristic features of the modern agricultural era. This period, dating roughly from World War II, has been marked by rapid and fundamental changes in agricultural production methods. Because agricultural chemicals have enabled farmers to obtain higher yields per unit of land with lower labor requirements and lower overall production costs, their use has become a standard feature of most of the country's major agricultural systems. Total use of fertilizers and pesticides has increased more than sevenfold since 1945 (1).

Despite the generally accepted benefits that fertilizers and pesticides provide, an initial period of unimpeded adoption and continuously increasing use was followed by a closer examination of their full range of implications and a growing concern over some of their unforeseen consequences. Thus, a recognition in the 1960's of the unintended effects of insecticides on nontarget organisms, possibly including man, eventually led to the banning in the 1970's of several important ones, especially chlorinated hydrocarbons. Nitrogen fertilizers have been implicated in some agricultural areas as a significant contributor to high nitrate levels in drinking supplies (often exceeding the U.S. Public Health Service recommended limit) (2). Finally, manufacture of virtually all major fertilizers and pesticides requires considerable inputs of fossil fuels (3).

Because of these concerns, farmers, agricultural researchers, and extension workers in the past several years have shown a greater interest in ways of using fertilizers and pesticides more efficiently and in giving a larger role to nonchemical alternatives, such as biological control of insect pests or fertilization with organic wastes. But the dominant place of chemical methods of fertilization and pest control remains unchallenged. The prevailing view seems to be that regardless of environmental and energy concerns, fertilizers and pesticides are an indispensable part of productive and profitable agriculture and that their use could not be sharply curtailed without drastic adverse consequences. A small minority of farmers has questioned this position, however, and farm without using either modern inorganic fertilizers or synthetic pesticides, a system that is commonly called "organic farming." In view of the virtually universal acceptance of agricultural chemicals, it is not surprising that such a radical departure from prevailing practices has been strongly criticized. Predictions of the consequences of its adoption on a large scale have ranged from a sharply lower standard of living, to a need for a massive return of labor to the country, to widespread famine and starvation (4). Critics and advocates of organic farming, the latter most commonly found outside the mainstream of agricultural research, have frequently exchanged very harsh accusations. This may help explain why very little research has been done on organic farming as a system of commercial agriculture (in contrast to home gardens or hobby farms), although there has been considerable work on ways of partially reducing the use of chemicals.

For environmental and energy reasons, this situation began to change somewhat in the mid-1970's, with research being conducted on the economics, energy efficiency, and social context of organic farming (5). The first and most intensive such study, summarized in this article, examined commercial organic farms in the Midwest from 1974 to 1978 from a range of viewpoints. Specific results from this work have been reported previously, including those on economic profitability and energy use (6-8), crop yields (9, 10), crop quality (11), and organic farmers' motivations and social relations (12, 13). In this article we integrate these separate investigations in order to present as thorough an overview as possible of organic methods as applied to a major type of farm in one of the nations leading agricultural regions.

Frequently, organic farming is discussed as though the only choices were "all or nothing." That is, such discussions typically are concerned with what would happen if all farmers began farming with completely organic methods. In the study reported here no attempt was made to answer this question. The results of the study are limited to a particular type of farm in a particular region, and all the data concern the performance of actual organic farms when such farms comprise probably less than 1 percent of all the farms in the region. Because of aggregate effects that are not manifest under such conditions (such as changes in crop prices when there are changes in the overall supply of various crops), no attempt was made to extrapolate the results to hypothetical situations in which either appreciable numbers of farms or all farms made major changes toward the practices used on the farms we studied. Nevertheless, the results give a qualitative indication of what some of the possibilities might be for the development of less chemical-intensive agricultural systems, and are relevant to the question of whether intensive use of chemicals always is essential for economically competitive farming.

Social Aspects of Organic Farming

Organic farming is commonly regarded as one facet of a broader "alternative agriculture" movement whose followers diverge from the mainstream in many more ways than simply in their fertilization and pest control practices (14). This view is shared by many supporters, as well as many critics, of organic farming. The former consider it as part of an approach to agriculture that is less resource-intensive, more sustainable, more personally rewarding, and less mechanized (15). Critics, in contrast, frequently assume that organic farming is simply old-fashioned farming, or that its advocates are people with a peculiar metaphysical outlook and little or no prior farming experience who are not interested in making money from farming (16).

We used a mailed questionnaire to examine the background, attitudes, and motives of 174 organic farmers in the Corn Belt. All of these farmers produced field crops (and usually livestock as well) on a commercial scale, which we took to mean at least 40 hectares (100 acres) (12). In general, except for their fertilization and pest control practices, these farmers were more like their neighbors who farmed conventionally than like the stereotypic organic farmers described by either supporters or critics (13). Over 80 percent of them had previously farmed with conventional methods, thus contradicting the common image of them as "back-to-the-landers." They were about the same age as their conventional counterparts in the Corn Belt (median about 50 years, with about one-fifth below 40 and one-fifth over 60). Therefore, they typically were neither older farmers who never got around to adopting modern chemicals and other modern methods nor members of any youthful counter-culture movement.

The organic farmers who had formerly used conventional methods converted to organic farming for a variety of reasons. By far the most common reason (mentioned by three-quarters of the sample) was a specific perceived problem or concern about chemical use, such as the health of their livestock or of their family, problems with their soil, or the ineffectiveness of chemicals. Far fewer (about one-third) mentioned a generalized dislike of chemicals, a concern about the environment, or religious principles. About half of the sample was influenced by proponents of organic farming, most often dealers for organic fertilizers and soil amendments. On the average, the farmers in our sample had adopted organic methods in 1971, or 6 years before they responded to our questionnaire.

The advantages they reported having experienced with organic methods were similar to their reasons for originally deciding to farm organically. However, we have no way of knowing whether their reports resulted from an independent evaluation after gaining some experience with their newly adopted methods, or were merely another manifestation of the views that first led them to adopt organic methods. In any case, the presumed advantages for their families' health and that of their livestock were by far the most frequently cited benefits, each being mentioned by about half of the sample. Soil quality, the environment, and religious factors were each mentioned by about one-fourth of the respondents. Only one of the four most frequently mentioned disadvantages was an agronomic one: weed problems. The other three were social or institutional in nature: difficulty in finding markets for organic products; lack of up-to-date information sources; and low opinion of organic farming on the part of others.

Thus, organic farmers of the type we studied seemed to be motivated more by pragmatic considerations than philosophical or ideological ones, although ideological considerations did play a role in their thinking. They resembled the majority of commercial farmers both in their heavy use of purchased inputs, including full-size machinery, and in their use of conventional marketing channels rather than specialty outlets (13). Close similarity to the majority of farmers also characterized most of their production methods and the results they obtained.

Farming Practices

Data on organic farming practices were obtained from three sources: a mail survey concerned with some basic features of 363 organic farms in the western Corn Belt (Illinois, Iowa, Nebraska, Missouri, and Minnesota), conducted from 1975 to 1978 (12); a study from 1974 to 1976 of the economics and energy use of crop production on 14 organic and 14 conventional farms in the same region (6, 10); and a similar study in 1977 and 1978 on 23 organic farms, primarily in Iowa (8). In all three studies, the organic farms were required to have field crops as the main crop enterprise and to have a minimum total size of 40 ha. "Organic farming" was defined almost strictly in negative terms, that is, no use of any of the following: inorganic nitrogen fertilizer or urea, acidified phosphorus fertilizer (superphosphate or triple superphosphate), conventional potassium fertilizer (muriate of potash), or synthetic herbicides or insecticides. (The only exception was that the farmer might use occasional spot applications of herbicides on an intractable weed problem.) No requirements were imposed concerning what positive steps, if any, were taken for fertilization and pest control. However, most of the organic farmers did take one step aimed at supplying fertility: they frequently added an "organic fertilizer." We made no attempt to evaluate the efficacy of such soil amendments of low nitrogen, phosphorus, and potassium content, but the cost of such fertilizers was considerable.

The organic farmers did not attempt to compensate for the nonuse of standard fertilizers and pesticides by adopting radically different practices from those generally used by conventional farmers. Differences between organic and conventional practices were, in many instances, ones of degree, even for weed control, insect control, and fertilization, areas in which one would expect the largest differences in practices between the two groups, since they are the areas where the two groups differ by definition.

Weed control. Compared to conventional farmers, the organic farmers used more mechanical cultivation of row crops (corn and soybeans) to control weeds. However, it also was not uncommon for conventional farmers to use mechanical cultivation in addition to herbicides (17). The conventional farmers typically did not use herbicides on other important crops, including hay, oats, or wheat.

Insect control. The organic farmers mainly used crop rotation, not exotic biological control techniques, to combat major pests. Organic farmers were not alone in their nonuse of insecticides. Almost half of the conventional farmers whose corn yields we measured did not use insecticides on their corn; in this respect they were similar to corn producers in general (18). The nonusers were apparently satisfied that rotation, particularly of corn and soybeans, gave adequate control.

Fertility. The organic farmers often applied commercial organic amendments that typically contain very low concentrations of plant nutrients. Livestock manure was applied, as available, on both organic and conventional farms. The rate of application of manure on the organic and conventional livestock farms was nearly identical (6). This rate provided only a small portion of the nutrient requirements of the crops (19). Most of the nitrogen fertility on organic farms apparently was provided by growth of legumes. Although conventional farmers used commercial nitrogen fertilizers, those who had livestock also grew a considerable amount of legume forage

(20). Thus although the two groups of farmers differed with respect to the kinds of commercial fertilizers they applied, other practices related to fertility were similar, the difference being one of emphasis.

Farm type. Management that relies on legume forage to supply nitrogen fertility naturally leads to a mixed crop and livestock operation, since it is simpler to use the forage for one's own livestock than to sell it. Not surprisingly, therefore, nine-tenths of the organic farmers in our survey had a substantial quantity of livestock, most commonly beef cattle, hogs, or dairy cows (12). Among conventional Corn Belt farmers, about half receive more than 50 percent of their income from livestock (20). Thus the type of enterprise in which the organic farmers are most commonly engaged is also common among conventional farmers. However, the conventional farmers have more flexibility in the sense that they can choose to have either a mixed crop and livestock operation or a cash grain enterprise, whereas strong pressures tend to restrict organic farmers to the former.

Crop mix. Although our three sources of data differed from each other slightly on this point, in part because of differences in geographic distribution within the Corn Belt, they all yielded the same qualitative conclusion: on the conventional mixed grain-livestock farms, the leading crops (in descending order of importance) were corn, soybeans, hay, oats, and wheat; on the organic farms, the order of hay and soybeans was reversed. On the conventional farms, an additional 15 to 20 percent of the cropland was in corn or soybeans compared to the organic farms, but about 10 percent less was in oats (planted as a nurse crop for legume forage) and wheat.

Farm size. The median size of the 363 organic farms with at least 40 ha was 86 ha (9). This is about 18 percent below that of all crop-livestock farms with at least 40 ha in the same region in 1974 (20).

Equipment. The median size of the organic farms' largest tractor was 80 horsepower, and more than four-fifths of these farms had at least one tractor over 60 horsepower (12). We found only negligible differences in the sizes of major harvesting machinery, tractors, and tillage implements (21).

Labor requirements. With their high degree of mechanization, the organic farms required slightly more labor than conventional farms: 12 percent per unit value of crop produced, or 3 percent more per unit of land (6). The organic farmers did not use exceedingly labor-intensive methods, such as picking off insects by hand. Both organic and conventional farmers resorted occasionally to hand-weeding of soybeans. The difference in labor inputs reflected the differences in crop mix and cultivation, rather than fundamental differences in production methods or machinery.

Economic Performance

We conducted two studies of the income, costs, and profitability of crop production on organic and conventional farms. The first, which covered the crop years 1974 to 1976, involved 14 organic crop-livestock farms in a five-state region (Illinois, Iowa, Minnesota, Nebraska, and Missouri); each such farm was matched with a nearby conventionally operated crop-livestock farm that was chosen to be roughly comparable in size and soil type (7). The second study dealt with 23 organic farms in 1977; 19 of these farms were also studied in 1978 (8). In this study, comparative data on conventionally operated farms were obtained from county-level statistical reports of yields and harvested area of major crops, from crop production budgets (22) and from the 1974 *Census of Agriculture* (20).

Farms in the first study were found by word of mouth. Those in the second study were drawn from the sample obtained by the mail survey mentioned earlier,

TABLE 25.1. Economic Performance of Organic and Conventional Farms. The Data are Averaged Over all Cropland (including rotation hay and pasture, soil-improving crops, and crop failures).

Year	Value of Production ($/ha)		Operating Expenses ($/ha)		Net Returns ($/ha)	
	Or- ganic	Con- ventional	Or- ganic	Con- ventional	Or- ganic	Con- ventional
1974*	393	426	69	113	324	314
1975*	417	478	84	133	333	346
1976*	427	482	91	150	336	333
1977/	384	407	95	129	289	278
1978/	440	527	107	143	333	384

*Data from 14 organic and 14 conventional farms (7).
/Data from 23 organic farms in 1977 and 19 in 1978; county-average data for conventional farms (8).

but included only farms located in Iowa, Illinois, and Minnesota that met the following criteria: (i) they raised beef or hogs, or both, but had no other major livestock enterprise; and (ii) their soil had been mapped. In addition, the organic farms in both studies had been managed organically for at least 4 years. The 14 organic and conventional farms in the first study had an average size of 172 and 194 ha, respectively; the 23 organic farms in the second study averaged 95 ha compared to 96 ha for all beef- and hog- producing farms in the same counties.

In both studies, data were initially collected through personal interviews with each participant, after which we used a series of mailed data forms. Additional interviews with the participants were conducted between the two crop years of the second study. For each field on each farm, including meadow in rotation with cultivated crops, but not permanent pasture (23), information was obtained on the following: yields; applications of fertilizers, manures, and other materials; tillage, cultivation, and harvesting operations; and seeding rates and varieties used. The results in this article are averages over all the cropland on each farm, including cultivated crops, rotation meadow, soil-improving crops, and crop failures.

Gross value per hectare was computed from reported yields and statewide market prices, regardless of whether the crop was sold or was consumed by livestock on the same farms, and regardless of whether the organic crops were sold at a premium. Operating costs included direct or variable costs only: materials, labor, fuel, equipment repairs, seeds, and crop drying. No fixed or overhead expenses were included. They were assumed to be similar on the two kinds of farms because of the similarity in implements and land value (21). Labor was charged at the prevailing wage rate, regardless of whether the work was done by hired labor or by the farm family.

The main results of these studies are summarized in Table 25.1. From 1974 to 1977 the organic farms produced between 6 and 13 percent less market value per hectare of cropland than the conventional farms. At the same time, however, their operating costs were also lower by about the same amount. Consequently, the two groups' income from crop production after operating costs were deducted were within 4 percent of each other each year from 1974 to 1977. The picture was somewhat different in 1978, when the organic farms' gross income per hectare was

TABLE 25.2. Measured Crop Yields on Organic and Conventional Farms, (10, 25).

| Crop | Number of measurements | Years | Yield (metric tons/ha) | | Difference |
			Organic	Conventional	
Corn	26	1975 to 1978	6.45	7.00	- 0.55 (8 percent)
Soybeans	7	1977 to 1978	2.44	2.57	- 0.13 (5 percent)
Wheat	4	1977 to 1978	1.88	3.28	- 1.40 (43 percent)

17 percent below that of the conventional farms. While their operating costs continued to be lower, this was not enough to offset the wider gap in gross income, and returns on the organic farms were an average of 13 percent below those of the conventional farms. In relating these figures on income per hectare to data for whole farms, it should be recalled that organic farms on average were about one-fifth smaller, according to our survey of 363 organic farms.

The difference between the results of 1978 and those of the other 4 years is probably a result of growing conditions. In 1978, conditions in the study region were very favorable, whereas there was serious drought in at least part of the region during each of the previous years. One can expect that when weather conditions are unfavorable there is less advantage in using agricultural chemicals (especially fertilizers), since other factors, such as soil moisture, limit yields. We present further evidence that this partly explains our results in our description of crop yields.

Crop Yields

Yields of corn, a crop that usually receives the heaviest fertilizer and pesticide applications under conventional management, typically were about 10 percent lower on the organic farms. Soybeans, which in the Corn Belt usually receive phosphorus, potassium, and herbicide but little or no nitrogen or insecticide, yielded about 5 percent less on the organic farms. The two groups' yields were about equal for oats and hay, which do not usually receive chemicals, except for light fertilizer applications on oats. The biggest difference was in wheat (a relatively insignificant crop on these farms), for which organic yields were about one-fourth lower. Thus, with the exception of wheat, which in the Corn Belt typically receives a complete fertilizer application but no herbicides or insecticides, the amount by which yields of various crops were lower on the organic farms was consistent with the importance on conventional farms of chemicals in the production of each crop; highest for corn, less for soybeans, negligible for oats and hay.

The data from which these conclusions are drawn were obtained over a period of 5 years from five different states. For corn, for example, we had 81 separate data points. However, these data were obtained from farmers' reports, not actual measurements, and the organic and conventional farms were only qualitatively matched by soil type and location. Therefore, we also conducted field measurements of crop yields under more carefully controlled conditions. Each data point consisted of a yield measurement on a pair of neighboring (frequently adjacent) organic and

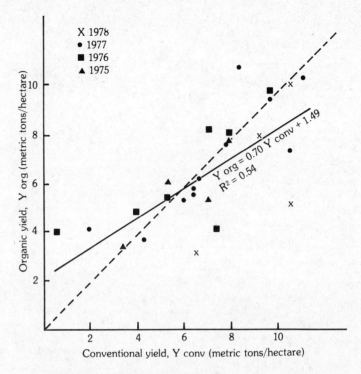

Figure 25.1. Corn grain yields of 26 matched pairs of organically and conventionally managed fields. The solid line is the best fit. The dashed line represents equal yields on the two kinds of fields (10).

conventionally managed fields of the same soil type, where the two farmers used the same variety and planted on or close to the same day (24, 25).

The results (see Table 25.2) corroborate the conclusions based on farmers' reports of yields. On organic farms the yields were much lower for wheat, moderately lower for corn and slightly lower for soybeans than those of conventional farms. For corn, we had sufficient data to examine this comparison in more detail. There was a significant correlation ($r = .58$: $P < .002$) between the proportional difference in yield on the two kinds of fields (conventional yield minus organic yield divided by the average) and the growing conditions in the particular location in the particular year, as measured by the deviation of the countywide corn yield from the 10-year county average. That is, when conditions were better than average, yields on conventionally managed fields were generally higher than those on the organic farms by more than the overall average of 8 percent; under poorer conditions, yields from the organic fields came closer to or even exceeded those of the conventional fields (Fig. 25.1). Yields on three of the 26 fields on organic farms exceeded 10 metric tons per hectare (159 bushels per acre), which would be considered an exceptionally good yield on any farm.

Energy Consumption

Although organic farming is generally less energy-intensive than conventional farming (3), some of this saving is offset by the greater reliance of organic farmers on

TABLE 25.3. Energy Consumption of Crop Production
on Organic and Conventional Farms.
See footnotes to Table 25.1 for sources
of data.

| Year | Energy Consumption Per Unit of Market Value (Mcal/$) | | |
	Organic	Conventional	Ratio
1974	1.8	4.3	0.42
1975	1.7	3.8	0.45
1976	1.8	4.8	0.38
1977	1.9	5.1	0.37
1978	1.8	4.1	0.44
Average	1.8	4.4	0.41

mechanical cultivation for weed control and by the lower yields on organic farms. We examined the overall energy requirements of crop production using the data collected for the studies of economic performance.

Since the two groups of farmers raised different relative amounts of crops, the results were aggregated for all the cropland on each farm, just as was done with the economic data. Also in analogy with the economic analysis, we ignored energy associated with capital equipment, limiting the computations to annual inputs: fuel for tillage, planting, and harvesting equipment; fuel for crop drying; and energy to manufacture fertilizers, pesticides, and other materials. Because the two groups differ in the value of crops produced per unit area, energy intensiveness was computed per unit value of production, rather than per unit area (26).

The results of this analysis are shown in Table 25.3. The pattern remains very similar through the 5 years covered by the two studies: the organic farms required about two-fifths as much fossil energy to produce one dollar's worth of crop. This difference arises from two main sources (27). First, energy consumption for corn is much lower on the organic farms, primarily because of nonuse of manufactured nitrogen fertilizer. Second, a greater fraction of cropland is in corn on the conventional farms, which contributes significantly to their higher energy intensiveness, since corn is the most energy-intensive crop.

Effects on Crop Quality and Plant Growth

The comparative nutritive value of crops raised by organic and conventional methods is a subject of considerable controversy, one on which the available evidence is extremely limited. We have examined the crude protein content of corn, wheat, and soybeans raised under both systems, as well as the amino acid composition of the corn protein. The samples used in these analyses were obtained from a subset of the fields used in the crop yield measurements. Consequently, within each organic-conventional pair, neighboring fields were matched by soil type, variety, and planting date.

The only clear difference in nutritive value occurs with corn, where the conventionally raised grain was consistently higher in crude protein (Table 25.4). For soybeans and wheat, differences within a pair went in both directions, and the average differences between the two samples were small and not statistically significant.

TABLE 25.4. Average Crude Protein Content of Grains From Organic and Conventional Farms (range given in parentheses).

| Crop | Number of Measurements | Average Protein Content* | | |
		Organic	Conventional	Difference
Corn	19	8.99 (6.63 to 11.06)	10.13 (7.88 to 11.56)	-1.14/ (-3.00 to -0.19)
Soybeans	7	41.62 (39.19 to 44.19)	42.06 (40.06 to 44.50)	-0.44 (-5.31 to +1.19)
Winter wheat	4	14.25 (12.19 to 16.06)	14.12 (12.69 to 15.56)	0.13 (-0.62 to +1.19)

*Percentage total N x 6.25.
/P less than .001 by two-tailed t-test.

The corn grain samples were analyzed for 16 amino acids. In terms of fraction of protein content, the organically raised samples were significantly higher (P < .01) in lysine (2.27 compared to 2.02 percent), an amino acid that limits the nutritive value of corn grain for monogastric species (28). The protein from organically grown corn was also higher in methionine, histidine, threonine, and glycine but lower in leucine and phenylalanine. However, in terms of fraction of total grain weight, none of the amino acids were higher in the organically grown grain. Moreover, in terms of the quantity produced per unit of area, the organically raised samples were significantly lower in all amino acids except methionine (11), since the grain yields per unit area and the protein content of the grain were both lower (see Tables 25.2 and 25.4).

Inadequate nitrogen availability on the organically managed fields could have caused the different amino acid patterns in the two sets of samples and could have been the factor that limited yields (28). A lack of nitrogen is also suggested by the crude protein content of the organic, but not the conventional, corn grain being slightly below the level usually achieved with adequate nitrogen (29). Moreover, the difference between the two fields' crude protein content was positively correlated with difference in yield. Presumably, a modest addition of nitrogen to the organically managed cornfields would reduce their yield disadvantage relative to conventional fields, while keeping a large portion of the advantage of the organic methods (lower production costs and lower energy consumption).

The lower nitrogen supply on the organically managed fields may have been why they largely avoided two other problems: stalk lodging (plants that have fallen over) and Diplodia stalk rot. Both of these problems were twice as prevalent on the conventional cornfields. An average of 10 percent of the conventionally grown corn plants on 25 fields had lodged, compared to 5 percent on the matched organic fields; 24 percent of plants on 14 conventional fields were affected by Diplodia, compared to 13 percent on the organic. Both of these differences were statistically significant (P < .02 and P < .05, respectively) (10).

Soil Nutrients and Erosion

Under conventional practice, inorganic fertilizers with a high available nutrient content are used both to provide the nutrients needed immediately for each year's crop, as well as to maintain the long-term levels of nutrients in the soil. In the conventional mixed crop-livestock farms of the type we studied, application of commercial inorganic fertilizers commonly occurs along with manure applications

TABLE 25.5. Soil Measurements on Matched Organically Managed and
Conventionally Managed Fields (10). The measurements
were conducted on 30 pairs of fields, except in the
case of organic carbon which was measured on 35 pairs.
N.S., not significant.

Soil Property	Organic		Conventional		Differ- ence	P
	Mean	Range	Mean	Range		
Organic carbon (%)	2.35	0.97 to 4.41	2.21	0.76 to 6.30	0.14	<.05
Total nitrogen (%)	0.233	0.109 to 0.422	0.221	0.080 to 0.588	0.012	<.1
Ratio of carbon to nitrogen	10.25	8.45 to 12.37	10.28	8.41 to 11.73	-0.03	N.S.
Available phosphorus						
P_1 (ppm)	25.2	5.9 to 72.1	33.8	2.2 to 121.0	-8.6	<.1
P_2 (ppm)	69.8	12.7 to 185.4	69.7	16.2 to 195.0	0.2	N.S.
Exchangeable potassium (ppm)	137.0	21.9 to 436.6	148.2	58.3 to 322.8	-11.2	N.S.
Cation exchange capacity (meq./100 g)	27.8	9.9 to 45.1	27.2	10.7 to 49.2	0.6	N.S.
pH	6.50	5.77 to 7.90	6.38	5.33 to 7.95	0.12	N.S.

and rotations with legume forage. In contrast, organic farmers use legume forage as the primary source of sustained soil fertility (along with small amounts of on-farm manure, purchased rock phosphate, and proprietary organic soil amendments of low nitrogen, phosphorus, and potassium content).

We examined possible differences in soil nutrient status resulting from these different practices by sampling soils from 30 pairs of fields used in the corn, wheat, and soybean measurements already described. Five pooled replicates per field were analyzed for total organic carbon content, total nitrogen, available phosphorus (Bray P_1 and P_2), exchangeable potassium, cation exchange capacity, and pH (organic carbon only was measured on an additional five pairs) (30).

The results are summarized in Table 25.5. The only difference that was statistically significant ($P < .05$) was the slightly higher organic carbon content on the organic fields. There was a weaker indication ($P < .1$) of higher nitrogen and lower available phosphorus (as measured by P_1 but not P_2) on the organic fields, with no other differences significant at the $P < .1$ level.

Although the soil analyses indicated no deficiency in available potassium on organic fields, and only a small deficiency in available phosphorus, over the long term these nutrients will probably become increasingly deficient, since a nutrient balance analysis revealed that more phosphorus and potassium were being removed with the crop than were being applied (31).

The nutrient status of the soil is also strongly affected by erosion (32). The two kinds of farms differed in two ways that affect soil erosion by water, a significant problem in the Corn Belt (33). The organic farmers were far less likely to use the moldboard plow, preferring instead the chisel plow or other reduced tillage methods (7). Since the moldboard plow turns all crop residues under, it leaves the soil much more vulnerable to erosion (34). Also, as noted earlier, the organic farmers had more land in rotation meadow, which is a very effective soil conservation strategy, than did the conventional operators.

We analyzed the effect of differences in rotations (but not tillage practices) for the 14 pairs of farms in the first economic study, using the universal soil loss equation (35). Averaging over all the cropland on each farm, we estimated that for a given set of physical conditions (soil type, slope, slope length, and rainfall), water erosion was about one-third less for the rotations used on the organic farms. This difference was consistent throughout the sample: in all but one pair, the expected erosion rate was lower on the organic farm. Because we did not have adequate information on the physical factors, and did not take tillage differences into account, we cannot quote the results in terms of actual soil loss. However, because the farms in each pair were matched by location and to some extent by soil type, the effects of these physical factors are approximately the same for the two members of each pair. (This analysis also does not consider any differences in the physical state, and hence the erodibility, of soil of a given type resulting from different management practices.) Had we taken into account differences in tillage on the two kinds of farms, the differences in erosion estimates would have been greater, since the organic farmers used less erosive tillage methods.

Significance of Results

The commercial-scale organic farmers in our studies made little use of methods that most farmers would regard as exotic; rather, as alternatives to chemical fertilization and pest-control methods they used rotations with legume forages and other practices similar to those found on many Corn Belt farms, but relied more heavily on these techniques than did conventional farmers. Because of the heavier reliance on legume forage as a nitrogen source, organic farmers may not be able to choose an exclusively cash grain operation, whereas for better or worse conventional farmers have this choice.

Slightly lower gross production per unit of cropland on the organic farms was largely offset by comparable reductions in operating expenses, so that crop production was about equally profitable on the two types of farms except in a year that had extremely favorable weather. The exact comparison appears to depend on growing conditions, with the organic farms doing relatively better under the abnormally poor conditions of the mid-1970's, but relatively poorer when conditions improved in 1978. Except for wheat, a minor crop in the Corn Belt for which organic farms had much poorer yields, yields of most organically raised crops generally ranged from about the same to about 10 percent lower than on the conventional farms.

A consequence of the organic farms' production methods is that less fossil energy is required per unit of crop output, so that these farms would be less severely affected by a deteriorating energy situation. Another benefit is that soil erosion is significantly reduced under the crop rotation and tillage methods used on the organic farms (although this benefit could also be obtained by conventional farmers who chose to use the same tillage methods and rotations while still using conventional chemicals). In soil nutrient status the picture was mixed, with the organic farms showing slightly higher levels of organic carbon and nitrogen but lower available phosphorus. With regard to crop quality, both the lower crude protein content in the organic grain and the different amino acid balance indicated a nitrogen deficiency. Organically managed cornfields showed a clear advantage with regard to lodging and *Diplodia* stalk rot.

Since our present agricultural system, in which agricultural chemicals are a key element, is one that basically works—indeed, that works very well by several important criteria—it is not surprising that most researchers apparently assume that these chemicals will continue to have a major role in any future agricultural system. Consequently, most research on alternative systems is concerned with relatively minor adjustments in the use of agricultural chemicals. The results of our studies suggest that this view may be too cautious and that a better approach might be to determine how far we can and should move in the direction of reduced agricultural chemical use. The organic farmers we studied had fared reasonably well without chemical fertilizers and pesticides and without the benefit of the scientific and technical assistance routinely available to farmers following more accepted practices. That their performance might have been better had they used just modest amounts of fertilizer is indicated by the protein content of the organically managed corn. Thus there may be intermediate systems that, from the combined viewpoints of productivity, profitability, and resource use, would prove more attractive than either of the two systems we studied.

Notes

1. U.S. Department of Agriculture, Economics, Statistics, and Cooperative Service, "Changes in farm production and efficiency, 1978" (Statistical Bulletin No. 628, Washington, D.C. 1980).

2. J.H. Dawes, T.E. Larson, R.H. Harmeson, in *Proceedings of the 24th Annual Meeting of the Soil Conservation Society of America* (Colorado State University, Fort Collins, 1968), pp. 94–102; D.H. Kohl, G.B. Shearer, B. Commoner, *Science* 174, 1331 (1971): National Academy of Sciences, *Panel on Nitrates and the Coordinating Committee for Scientific and Technical Assessment of Environmental Pollutants* (Washington, D.C., 1978), p. 241.

3. C.H. Davis and G.M. Blouin, in *Agriculture and Energy*, W. Lockeretz, Ed. (Academic Press, New York, 1977), p. 315.

4. E. Butz, quoted in *Yearbook of Spoken Opinion: What They Said in 1971.* (1972) p. 123: R. White-Stevens, in *Fertilizer and Agricultural Residues*, R.C. Loehr, Ed. (Ann Arbor Science, Ann Arbor, Mich., 1977).

5. K.J. Roberts, thesis, University of Missouri, Columbia (1977); G.M. Berardi, *Agro-Ecosyst.* 4, 367 (1978); S.L. Kraten, thesis, Wathington State University, Pullman (1979); R.C. Oelhaf, *Organic Agriculture: Economic and Ecological Comparisons with Conventional Methods* (Allanheld, Osmun, Montclair, N.J., 1978); C. Alexander, thesis, University of Missouri, Columbia (1977); D. Buesching, paper presented at the Annual Meeting of the Rural Sociological Society, Burlington, August, 1979; C.K. Harris, S.E. Powers, F.H. Buttel, *Newsline* (*Rur. Sociol. Soc.*)8, 33 (July 1980); D.Vail and M. Rozyne, in *New Principles of Food and Agriculture*, D. Knorr. Ed. (AVI. Westport, Conn., in press); U.S. Department of Agriculture, *Report and Recommendations on Organic Farming* (Government Printing Office, Washington, D.C., 1980).

6. R. Klepper, W. Lockeretz, B. Commoner, M. Gertler, S. Fast, D. O'Leary, R. Blobaum, *Am. J. Agric. Econ.* 59.1 (1977).

7. W. Lockeretz, G. Shearer, R. Klepper, S. Sweeney, *J. Soil Water Cons.* 33, 130 (1978).

8. G. Shearer, D.H. Kohl, D. Wanner, G. Kuepper, S. Sweeney, W. Lockeretz, in preparation.

9. W. Lockeretz and S. Wernick, *Rural Soc.*, in press.

10. W. Lockeretz, G. Shearer, S. Sweeney, G. Kuepper, D. Wanner, D.H. Kohl, *Agron. J.* 72, 65 (1980).

11. J.L. Wolfson and G. Shearer, in preparation.

12. S. Wernick and W. Lockeretz, *Compost Sci.* 18 (No. 6), 20 (1977).

13. W. Lockeretz and S. Wernick, *Compost Sci. Land Util.* 21 (No. 2), 40 (1980).

14. G. Youngberg, *Policy Stud. J.* 6, 524 (1978).

15. W. Berry, *New Farm* 1, 74 (1979); R. Merrill, in *Radical Agriculture*, R. Merrill, Ed. (Harper & Row, New York, 1976), p. xv; M. Bookchin, in *ibid.*, p.3.

16. S.B. Aldrich, *Illinois Issues* 3, 19 (1977); L.H. MacDaniels, *Facts about Organic Gardening* (Information Bulletin 36, Extension Service, Cornell University, Ithaca, N.Y., 1975); S. Margolius, *Health Foods Facts and Fakes* (Walker, New York, 1973).

17. W. Lockeretz, R. Klepper, B. Commoner, M. Gertler, S. Fast, D. O'Leary. *Organic and Conventional Crop Production in the Corn Belt: A Comparison of Economic Performance and Energy Use for Selected Farms* (Publ. CBNS-AE-7, Washington University, St. Louis, 1976).

18. T.R. Eichers, P.A. Andrilenas, T.W. Anderson. *Farmers' Use of Pesticides in 1976* (Department of Agriculture, Economics, Statistics and Cooperatives Service, Agricultural Economics Report No. 418, Washington, D.C., 1978).

19. S.L. Tisdale and W.L. Nelson, *Soil Fertility and Fertilizers* (Macmillan, New York, ed. 3, 1975), p. 576.

20. U.S. Department of Commerce, Bureau of the Census, 1974. *Census of Agriculture* (Government Printing Office, Washington, D.C. 1977).

21. W. Lockeretz, R. Klepper, B. Commoner, M. Gertler, S. Fast, D. O'Leary, R. Blobaum, *A Comparison of the Production, Economic Returns, and Energy Intensiveness of Corn Belt Farms That Do and Do Not Use Inorganic Fertilizers and Pesticides* (Publ. CBNS-AE-4, Washington University, St. Louis, Mo., 1975).

22. U.S. Department of Agriculture, Economics, Statistics, and Cooperatives Service, *Firm Enterprise Data System*, (Oklahoma State University, Stillwater, various years).

23. Permanent pasture, which generally has a lower value of production than crops, was not included. Thus the value of production per hectare would have been lower than reported if we had included any land that might have been suitable for crop production but that was used for permanent pasture instead. In the 1974-1976 study, 78 and 85 percent of land suitable for cropland was used for crops on organic farms and conventional farms, respectively (17). Thus a small bias in favor of the organic farmers was introduced in this study by the exclusion of land that might have been in crops but was not. In the later study, 94 percent of land suitable for crops was used for crops on organic farms raising beef, cattle, and hogs. Comparable data were not available for conventional farms, but it is unlikely that more than 94 percent of such land was used for crops (8).

24. For details on the methods of measurement and comparative yields and practices, see Lockeretz *et al.* (10, 25).

25. W. Lockeretz, S. Sweeney, G. Kuepper, D. Wanner, paper presented at the 70th Annual Meeting of the American Society of Agronomy, Chicago, 1978.

26. For details on the methods, see Klepper *et al.* (6).

27. W. Lockeretz, paper presented at the International Federation of organic Agriculture Movements Agricultural Techniques Conference, Montreal, Canada, 1978.

28. V.V. Rendig and F.E. Broadbent, *Agron. J.* 71, 519 (1979).

29. W.H. Pierre, L. Dumenil, V.D. Jolly, J.R. Webb, W.D. Shrader. *Agron. J.* 69, 215 (1977).

30. For details on the methods of sampling and analysis, see Lockeretz *et al.* (10).

31. W. Lockeretz, R. Klepper, B. Commoner, M. Gertler, S. Fast, D. O'Leary, R. Blobaum, in *Agriculture and Energy.* W. Lockeretz, Ed. (academic Press, New York, 1977), p. 85.

32. R.F. Holt, *J. Soil Water Cons.* 34, 96 (1979).

33. U.S. Department of Agriculture, Soil and Water Resources Conservation Act. "Appraisal 1980. Review Draft Part I" (Washington, D.C. 1980).

34. W.A. Hayes and L.W. Kimberlin, in *Crop Residue Management Systems* (American Society of Agronomy, Crop Science Society of America and Soil Science Society of America, Madison, Wis. 1978), p. 35.

35. W.H. Wischmeier and D.D. Smith, *U.S. Dep. Agric. Agric. Handb. No. 282* (1965).

36. This research was conducted at the Center for the Biology of Natural Systems, Washington University, from 1974 to 1979, under NSF grants AER-74-18438 and AER-77-17031.

26

Critique of "Organic Farming in the Corn Belt"

T.H. Jukes, S.R. Aldrich, D.F. Cox, W. Lockeretz, D.H. Kohl and G. Shearer

The study conducted by Lockeretz et al. (see Chapter 25) generated considerable controversy. Some of the critics' replies appear below. Lockeretz et al. responded directly to their criticisms.

Organic Farming

Lockeretz et al. (6 Feb., p. 540) make a comparison of "organic" and conventional farming, based in part on mail surveys and personal interviews. Such anecdotal methods are inadequate by comparison with those used by agronomists, in which an investigator typically makes side-by-side comparisons of two or more experimental units, such as plots, with measurements of yield, and chemical analyses of soils and of crops produced. The distinction between organic and conventional farming drawn by Lockeretz et al. is unclear; for example, they mention occasional use of herbicides by organic farmers. No analyses for pesticide content of organic crops are given, although in another report (1) organic foods were found to contain pesticide residues more frequently than did the average of all foods analyzed.

Organic farming is defined as including no use of urea, but organic farmers "frequently added an 'organic fertilizer,'" that is manure, which inevitably contains urea. Organic farmers hence imply a nonexistent difference between synthetic and natural urea, shown by Wohler 152 years ago to be identical (2). His experiment is commonly cited as erasing the "vital force" concept of bio-chemical synthesis. No single example is a clearer illustration than this of the unreality of "organic farming" ideas about fertilizers.

The adjective "organic" properly refers to compounds of carbon, as in "organic chemistry." Its neologic application to food and farming, introduced in 1942 (3), was, and is, accompanied by the allegation that food produced without chemical fertilizers is "more healthful" than food conventionally produced (1). This claim cannot be substantiated (4).

Reprinted with permission from Science 213 (4509): 708–712 (14 August 1982). Copyright 1982 by the AAAS.

Lockeretz et al. state that the protein from organically grown corn was higher in lysine, methionine, histidine, threonine, and glycine, but lower in leucine and phenylalanine than that from "conventional" corn and that this difference could have been caused by "inadequate nitrogen availability." The customary belief is that the amino acid distribution in proteins is controlled genetically by nucleotide sequences in DNA molecules.

Thomas H. Jukes

Although the article by Lockeretz et al. makes a contribution to the comparison of organic and conventional farming, the study on which it is based is seriously flawed in several respects. This article should, therefore, be examined in conjunction with earlier reports from the study.

In a previous publication (1), the study team acknowledged that the organic farms were selected after "a preliminary judgement of each organic farmer's competency as a farm manager." The conventional farmers were reported to be "top management" farmers, but their yields were only slightly above county average, and fertilizer applications were no more than the state average. Some bias in favor of the organic group seems likely.

The data for 14 paired farms from 1974 to 1976 are all farmers' estimates rather than carefully measured yields. The first year data are thus farmers' recollections of fertilizer, manure, and pesticide applications; days and number of livestock grazed; and crop yields in the preceding year. Such data are highly unreliable.

In an earlier publication (2), the organic farms are reported to have a 2 percent advantage in soil productivity potential.

On the eight farms for which soil maps were available, the conventional farm had 9 percent more of their land as harvested crops (of land that was deemed suitable). Because the Washington University team presents "economic performance" data on a per hectare of cropland basis, this considerable advantage for conventional farms is lost. The authors state, however, that if land in permanent pasture on organic farms is credited with production value equivalent to hay and rotation pasture the advantage for conventional farming as a result of more harvested cropland falls to only 3 percent. It would be more accurate to credit permanent pasture with no more than one half as much productive value because of the lower productivity of native pasture species and typically fewer fertility treatments. The disadvantage of the organic farms for this factor would then stand at 6 percent.

The economic performance of organic farms in 1974 and 1975 would have been considerably less favorable if the prices in those years had not been atypically high and the estimated hay yields unrealistically high (47 percent above conventional in 1974 and 15 percent in 1975). The likely explanation for the high hay yields is that farmers have less precise bases for estimating hay yields than grain yields and simply overestimated them. Although the hay yields averaged 31 percent higher on organic farms from 1974 to 1975, Lockeretz et al. state that "The two groups were about the same for oats and hay."

When appropriate adjustments based upon the preceding paragraphs are made with data from earlier publications, the real "economic performance" for organic farms is at least 20 percent less than for conventional farms.

To replace 20 percent lost production on present cropland would require at least 30 percent additional land because the available land is much less productive (3). Furthermore, much of this land, which is now idle, in permanent pasture, or forested, is relatively steep, hence highly erosive. Consequently, although erosion on individual farms is calculated by Lockeretz et al. to be less in cropping systems characteristic of organic farming (fewer row crops, more close-growing, small grains and hay), the aggregate erosion on a regional or national basis would be greater if organic farming were widely adopted. . . .

Lockeretz et al. suggest that there may be "intermediate systems" which are more attractive than the two extremes studied. That would appear to consist of applying fertilizers at the optimum economic rate and applying pesticides only as needed. That is, in fact, the program suggested by the extension services of state colleges of agriculture as typified by the current widespread attention to integrated pest management. There is, however, no intermediate between growing a leguminous crop to supply homegrown nitrogen and a nonleguminous crop on a field in a given year.

Samuel R. Aldrich

Lockeretz et al. state that, if the yield of corn under conventional management is low, a comparable field under organic management will give an equal or higher yield. If the conventional yield is high, a comparable organic yield will be equal or lower. They speculate that a crop may be unable to take advantage of conventional practices when some factors, such as moisture, are limiting. Two statistics are used to justify this belief and speculation. First, the slope of a line, fitted by the method of least squares, through 26 points representing yields of pairs of fields managed by organic and conventional methods, was less than 1. Second, the correlation between the proportional difference in yield on the two kinds of fields and the growing conditions at that location in that year was negative, -.58 (the negative sign is omitted in the article).

There are other reasons why the slope of the fitted line may be less than 1, and these cannot be disentangled here from the one the authors propose. The conventional yield, the independent variable in the statistical model used, is measured with error. The error includes, but is not restricted to, the sampling errors involved in measuring the yield of a field by harvesting several small plots. All errors in measuring the independent variable tend to make the slope lower than what it would be if the errors were not present. Any interpretation of the slope must recognize this bias.

The correlation cited is correct but has an unusual dependence on two extreme values of the proportional difference that arise in pairs of fields with the lowest conventional yields. Without these two points, less than 10 percent of the data, the correlation drops to a nonsignificant -.27. The authors have drawn important conclusions and used undeniably plausible explanations. The supporting evidence, however, is not so strong as is implied.

D.F. Cox

Cox raises a valid caution regarding the interpretation of the organic-conventional yield differences in relation to growing conditions. We agree that we presented nothing more than "undeniably plausible explanations." If our inference was not correct—that is, if organic farmers do not fare relatively better under poorer conditions—then the relatively good performance they showed in our study was not helped by the adverse conditions during much of the study period and is more generally valid. [One minor technical point to clarify a possible misunderstanding for any readers who may wish to pursue Cox's point themselves; because this article defined the organic-conventional yield difference in the opposite sense from that in an earlier article (1) there no longer should be a negative sign in the correlation coefficient.]

Before we respond to Aldrich's letter, two general points must be made. First, although over the 5 years of our study we used many different techniques and studied several different samples of farms from a range of viewpoints, all of Aldrich's criticisms refer only to the first of two economic studies. Our subsequent work, including not only a new economic study but also soil analyses, yield measurements, and a sociological study, was designed largely to overcome the shortcomings and remove some of the limitations we discussed when we reported our initial efforts (2). Apparently we were successful, because 6 years after his first published criticism of our work (3), Aldrich still confines himself to this initial phase. (Moreover, whenever subsequent studies permitted explicit comparison, it turned out that our preliminary conclusions held up fairly well.)

The second problem in responding to Aldrich is that on several previous occasions he has criticized the very same work using the opposite reasoning. When he was trying to explain away the high energy inputs we found on conventional farms, he concluded that the fertilization rate was "unnecessarily high . . . thus raising the energy input above that needed on these farms" (4). Now this same rate apparently is too low, being "no more than the state average," thus showing that the conventional farmers weren't top managers. Likewise, Aldrich initially criticized us for presenting the data on a per hectare basis, since "the only valid comparison is on a whole-farm basis" (3); the same study was later criticized on the grounds that "a whole-farm system is simply not a suitable research entity" (5), while the current letter seems to rediscover the value of the whole-farm approach.

Aldrich expresses doubt that our sample was made up of "top management" conventional farmers. The evaluation "top management" was not made by him. All conventional farmers who served as part of the matched pairs were "'top management' operators as judged by local ASCS [Agricultural Stabilization and Conservation Service] personnel" (6). No such recommendation was requested for the organic farmers. Thus, if there is a "bias" at all, it could very well be in favor of the conventional farmers. And of course this whole issue—as Aldrich does not point out—applies only to the first economic study, since the second study used all the organic farmers we could find who met certain objective criteria, while the control group consisted of all the farmers in the same counties (7).

Aldrich also expresses concern regarding the validity of farmers' estimates of yields. He neglects to mention that measured yield comparisons were entirely consistent with those based on yields reported by farmers, as we noted previously (1). Furthermore, the yield comparisons in the first year of the study (which depended on recollection) were quite consistent with those of the last years of the study, during which time concurrent records were kept. Aldrich's concern for the large differences in hay yield is again the result of his apparent preference for the smaller of our two studies. In the initial study (6) we explicitly warned that differences in hay yield (in contrast to corn and soybean yields) "may be less meaningful because there were so few (pairs of) farms" growing this crop. Data from all 5 years included in both economic studies (6-8) showing hay yields on organic and conventional farms were about the same.

Aldrich points critically to the bias introduced by differences in land use and land quality between the two groups in our first study. We fully discussed this bias in favor of the organic farmers in our report of this study (8). We estimated the bias to be between 3 and 9 percent. (It is curious that Aldrich calls the reader's attention only to the 3 percent polar case and then proceeds to "correct" our stated 3 to 9 percent estimated range to his own estimate of 6 percent!) Nor does Aldrich note that in the second, larger study (7) no such bias existed; yet the results of the comparisons were similar.

Aldrich notes that the organic farmers wouldn't have done so well if crop prices hadn't been so high in 1974 and 1975. True. But he does not note that, because conventional farmers have a higher output, they benefited even more from the high prices.

But when all is said and done, arguing over whether or not Aldrich is right each time he tries to find a few percentage points here or there for the conventional farmer misses the main point of our conclusions: the amount by which the organic farmers fell below the conventional farmers in yield and productivity was *much less* than had been commonly supposed and certainly gives no support at all to the frequently expressed view that adoption of organic farming—or even of certain features of organic farming—would consign an enormous number of people to starvation and famine. Organic farmers have achieved the results we reported largely without benefit of assistance from agronomic researchers. (Surely agronomic researchers must believe that such assistance is worth at least a few bushels an acre.) Further, from the point of view of the organic farmer, the relatively small deficit in crop production is almost entirely offset by the lower cost of producing crops and the additional advantage of being insulated from shortages and future price increases of energy-intensive inputs. Thus there is good reason to give serious consideration to intermediate systems between the two that we studied, since such systems might offer many of the resource advantages of organic farming with little or no loss of the high productivity of conventional farming. To Aldrich, "intermediate" means no more than eliminating wasteful use of fertilizers or pesticides, which would correspond to an economically optimal version of conventional practice, as currently recommended by extension advisers. But organic and conventional practices differ in many more ways than simply in the quantity of fertilizers and pesticides used. Thus there is quite a difference between Aldrich's suggestion of reducing somewhat the use of these materials in the context of conventional practice and starting with organic farmers' rotations, tillage practices, and so forth, and then adding a modest amount of certain agricultural chemicals to the extent that it is advantageous to do so. (We conjectured, for example, that the small yield difference in corn between the two groups might be largely eliminated if organic farmers applied a small fraction of the amount of nitrogen fertilizer typically used with conventional practices. This rate would be much lower than the "economically optimal" rate under conventional practice.)

Jukes' characterization of mail surveys and interviews disposes of a lot of agricultural research. Actually, besides using these methods, we also did the things he regards as better: side-by-side yield comparisons; chemical analyses of soils; and chemical analyses of crops. (Jukes is right that we didn't analyze pesticide residues in crops, a topic about which our article says absolutely nothing.) Moreover, where the field measurements and the interviews covered the same topic (that is, crop yields), we checked the two for consistency and found good agreement, as noted above. Neither Jukes nor Aldrich, who, respectively, criticized our use of farmers' reported yields as "anecdotal" and "highly unreliable," mention this corroboration. (For that matter, they do not mention the field measurements at all.)

Jukes' implication that protein composition depends only on the nucleotide sequence of DNA does not entitle him to label this the "customary belief." The literature on protein synthesis is full of examples of environmental control of gene expression. In particular, it is well established that amino acid composition of grain grown from seeds with homogeneous genomes varies with nitrogen fertilization (9).

Jukes' criticism of the term "organic farming" is a quibble. The point of words is to communicate ideas. We are confident that every reader knows what "organic" means when it modifies "farming" as opposed to its meaning when it modifies "chemistry" (especially since we set down explicitly the criteria for being included in the sample of organic farms). In addition, a quick check of any dictionary will show that before the word "organic" was applied to chemistry, it had—and still has—other senses that make the term "organic farming" a reasonable one that hardly illustrates the "unreality" of "organic farming" ideas.

Jukes' obvious (but irrelevant) point that urea in manure is identical to synthetic urea says nothing about organic farmers' knowledge of fertilizers. They value manure because it contains many things (which give it a characteristic non-urea-like color, texture, and smell) besides urea, including several that are beneficial to crops and soils. Organic farmers are not alone in recognizing the agricultural value of manure. The conventional farmers in our study applied not only conventional fertilizers (including urea) but also manure to their fields at approximately the same rates as did organic farmers (6). Whatever Jukes' view of this issue, the reader may be assured that organic farmers, at least, do know the difference between manure and urea. For instance, were an organic farmer sufficiently incensed by the tone of Jukes' instruction and decided to respond heatedly, he would certainly not make the mistake of asserting that Jukes' ideas on organic farming were full of urea.

William Lockeretz
Daniel H. Kohl
Georgia Shearer

Notes

Thomas H. Jukes

1. *New York State Public Hearing in the Matter of Organic Foods* (State of New York, 1 December 1972).
2. F. Wohler, *Ann. Phys.* 12, 243 (1828).
3. C. Jackson and J.I. Rodale, *Apostle of Nonconformity* (Pyramid, New York, 1974), p. 63.
4. R.M. Leverton, *J. Am. Diet. Assoc.* 62, 501 (1973).

Samuel R. Aldrich

1. R. Klepper, W. Lockeretz, B. Commoner, M. Gertler, S. Fast, D. O'Leary, R. Blobaum, *Am. J. Agric. Econ.* 5, 1 (1977).
2. W. Lockeretz, G. Shearer, R. Klepper, S. Sweeney, *J. Soil Water Conserv.* 33, 130 (1978).
3. S.R. Aldrich, W.R. Oschwald, J.B. Fehrenbacher, *Ill. State Geol. Surv. Environ. Geol. Notes,* 46 (1971), p.7.

William Lockeretz, Daniel H. Kohl, Georgia Shearer

1. W. Lockeretz, G. Shearer, S. Sweeney, G. Kuepper, D. Wanner, D.H. Kohl, *Agron. J.* 72, 65, (1980).
2. W. Lockeretz, R. Klepper, B. Commoner, M. Gertler, S. Fast, D. O'Leary, R. Blobaum. *A Comparison of the Production, Economic Returns, and Energy Intensiveness of Corn Belt Fertilizers and Pesticides* (Publication CBNS-AE-4, Washington University, St. Louis, Mo., 1975)
3. S.R. Aldrich, *Science* 190. 96 (1975).
4. Organic and Conventional Farming Compared (Report No. 84, Council for Agricultural Science and Technology, Ames, Iowa, 1980), p.23. This report was prepared under the chairmanship of S.R. Aldrich.
5. S.R. Aldrich, *Ill. Issues* (Sept. 1977), p. 19.
6. R. Klepper, W. Lockeretz, B. Commoner, M. Gertler, S. Fast, D. O'Leary, R. Blobaum, *Am. J. Agric. Econ.* 59, 1 (1977).

7. G. Shearer, D.H. Kohl, D. Wanner, G. Kuepper, S. Sweeney, W. Lockeretz, *ibid.* 63, 264 (1981).

8. W. Lockeretz, G. Shearer, R. Klepper, S. Sweeney, *J. Soil Water Conserv.* 33, 130 (1978).

9. S. Dubetz, E.E. Gardiner, D. Flynn, A.L. DeLaRoche, *Can. J. Plant Sci.* 59, 299 (1979); M. Byers and J. Bolton, *J. Sci. Food Agric.* 30, 251 (1979); V.V. Rendig and F.E. Broadbenx *Agron. J.* 71. 509 (1979).

27

World Champions:
A Survey of American Farming
(down on the campus)
An Anonymous Author

The Economist provides a brief introduction to the ongoing debate over the type of (and source of support for) research conducted at the land grant colleges. Also discussed is some work of the extension service of the land grant colleges.

If Old MacDonald visited the farms of the co-op members he just would not believe his eyes. Iowa and Illinois grow one sixth of all the maize in the world; Kansas and North Dakota produce more wheat than the whole of South America. It was not always so. Back in the 1930s American farmers were no more productive than those in the third world. Their grain yields then averaged less than 1.5 tonnes per hectare. Yet now American yields are around 3.5 tonnes per hectare while those in the third world have remained stuck at under 1.5 tonnes. Why?

In trying to answer this almost impossible question, economists have dwelt more on the failures of the third world than the triumphs of the United States. This has meant that the importance of the remarkable co-operation that exists and persists between the universities and the farmers in the United States has been underrated. It goes back to at least 1862, when President Lincoln in response to demands from farmers for "people's universities" signed into law the Morrill Land Grant Act. This legislation granted an endowment of public land to states that agreed to use the income from the land to establish agricultural and mechanical colleges. The states received 30,000 acres for each senator and representative they had in the congress.

The colleges were not much better than trade schools, teaching such simple courses as "How to plough", until 1887 when congress gave them a chance to graduate into scientific institutions when it passed the Hatch Act. Under this legislation the federal government agreed to help finance agricultural experiment stations attached to the land grant colleges. The act said in part:

It shall be the object and duty of the state experimental stations through the expenditures of the appropriations hereinafter authorised to conduct original and other researches, inves-

Reprinted with permission from The Economist: 9-10 (5 January 1980).

tigations and experiments bearing directly on and contributing to the establishment and maintenance of a permanent and effective agricultural industry in the United States, including researches basic to the problems of agriculture in its broadest aspects, and such investigations as have for their purpose the development and improvement of the rural home and rural life and the maximum contribution by agriculture to the welfare of the consumer.

The keystone was then slotted into place in 1914 with the Smith-Lever Act. This added an extension service to the land grant colleges, to carry their findings and teachings directly to the farmers. Extension officers, at least the best of them, are tireless busybodies in discovering exactly what the academics and experimenters are up to and then on briefing county agents and farmers on ways this academic work can be exploited to breed bigger and better animals faster or to grow more food at less cost and more profit.

The ways are not always obvious. In cotton, for example, where insects can reduce yields by 90%, farmers have an understandable temptation to go in for overkill, spraying everything that moves with poison enough to provide corpses for a dozen Agatha Christie novels. It is usually a big mistake. Over-frequent use of poisons tends to hasten the speed at which insects mutate around the poison and produce super-offspring resistant to it. The poison damages the environment and sometimes the farmer's own health. It is also very costly and often counterproductive since beneficial insects such as the ladybug (ladybird to non-Americans), the green lacewing, the assassin bug and the predaceous stink bug are wiped out along with boll weevils, bollworms, cotton fleahoppers and other pests.

Experimental stations have therefore worked out a combination of cultural, biological and chemical practices that cut down on the use of insecticides and extension officers have tried to coax farmers to switch from indiscriminate poisoning to "effective management of insects". Cotton growers are advised to "count" the number of pests in their fields (a simpler task than it sounds) and then, in consultation with an entomologist, to use insecticides only when pest insects reach a population level where the damage they will cause is expected to exceed the cost of control.

In cotton insect management, as in other new farming techniques, the extension officer needs only to persuade a few farmers to try out a good new money-making idea for most of the others eventually to become converts. For if the technique works and reduces cost it puts obstinate fellows who refuse to use it at a competitive disadvantage.

When an agricultural technology or technique is introduced it generally has only a tiny impact on national productivity at first. Only a few intrepid farmers adopt it initially and they cannot usually quickly measure its effectiveness. But once the pioneers can show big benefits other farmers rush in to follow their lead. Productivity then grows at an exponential rate.

The land grant college/extension system cannot, of course, grab all the credit for the great leap forward in yields that has come during the second, mechanical/chemical revolution, in agriculture. Advances by commercial interests, notably the farm machinery and seed companies, have also helped. So has the use of fertiliser, with farmers currently spreading 50m tons of the stuff, excluding manure, every year. So have government policies that have supported farm prices at profitable levels, and handed farmers a disguised subsidy by paying them not to grow crops on what was usually their most marginal land.

Still, most farmers agree (and they are notoriously people who agree on hardly anything) that the land grant college/extension system has made an immense contribution to reducing the gap between yields on the best farmed farms and average ones, and also towards cutting the time it takes for a practitioner to benefit from academic research.

Even so the system has become more controversial. Farmers resent the way the extension service, in trying to butter up congressmen from urban districts, has put more effort into "home economics". City folk are shown how to make jam or mow a lawn. At the other extreme, a book in the finest American muckraking tradition, called "Hard Tomatoes, Hard Times", caused a big stir in congress when it said the land grant college/extension system had become the handmaiden of agribusiness interests. The author, Jim Hightower, has more than a trivial point when he criticises institutions financed by public funds for research work that benefits those who can well afford to do the research themselves.

Chicken farming is such an activity. The 60 biggest broiler companies in the United States control 90% of the broilers. One of the biggest is the Federal Company, with its headquarters in Memphis, Tennessee. Its Holly Farms subsidiary maintains a 1.5m breeder hen flock to obtain 5m broilers a week for its processing plants and it is fully vertically integrated: breeding, hatching, growing, processing and marketing its broilers.

Though people can and do grouse about the bland taste of the chickens produced on this and other farm assembly lines, their efficiency must be conceded. In 1940 it took from 12 to 14 weeks to produce a 4lb chicken and the chicken ate 4lb of feed for each 1lb of weight it gained. Now the same sized chicken is raised in less than eight weeks and eats only 1.9lb of feed for each 1lb it gains in weight.

Such businesses are rich and ought indeed to foot the bill for their own research. But few areas of farming are as concentrated, or likely to become so. The farm family remains the mainstay in most sectors of agriculture, and it benefits mightily from the land grant college/extension system.

Americans, particularly the capitalist ideologues of the Chicago School, are often loth to face up to the fact, but it is no coincidence that their country's two most successful export industries—agriculture and defence—are those in which the government is a generous patron.

Back at the Lab

What will be the next big technological breakthrough in farming? Futurologists at the department of agriculture have asked themselves and imaginative agricultural scientists/researchers this question. Among the predictions:

* Cows that routinely have twins and ewes that usually give birth to triplets.
* New crops from hybrid breakthroughs (wheat? cotton?) and a successful search for other food crops.
* The conversion of unpalatable raw products, such as cellulose and petroleum products, into edible protein, carbohydrates, and fats to provide additional animal feeds.
* Double cropping and intensive cropping to increase crop yields on land.
* Reduced tillage techniques that save fuel by cutting the number of times a farmer must cultivate a field.
* More reliance on biological controls (for example, the release of sterile male insects into a field) and less on poisons to control insect pests.
* The development of anti-transpirants that inhibit a plants' tendency to lose water through evaporation.

* Enhancement of photosynthetic efficiency: improving the process by which living plants form carbohydrates through genetic selection, physical modification and chemical modification; enhancing the biological capacity of living plants to absorb nitrogen for protein synthesising; and enhancing plant growth through elevating atmospheric levels of carbon dioxide.

* Plants that generically resist drought better and thrive on salty water.

* The greater use of natural and synthetic compounds which make plants ripen quicker or all at the same time, and which slow the speed at which fruit and vegetables go rotten after they are harvested.

28

Biotechnology, Seeds, and the Restructuring of Agriculture
(excerpts)

Jack Kloppenburg Jr. and Martin Kenney

In what may be the single most important article in this section, Jack Kloppenburg and Martin Kenney discuss the "gene revolution" in agriculture by which there will be a complete integration of the chemical and seed industries, and thus total control over the agricultural production process. The authors argue that it is not surprising commodity prices and farm incomes have dropped, debt load is intolerable and overproduction is endemic in the United States. Social relations were reshaped concomitant with capital accumulation in agriculture; new social relations in agriculture are being generated with the deployment of biotechnology. A primer on capitalism and the farmer is offered, but emphasis is put on biotechnology and its effects on both developing and developed economies. The "gene revolution" in agriculture promises advances in nitrogen fixation, stress tolerance and disease resistance as well as the acquisition of seed companies by transnational petrochemical corporations, integration of the chemical and seed industries and unprecedented linkages between private companies and universities. The authors speculate on the positive and negative impacts of a "bio-revolution" in the developing countries; the potential for both "liberation and domination" is ever present.

The New Biotechnologies

In 1974 Stanford and University of California, San Francisco researchers Stanley Cohen and Herbert Boyer succeeded in removing a DNA sequence from a gene of one organism and inserting it into the genetic coding of another. Together with breakthroughs in cell and tissue culture this achievement opened a vast new frontier for those industries in which biological processes and organic chemicals are important components of the production process (OTA, 1981). Rather than a purely empirical or descriptive knowledge of life processes, a new understanding based on a precise knowledge of the operation of organisms became possible. The key to understanding

The authors wish to thank Frederick Buttel for his support and advice in the course of their research and the preparation of this manuscript. Reprinted with permission from *The Insurgent Sociologist* 736 PLC. Department of Sociology, University of Oregon; Eugene, Oregon. [1985.]

the new biotechnology is to think of the DNA in every cell as information, a program which controls the behavior of that cell.

The manipulation and alteration of the genetic or cellular integrity of an organism in order to create novel forms engineered for specific functions promise to revolutionize chemical and pharmaceutical development and production, pollution and waste management, energy generation, food processing, and plant and animal breeding. The market for agriculturally-related genetic engineering products and processes is expected to surpass even that for medical/pharmaceutical applications, and sales for the agricultural sector alone are projected to reach $50-$100 billion annually by the year 2000 (Sheasly, 1981: 23).

Biotechnology introduces the reality of vastly more efficient breeding and selection methods in the short run, and the possibility of fully engineered plants in the long run. Advances in tissue culture and protoplast fusion have already greatly enhanced the speed and efficiency of conventional breeding programs (Meredith, 1982). Clonal propagation of asexually reproduced species ensures disease free plant material and reduces the time needed to grow out planting stock by as much as a factor of 30 (Strohl, 1981: 43). Such procedures have already had a commercial impact on oil palms, cassava, potatoes, strawberries and even redwood trees. The new techniques profoundly affect the breeding of sexually reproduced species as well. Tissue culture and related procedures enable the evaluation of germplasm and the selection of desirable characteristics to be performed on a growing mass of cells in a petrie dish rather than on actual plants in the field (Crops and Soils Magazine, 1982: 17; Shepard, 1982: 157). Such procedures reduce by half the 10 to 12 years traditionally needed to develop a new crop variety.

But it is the potential capacity to wholly circumvent conventional barriers of genetic incompatibility which gives biotechnology in agriculture its truly revolutionary character (Schmeck, 1982). It should be possible to move genes controlling particular features between varieties and even between species; that is, to actually design novel plant varieties engineered to meet specific economic goals. While such engineered varieties have not yet been developed, both the corporate giants and the venture capital rDNA firms are assiduously pursuing their development across the entire spectrum of commercial crops. Principal areas of research include nitrogen fixation, stress tolerance (especially to cold, moisture, salinity and aluminum toxicity), disease and pest resistance, enhanced photosynthetic efficiency, growth regulation, herbicide immunity, and, of course, hybridization in pure-line crops. Forecasts of when engineered varieties might be available have varied widely, but there is a growing consensus among researchers that initial commercial applications will be realized within a decade (Pramik, 1982:15; [Seedsmen's Digest, 1982c: 8]).

Centralization of the Agricultural Inputs Sector

Galvanized by continued scientific advances and the broad range of sectors over which the new bioengineering techniques are commercially exploitable, business interests have made massive investments in biotechnology. In the last few years the establishment of small genetic engineering research firms has attracted extensive attention in the business, scientific, trade and popular media (e.g., Bylinsky, 1980; Walsh, 1981; Wittwer, 1982; Cowen, 1981). Transnational corporations such as Allied, American Cyanamid, ARCO, Chevron, Ciba-Geigy, Dow, DuPont, FMC Corporation, Hoechst, Monsanto, Occidental Petroleum, Pfizer, Rohm and Haas, Sandoz, Shell, Stauffer, and Upjohn, have responded to the new opportunities by purchasing equity interests in the venture firms, and by rapidly enhancing their in-house research and development capabilities with regard to bioengineering.

Many of these same companies have also attracted attention for their participation in the wave of acquisitions and mergers that has been sweeping the seed industry (Mooney, 1979; Fowler, 1980). Since 1973 over 50 seed companies have undergone changes of ownership (Davenport, 1981: 9). Of the principal American seed firms only Pioneer Hi-Bred has maintained its independence. Such well known companies as Northrup King, Asgrow, Trojan, and Funk have been absorbed into the corporate folds of transnational petrochemical and pharmaceutical giants (Table 28.1), and DeKalb Ag Research has undertaken a joint venture with Pfizer Genetics.

Seed company acquisitions were initially independent of consideration relating to biotechnology and many of the most significant transactions occurred prior to 1976, before the bio-boom took hold. It was the 1970 passage of the Plant Variety Protection Act (PVPA), extending patent-like protection to newly developed non-hybrid plant varieties, which touched off the scramble. But those agrochemical producers that purchased seed companies in the first half of the 1970s today find themselves uniquely poised to take advantage of the biotechnological revolution in agriculture. Biotechnology has reinforced the acquisition trend and given it new urgency.

The trend to integration of the agrochemical and seed industries has an inherent and compelling logic. The plant breeder and the agrochemical researcher are frequently working on the same problem, albeit from different perspectives, and chemical solutions (e.g., growth regulators, pollen sterilants, etc.) have often been sought for difficulties which appeared intractable to the breeder.

Research and development in the seed companies and their parent corporations has profound synergistic potential. The genetic manipulation of bacteria, for example, is relevant to both the refinement of industrial fermentation processes and to the improvement of nitrogen-fixing microbes which inhabit the roots of certain crops. Research in one area may well have important and unexpected significance for work in another. For example, human interferon has recently been found to be an effective fungicide (New Scientist, 1982a: 554). Biotechnology has in large measure dissolved the boundaries between the chemical and biological inputs sectors in agriculture and welded their products as well as their producers. There are tremendous opportunities to rationalize and coordinate research, development and marketing of the full range of agricultural inputs.

The seed is the form in which biotechnological research in arable agriculture must be realized. It is important to understand that the techniques of genetic engineering complement and expand rather than supersede conventional plant breeding methods. The need for the traditional plant breeder has not been eliminated, nor is it likely to be. Except for a few vegetatively propagated crops, there is no way to bring a new variety to the consumer except via the seed. The seed is itself the end product of the entire research and development program and it is as a seed that the plant must enter the market.

Thus, a plant breeding capability, seed production and processing facilities, and distribution and marketing networks are critical to the rapid and efficient commercialization of biotechnology in arable agriculture. It is these features which the large petrochemicals and pharmaceuticals now enjoy through their recent and continuing acquisitions of established seed companies. Purchase of the Joseph Harris Seed Company in 1979 provided Celanese with the Carl L. Warren Laboratory, a cadre of 30 experienced researchers, an extensive proprietary collection of vegetable germplasm, and an established clientele. By acquiring Funk Seeds in 1976, Ciba Geigy gained control of a company with a strong position in the lucrative seed corn market and extensive international research and marketing facilities. Seed

TABLE 28.1. Some Recent Seed Company Acquisitions and Characteristics of Acquiring Firms

Acquiring Company	Seed Subsidiaries	In-House Biotech	Biotech Venture Firm Interests
ARCO	Dessert Seed Co	X	IPRI Ingene Bioengineering Center
Celanese	Celpril, Inc. Moran Seeds Joseph Harris Seed Co.	X	
Ciba-Geigy	Ciba Geigy Seeds Funk Seeds Louisiana Seeds Hybridex	X	
FMC Corporation	Seed Research Associates	X	Centocor Immunorex
Monsanto	Farmers Hybrid Co.	X	Genex Biogen Genentech Collagen
Occidental Petroleum	Ring Around Products Excel Hybrid Missouri Seeds Moss Seeds	X	
Pfizer	Trojan Seed Co. Jordan Wholesale Co. Clemens Seed Farms Warwick Seeds	X	
Sandoz	Northrup King National N-K McNair Sees Gallatin Valley Rogers Brothers Ladner Bet	X	Zoecon
Shell	North American Plant Breeders Nickerson Seed Co. Apripro, Inc. Tekseed Hybrid	X	Cetus
Stauffer	Stauffer Seeds Blaney Farms Prairie Valley	X	
Upjohn	Asgrow Seeds Associated Seeds	X	

companies, and by extension their transnational parents, are capable of setting their own breeding agendas according to their own criteria—profitability.

The Seed: Nexus of the Production Process

Critics of the PVPA have seen the Act as the catalyst permitting the consummation of what they regard as an unholy marriage between the chemical and seed industries (Mooney, 1978; Fowler, 1980). In particular they fear the institution of a "chemical bias" whereby the transnational corporations will encourage their seed company subsidiaries to develop plant varieties requiring large inputs of fertilizer and pesticide, in which they hold substantial interests. While such concerns are not without validity, they do not adequately reflect the technological transformation of the past few years. The powerful synergy which biotechnology confers on the chemical/seed linkage and the revolutionary potentials inherent in genetic engineering raise the issue to a qualitatively different plane: what is at issue now is not mere fertilizer-pesticide "bias", but the possibility of establishing a high degree of control over the determination of the agricultural production process itself.

As it matures, biotechnology will permit plant breeding agendas to be set with unprecedented specificity. In seeds are encoded the programs which control the biosynthetic processes by which plants develop and respond to the environment. To the extent that genetic engineering permits the reprogramming of detailed parts of the genetic code, plant breeders and molecular biologists will be able to determine where the plant may be grown, under what environmental conditions, the requisite inputs, the timing of cultural and labor activities, the mode of harvest, the manner of processing, and, of course, the characteristics and quality of the vegetable product itself. In sum, the seed becomes the nexus of control over the determination and shape of the production process in agriculture.

Though agricultural genetic engineering is still an embryonic technology, the trajectory of its application to production processes can already be discerned. Biotechnology holds out the possibility of designing plants in such a way that they are complemented by selected chemicals or organisms, and vice versa. The systematic search for herbicide antidotes and timed release fertilizers in which the agrochemical corporations have been engaged, has begun to yield results (Geissbuhler et al., 1982: 507). Funk Seeds has introduced eight chemically treated sorghum varieties which may safely receive applications of parent Ciba-Geigy's proprietary herbicides (*Farm Chemicals*, 1979: 55). Northrup King (Sandoz) is close to commercializing herbicide-coated alfalfa seed (*World Crops*, 1982: 30). Industry spokesmen are quite explicit regarding their strategic intentions. Dr Klaus Saegebarth, DuPont's director of agrichemicals research, sees "the breadth of DuPont's line of crop protection chemicals as literally representing a DuPont Crop Management System" (*Farm Chemicals*, 1981: 21).

The dominant position among giant pharmaceutical and petrochemical firms with regard to biotechnology ensures that the plant/chemical inputs linkage will exert a powerful influence on future development of genetically engineered crop varieties. Important though it is, it would be a mistake to focus exclusively on this feature. Having gained access to the instructions encoded in the DNA at the molecular level, a "package" approach to crop development potentially encompasses any or all plant traits relevant to the production process including, but by no means limited to, response to chemical inputs.

In addition to investigation into herbicide resistance, pesticide compatibility, and chemical growth regulation, both private and public plant breeders are using the techniques of genetic engineering to focus research on an array of important agronomic traits including plant architecture, harvestability, maturation, photo-period, stress (temperature, moisture, soil chemical, soil structure) tolerance, photosynthetic efficiency, nutrient utilization, disease resistance and nutritional quality. As biotechnology enhances control over the particular form the expression of these features takes, specific varieties will be developed for specific purposes. Such varieties will be complex, detailed, and carefully balanced combinations of agronomic traits. As such, they will require the application of sophisticated variety specific management and monitoring packages if their productive potential is to be realized (Hanway, 1978b: 5) (1).

Up to the present the farmer has retained a substantial degree of control over the farm production process and his own labor process. Biotechnology permits the external determination of these processes by their embodiment in the seed itself. It would be naive to think that control over the seed by transnational agribusiness will not be used to establish and defend market positions in proprietary input packages. In selecting the seed of a particular plant variety the farmer will in essence also be choosing his entire production process. Control may be exerted from both the input and product stages, for a number of food processors have joined the inputs corporations as owners of seed companies and investors in biotechnology. The farmer will certainly become more deeply enmeshed in the web of contractual relations which bind him to large-scale capital. Contractual integration will become more widespread and the contracts themselves will be more stringent. Processors frequently specify the variety to be grown and, in an arrangement known as "bailment", the processor also supplies the seed and retains title to both the seed and the crop which grows from it (Pfeffer, 1982: 77). Biotechnology will help render the farmer ever more a "propertied laborer" (Davis, 1980): on the one hand a landlord and on the other a laborer who cares for corporate plants.

The Changing Role of Public Agricultural Research

The potentially determinate relationship between the seed and agricultural production processes which is emerging from biotechnological advances makes control over plant breeding an item of paramount importance. Yet this is the very area in which public agricultural research agencies enjoy a measure of preeminence vis a vis private industry. However, capital achieved a major precondition for the effacement of public research in 1970 with passage of the PVPA. Since that time seed companies have been attempting to redefine the role that is played by the public breeder (see Roberts, 1979; Sprague, 1980; Pardee et al., 1981; Peterson, 1981; Leffel, 1982; Ruttan, 1982). Biotechnology renders the need for capital to circumscribe public breeding activities yet more urgent, for the seed is now the gateway to control over the production process as a whole.

Prior to the enactment of the PVPA, varietal development in pure-line (non-hybrid) crops was almost exclusively the province of the public breeder. The activities of private companies in these crops were mostly limited to the production, processing and marketing of the seed of "college bred" varieties (Christensen, 1957; White, 1959; [Copeland, 1976: 214]; Duvick, 1982: 34; Padwa, 1982: 98). Without some form of patent-like protection there was little incentive for the investment of private capital in the costly and time-consuming process of research and varietal development. However, when hybrid corn was introduced in the 1920s seed companies had taken advantage of the "natural" protection provided by proprietary control of inbred parents and moved quickly to displace the public development of commercial corn lines (Ruttan, 1982: 25). With the example of the profits possible in hybrid corn before them, seedsmen sought to gain "breeder's rights" by legislative fiat. In 1970, despite the lack of evidence that public breeding had been anything but "remarkably effective" (Ruttan, 1982: 25), the PVPA became law.

Industry would like to see the activities of the public sector confined exclusively to those areas not attractive to private investment: education and training, the evaluation and development of germplasm, and basic research. Applied research, by which is meant the release of finished commercializable varieties, is explicitly seen to be the responsibility of the private sector (Roberts, 1979: 45). The elimination of "duplicative" and "redundant" public research would give private industry virtually complete control over all crop varieties entering the market. Reduced to the provision of inbred lines to private breeders they themselves had trained, the land grant universities would provide a cheap subsidy to the seed industry which would then extract high profits from farmers.

Though publicly developed lines yet account for more than 80 percent of the varieties of rye, wheat, oats, soybeans, rice, barley and peanuts used in commercial production (Hanway, 1978: 5), public agency hegemony in plant breeding is being steadily eroded. Fully 86 percent of the varieties receiving protection over the first decade following enactment of the PVPA were bred by private companies. The USDA's Agricultural Research Service has made disengagement from applied breeding one of its institutional objectives (Skarien, 1982: 6).

The Experiment Stations and the land grant universities (LGUs) are hard pressed even to maintain current levels of activity. Public institutions face declining state and federal aid for plant breeding research. They are finding it increasingly difficult to recruit and retain staff and to keep operating funds at a reasonable level (Peterson, 1981: 24; Pardee et al., 1981: 9). Several state programs have shifted their focus from varietal development to germplasm development and population improvement, and a general trend to enhanced cooperation with corporate breeding is evident (Hanway, 1978: 6). With some 56 private companies currently constituting the National Council of Commercial Plant Breeders, the LGUs are under continuous pressure to abandon those areas of research which can profitably be undertaken by private enterprise.

Corporate interest in biotechnology has also stimulated the formation of unprecedented linkages between private companies and universities (for a full discussion see Kenney et al., 1982). Such arrangements, while allowing scientists to remain within the university, introduce important conflicts of interest and secrecy concerns into the academic environment. University breeding programs, where not weakened by loss of personnel to expanding private breeding concerns, are brought increasingly under corporate influence. It would appear unlikely that public breeding programs, many of which are already in financial straits, will be in a position to exploit the new technologies as rapidly or easily as private industry. Should genetic engineering become an integral part of crop improvement the LGUs and the experiment stations may even find themselves with plant breeding—or engineering—capabilities decidedly inferior to those of the private sector. Under such conditions public agricultural institutions would have little choice but to engage in the residual activities which private capital chooses not to undertake.

For all its promise, genetic engineering is as yet an embryonic technology. The outcome of any one line of research is highly uncertain and while progress is being made daily there are yet many fundamental problems to be overcome and much research to be undertaken before extensive commercialization of "engineered" products can be realized ([Rachie and Lyman, 1981]; Nilan, 1981). The concrete imperative of profitability makes absorption of expensive and indeterminate basic research costs by the government a desirable option from the corporate point of view. Yet the present structure of the USDA and the LGU system is not geared to the efficient pursuit of the new lines of research which advances in biological knowledge have opened up. It is to this constraint that the corporations and their institutional allies have now turned.

The Rockefeller Foundation and the White House Office of Science and Technology Policy (OSTP) recently issued a joint report (2) bluntly indicting the USDA for its parochialism, bureaucratic rigidity, regional geopolitics, and inability to identify research areas of critical importance. A substantial portion of the problem is attributed to the dispersed and decentralized nature of the Agricultural Research Service and to lack of control over the block grants which support research in the land-grant universities and associated state experiment stations. The report recommends a restructuring of the American agricultural research system. The principal features of this realignment would be the consolidation and rationalization of ARS stations and programs, a concentration on basic "cutting edge" biological research, and the expansion of the currently modest competitive grants program (The Rockefeller Foundation 1982).

Implementation of the recommendations could well result in a transformed LGU system that is increasingly replaced by a structure based on the Rockefeller model of highly centralized research facilities in a few locations (Kohler, 1976). The new system of "managed" and "rationalized" research would function to serve corporate capital which would be permitted to determine research goals. The Rockefeller/OSTP report asserts that

Private sector expertise should be fully utilized in efforts by the public sector to identify future research needs, estimate future demand for scientific and technical manpower, and define appropriate, complementary roles and responsibilities for the various sectors and institutions involved in science for agriculture. Mechanisms should be developed for strengthening the linkages between the findings of basic and applied research performed in the public sector and their development and commercialization by industry.

Tellingly, no mention is made of the role of farmers, labor, consumers, or environmental groups. Stimulated by the revolutionary potential of biotechnology, capital is attempting to establish control not only over the crucial plant breeding process, but over the shape of basic research as well.

Genetic Vulnerability

An issue which has received much attention in recent years is that of genetic vulnerability. Assertions to the contrary (Mooney, 1979; Fowler, 1980; Schapiro, 1982) notwithstanding, seed companies and their transnational parents are interested in preserving and enlarging, not narrowing, the genetic diversity available to plant breeders. Germplasm is, after all, the breeder's raw material. The continual development of new varieties in response to competitive pressure and to changes in the disease, pest or climatic spectra requires a substantial collection of germplasm from which to work. Neither the corporate nor the public breeder has an interest in intentional genetic erosion. Why then does Pioneer sell hybrid corn to the Mexican campesino, thus displacing traditional varieties? And why is it that the National Academy of Sciences can call American crops "impressively uniform genetically and impressively vulnerable"?

The answer is to be found not in the PVPA but in the very nature of capitalist competition. Whatever Pioneer's ultimate interest in the preservation of native varieties of Mexican maize, the concrete imperatives of competition and profitability will drive the company to sell hybrids to the Mexican farmer, thus overriding long-term genetic diversity considerations. Worldwide, genetic erosion will continue; traditional cultivars will continue to be replaced by commercial varieties. Similar pressures act on the American farmer as well. In general the farmer must select the highest yielding seed available since he is also driven by the profit motive. Choices are not made on the basis of the public interest, for only those who outproduce their competitors survive.

Thus, *the market itself produces a lack of genetic diversity* in the crop varieties being grown at any given time. In the absence of national agricultural planning or of controls on seed companies or farmers, the best we can do is to keep our germplasm banks filled and to maintain our research capabilities at such levels as will permit us to deal effectively and quickly with such problems as arise.

The American seed industry clearly supports germplasm collection and preservation and has a major influence on international and domestic policies through representation on both the International Board for Plant Genetic Resources and the National Plant Genetic Resources Board. Private companies currently maintain extensive proprietary genetic collections of their own and support the strengthening of the National Seed Storage Laboratory (NSSL) and associated facilities. Though private companies will willingly permit the government to subsidize the storage and preservation of the bulk of national germplasm resources, they are unlikely to submit their own advanced breeding lines to the NSSL since its collection is open to any bona fide researcher.

Seed companies have historically not been as deeply involved as public agencies in plant exploration, the collection of wild varieties, or in the basic screening and evaluation of such materials. These costly activities will probably remain the province of the government and the LGUs. How much of the current universe of world germplasm will be preserved will largely be determined by how well public agencies fulfill this role (3). The potential consequences of an inadequate pool of genetic resources is now widely recognized (Ruttan, 1982: 26). Since all of the principal crops grown in the United States and most advanced capitalist nations are native to other parts of the world, American germplasm collection teams are currently scouring the world for useful materials (*Diversity*, 1982: 14; Vicker, 1982: 54).

Such plant genetic resources, acquired free of charge from the gene-rich LDCs, can be worth a great deal. Incorporation of an Ethiopian gene conferring striped rust resistance into American barley varieties has saved U.S. farmers an estimated $150 million per year (*New Scientist*, 1982b: 218). In a classic example of imperialism, these varieties are sold back to the very nations which furnished the genetic material at no charge in the first place. Pressures on the LDCs to institute variety protection legislation similar to that in the developed world are being applied by the FAO and the International Board for the Protection of Plant Genetic Resources. Such legislation would ease commercial access to LDC seed markets and greatly enlarge possibilities for profit. Genetic material will increasingly be recognized as a strategic resource.

Already some LDCs have closed their borders to plant hunters and, despite an avowed policy of free access, the United States has refused certain nations access to genetic material in the National Seed Storage Laboratory on political grounds.

Biotechnology could, however, significantly alleviate many of the problems associated with genetic vulnerability. Of the germplasm already in American collections only a very small proportion has actually been evaluated. The genetic variability available in corn is perhaps the best documented, yet 90 percent of the germplasm available for that crop has not been utilized as a source of varietal improvement (Zuber and Darrah, 1980: 248). Much of the genetic resources currently available are unusable because breeders simply don't know their characteristics. The new genetic technology allows the evaluation of 100 million cells, each a potential plant, in a single petrie dish (Meredith, 1982: 6). Enormous savings in time, space and money will permit extensive evaluation of current germplasm accessions, thereby greatly expanding the genetic material available to the breeder in practical form.

Such savings apply to the actual process of breeding as well as to germplasm evaluation. Moreover, biotechnology will further extend the genetic diversity available to the plant breeder by allowing the incorporation of traits from different species and, ultimately perhaps, from other organisms. Breeders will no longer be limited by the heretofore rigid parameter of speciation. Not only are mutagenic techniques improved by biotechnology, but variability can actually be engineered via protoplast fusion and rDNA transfers (Nilan, 1981: 29; Padwa, 1982: 101). Advances associated with genetic engineering may also reduce genetic vulnerability by permitting the selection or construction of plants with multiple tolerance genes ("horizontal" resistance) rather than unstable single gene ("vertical") resistance (Orton, 1982: 23).

However, if genetic engineering addresses many of the material consequences of genetic erosion, it will not halt the process of erosion itself since that is a product of capitalist competition. In this sense biotechnology treats the symptoms rather than the disease. If the new technologies are viewed as a solution rather than as a palliative, genetic engineers and plant breeders may yet find themselves without sufficient genetic resources to deal with crises of genetic vulnerability.

A "Bio-Revolution" in the LDCs?

There has been widespread recognition of the potential value of biotechnology to the LDCs (Plucknett and Smith, 1982; Gandhi, 1982; Brady, 1982; Bodde, 1982). India and the Philippines have established national institutes of biotechnology, and at the request of the U.S. Agency for International Development the National Academy of Sciences has convened a conference on "Priorities in Biotechnology Research for International Development" (Swaminathan, 1982). Visions of a "bio-revolution" to take up where the Green Revolution left off are already commonplace (Sojka, 1981).

Would such a bio-revolution have a more positive impact on the poor of the LDCs than did the Green Revolution? Much would appear to depend on the role and strategy undertaken by the International Agricultural Research Centers (IARCs). Even assuming that the IARCs are suitable agencies for the development and introduction of socioeconomically desirable bioengineered plant varieties, there is reason to doubt that they will be in a position to assume this responsibility. The changing articulation of public and private plant breeding in the advanced capitalist nations is having parallel effects on international institutions.

The IARCs currently find themselves in financial straits akin to those suffered by the American land grant system. Funding for the IARCs in 1983 will fall short of inflation by 6 percent and virtually all 13 centers are cutting back on research and training programs (Lewin, 1982; Plucknett and Smith, 1982). They are also turning increasingly to arrangements which are highly advantageous to private capital. For example, CIMMYT, the Mexico-based international maize and wheat research institute where Norman Borlaug did his Nobel Prize-winning work, has found it necessary to ask Pioneer Hi-Bred to grow out its varieties for purposes of maintaining the viability of its germplasm collection—an expensive process CIMMYT could not afford (*Diversity*, 1982). In return, Pioneer is allowed to retain a copy of all genetic material it reproduces. As with the LGU system, the IARCs will receive new tasks as their budgets are decreased.

Transnational agribusiness clearly views the Third World as both a lucrative market for bioengineered products and a source of much needed genetic diversity. With the plant breeding process itself becoming a crucial link in the valorization of biotechnology research, private industry may well find it useful to confine the IARCs, based as they are in the LDCs and espousing the ideology of working for the common good, to basic research and the collection, preservation and evaluation of germplasm. The shape of the Bio-Revolution will ultimately be determined by the needs of transnational capital.

Bioengineered crop varieties adapted to low levels of fertility or tolerant of saline conditions could raise productivity in vast areas of marginal land where conventional HYVs are not suitable. In the Green Revolution the poor were driven from the good land by the developing capitalist sector; the Bio-Revolution will extend the process of displacement to heretofore marginal areas where subsistence and petty commodity production has persisted. Clonal propagation of improved tree crops could greatly alleviate fuelwood and deforestation problems, but these are not the uses to which genetic engineering is being put. It is the large plantation owners and forestry corporations such as Unilever, Sime Darby, and Weyerhauser that have access to the new technology and their goal is simply profit. Tissue culture has reduced the time necessary to develop improved oil palm varieties by a factor of 30. Thousands of micropropagated oil palms, designed to be uniformly short to reduce labor costs, have already been planted on the commercial plantations of Southeast Asia (Strohl, 1981).

Introduction of engineered plant varieties may also have far-reaching effects on the international division of labor in agriculture. The tropics have a number of advantages over temperate zones including year round warmth and more intense sunlight. Biotechnology could conceivably permit the development of varieties of, say, corn or soybeans amenable to continuous culture outside the temperate zone—with devastating effect on the farmers of North America and Europe. On the other hand, industrial applications of biotechnology have already had negative impacts on markets for LDC sugar, pyrethrums (organic pesticides derived from a member of the daisy family) and opiates as bioengineering techniques permit the production of substitute or synthetic commodities. For example, development of immobilized enzymes in the early 1970s slashed production costs of high fructose corn syrup by 40 percent, devastating the cane sugar market. In 1982 corn syrup accounted for 38 percent of the industrial sweetner market and by 1987 this figure is expected to rise to at least 60 percent (Hannigan, 1982: 77).

Moreover, the development of tissue culture techniques is making possible the industrial production of medicinal products formerly only derivable from whole plants or synthetic processes involving expensive petrochemicals. Tissue culture, the growing of plant or animal cells in a nutrient medium, allows individual cells to produce substances in isolation from the remainder of the original organism. The cells produce the desired substance which is then extracted. The increased capital intensity of this production process is obvious: no plants to be planted, husbanded and harvested; lower transportation and processing costs, and better quality control. Production becomes more predictable and dependable, and is no longer even "agriculture." Many products will be affected in this fashion by tissue culture developments. In each case workers will be displaced and many LDCs will find markets for their agricultural commodities being eroded by bio-industrial substitutes.

Political Initiatives

At present private enterprise operates under minimal constraints in the development and commercialization of the new biotechnologies. It is imperative that citizen's groups gain an understanding of and a significant measure of control over the manner in which the world's gene pool will be exploited. We have tried in this paper to establish the trajectories along which biotechnology in agriculture will likely be implemented, and to explore the impact that biotechnical innovation could have on the organization of production and the structure of the world agricultural system. It should be clear that if capitalist designs for the deployment and commercialization of biotechnology are not modified there will be serious consequences for the environment and for farmers and agricultural workers of both the LDCs and the advanced capitalist nations.

The advent of genetic engineering has already sparked a number of controversies which have received significant public attention. Ever since the perfection of techniques of DNA recombination in the 1970s, genetic engineers have had to contend with criticisms from environmental groups regarding the possibility of ecological disaster should genetically modified organisms escape containment. Some city governments have gone so far as to apply zoning regulations in an attempt to restrict and control rDNA research (see Krimsky, 1982). The ethical implications of the manipulation of life forms, and especially prospects for "engineering" the human species, have attracted the concern of many humanitarian and religious organizations. Plant patent legislation such as the American PVPA and similar bills now pending in Canada and Australia continue to arouse populist anti-corporate sentiment and to elicit important opposition from such U.S. groups as the National Sharecroppers Fund and the People's Business Commission.

Though concerns with the environment, ethics, and patent law are extremely important and have established a popular base of opposition to the unregulated commercialization of biotechnology, a more strategic focus for struggle may be the battle for control over the direction and uses of publicly funded research. Biotechnology has in some ways dissolved the distinction between basic and applied science. The goals established in basic research directly and materially condition the form of the final product and the possibilities of commercialization. Capital has clearly recognized this connection and is now attempting to restructure the public agricultural research apparatus to its own specifications. Defending the relative autonomy of the university from this assault is a prerequisite to gaining social control over the direction future research will take.

If the commercial potential of biotechnology has made private industry eager to buy access to academic research, declining levels of government support have rendered university administrators more than willing to consummate the transaction. Critics of the accelerating penetration of the university by capital found a public forum for their concerns in hearings before Congressman Albert Gore (U.S. House of Representatives 1981). More recently, Ralph Nader, Albert Meyerhoff, and David Noble have formed the Special Commission on the Corporate Control of Academic Science (4) in order to lobby for the creation of "a democratic mechanism that would oversee university-based research activities in order to render science and technology compatible with democracy and the public interest" (Noble 1983: 52). With a similar end in mind the California Rural Legal Assistance (CRLA) agency has already undertaken direct action. Addressing possible conflicts of interest, CRLA sued the University of California to force faculty members to disclose their financial interests in private companies supporting their research (Divoky 1983: B2).

Congressman Gore's subcommittee has also been the arena for discussions regarding the possibility of using newly developed biotechnical procedures to genetically screen workers for susceptibility to diseases associated with the industrial environment (U.S. House of Representatives 1982). Selection of a labor force "tolerant" of workplace conditions is appealing to capital for obvious reasons. The prospect of new forms of managerial control and employment discrimination has begun to awaken labor organizations to the importance of biotechnology and to the uses to which it can be put. Representatives of a variety of labor, consumer, academic, and environmental groups have recently established the Committee for Responsible Genetics (5). This organization will function as a clearing-house for the exchange of information among citizens' and public interest groups addressing the far-reaching political, economic, environmental, and ethical questions posed by the new biotechnologies.

Biotechnology is pregnant with potential for both liberation and domination. Which way it develops will depend upon who wields it and upon the parameters that society can establish to guide its use. We hope that other researchers will find in our paper an agenda for further study and a basis of information with which to build struggle against capitalist hegemony. The time for action is now—before the new technologies are irretrievably deployed.

Notes

1. Agricultural production will become increasingly systems oriented. The management sophistication demanded by new plant varieties will certainly reinforce the trend to on-farm utilization of advances in electronic data evaluation and processing techniques (Geissbuhler et al., 1982:505). As varietal sensitivity or responsiveness to inputs and environmental factors is increased, it becomes ever more important that growing conditions be monitored closely. A variety of crop or function specific (e.g., integrated pest management) computer programs have already been developed by the USDA and private firms.

2. The report is the product of a meeting held in June 1982 at the Winrock Conference Center. The fifteen participants in the Winrock meeting included Denis Prager (OSTP), John Pino (Rockefeller Foundation), Judith Lyman (Rockefeller Foundation), Winslow Biggs (Carnegie Institution), Irwin Feller (Institute for Policy Research and Evaluation), Ralphy Hardy (DuPont), John Marvel (Monsanto), Representative George Brown (D-California), Perry Adkisson (Texas A&M University), James Bonnen (Michigan State University), James Kendrick (University of California, Berkeley), Lowell Lewis (University of California, Berkeley), James Martin (University of Arkansas), Terry Kinney, Jr. (USDA-ARS), Peter van Schaik (USDA).

3. Certain provisos need to be made on this point. Particular companies deeply dependent on single crops have engaged in extensive collection work. United Fruit is thought to hold as much as two thirds of the world's banana germplasm (Mooney, 1979) and such companies as Campbells and Heinz have comprehensive tomato germplasm inventories. Moreover, pharmaceutical companies have been very active in medicinal plant collection and such activities may also become a component of the strategies of their newly acquired seed companies.

4. For information contact the Special Commission on the Corporate Control of Academic Science, c/o The Center for Study of Responsive Law, P.O. Box 19367, Washington, D.C., 20036, (202) 387-8034.

5. For information contact The Committee for Responsible Genetics, P.O. Box 759, Cambridge, MA, 02238.

References

Bodde, Tineke. 1982. "Biotechnology in the third world." *BioScience* 32:9 (October):713–716.

Brady, Nyle C. 1982. "Chemistry and world food supplies." *Science* 218 (26 November):847–853.

Bylinsky, Gene. 1980. "DNA can build companies too." *Fortune* (16 June):144–160.

Christensen, Ken. 1957. "Value of applied research to the seed industry." Proceedings of the Second Farm Seed Industry-Research Conference, Washington, D.C.: American Seed Trade Association.

Cowen, Robert C. 1981. "Genetic engineering: hopes for high profits mount; ethical and social questions persist." *The Christian Science Monitor* (27 October): 12–13.

Crops and Soils Magazine. 1982. "New test allows quicker gene selection." *Crops and Soils Magazine* 34:7 (April-May):17.

Davenport, Caroline. 1981. "Sowing the seeds—research, development flourish at Dekalb and Pioneer Hi-Bred." *Barron's* 61:9:9–10,33.

Davis, John E. 1980. "Capitalist agricultural development and the expropriation of the propertied laborer." in F.H. Buttel and H. Newby (eds.), *The Rural Sociology of the Advanced Societies.* Montclair: Allenheld, Osmun and Company.

Diversity. 1982. "NWPGR research director reports on successful East Asian exploration." *Diversity* 1:1 (Spring):14-15.

Divoky, Diane. 1983. "UCD starts checking on faculty conflicts of interest." *Sacramento Bee* (22 February):B2.

Duvick, D.N. 1982. "Genetic engineering: status and potential for cotton." Proceedings of the 1982 Beltwide Cotton Production-Mechanization Conference, Las Vegas. January 6-7.

Farm Chemicals. 1979. "Ciba-Geigy introduces unique 'package' for sorghum." *Farm Chemicals* 142:7 (July):55.

Farm Chemicals. 1981. "The DuPont agrichemicals story." *Farm Chemicals* 144:3 (March) : 13-35.

Fowler, Cary. 1980. "Sowing the seeds of destruction." *Science for the People* (September/October):8-10.

Geissbuhler, Hans, Paul Brenneisen and Hans-Peter Fischer. 1982. "Frontiers in crop production: chemical research objectives." *Science* 217 (6 August):505-510.

Gandhi, Indira. 1982. "Scientific endeavor in India." *Science* 217 (10 September):1008-1009.

Hannigan, Kevin J. 1982. "The sweetener report 1982-1987." *Food Engineering* (July):75-85.

Hanway, D.G. 1978. "Agricultural experiment stations and the variety production act." *Crops and Soils Magazine* 30:6 (March):5-7.

Kenney, Martin, Frederick Buttel, Tadlock Cowan, and Jack Kloppenburg. 1982. "Genetic Engineering in Agriculture." Rural Sociology Bulletin No. 125, Cornell University.

Kenney, Martin. 1983. "Biotechnology: a blessing for the Third World?" An unpublished manuscript.

Kenney, Martin and Jack Kloppenburg. 1983. "The American agricultural research system: an obsolete structure?" *Agricultural Administration* (forthcoming).

Kohler, Robert E. 1976. "The management of science: the experience of Warren Weaver and the Rockefeller Foundation programme in molecular biology." *Minerva* 14 (Autumn): 279-306.

Krimsky, Sheldon. 1982. *Genetic Alchemy: the social history of the recombinant DNA controversy.* Cambridge: MIT Press.

Leffel, Robert C. 1982. "The future of public soybean improvement programs." *Seedmen's Digest* 33 (February):12-17.

Lewin, Roger. 1982. "Funds squeezed for international agriculture." *Science* 218 (26 November):866-867.

Meredith, Carole P. 1982. "The new techniques and their potential." *California Agriculture* (August):5.

Mooney, Pat Roy. 1979. *Seeds of the Earth.* Ottawa: Inter Pares, Canadian Council for International Cooperation and the International Coalition for Development Action.

Murray, James R. and Alexander Hiam. 1981. "Biological Diversity and Genetic Engineering." Paper presented at the United States Department of State Strategy Conference on Biological Diversity, November, Washington, D.C.

New Scientist. 1982a. "Plants respond to animal interferon." *New Scientist* 95 (26 August):554.

New Scientist. 1982b. "Foreign fields save Western crops—free of charge." *New Scientist* 96 (28 October):218.

Nilan, Robert A. 1981. "Genetic Engineering in Plants." Proceedings of the 27th Annual Farm Seed Conference. Washington, D.C.: American Seed Trade Association.

Noble, David. 1983. "Academia incorporated: selling the tree of knowledge." *Science for the People* 15:1 (January/February):7-11, 50-52.

Office of Technology Assessment [OTA]. 1981. *Impacts of Applied Genetics.* Washington, D.C.: Government Printing Office.

Orton, Thomas J. 1982. "New concepts in whole-plant genetics." *California Agriculture* (August):22-23.

Padwa, David. 1982. "Future impacts of genetic engineering." Proceedings of the International Conference on Genetic Engineering, Preston, Virginia: Battelle Memorial Institute, Volume 5, pp.97-102.

Pardee, William, David Phillipson, et al. 1981. "Panel discussion—public vs. private research." Proceedings of the 27th Annual Farm Seed Conference, Washington, D.C.: American Seed Trade Association.

Peterson, C.E. 1981. "We need them both." *Seedsmen's Digest* 32 (March):24–29, 46–48.

Pfeffer, Max John. 1982. "The labor process and capitalist development of agriculture." *The Rural Sociologist* 2 (2):72–80.

Plucknett, Donald L. and Nigel J.H. Smith. 1982. "Agricultural research and Third World food production." *Science* 217 (16 July):215–220.

Pramik, Mary Jean. 1982. "Atlantic Richfield builds research team for agricultural applications in biotechnology." *Genetic Engineering News* 2 (May/June):14–15P.

Roberts, Thomas H. 1979. "Public and private roles in seed improvement." *Seedmen's Digest* 30 (September):42–47.

The Rockefeller Foundation and The Office of Science and Technology Policy. 1982. *Science for Agriculture*. Report of a Workshop on Critical Issues in American Agriculture. New York: The Rockefeller Foundation.

Ruttan, Vernon W. 1982. "Changing role of public and private sectors in agricultural research." *Science* 216 (2 April):23–23.

Schapiro, Mark. 1982. "Seeds of Disaster." *Mother Jones* 7 (December):11–15,36,37.

Schmeck, Howard M. Jr. 1982. "Rat gene implant in mice reported." *New York Times* (17 December):A1,B14.

Sheasly, Jeffrey L. 1981. "Bioengineering: scientific facts or fancy." *Farm Chemicals* 144 (October):23–40.

Shepard, James F. 1982. "The regeneration of potato plants from leaf-cell protoplasts." *Scientific American* 246 (May):154–166.

Skarien, Kenn. 1982. "USDA role in future plant breeding." *Seedsmen's Digest* 33 (July):6.

Sojka, Gary A. 1981. "Where biology could take us." *Business Horizons* (January/February):60–69.

Sprague, G.F. 1980. "The changing role of the private and public sectors in corn breeding." Proceedings of the 35th Annual Corn and Sorghum Research Conference. Washington, D.C.: American Seed Trade Association.

Strohl, Richard. 1981. "Micropropagation: new technology for perennials." *Agribusiness Worldwide* (January):42–48.

Swaminathan, M.S. 1982. "Biotechnology research and Third World agriculture." *Science* 218 (3 December):967–972.

U.S. House of Representatives. 1981. "Commercialization of academic biomedical research." Hearings before the Subcommittee on Investigations and Oversight and the Subcommittee on Science, Research, and Technology of the Committee on Science and Technology, June 8,9, Washington, D.C.: United States Government Printing Office.

U.S. House of Representatives. 1982. "Genetic screening in the workplace." Hearings before the Subcommittee on Investigations and Oversight of the Committee on Science and Technology, June 22, Washington, D.C.: United States Government Printing Office.

Vicker, Ray. 1982. "U.S. scientists are collecting germplasm as a safeguard against an agricultural disaster." *The Wall Street Journal* (21 July):54.

Walsh, John. 1981. "Biotechnology boom reaches agriculture." *Science* 213 (18 September):1339–1341.

White, Allenby L. 1959. "Research problems as observed by the seed industry." Proceedings of the Fourth Farm Seed Industry-Research Conference, Washington, D.C.: American Seed Trade Association.

Wittwer, Sylvan H. 1982. "The biological revolution." *Farm Chemicals* 145 (September):33,36.

World Crops. 1982. "Americans increase seed viability with herbicide coating." *World Crops* 34 (January/February):30–31.

Zuber, M.S. and L.L. Darrah. 1980. "1979 U.S. corn germplasm base." Proceedings of the 35th Annual Corn and Sorghum Research Conference, Washington, D.C.: American Seed Trade Association.

Part V

NUTRITION AND MALNUTRITION IN THE UNITED STATES

29

Diet for a Small Planet
(excerpts)
Frances Moore Lappé

Frances Moore Lappé tells the story of how in 1969 she discovered that half of the harvested acreage in the U.S. was devoted to feeding livestock. Furthermore, it took 16 pounds of grain and soybeans (the animals scientists who guest lecture in my classes at Cornell University argue that it is less; nevertheless, they recognize the inefficiency) to produce one pound of beef in the United States. These facts, coupled with nutritional concerns about excess protein in the average American's diet prompted Lappé to write *Diet for a Small Planet* in 1971. When she first published the book, many people understood her to be supporting the idea that food resources were scarce and thus we had to cut back on consumption. Agricultural scientists were particularly irate and responded defensively (see Chapter 30). Lappé dismissed the scarcity notion in a coauthored work, *Food First* (see Chapter 3). Some excerpts from the 1982 edition of *Diet for a Small Planet* are given here to present the reader with the changes in the U.S. diet that warrant nutritional and health concern, and to acquaint the reader with the basic concepts of protein complementarity. The reader is strongly encouraged to read the entire text of *Diet for a Small Planet* to understand the political as well as health implications of our diet, and ways in which we can avoid eating protein and other nutrients in excess.

1. America's Experimental Diet . . .

Never has a people's diet changed so much so fast as ours has over the last 80 years. . . . I will discuss each change separately, but as nutritionist Dr. Joan Gussow wisely observes, our bodies don't experience these changes separately. . . . So we have to look at the whole cluster.

Dangerous Change No.1:
Protein from Animals Instead of Plants

Contrary to what I thought, the dramatic change is not in our protein consumption. It has actually varied little over the last 65 years, fluctuating between 88 grams and

---

104 grams per person per day (roughly twice what our bodies can use). The change is in how our protein is packaged. Sixty-five years ago we got almost 40 percent of our protein from grain, bread, and other cereal products. Now we only get 17 percent of our protein from these sources. In their place, animal products, which then supplied about half of our protein, now contribute two-thirds.[1]

U.S. consumption of animal products began to climb after World War II, with beef consumption almost doubling and poultry consumption almost tripling by the late 1970's.[2]

The Risks. There is no medical consensus about the risks of diets high in protein generally or about diets high in animal protein specifically. (There is general agreement about the risks of what results from this new "packaging" of our protein—more fat and less fiber. But I'll deal with those risks later.) While no consensus exists, there are some intriguing warning signals.

The Senate Select Committee notes: "One series of investigations found that diets that derive their protein from animal sources elevate plasma cholesterol levels to a much greater extent than do diets that derive their protein from vegetable sources. Another line of basic research demonstrated that, in almost all cases, high protein diets are more atherosclerotic than are low protein diets."[3] (Atherosclerosis is a hardening of the arteries caused by fatty deposits accumulating along the artery walls.) . . .

Dangerous Change No.2:
More Fat

Americans eat 27 percent more fat than did our grandparents in the early 1900s. And more than one-third of that increase has come just in the last ten years. As a result, fat's contribution to our total calorie intake climbed from 32 to 42 percent, though there are signs that the average may be lowering.

The Risks. The risks appear to lie in too much total fat, too much saturated fat, and too much cholesterol. Saturated fats found in animal foods and in some vegetable foods (especially palm and coconut oil), and cholesterol, found only in animal foods (especially eggs, some seafood, and organ meats), generally increase the blood cholesterol level. Eating saturated fat raises blood cholesterol levels more than does eating cholesterol itself.[4] As Patricia Hausman explains in *Jack Sprat's Legacy*, the higher the blood cholesterol, the greater the rate of fatty deposits that harden the arteries. The more severe the fatty deposits in the arteries, the greater the risk of heart disease, stroke, and other complications of atherosclerosis.

Reducing the cholesterol in the diet does not automatically reduce the cholesterol in the blood for everyone. There may be genetic factors which determine why some people respond to lowered dietary cholesterol and others do not. But, to be on the safe side, it would seem prudent to assume that lowering our cholesterol consumption will make a difference.

In a survey of 200 scientists in 23 countries, 92 percent recommended that we eat less fat to reduce our risk of heart disease.[5] In addition to increased risk of heart disease, says Hausman, "studies, spanning up to 40 countries worldwide, confirmed that the total amount of fat in the diet does correlate with some forms of cancer. Studies link six forms of cancer with dietary fat, including cancers of the breast and colon, two of the top cancer killers in the United States."[6] . . .

Dangerous Change No.3:
Too Much Sugar

Since the turn of the century Americans have doubled their daily sugar dose; just since 1960 it's gone up 25 percent. One-third of a pound of sugar is now consumed each day for every man, woman, and child in America.[7]

The Risks. The problem with sugar is both what it does to us and what it displaces. The link between sugar and tooth decay is well established. In virtually all societies studied, the incidence of tooth decay rises as people eat more sugar. Half of all Americans have no teeth at all by the time they rech the age of fifty-five.

Sugar also fills us up with calories while giving us no nutrients or fiber. Filled on sugar calories, we inevitably eat less of other nutrient-rich foods such as breads and cereals, fruits and vegetables. Unfortunately, sugar makes us need the nutrients in these foods even more. Sugar increases the body's need for thiamin and perhaps the trace mineral chromium as well, according to Dr. Jean Mayer.[8] . . .

Dangerous Change No.4:
Too Much Salt

Americans now eat 6 to 18 grams of salt (sodium chloride) a day—10 to 30 times the average human requirement, and as much as three times the recommended level.[9] *Dietary Goals for the United States* recommends that we eat no more than one teaspoon of salt (5 grams) a day (about 2,000 mg of sodium). Since the average human *requirement* for salt is probably one-twentieth the recommended maximum of one teaspoon, there is virtually no danger of insufficient salt even if we never add salt to any food ourselves.[10]

The Risks. Health scientists are widely agreed that high salt intake markedly increases the risk of hypertension, or high blood pressure, and they estimate that as many as 40 percent of the older people in the United States are susceptible to hypertension. High blood pressure increases the risk of heart attack and stroke. High-salt diets also cause edema, or water retention, in some people. . . .

Dangerous Change No.5:
Too Little Fiber

Until very recently, most of us did not know that lack of fiber in the diet was a risk; most of us didn't even know what fiber was. Scientists define dietary fiber as the skeletal remains of plant cells that are not digested by our bodies' enzymes.

As significant as any other change in the human diet over the last 20,000 years is the "fiber revolution." The diets of our early ancestors probably contained ten times the dietary fiber of contemporary diets.[11] Our long digestive tract undoubtedly evolved to handle this higher-fiber diet. The antifiber revolution has taken its most extreme form in the United States, where today 70 percent of our calories come from food containing little or no fiber.[12]

The fiber in fruits, grains, beans, seeds, and vegetables differs, and serves different beneficial functions. Some, for example, shorten the time it takes food to pass through the intestines; others promote the growth of bacteria useful in altering potentially harmful substances. So it is important to eat a variety of fiber.

The Risks. Of all the diet-disease connections, the role of dietary fiber may be hardest to pin down, since the fiber content of our diet has no direct biochemical effects but promotes physical and secondary physiological changes. Nevertheless, low-fiber diets have been implicated in heightened risk of bowel cancer and other intestinal diseases. "Dietary fiber appears to aid in reducing the onset and incidences of diabetes, cardiovascular disease, diverticulosis, colon and rectal cancer, and hemorrhoids," states Dr. Sharon Fleming of the Department of Nutritional Sciences at the University of California, Berkeley.[13] More than one scientist believes that fiber in the diet appears to be even more strongly linked to reduction of blood cholesterol levels than does a lowering of fat consumption.[14] Another problem associated with lack of fiber is plain old constipation. . . .

Dangerous Change No.6:
Too Much Alcohol

Ever since Prohibition, Americans have been drinking more alcohol. They drank the equivalent of 2.69 gallons of pure alcohol per person in 1975, 24 percent more than during the 1961-65 period. Of course, this figure is misleading, because while many people drink little or no alcohol, others drink far more than their share.[15] The biggest increases have come in wine, with 490 million gallons sold in 1979, and beer, up from 82 million barrels in 1950 to 175 million barrels in 1979.[16] (Some 25 percent of the cereal grains directly consumed in the United States are used to make alcoholic beverages.)[17] . . .

The Risks. Alcohol leads to cirrhosis of the liver, the sixth leading cause of death in the United States. It can also cause birth defects and mouth cancer. Even more deadly is alcohol's effect in traffic accidents: half of all traffic deaths involve a drinking driver. Moreover, alcoholism destroys—only more slowly—the lives of millions of Americans every year. . . .

Dangerous Change No.7:
More Additives, Antibiotic Residues, and Pesticides

Food Additives

"It is impossible to know exactly how many pounds of artificial colors, flavors and preservatives we ingest annually" is the sober assessment of Letitia Brewster and Michael Jacobson. In *The Changing American Diet*, these authors note that the only accurate records made public are the amounts of coal-tar-based colors certified each year by the Food and Drug Administration. But Brewster and Jacobson suggest that the increase in the use of food coloring is probably a pretty good indicator of the increase in other additives. The use of certified food coloring has increased about *elevenfold* since 1940.[18]

The Risks. The debate over the risks of food additives continues. The Center for Science in the Public Interest, co-founded by Jacobson, has spent ten years looking into these risks. Jacobson's first book, *Eater's Digest* (Doubleday, 1972), is a valuable encyclopedia of food additives and their risks.

"But there are hundreds of common additives," I said to Michael Jacobson in a recent phone conversation. "What do *you* tell people to do?" He answered with a list of five additives about which he believes there is enough evidence to warrant concern.

Read labels and avoid these additives, Michael suggests. "But it's not so difficult," he says. "Basically, if you avoid junk food, you'll avoid most of them." . . .

Dangerous Change No.8:
Too Many Calories

I probably don't have to present evidence to convince you of one of the key consequences of the new American diet. A government study confirms what our scales are telling us: as of the early 1970s the average American man was six pounds heavier and the average woman seven pounds heavier than their counterparts of 15 years earlier.[19] Twenty percent of all Americans are either clinically overweight or obese.[20]

The Risks. Extra pounds can aggravate hypertension and heart disease.[21] (Even a 10 percent reduction in weight can lower blood pressure significantly, according to a recent study.[22]) It is less widely known that obesity is also believed to promote diabetes.

But why are Americans getting fatter?

We are not eating more calories, but we are burning up less because our lives are more sedentary. Moreover, with the typical American high-fat, low-fiber, high-sugar diet you can eat a lot of calories without eating very much bulk, so you just don't feel full. A gram of fat has more than twice as many calories as the gram of carbohydrate. This means that for the calorie "cost" of just one pat of butter or two bites of hamburger, you could eat a whole cup of plain popcorn, a slice of bread, most of a small potato, a cup of strawberries, or an entire head of lettuce. . . .

The Good News

The flip side of the message in this chapter—that so many of our most dreaded diseases are related to the food we now eat—is the good news: *we* can reduce our chances of getting these diseases since we control what we eat. And it's easy. We don't have to memorize a book of tables and walk through the grocery store with an electronic calculator, adding up grams of fat, salt, and sugar. Since the eight threats to our health derive mainly from animal foods and processed foods, achieving a healthy diet involves only a few steps: reducing our consumption of animal foods (limiting eggs to three a week and cutting back on full-fat dairy products), enjoying a variety of *whole* foods, and using safflower, sunflower, corn, or soybean oil at home. Remember, what the medical authorities are recommending today is not some newfangled way of eating that requires a Ph.D. to put together. It is a pattern of eating that sustained human life for thousands of years. . . .

3. Protein Myths: A New Look

HAVING READ of the vast resources we squander to produce meat, you might easily conclude that meat must be indispensable to human well-being. But this just isn't the case. When I first wrote *Diet for a Small Planet* I was fighting two nutritional myths at once. First was the myth that we need scads of protein, the more the better. The second was that meat contains the *best* protein. Combined, these two myths have led millions of people to believe that only by eating lots of meat could they get enough protein.

Protein Mythology

Myth No.1: *Meat contains more protein than any other food.*
Fact: Containing 20 to 25 percent protein by weight, meat ranks about in the middle of the protein quantity scale, along with some nuts, cheese, beans, and fish. . . .

Myth No.2: *Eating lots of meat is the only way to get enough protein.*
Fact: Americans often eat 50 to 100 percent more protein than their bodies can use. Thus, most Americans could *completely eliminate* meat, fish, and poultry from their diets and still get the recommended daily allowance of protein from all the other protein-rich foods in the typical American diet.

Myth No.3: *Meat is the sole source for certain essential vitamins and minerals.*
Fact: Even in the curent meat-centered American diet, nonmeat sources provide more than half of our intake of each of the 11 most critical vitamins and minerals, except vitamin B12. And meat is not the sole source of B12; it is also found in dairy products and eggs, and even more abundantly in tempeh, a fermented soy food. Some nutrients, such as iron, tend to be less absorbable by the body when eaten in plant instead of animal foods. Nevertheless, varied plant-centered diets using whole foods, especially if they include dairy products, do not risk deficiencies.

Myth No.4: *Meat has the highest-quality protein of any food.*
Fact: The word "quality" is an unscientific term. What is really meant is usability: how much of the protein eaten the body can actually use. The usability of egg and milk protein is greater than that of meat, and the usability of soy protein is about equal to that of meat.

Myth No.5: *Because plant protein is missing certain essential amino acids, it can never equal the quality of meat protein.*
Facts: All plant foods commonly eaten as sources of protein contain *all* eight essential amino acids. Plant proteins do have deficiencies in their amino acid patterns that make them generally less usable by the body than animal protein. However, the deficiencies in some foods can be matched with amino acid strengths in other foods to produce protein usability equivalent or superior to meat protein. This effect is called "protein complementarity."

Myth No.6: *Plant-centered diets are dull.*
Fact: Just compare! There are basically five different kinds of meat and poultry, but 40 to 50 kinds of commonly eaten vegetables, 24 kinds of peas, beans, and lentils, 20 fruits, 12 nuts, and 9 grains. Variety of flavor, of texture, and of color obviously lies in the plant world . . . though your average American restaurant would give you no clue to this fact.

Myth No.7: *Plant foods contain a lot of carbohydrates and therefore are more fattening than meat.*
Fact: Plant foods do contain carbohydrates but they generally don't have the fat that meat does. So ounce for ounce, most plant food has either the same calories (bread is an example) or considerably fewer calories than most meats. Many fruits have one-third the calories; cooked beans have one-half; and green vegetables have one-eighth the calories that meat contains. Complex carbohydrates in whole plant foods, grain, vegetables, and fruits can actually aid weight control. Their fiber helps us feel full with fewer calories than do refined or fatty foods.

Myth No.8: *Our meat-centered cuisine provides us with a more nutritious diet overall than that eaten in underdeveloped countries.*
Fact: For the most part the problem of malnutrition in the third world is not the poor quality of the diet but the inadequate quantity. Traditional diets in most third world countries are probably more nutritious and less hazardous than the meat-centered, highly processed diet most Americans eat. The hungry are simply too poor to buy enough of their traditional diet. The dramatic contrast between our diet and that of the "average" Indian, for example, is not in our higher protein consumption but in the amount of sugar, fat, and refined flour we eat. While we consume only 50 percent more protein, we consume eight times the fat and four times the sugar. Our diet would actually be improved if we ate more plant food. . . .

How Much Is Enough?

The protein allowances I use in this book are those recommended by the Committee on Dietary Allowances of the National Academy of Sciences, Food and Nutrition Board. It's interesting to learn how the committee arrives at these recommended allowances. Keep in mind that the procedure is full of *assumptions* (some of which are disputed within the scientific community), *estimates*, and *averages*. Realizing this, R.J. Williams's advice takes on even greater importance: observe your own body carefully to find out what is best for you.

To come up with the recommended allowance for an entire population, the committee followed four steps:

Step 1. Estimating average need. . . .
Step 2. Adjusting for individual differences. . . .
Step 3. Adjusting for normal eating compared to experimental conditions. . . .
Step 4. Adjusting for protein usability. . . .

4. Protein Complementarity: The Debate . . .

Complementing Your Proteins

Because different food groups have different amino acid strengths and weaknesses, eating a mixture of protein sources can increase the protein value of a meal; here's a case where the whole is greater than the sum of its parts. The EAA [Essential Amino Acid] deficiency in one food can be countered by the EAA contained in other food. For example, the expected biological value of three parts bread and one part cheddar cheese would be 64 percent if eaten separately. Yet, if eaten together, their biological value is 76 percent because of the complementary relationship. The "whole" is greater largely because cheese makes up for bread's lysine and isoleucine deficiencies. Such protein mixes *do not result in a perfect protein* that is fully utilizable by the body (only egg is near perfect). But combinations can increase the protein quality as much as 50 percent above the average of the items eaten separately.

Eating wheat and beans together, for example, can increase by about 33 percent the protein actually usable by your body. Figure 29.1 will help you see why. It shows the four essential amino acids most often deficient in plant protein. On each side, where beans and wheat are shown separately, we see large gaps in amino acid content as compared to egg protein. But if we put the two together, these gaps are closed.

Figure 29.2, "Summary of Complementary Protein Relationships," illustrates the basic combinations of foods whose proteins complement each other. The dishes

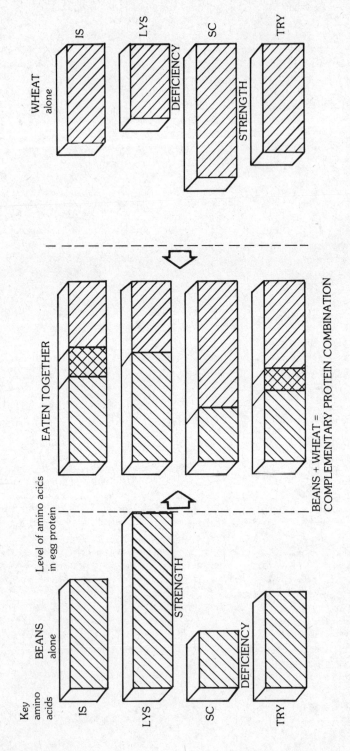

Figure 29.1. Demonstrating protein complementarity. [Source: *Amino Acid Content of Foods and Biological Data on Proteins*, Food and Agricultural Organization of the U.N., Rome, 1970]

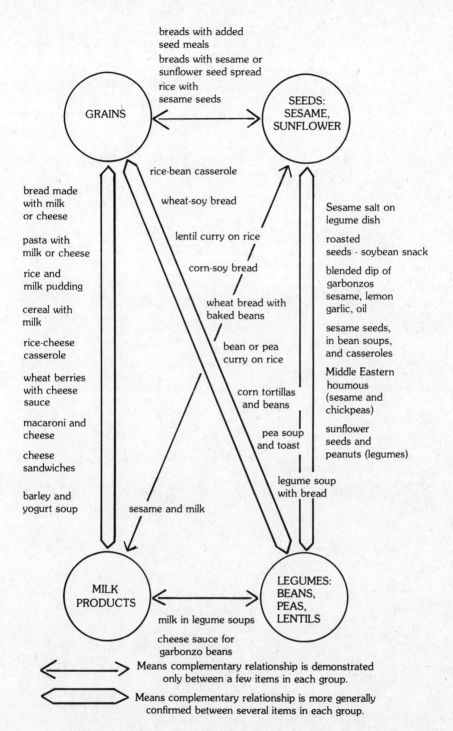

Figure 29.2. Summary of complementary protein relationships.

listed are meant to be suggestive of the almost endless possibilities using each combination. (Complete protein tables are listed in Appendix E of *Diet for a Small Planet*). . . .

Notes

1. Letitia Brewster and Michael Jacobson, *The Changing American Diet*, Center for Science in the Public Interest, 1744 S. St. NW, Washington, D.C. 20009, pp. 64–65.
2. Ibid. pp. 35, 43.
3. Dietary Goals for the United States, Second Edition, prepared by the staff of the Select Committee on Nutrition and Human Needs, United States Senate, December 1977, reproduced by the Library of Congress, Congressional Research Service, March 31, 1978, p.xi.
4. Patricia Hausman, *Jack Sprat's Legacy: The Science and Politics of Fat and Cholesterol*, Center for Science in the Public Interest (Richard Marek Publishers, 1981), pp. 58–59.
5. *Dietary Goals*, op. cit., p.xxx.
6. *Jack Sprat's Legacy*, op. cit., pp. 105–106.
7. *The Changing American Diet*, op. cit., p.46, and U.S. Department of Agriculture, Economics and Statistics Service, *Food Consumption, Prices, and Expenditures*, Statistical Bulletin No. 656, February 1981, p.2.
8. *Dietary Goals*, op. cit. p.32.
9. Ibid. pp. 40–49.
10. Ibid. p. 49.
11. Gene A. Spiller with Ronald J. Amen, *Topics in Dietary Fiber Research* (Plenum Press, 1978), p. 78.
12. U.S. Department of Agriculture, *Handbook of Agricultural Charts, 1978*, p. 56.
13. Dr. Sharon Fleming, personal correspondence, February 26, 1981.
14. M.G. Hardinge, A.C. Chambers, H. Crooks, and I.J. Stare, "Nutritional Studies of Vegetarians III. Dietary levels of Fiber," *American Journal of Clinical Nutrition*, 1958, 6:523.
15. *The Changing American Diet*, op. cit., p. 13.
16. Milton Moskowitz, Michael Katz, and Robert Levering, *Everybody's Business: An Almanac* (Harper and Row, 1980), p. 785.
17. Wayne Anderson, "More Meat - or less - on the Dinner Table," *Feedstuffs*, May 12, 1975, p. 116.
18. *The Changing American Diet*, op. cit. pp. 27–28.
19. Ibid. p. 50.
20. Graham T. Molitor, "The Food System in the 1980s," *Journal of Nutrition Education*, volume 12, no.2 Supplement, 1980, pp. 103 ff.
21. *The Changing American Diet*, op. cit., p. 58.
22. *New England Journal of Medicine*, vol. 304, no. 16 (April 6, 1981), pp. 930–933.

30

The Need to Know About Animals
(excerpts)
Robert McDowell

To avoid a misunderstanding about the role of livestock in the world economy, Robert McDowell has written an article discussing the benefits of raising livestock. The article is included here to highlight the important role that animals play in developing countries' economies, lest the reader should interpret Lappé's messsage in Chapter 29 as a call to eradicate the yak and the llama from the developing world!

The population of ruminant species of animals, such as buffaloes, cattle, goats, sheep, camels, alpacas, deer, and antelopes, that make some contributions of food and nonfood uses to humans is near 3 billion. In addition 0.62 billion pigs and 5.7 billion poultry are kept for food production. Species lesser in number, like the horse, kangaroo, rabbit, capybara, guinea fowl, pigeon, and duck, contribute more than 0.5 million kg of animal protein per year. These sources are exclusive of fish and other marine life. Most domestic species of animals are expanding at the rate of 1 to 2 percent per year. In many areas, an important issue has become the limitation of feed supplies.

  With rising human and animal numbers, a fundamental question is, How do we utilize our land resources most effectively for humankind? What proportions shall we use for residential or industrial purposes, agriculture, recreation, forests, or forever leave wild? If land use is for agriculture, how much should be planted to food crops, nonfood crops (coffee, tea, etc.), crops to feed animals, or flowers? Choices vary widely because of numerous factors in any area, such as soil fertility, temperature, rainfall, labor, and capital, which govern agriculture enterprises. In addition, there are external elements, such as distance to market, prices for products, and political decisions, that influence decisions on land use. All factors considered animal production is the enterprise of "best use" for much of our less-productive land. Ruminant animals are scavengers and can utilize plant materials and land areas suitable for little else. Is there a better use for the poorly drained clay soils of St. Lawrence

This paper is one in a series of eighteen papers on world food issues, which can be obtained from the Distribution Center, 7 Research Park, Cornell University, Ithaca, NY 14850. Reprinted with permission from Papers on World Food Issues. 1984. Ithaca: Distribution Center, Cornell University.

TABLE 30.1 General Order of Priorities for Use of
Livestock in the United States and Developing
Countries

United States	Developing Countries
Derive income from	Reduce risks from cropping
Milk	Generate capital
Meat	Render services
Eggs	Traction
Fiber	Fuel
Diversify farm operations	Fertilizer
Derive returns from non-	Satisfy cultural needs
arable lands	Ensure status or prestige
Provide status symbol	Provide food
Generate Capital	Generate Income

Source: McDowell 1980.

County, New York, the mountain ranges of the Rockies, the sand hills of Nebraska than for livestock?

With the need for human food putting pressure on land use, many have come to view animals and fowl as competitive with humans for food and having relatively low efficiency for providing human food. Although few would contest certain points, such as the comparative inefficiency of producing food from animal sources on lands suitable for intensive food production, those who hold that animals are highly competitive with humans have a narrow basis for such a conclusion. Overall, less than 1 percent of the animals useful to humans receive foods directly consumable by the humans. Much more food grains are lost in storage to rats, insects, and molds than are fed to domestic animals.

In the United States we depend upon animal products (eggs, meat, milk, and milk products) to provide 64% of the protein and 31% of the energy we ingest. As human population expands, we may need to consider modifying consumption of animal products, but to extrapolate our situation to countries where food supplies are already limited is subject to serious challenge. In the countries classified by the Food and Agriculture Organization (FAO) as developing are found 64% of the world's cattle, over 90% of the buffaloes and goats, and 50 to 55% of the sheep, pigs and poultry. If we consider animal products resulting from the use of cereal grain feeding as affordable largely in affluent societies, why do the poor regions of the world possess so many domestic animals and poultry? India has the world's largest population of cattle and buffaloes. China is number one for pigs. Africa is the second ranking continent in number of domestic animals and with its wildlife has the largest biomass of animals. Its economy is highly dependent on animals. Annual output from domestic livestock is near $10 billion, with 50% attributed to products (meat, milk, fiber, and skins) and the remainder from services from nonfood products such as manure, traction, and transport. The game population contributes $3.5 billion, with about 70% from tourism and trophies and 30% from meat and skins. An additional $3-4 billion is from fish out of streams, lakes and coastal waters. The total contributions could be as much as $18 billion. Africa's annual cereal grain output is estimated at $8.5 billion. With low production of food legumes, the protein from meat and milk fills a vital role in human nutrition and permits many Africans to survive on high starch diets.

In general, there is a sharp contrast in the order of priorities for the use of animals in the United States and the developing countries (Table 30.1). The highest priority in the United States is to derive income from the sale of animal products, whereas generation of income ranks much lower in the developing countries.

As we plan for the future in the United States, we may wish to seriously examine the wisdom of using 60 percent of our cereal grain production for animal feeding. For the developing countries, the interdependence of people and animals will become an important feature in planning, not only in land use, but also in employment. In India, approximately 70 percent of all milk is produced by landless or near landless (less than 2 ha) people. Currently, there are nearly 40 million people owning about 80 million livestock units in the sub-Sahara part of Africa. These animals use 526 million hectares of land unsuitable for crop production.

References

Baker, P.R. 1978. Nomadism in Africa. In Animal Husbandry in the Tropics, 3rd ed., ed. G. Williamson and W.J.A. Payne. Longman, London.

Barat, S.K. 1975. Hides, skins and animal by-products. World Animal Rev. 14: 20–25.

Barnett, M.L. 1978. Livestock, rice and culture. Rockefeller Foundation report of working papers on integrated crop and animal production to optimize resource utilization on small farms in developing countries. Bellagio, Italy (Oct. 18-23, 1978).

Cockril, W.R., ed. 1974. The husbandry and health of the domestic buffalo. Food & Agric. Organ., Rome.

Fernandez-Baca, S. 1975. Alpaca raising in the high Andes. World Animal Rev. 14:1–8.

Food and Agriculture Oganization of United Nations (FAO). 1981. Production yearbook 1980. Vol. 34. Rome.

Goe, M.R. and R.E. McDowell. 1980. Animal traction: Guidelines for utilization. Cornell Int. Agric. Mimeo 81. NYS College of Agric. and Life Sci., Cornell Univ., Ithaca.

Goldshmidt, W. 1973. The bride price of Sebei. Sci. Am. 229: 74–85.

Gonzalez-Jimenez, E. 1977. The capybara, an indigenous source of meat in Latin America. World Animal Rev. 21: 24–30.

Guilliver, P.H. 1966. The family herds: A study of two pastoral tribes in East Africa, the Jie and Turkana. Routledge and Kegan Paul, London.

Harris, M. 1974. Cows, pigs, wars and witches: The riddles of culture. Random House, New York.

Harwood, R.R. 1979. Small farm development: Understanding and improving farming systems in the humid tropics. Westview Press, Boulder, Colo.

International Livestock Centre for Africa. (ILCA) 1982. Livestock production in Mali. ILCA Bull. No.15. Addis Ababa, Ethiopia.

McCammon-Feldman, B., P.J. Van Soest, P. Horvath, and R.E. McDowell. 1981. Feeding strategy of the goat. Cornell Int. Agric. Mimeo. 88. NYS College of Agric. and Life. Sci., Cornell Univ., Ithaca.

McDowell, R.E. 1977. Ruminant products: More than meat and milk. Winrock Rept. No. 3. Winrock Int. Livestock & Train. Center, Morrilton, Ark.

_____. 1980. The role of animals in developing countries. In Animals, feed, food and people, ed. R.L. Baldwin. Westview Press, Boulder, Colo.

_____. 1982. Limitations for dairy production in developing countries. J. Dairy Sci. 64: 2463.

Makhaijavi, A., and A. Poole. 1975. Energy and agriculture in the third world. Ballinger Pub. Co., Cambridge Mass.

31

Cancer Is Not Inevitable
Thomas H. Maugh II

Thomas Maugh II summarizes the National Research Council's "interim dietary guidelines" that are suggested to reduce the risk of cancer. The suggestions are similar to those made by the American Heart Association issued in 1977 by the Senate Committee on Nutrition and Human Needs. The landmark report (previously, official groups had been reluctant to suggest a diet-cancer connection) also summarizes the current state of knowledge about dietary links to cancer. Some of these links, in particular regarding fats (the American Meat Institute took particular offense to the panel's recommendation to reduce dietary fat) and dietary fiber, were controversial.

"It is highly likely that the United States will eventually have the option of adopting a diet that reduces its incidence of cancer by approximately one-third," according to a new report issued this month by the National Research Council. "The evidence is increasingly impressive," says Clifford Grobstein of the University of California, San Diego, chairman of the panel that prepared the report, "that what we eat does affect our chances of getting cancer, especially particular kinds of cancer. This is . . . good news because it means that by controlling what we eat we may prevent such diet-sensitive cancers."

The bad news, he continues, is that the committee "does not yet think it possible to say . . . how much the incidence of particular cancers might be reduced by dietary alteration. Certainly we have no ideal cancer-preventing diet to announce." What the panel did announce was some modest suggested changes in dietary habits that should at the very least, in Grobstein's words, "reduce anxiety" about cancer. The suggestions are similar to the "prudent diet" recommended by the American heart Association to minimize heart disease, to the "Dietary Goals for the United States" issued in 1977 by the Senate Select Committee on Nutrition and Human Needs, and to the unofficial guidelines recommended in 1979 by Arthur Upton, then director of the National Cancer Institute, in testimony before the Senate committee. Nonetheless, the report marks the first time that any official body has suggested that the risk of cancer can be alleviated by dietary changes.

The "interim dietary guidelines" fall into four major categories:

Reprinted with permission from Science 217 (4554): 36–37 (2 July 1982). Copyright 1982 by the AAAS.

* The proportion of calories in the diet provided by fats should be reduced from 40 percent to 30 percent. "Of all the dietary compounds (the panel) studied, the combined epidemiological and experimental evidence is most suggestive for a causal relationship between fat intake and the occurrence of cancer"—especially cancers of the colon, breast, and prostate. This is in sharp contrast to a 1980 report *Toward Healthful Diets* by the Food and Nutrition Board of the National Academy of Sciences, which concluded that "there is no basis for recommendations to modify the proportions (of fat) in the American diet at this time." Questioned about this at a press conference, Grobstein said "We know more now."

* The daily diet should include wholegrain cereals, fruits, and vegetables, especially those in vitamin C and B-carotene, which is converted by the body into vitamin A. These foods include citrus fruits, dark-green and deep-yellow vegetables, and members of the family Cruciferae (such as cabbage, broccoli, cauliflower, and Brussels sprouts). "In laboratory experiments," says Grobstein, "these vitamins, the mineral seleniuim, and some nonnutritive chemicals present in cruciferous vegetables inhibit the information of cancer-causing chemicals or reduce cancer incidence in other ways." The report strongly recommends against injudiciously supplementing diets with these substances because of potential side effects.

* The consumption of salt-cured, salt-pickled, and smoked foods should be minimized because they are associated with an increased incidence of cancers at certain sites, particularly the stomach and the esophagus. In the United States, such foods include sausages, smoked fish and ham, bacon, and hot dogs.

* Excessive consumption of alcohol should be avoided, particularly in combination with cigarette smoking. Such consumption has been associated with an increased risk of cancer of the upper gastrointestinal and respiratory tracts, as well as with other adverse health effects.

The report was commissioned by the National Cancer Institute during the Carter Administration, in 1980. Its fate under the Reagan Administration seems problematic. That Administration's view is thought to have been summarized by Agriculture Secretary John R. Block, who testified during his confirmation hearings that "I'm not so sure government should get into telling people what they should or shouldn't eat." The report's principal value may thus lie not in its guidelines but rather in its summarization of the current state of knowledge about dietary links to cancer.

The subject is a particularly difficult one to study—a "minefield" in the words of the panel's vice chairman, John Cairns of the Harvard School of Public Health. The complex nature of cancer initiation, the formidable task of determining what an individual consumed 20 or even 30 years before the onset of a tumor, the difficulties of regulating the components of diet for experimental animals, the heterogeneity of the human population, and the wide variety of changing life-styles are just some of the problems that confront researchers.

The foundation for the link between diet and cancer rests on two key facts. The first is that, with the exception of lung cancer resulting from smoking, the incidence of most types of cancer has not changed appreciably during the 20th century. This, and the observation that the incidence of many types of cancers is higher in nonindustrialized countries such as New Zealand than in the United States, indicates that the most common cancers "are related, for the most part not to industrialization but to various other long-standing features of our life-style, especially diet."

The second key fact is that the incidence of various types of cancers varies from country to country. When people migrate from one country to another, "they tend to acquire the pattern of cancer that is characteristic of their new homes. This is surely the most comforting fact to come out of all cancer research, for it means that cancer is in large part, a preventable disease."

The evidence associating fats with cancer, in fact, first came from studies of Japanese who migrated to the United States, abandoning their traditional low-fat diet in favor of a meatier one in the United States. Evidence for the link was subsequently strengthened by a large number of epidemiological studies as well as by studies of laboratory animals. Most investigators now believe that dietary fats act as promoters, agents that do not themselves cause cancer but that enhance the activity of carcinogens.

The recommendation to reduce dietary fat has so far been the most controversial aspect of the report. The American Meat Institute, a trade group of cattle growers, charged the panel with promoting "misleading advice which does no service to the public." Commented Grobstein: "I don't think we're disseminating unproved theories." The panel may also come into conflict with the American Heart Association, which has been promoting not only a low-fat diet but also a shift to polyunsaturated fats. Animal evidence cited in the report indicates that in a low-fat diet, polyunsaturated fats are more effective than saturated fats in promoting tumor formation. Panel member Anthony B. Miller of the National Cancer Institute of Canada predicted that it will be some time before the effects of polyunsaturated fats is known in humans.

Another potentially controversial aspect of the report involves dietary fiber. Several investigators, led by Denis P. Burkitt of St. Thomas's Hospital in London, argue that a high proportion of nonnutritive fibers, such as cellulose, lignin, gums, and pectins, in the diet protect against cancer of the colon and rectum. The fiber is believed to act primarily as a bulking agent, diluting the concentration of potential carcinogens in the feces and hastening their passage through the bowels.

The panel, however, concluded that there is "no conclusive evidence to indicate that dietary fiber . . . exerts a protective effect." If such an effect does exist, furthermore, it is most likely to be "related to the intake of one fiber component—the pentosan fraction," found primarily in whole wheat products. Burkitt contends that the evidence is sufficiently strong to advocate a significant daily consumption of fiber.

The status of other dietary components reviewed in the report is less controversial but no less complex. For most of them, the evidence is suggestive but inconclusive. Protein is a good example. Epidemiological studies have suggested an association between high consumption of protein and increased risk of cancer at several sites, including breast, large bowel, pancreas, prostate, and kidney. These studies are clouded, however, by the close association of protein and fats in the diet. Studies in laboratory animals indicate that carcinogenesis is suppressed when protein consumption is at or below the minimum level required for optimal growth. The panel thus concludes that "high protein intake *may* be associated with an increased risk of cancer at certain sites."

A similar situation exists for carbohydrates. High consumption of sugar is associated with an increased risk of pancreatic cancer in women, and a high intake of potatoes is associated with liver cancer in both sexes. Frequent consumption of starches has also been associated with gastric and esophageal cancer, while a high intake of sugar combined with a low intake of starch has been associated with an increased incidence of breast cancer. The total evidence, however, "is too sparse to suggest a direct role for carbohydrates in carcinogenesis. However, excessive carbohydrate consumption contributes to caloric excess, which in turn has been implicated as a modifier of carcinogenesis."

There is little information about vitamins, apart from A and C. Vitamin E, like C, inhibits the formation of carcinogenic nitrosamines, but it is present in so many different commonly consumed foods that it is difficult to identify population groups that do not receive enough. There is virtually no information about the B vitamins.

Results are also scanty for minerals. Both epidemiological and laboratory studies suggest that selenium may offer some protection against cancer, but many of those studies used near toxic levels of seleniuum. Iron deficiency has been indirectly associated with cancer of the upper alimentary tract, and perhaps also with gastric cancer. Zinc may be associated with tumor formation, but experiments in animals suggest that it both enhances and retards carcinogenesis, depending on concentration and experimental design. Molybdenum deficiency may be associated with an increased risk of esophageal cancer. Both an excess and a deficiency of iodine may be associated with an increased risk of thyroid cancer.

Of perhaps greater concern in the long run is the large number of hazardous extraneous chemicals in the diet. These include hazardous constituents of foods themselves, environmental contaminants, mutagens produced during cooking, and both intended and inadvertent food additives. There are some 3000 food additives that are used intentionally, an estimated 12,000 that are added inadvertently during processing and packaging, and an unknown but presumably large number of natural constituents and environmental contaminants. Most of these fortunately, are present at quite low levels and their effects may be negligible. It is "reassuring," the panel argues, that cancer incidence rates have not increased during this century, for this suggests that these nonnutritive substances have either a small constant effect or little effect at all. The panel cautions, however, that any effects attributable to the greatly increased use of processed foods and changes in cooking habits in the last 20 to 30 years may not yet have become apparent.

One of the most important questions that remains to be answered is the relation between mutagenesis and carcinogenesis. Mutagens are widely distributed in the diet. Many vegetables contain mutagenic flavonoids, and mutagenic activity has been observed in extracts from many foods, including coffee, tea, and alcoholic beverages. Mutagens are produced in meat and fish by the high-temperature pyrolysis of proteins, and recent studies have shown that even low-temperature cooking also leads to production of mutagens.

Most of the mutagens that have been found in foods have not been tested for carcinogenic activity, but there is a growing body of evidence suggesting that mutagens are likely to be carcinogens. Some scientists, however, argue that the link is inconclusive and that the association should not be used as a basis for regulation. Cairns espouses what seems to be a majority viewpoint when he notes that it would be foolish to believe that any compound which is a potent mutagen in bacterial or animal systems is not a hazard to humans. Even if mutagens should prove carcinogenic, though, difficult decisions will be necessary. Cooking of meat and fish, for example, may produce mutagens, but it also destroys pathogenic microorganisms and parasites. Some vegetables that contain mutagens also have high nutritive value.

The report emphasizes that "the weight of evidence suggests that what we eat during our lifetimes strongly influences the probability of developing certain kinds of cancer, but that it is not now possible, and may never be possible, to specify a diet that protects all people against all forms of cancer." Nonetheless, concludes Grobstein, "it is time to further spread the message that cancer is not as inevitable as death and taxes."

32

Jane Brody's The New York Times Guide to Personal Health
(excerpts)
Jane E. Brody

Jane Brody is one of America's most respected news columnists. Her weekly "Personal Health" column, which appears regularly in *The New York Times* and over 100 other newspapers, is read by lay people as well as academic and medical professionals. *Jane Brody's The New York Times Guide to Personal Health* (the entire text of which is strongly recommended for further reading) was written in the same year as the National Research Council's report, "Diet, Nutrition, and Cancer" (Chapter 31). Brody's summary of relevant diet and nutrition research echoes that of the Council's. Excerpts from "Cutting Down on Hidden Fat" and "Starches: Not Fattening and Good for You" appear below.

Cutting Down on Hidden Fat

Most of the fat in our diets is *hidden* fat. It is the hard-to-notice marbling in meat. It is an integral part of hard cheeses and cream cheese, fish, deep-fried foods, nuts, seeds, cream soups, ice cream, and chocolate. It is a major ingredient in a wide variety of factory-prepared products, including baked goods (especially cakes, pies and cookies), processed meat (frankfurters, bologna, and the like), instant meals, coffee whiteners, whipped toppings, snack foods, and granolas. Even one popular diet product, Pillsbury's Figurines, has fat as its main ingredient.

Yet those who advocate more healthful diets that are not overly dependent on red meat often substitute fattier foods than the ones they reject. Examples include the quiches, avocado salads, nuts and seeds, nut butters, sesame paste, and granolas featured in health food restaurants and stores. A quiche is made from cheese in which three-fourths of the calories come from fat that is more saturated than meat fat, cream in which nearly all the calories are fat, and piecrust in which more than half the calories are fat calories.

Similarly, 85 percent of the calories in nuts come from fats, and three-fourths of the calories in seeds (for example, sunflower seeds) and avocados are fat calories.

Whereas most breakfast cereals contain little or no fat, granolas derive about a third of their calories from the fat in nuts, seeds, coconut, and added oil.

Don't assume that a label claiming "high in polyunsaturates" means you can eat all you want. High compared with what? It may also be high in saturates and cholesterol. Besides, the idea in the prudent diet is not simply to add polyunsaturates to your current diet. Rather, the goal is, first, to reduce your total fat intake and second, to substitute polyunsaturates for saturates wherever reasonable.

The meals you eat in restaurants also may contain far more fat than you may suspect. You may pass up the butter on your bread, the sour cream for your baked potato, and dishes that are deep-fried. But your soup, gravy, and sauces may be swimming with hidden fat; your steak (already three-fourths fat calories) or your fish may be broiled with butter; your salad may be loaded with a fatty dressing; and your rich desserts may contain far more fat than sugar.

Nutrition and Health, a newsletter prepared by the Institute of Human Nutrition at Columbia University, advises that you avoid certain dishes on restaurant menus: those called creamed, in cream sauce or in its own gravy; sauteed, fried, pan-fried or crispy; escalloped, au gratin, or with cheese sauce; buttery, buttered, or in butter sauce; au lait, a la mode, or au fromage; marinated, stewed, basted, or casserole; prime, hash, pot pie, or hollandaise.

Instead, the institute suggests that you choose dishes described as pickled, in tomato sauce or with cocktail sauce, steamed, in broth, in its own juice, poached, garden fresh, roasted, or stir-fried. . . .

Starches: Not Fattening and Good for You

There's one simple way to save calories and money in your daily food budget: Eat the potatoes. Also the rice, pasta, corn, beans, and bread. Strange advice, coming in a book on healthful living? Aren't these the starchy foods, high in calories and low in nutrients, that our forefathers were forced to live on but that we, in our late-twentieth-century affluence and abundance, can afford to pass up or merely sample now and again?

The answer is yes—and no. Yes, these are starchy foods, laden with so-called complex carbohydrates (as opposed to sugars, which are simple carbohydrates). No, they are not high in calories. Ounce for ounce, they have no more calories than pure protein, and they have fewer than half the calories in fat.

A five-ounce potato, without butter or sour cream, has 110 calories, whereas a five-ounce T-bone steak has about 550. That's because the steak has more fat than protein, and fat is our most calorie-laden nutrient. Yet, those watching their weight are likely to leave the potato on the plate and down every morsel of the meat. Dieters also pass up the rice (154 calories in five ounces) and the pasta (210 calories). Even five ounces of bread, at 390 calories, are less fattening than the steak.

In addition to saving you calories, the starchy carbohydrates can save you money if you eat them in place of some of the more costly fat-rich protein foods that most Americans consume to great excess.

Experiments with high-carbohydrate diets have shown that they can produce painless weight loss because the dieter feels satisfied without eating too many calories. In one such study, overweight college students consumed twelve slices of bread a day as part of their regular meals and lost, on the average, sixteen pounds in eight weeks. Those eating a high-fiber bread lost the most. The bulk provided by many complex carbohydrate foods, particularly fruits, vegetables, and whole grains, can fill the dieter far better than calorie-dense fats and sweets.

TABLE 32.1. The Amount of Fat in Food

Percent of Calories From Fat   Type of Food

DAIRY PRODUCTS
More than 75%   Butter
                       Cream--half-and-half, heavy, and sour
                       Cream cheese
                       Whipped cream

50 to 75%   Rich ice cream
                       Hard cheeses--cheddar, Swiss, American, etc.

40 to 50%   Regular ice cream
                       Whole milk
                       Whole-milk yogurt

30 to 40%   2% milk
                       Creamed cottage cheese
                       Ice milk
                       Low-fat yogurt

20 to 30%   Thick shake
                       1% milk
                       1% fat cottage cheese

Less than 20%   Skim milk
                       Buttermilk
                       Uncreamed cottage cheese
                       Farmer's cheese
                       Frozen yogurt

                       FISH
More than 75%   (none)

50 to 75%   Fried perch
                       Tuna with oil
                       Tuna salad

40 to 50%   Sardines, drained
                       Mackerel
                       Canned salmon

30 to 40%   Fried flounder or haddock
                       Broiled halibut
                       Tuna in oil, drained
                       Scallops and shrimp, breaded and fried

20 to 30%   Broiled cod
                       Raw oysters

Less than 20%   Broiled ocean perch
                       Scallops and shrimp, steamed or broiled
                       Tuna in water

	RED MEATS
More than 75%	Bacon
	Choice sirloin
	Regular hamburger
	Cold cuts (bologna, salami, etc.)
	Frankfurters
	Pork sausage
	Spareribs
50 to 75%	Corned beef
	Rib lamb chops
	Pork loin
	Ham
40 to 50%	Lean T-bone
	Lean hamburger
30 to 40%	Flank steak
	Lean chuck pot roast
20 to 30%	Sirloin tip
Less than 20%	(none)

	VEGETABLE AND GRAIN-BASED FOODS
More than 75%	Avocado
	Coconut
	Cole slaw
	Nuts and peanut butter
	Olives
50 to 75%	Pound Cake
40 to 50%	Chocolate cake with icing
30 to 40%	Yellow or white cake without icing
	Granola
	Pizza
20 to 30%	Corn muffin
	Pancakes
	Wheat germ
Less than 20%	Angel food and sponge cake
	Dried beans, peas, and lentils
	Bread
	Grains--bulgur, couscous, rice, millet, etc.
	Pasta
	Breakfast cereals (except granola)
	Vegetables and fruits (except those listed above)

And no, starchy foods are not necessarily low in nutrients. Most starchy foods, particularly those made from whole grains and beans, are rich sources of vitamins, minerals, and trace nutrients. The potato, for example, is a nutritional bargain in terms of its calories. It supplies, among other nutrients, nearly 5 percent of the protein, 5 percent of the iron, 8 percent of the phosphorus, 10 percent of the thiamin, 11 percent of the niacin, and 50 percent of the vitamin C needed in an adult's daily diet, but only 4 to 5 percent of the calories. Starchy foods also contain fiber, or roughage, the noncaloric, undigestible plant materials that are important aids to digestion and may help prevent various diseases of the colon, including cancer. . . . And like the potato, most starchy foods contain small but significant amounts of protein. The protein content of some beans, in fact, is on a par with meat.

33

PCBs for Breakfast and Other Problems of a Food System Gone Awry

Joan Gussow

Joan Gussow focuses on the quality of the U.S. food supply, specifically the chemical contamination of food and water in the United States. Many highly toxic persistent chemicals have been and will be incorporated into the human food chain through carelessness and greed alike. What should be our response to such contamination problems? Outrage . . . indifference . . . or perhaps we should ship our toxic wastes to other countries? Perhaps more importantly, Gussow asks, "Whose job is it to worry about the U.S. food supply?" The question is almost rhetorical and yet the author warns that nutrition professionals, in particular, need to recognize that concern about the chemical contamination of the food supply is "part of [their] job."

When I first became concerned about the relationships between food and the larger environment, some 14 years ago, I had a vague awareness that there were environmental constraints on food production, a vagueness only partially dispelled by an issue of *Scientific American* on the biosphere in which Lester Brown had one of his characteristically alarming articles—this one entitled "Human Food Production as a Process in the Biosphere."

By the time I began teaching a course in nutritional ecology, I called the session on food and population "The photosynthetic limits." My perception of the problem then, in keeping with the understanding put forward in the early 1970s, was that there were limits to growth and that they were largely material limits. We would use up the natural gas we needed to make fertilizer (that seemed obvious even then) or the phosphate rock which we needed for the same purpose (but kept flushing down our sewers as dirty detergent just as if it were not a life-essential). Or we would run out of water or arable land (erosion was—and is—a terrifying problem).

It seemed clear that even if we overcame all those resource limits (as many people were urging that we most assuredly would), then ultimately we would come up against the fact that there was only so much solar radiation—only so much light available to power photosynthesis and make the plants grow. That led me to the understanding early in 1970 that energy was probably the limiting ingredient in our

Reprinted with permission from *Food Monitor*: pp. 16-19, 28 (May-June 1982).

food systems. Even if we turned ultimately to synthesizing food, we would need energy to do so.

It was only in the course of putting together my book The *Feeding Web* that I began to perceive that the real limits were other than strictly "substantial" ones. Perhaps, indeed, the manganese nodules at the bottom of the sea—those nodules Howard Hughes' big boat was ostensibly going out to mine—were but exemplars of the fact that there would always be sources of raw materials. Perhaps the Federal Government was right when in response to the publication in 1972 of the volume *Limits of Growth* it pointed out that "the notion of resource exhaustion is ultimately unrealistic . . . the entire globe is at our disposal." And should we run out of earth, there was always physicist Gerard O'Neill assuring us that we could live in person-produced space colonies grinding up asteroid after asteroid for what useful materials they contain.

What began to become clearer, however, was that things kept going wrong that seemed to have nothing to do with our running out of materials—that might, in fact, only get worse if materials were unlimited. We were beginning to perturb biological systems on whose continued functioning our survival depends. A reporter recently wrote of what he called the "humbling complexity" of some of the systems of mutual plant and animal interaction in the Amazon. He was responding both to the ongoing destruction of the Amazon jungle, which has been called "the lungs of the world," and to the clumsiness our species exhibits as we move toward simplifying the immensely complex system out of which we once evolved.

What is becoming frighteningly evident, where biological systems are concerned, is that we are utterly unable not only to control what will happen to them—we will not, as a headline suggested, "outwit" nature to produce more food—we are not even able to *predict* with any certainty what will happen in those systems *which we are most aware of being dependent upon.*

Climatologists tell us that we shall for a certainty have more "unstable" weather, though no one seems able to predict for sure whether the combined effects of our activities will cool or warm the earth. Either would wreak havoc with our established cropping systems, though only one would melt the polar ice-caps and flood the coastlines. That we are dissipating the ozone layer with flouro-carbons—and perhaps other substances as well—seems confirmed, through we are uncertain at what point we shall markedly increase skin cancer among humans, and perhaps among livestock, who are without the partial protection of houses and clothing.

There is no shortage of problems from which to choose if one wishes to be concerned with the effects of our interventions into the biological systems which sustain us. One I wish to consider is chemical contamination of the food and water supply—not because it is necessarily the most important problem but because it is currently a matter of grave concern to a great many communities.

I have a number of clippings from the *Los Angeles Times* on the contamination of more than 50 Southern California wells with a solvent called TCE. I am especially sensitive to stories about trichloroethylene, since 12 wells along a single road in the county where I live in New York State had to be closed last year because of gross TCE contamination. And, as is the case in Los Angeles, no one knows where the pollutant came from.

Now there are several possible reponses to this sort of ground-water contamination. Outrage is a common response: many residents consider pure water their right as citizens. Indifference is another response: one El Monte man interviewed by the *Los Angeles Times* said he only drank Sparkletts and Coors anyway. One woman said she'd go on drinking the water because she had to die of something.

A spokesperson from one health department reflected what seemed a common *official* response, suggesting that the offending chemical could well have been dumped 20 or more years ago and that "standards for the disposal of such chemicals were less strict in the past." The implication, of course, is that even though we may have past messes to clean up we are now getting things under control. But are we?

In 1976 Congress passed the Toxic Substances Control Act which is supposed to give the government control over chemicals not already regulated under other laws, as well as to give the EPA the right to "clear" new chemicals *before* they enter the marketplace. But before the EPA could begin to regulate *new* chemicals, they naturally had to discover what was already out there. The pre-clearance law could not be implemented until the inventory was complete. According to the *EPA Journal* for January 1980, the inventory was completed on June 1, 1979 (three years after passage of the law) when a list was published of 43,278 compounds then in use.

Estimates of the number of new chemicals entering the marketplace every year range from an industry low figure of 100 "significant" ones to a high estimate of 1,000 new chemicals per year. According to a Presidential Toxic Substances Strategy Committee, production of all chemicals and allied products doubled in the 12 years ending in 1979. One EPA official estimated that in order to keep up with new introductions, the agency would have to rule on four new-chemical applications every working day.

Let us assume for the moment that the low figure for new chemicals is correct, and let us further assume that the EPA has been given sufficient funds to hire the personnel to carry out their mandate—an admittedly wishful assumption in a time of budgetary stringency and an administration determined to gut the agency and deregulate everything possible. What are they going to be asked to rule on? They are going to have to rule on whether the chemical is safe enough to be let out into the environment. I need not rehearse the difficulties inherent in coming to a rational safety decision regarding human exposure to chemicals which ethically only can be tested on animals. Such decisions have been difficult enough in regard to chemicals which are *intended* to enter the food supply in regulated amounts— intentional additives. Consider as an object lesson the fact that the National Academy of Sciences was unable to apply its own proposed safety criteria to a single substance, saccharine, which it had extensively studied. On what basis, then, will we make safety decisions about chemicals which are intended *not* to enter the food supply at all, and which, when they do enter it, do so accidentally in uncontrolled amounts?

Consider, for example, the chemical PBB—polybrominated biphenyls—a known toxin which entered the Michigan food chain accidentally in 1974 when one or more bags of PBB-containing fire retardant accidentally were mixed into animal feed. The economic interests of the companies involved, the fears of elected officials, and the moral compunctions of farmers combined in that circumstance to obscure facts about the damage done in a maze of accusations and denials. The five-year chronology of the Michigan PBB case makes fascinating reading for those who optimistically hope that regulation, followed by careful monitoring, followed by prompt discovery, followed by rapid condemnation of the contaminated food will be the standard scenario when accidents occur in an environment full of toxic chemicals.

PBBs, flame-retardant chemicals used in varied manufacturing processes, are known to cause cancer in laboratory animals, as are their chemical analogs, PCBs. In the Michigan case, when 2,000 pounds of PBBs accidentally were substituted for a feed additive for farm animals, it took almost a year for the trouble to surface and the source to be discovered.

During this period Michigan had marked decreases in milk production and increases in illness among cattle. Contaminated hens stopped laying eggs. Before the nature of the problem was determined, some of the animals had been recycled into feed for livestock. The poison thus went from farm animals to people on farms, then to their customers, through milk, meat, butter, eggs and cheese.

As a result, 30,000 cattle were destroyed, plus 1.5 million chickens and 7,700 other farm animals. Some farmers were forced into bankruptcy. There have been reports of damage to the nervous systems, livers and immune systems in farm residents.

In 1978, five years after the accident, two companies, the Michigan Chemical Company (Velsicol) and Farm Bureau Services, Inc., pleaded no contest to charges stemming from the event and were fined $4,000 each.

Or consider polychlorinated biphenyls—PCBs—which used to be manufactured up the Hudson River from where I live in New York State. Such quantities of waste PCBs were dumped in the river that without extensive bottom dredging (which may not even work) fish from the river will be unsafe for generations. But PCBs are not supposed to be manufactured any more, and they are also supposed to be sealed into transformers where they are out of harm's way. Let me review briefly one documented PCB accident.

This one began in June 1979 when a broken transformer spilled 200 gallons of PCBs into a wastewater system at the Pierce Packing Company in Billings, Montana. By-products scooped from the wastewater were cooked into meat meal for animal food. By the time the problem was discovered it was necessary to investigate possible contamination in Arizona, California, Idaho, Illinois, Iowa, Kansas, Minnesota, Montana, Nebraska, New Jersey, North Dakota, Ohio, Oregon, Pennsylvania, South Dakota, Utah, Washington, Wisconsin and British Columbia!

A shipment of contaminated industrial grease on its way to Japan was turned back at sea. Seven million eggs, 1.2 million chickens, 30,000 turkeys, 5,300 hogs, two million pounds of industrial grease, 800,000 pounds of animal feed and 71,000 bakery items (as a minimum estimate) had to be destroyed.

What could have happened? How did the pollution spread so far before the problem was detected? As reported in The New York Times in September 1979 and in Science in January 1980; on July 6, 1979, in a routine inspection, a government poultry inspector sampled the chickens at Jolly Wholesale Poultry in Provo, Utah. He put the samples in a freezer and went on vacation for seven days. Five days after he returned the samples arrived at a San Francisco testing laboratory, where, after 10 days of testing, it was discovered that there was a problem: the chicken samples contained five times the allowed levels of PCB. Nine days later these samples arrived at the Meat and Poultry inspection regional office in Alameda. Three days later the agency's office in Boulder, Colorado, got word of the contamination. It took nine days to trace the chickens back to Jolly Wholesale Poultry. Five days later PCB was found in meat meal and a week later—59 days after samples were taken—the company announced it would destroy the contaminated chickens. It took twelve more days to trace the contamination to the leaking transformer at Pierce Packing Company in Billings, Montana, by which time the PCBs had been consumed by a variety of humans and animals.

A study by the Office of Technology Assessment concluded that despite an apparently elaborate system of safeguards, there have been a frightening number of such incidents involving "wide distribution and partial consumption of food" tainted with chemicals never intended to enter the food chain. We are assured that so far there is no imminent threat to public health, although it is unclear just what that means when the import of the OTA report is that no one is really sure who has eaten how much of what. It has been suggested that the FDA should set up pilot programs to look for "unanticipated" chemicals in the food supply, though the cost is daunting: two million dollars for each state or regional laboratory set up to look for "unanticipated chemicals" and the cost for testing for each "unanticipated" chemical is about $10,000.

Now what does all this have to do with limits to growth and with the kinds of solutions which might be most appropriate if we are to maintain a sustainable food system? I began by saying I originally believed the limits to our present patterns of food production were "substantial"—that we would be limited by running out of something—phosphate, topsoil, energy—which we needed to make the food system go. As my understanding evolved, I came to recognize that before we ran out of anything material, we would exhaust the earth's capacity to tolerate our disruption of natural systems. We would be stopped when the effluents from our affluent culture perturbed some vital system beyond recovery.

But in the last two years I have come to understand that the real limit is one we have already reached—it is a limit on the size and the complexity of the systems which we ordinary humans can safely manage. This far-flung food chain on which we depend is run by people like you and me—people who go on vacation, who get bored with routine jobs, who fail to recognize "unanticipated" problems simply because they are unanticipated, who would rather not rock the boat. And what may be an even more important understanding is the fact that *the problem will not be solved* by setting up more sophisticated automated monitoring systems controlled by computers and other electronic gadgetry. For *even* if you trust the computers you cannot trust the humans who watch them. The more routine we make the human task, the more vulnerable the human becomes to boredom and inattention and the less safe we become.

Hazel Henderson, a brilliant economic visionary, has suggested that industrial cultures are approaching an evolutionary cul-de-sac which she calls the "entropy" state. "The entropy state," she writes, "is a society at the stage when complexity and interdependence have reached such unmanageable proportions that the transaction costs generated equal or exceed its productive capabilities. In a manner analogous to physical systems," she goes on, "the society winds down of its own weight, and the proportion of its gross national product that must be spent in mediating conflicts, controlling crime, footing the bill for all the social costs generated by the 'externalities' of production and consumption . . . begins to grow exponentially." One might well consider such an exponentially growing cost the assessment of some portion of 43 thousand-plus chemicals times $10,000 per chemical times however many state or regional laboratories will be brought into action in an attempt to guarantee that a single spill of PCB from a single broken hose in Billings, Montana, does not contaminate the food supply of 19 states.

Ground water contamination from carelessly disposed wastes can theoretically be controlled by setting up regulated clay-lined dump sites which will isolate the deadly wastes from local aquifers. But who will make sure that each small manufacturing plant, faced with rising costs and lowered profits, will use the "safe" dump and will not instead send its loaded trucks out at night to dump their contents on a vacant lot in the South Bronx or Oakland? Only recently has it come out that some people are hoping to ship their toxic wastes abroad—to developing countries with less strict (!) laws than ours. Current U.S. policy does not forbid such shipments—leaving it to the receiving countries to make their own decisions. The notion of sending it all *away* becomes less enticing when one recalls that on a globe there *isn't* any away—that what we throw over our shoulder today will come over the horizon and hit us in the face tomorrow. At the least we should probably exercise caution—avoiding importing food from countries to which we ship our toxic wastes.

One of my students, investigating the possible contamination of a major New Jersey acquifer by a waste dump built on top of it, found herself looking at a table of parts per million of various hydrocarbons found in the water from a nearby well. Feeling unqualified to judge what the figures meant, she went to the local health department and asked the person in charge "What *should* water have in it?" He looked at her and said "H_2O." She and I found it striking that she should have had to ask. Taken en masse, my students' investigative term papers this year convinced me that once highly toxic persistent chemicals have been manufactured, they *will* get into the human food chain through human ignorance, carelessness, indifference or greed.

You can work out within your own frames of reference the implications of that possibility. For myself, it is probably clear from what I have said that I believe we must work toward smaller, more localized food systems over which we have some measure of personal control, and that we must also work toward the total elimination of manufactured substances which have certain combinations of persistence and toxicity. But what I believe most strongly is that some significant portion of nutrition professionals must come to recognize that helping make such decisions is part of our job. It is often non-nutritionists for example—among them Frances Moore Lappé and Joseph Collins, co-founders of the Institute for Food and Development Policy, who do the most provocative thinking about the world food crisis.

Whose job is it to worry about the U.S. food supply? Whose job is it to think about what our food system will look like in the year 2000? Who should be worrying about whether people will be able to buy enough food at a price they can afford, and whether they will know what kinds of foods to buy to maintain their health? Whose job is it to worry what will be in that food—both advertently and inadvertently?

Is that the job of food processors, the agricultural economists, the farmers, the government? Whose fault is it that we have built over much of the best farmland in the United States and that we are letting much of the rest of it run off in rivers of topsoil? Whose responsibility was it that we developed an agriculture that is both ruinous to cropland, heavily dependent on energy and toxic chemicals, dangerously narrow genetically, and economically structured so as to be ruinous to the stability of rural life and to the livelihood of the small farmers whom Jefferson saw as the backbone of our society? Who is responsible for the fact that we have a food supply notable for its sheer abundance, its illusion of variety and its tastelessness (in both senses of that word), as well as for its level of nutrient fortification, in a country which has the highest per capita ownership of refrigerators *and* the highest per capita consumption of food additives? If it is not our job to worry about these things, whose job is it? Is it really a matter of consumer choice when a culture takes two foods: corn and rice—foods which have a nearly zero storage energy cost—and turns them into frozen popcorn and Birdseye Frozen Italian Rice?

Either someone thinks about the system as a whole—and about the implications for the future of food of toxic chemicals and topsoil loss, insect resistance to pesticides, the loss of genetic diversity, the waste of energy in food processing and so on—or we simply go on pretending nutrition has only to do with what happens after food leaves the throat, ignoring the abberations of a system so vulnerable to human error that it may one day soon leave us short of wholesome food to put in our mouths.

I do not intend to suggest that I have discovered the right answers to these rather terrifying and complex problems that face this country and the world in the next decades. I will be happy, however, to defend my conviction that I am asking some of the right questions. I feel very strongly that someone in the field of food and nutrition—as well as everyone else who eats—must begin to worry about the systems that bring us food—and about whether they are sustainable enough so our children and their children will have something safe and healthful to eat.

Update

Five years after the toxic chemical PBB was found in some livestock feed in Michigan, 97 percent of the residents of that state are believed to have residual levels of the toxic chemical in their bodies.

That was announced by scientists from the Environmental Sciences Laboratory of the Mount Sinai School of Medicine, and reported in the April 16, 1982, issue of the *Journal of the American Medical Association*.

An accompanying editorial by Dr. Dean W. Roberts of Hahnemann Medical College in Philadelphia expressed "concern" with "potential delayed effects attributable" to the shortage of PBB in fatty tissue and possibly other tissues. The editorial added that "in view of the carcinogenesis lag time of up to two or three decades, it will be important to monitor a sample of the exposed population over a prolonged period."

Part VI

INTERNATIONAL NUTRITION AND MALNUTRITION

34

Nutrition and Infection in National Development
(excerpts)
Michael C. Latham

The nutritional problems characteristic of developed countries stand in sharp contrast to those of the developing countries. Whereas an excess of certain nutrients is quite often the cause of health problems in the former group, the latter group's problems are in large part due to deficiency of those same nutrients, in particular, calories. Nutritionists have for many years recognized the relative importance of calorie deficiency vis-à-vis protein deficiency in malnutrition (see excerpts from Michael Latham's article below), and yet many food scientists continue to see the problem differently.

In a similar way it is now widely accepted that most of the malnutrition in the Third World is due simply to inadequate intake of food. Protein deficiency is not the most important nutrition problem in the world. In most populations where the staple food is a cereal such as rice, wheat, corn, or millet, serious protein deficiencies, although common, seldom occur except where there is also a calorie or overall food deficiency (1). There has been an overemphasis on the protein problem and too much stress on protein deficiencies with a relative neglect of the first goal of a food policy, which should be to satisfy the energy needs of the population. Most cereals contain 8 to 12 percent protein and are often consumed with moderate quantities of legumes and vegetables. If calorie requirements are met on these diets, protein deficiencies usually become uncommon, and are certainly confined mainly to very young children with increased nitrogen losses due to frequent infections. The situation in those whose staple food is plantain, cassava, or some other low protein food may be very different.

The lesson to be learned is that commercial production of relatively expensive protein-rich foods, the amino acid fortification of cereal grains, the production of single cell protein, and several other ventures that a few years ago were offered as panaceas for the world's nutrition problems can only reduce the problem of protein-calorie malnutrition to a very small degree. Similarly, genetic efforts to change by

Reprinted with permission from Science 188 (4188): 561–565 (9 May 1975). Copyright 1975 by the AAAS.

small amounts the amino acid pattern of cereal grains are much less important than increasing the yields per acre of these cereals, and of other food crops.

A modest increase in cereal, legume, and vegetable consumption by children will greatly reduce the prevalence of protein-calorie malnutrition and growth deficits of children in the Third World, especially if combined with control of infectious diseases. Breast feeding during the first few months of life can assure an adequate diet, whereas bottle feeding as discussed elsewhere in this issue (2) is a major cause of diarrhea and nutritional marasmus.

Notes

1. P.V. Sukhatme, *Indian J. Agric. Econ.* 22, 7 (1972); D.S. McLaren, *Lancet* 1974-II, 93 (1974).

2. D.B. Jelliffe and E.F.P. Jelliffe, *Science* 188, 557 (1975).

35

Food Science and Nutrition:
The Gulf Between Rich and Poor
(excerpts)
Joseph H. Hulse

In an excerpt from an article that appeared in *Science* in 1982, Joseph Hulse argues that even when calorie intake is sufficient, the diet of many young children is nutritionally inadequate. This view is in contrast to that of the previous author (Chapter 34). Some problems with food scientists' solutions to malnutrition problems (and their sometimes narrow-minded perspective) are presented in Chapter 37.

Malnutrition in Developing Countries

While food science has made an immense contribution to the physiological, economic, and social well-being of people living in the world's wealthier countries, such is not the case among the rural poor in Africa, Asia, Latin America, and the Middle East. In these countries the underprivileged struggle to find food sufficient to survive, and must often walk many miles in search of wood with which to cook it.

Though for the poorest, malnutrition is a condition close to starvation, malnutrition in its broadest sense results from a diet inadequate to maintain satisfactory nutrition . . . impairs the capacity for work output and lowers resistance to infection. Infection, in turn, increases the food nutrient demand to repair the damage wrought by disease. Malnutrition and chronic infection impair learning ability which further reduces the capacity for effective work. Consequently, malnutrition begins a vicious circle broken only by provision of an adequate diet.

In countries of the African Sahel, where 70 to 80 percent of the energy is provided by cereals, seasonal variations in available food energy occur every year (1). During the months immediately before the harvest energy intake generally averages 25 to 30 percent less than the intake immediately after harvest. In the drought years of the early 1970's, energy intake deficiencies of close to 50 percent were recorded (1). The survey data available (1) illustrate the wide variability in available food among years, among seasons, among communities, among age groups,

Reprinted with permission from *Science* 216 (4552): 1291–1294 (18 June 1982). Copyright 1982 by the AAAS.

and between settled and nomadic life-styles. Even when, among the rural poor, calorie intake is sufficient, the diet of many young children is nutritionally unsatisfactory. This is largely because the protein content and amino acid composition of the locally grown cereals, whatever the quantity ingested are inadequate to satisfy a child's needs.

The chemist can analyze the relative composition and levels of concentration of most known nutrients, but chemistry alone cannot determine nutritional adequacy. The adverse effects of grossly excessive or inadequate nutrient intakes are often demonstrable, but what constitutes an ideal diet for any condition of man, woman, or child is far from certain.

In domestic and farm animals nutritional balance can be determined according to such desirable characters as rate of weight gain and carcass composition. Nutritional requirements for human health cannot be so easily prescribed since they involve such complex criteria as resistance to infection, healthy longevity, physical fitness, and intellectual capacity, not one of which is very easily quantified.

Nutritional studies with human subjects are expensive and time-consuming; humanitarian and ethical considerations restrict the range of variables that may be studied, the techniques of assessment that can be used, and the period of time over which any experiment may be continued. Consequently, recommended daily allowances of all dietary standards are the results of professional judgments based on the best available evidence. Recommended daily allowances of known essential nutrients have changed over the years and are still not uniform among all countries.

In the mid-1930's the League of Nations Committee on Nutrition wrote in its report (2): "The movement towards better nutrition in the past has been largely the result of the unconscious and instinctive groping of men for a better and more abundant life. What is now required is the conscious direction towards better nutrition. Such direction constitutes policy. Nutrition policy . . . must be directed towards two mutually dependent aims: first, consumption, bringing essential foods within reach of all sections of the [world] community; second, supply." The report then listed several courses of action necessary to ensure an adequate consumption and supply, including the recognition of nutritional policy as of primary national importance; better education on human nutrition; and a more equitable distribution of income since it is "the poorest people who are the most nutritionally deprived."

Notes

1. *Nutritional Status of the Rural Population of the Sahel*, Report of a Working Group. Paris, France, 28 to 29 April 1980 (Publication No. IDRC-160c. International Development Research Centre, Ottawa, Canada, 1980).

2. League of Nations, *The Relation of Nutrition to Health, Agriculture and Economic Policy* (League of Nations, Geneva, 1937).

36

Hope in Dark Times

Sheila Dillon

According to UNICEF (as reported in *Food Monitor*; a similar report appeared in the December 25, 1982 issue of *The Economist*, p.10), there are four inexpensive and simple ways to reduce malnutrition and infectious diseases among the child population in developing countries. The oral rehydration therapy, in particular, has been heralded as a major medical finding. The question remains as to whether or not there are bureaucratic and political structures that will commit funds and personnel to the activities UNICEF recommends.

In 1982, 40,000 young children died every day from malnutrition and infection, says UNICEF's new report, "The State of the World's Children 1982-1983". In much of the developing world malnutrition and infection are two sides of the same problem. If you are malnourished you are most susceptible to infections, and infections—particularly the very common diarrhoeal infections—suppress the appetite and diminish the body's ability to absorb food. This is the hidden hunger of the third world. No dramatic pictures of skin and bones, just a lifetime of too little food and chronic sickness.

The hard rock of malnutrition is as UNICEF says, the lack of food itself. "For those who simply do not have enough to eat, the long-term solution lies in having either the land with which to grow food or the jobs and the incomes with which to buy it." UNICEF is surprisingly blunt about the need for land reform and the control of the large-scale mechanization of agriculture in the third world as the basis for any long-term solution to hunger. "However important increasing production may be, it is clearly not the central problem. And the answer to hunger is therefore not ultimately technological. The problem is rather one of what crops are grown by whom on whose lands and for whose benefit. And the solution lies in political and economic change to allow the poor to both participate in, and benefit from, the increases in production which can most certainly be achieved."

But long-term is just that—long term. This year in the midst of a world-wide recession UNICEF has chosen to concentrate its report, and its efforts over the next year, on the promotion of four cheap, simple ways to cut the mortality rate of children and break the cycle of malnutrition and infection.

Reprinted with permission from *Food Monitor*: p.29 (January - February 1983).

* Oral Rehydration Therapy is a weighty name for a simple home-made mixture of sugar, salt and water that can stop the fatal dehydration that is the end result of many diarrhoeal infections. About 5 million children die every year as a result of these infections—by far the biggest single cause of death among children in the developing world.

Until recently rehydration could only be done intravenously in a hospital by nurses or doctors. The salt, sugar and water mixture was first discovered in the early 1960s, said Tony Hewett, chief of editorial and publications services at UNICEF in New York, but it was only in 1975 that the technique was developed sufficiently for mass use. The *Lancet*, the leading British medical journal, called this simple therapy "potentially the most important medical advance [of] this century."

* Universal Child Immunization is the second of UNICEF's goals for 1983. It is now feasible, says UNICEF, to immunize all children against measles, diptheria, tetanus, whooping cough, polio, and tuberculosis. It is feasible in 1983 for two reasons: first, because there are now enough community organizations and para-professional development workers in the third world to administer the necessary booster injections and to organize the primary injections of new-borns. Second, new vaccines are now more heat stable and therefore more portable—the sensitivity to heat of several vaccines has been one of the main problems in the development of vaccination programs in rural areas.

* Breastfeeding is UNICEF's third "low-cost opportunity to significantly accelerate progress in the nutrition and survival of infants." Breast milk is cheap, incomparably more nutritious than its commercial substitutes, convenient and—most crucial in the third world—a safeguard against infection. Numerous studies in the third world show the disastrous effects of bottle feeding on children in poor families. A World Health Organization study found that in Chile babies who were bottle-fed for the first three months of life were three or four times more likely to die than their siblings who had been exclusively breastfed. A 1980 study in Brazil showed that bottlefed babies were between three or four times more likely than breastfed babies to be malnourished.

* The mass use of simple Growth Charts is the fourth part of UNICEF's fight against child malnutrition. Because much child nutrition is invisible, even to mothers, UNICEF believes that simple charts kept on a regular basis at home will serve as warning signs. "Apart from being a scientific early-warning system, such charts can offer encouragement by making the solutions as visible as the problems."

These four things are, says UNICEF, "all low-cost, low-risk, low-resistance, people's health actions which do not depend on the economic and political changes which are necessary in the longer term if poverty is to be eradicated." Taken together and seriously promoted by governments and international agencies they could promote further improvements in health care and could save the lives of up to 20,000 children each day by the end of the decade.

UNICEF believes that the programs they propose will save and improve lives. They also believe that in doing that they will make it easier for the world's poorest citizens to "participate more fully in, and benefit more fully from, the wider social and economic changes which are necessary to abolish the poverty from which that hunger grows."

37

Fish Protein Concentrate: Lessons for Future Food Supplementation

E.R. Pariser and *M. Wallerstein*

The authors discuss why Fish Protein Concentrate (FPC) has failed to alleviate malnutrition. FPC and other high technology nutrition interventions have been offered as "quick and painless technological fix[es]." The authors also discuss the emphasis on protein deficiency in the 1960s and identify critical areas of neglect in food science. We can conclude that the high technology food product is more often than not an albatross rather than a panacea. The nutritional status of a population cannot be improved unless intervention programs are conducted with a sensitivity to the political, economic and cultural setting of the target population.

When the record of 'engineered' food supplementation during the past 25 years is examined a number of aspects merit further discussion, both in terms of food and nutrition policies in low income countries, and in terms of the development of new foods and food components. It is our intention here to isolate certain generalizable observations arising out of a recent, retrospective analysis we have conducted regarding the development of fish protein concentrates (FPC) in over forty countries.[1] We have chosen this point of reference because the case exemplifies particularly well what can happen when attempts are made in industrialized countries to address the complex, multidimensional problem of malnutrition in less developed countries through the application of purely technological instruments.

As developed in Canada, the USA, and elsewhere, fish protein concentrate is a stable, wholesome protein supplement of high nutritive value and low calorific content prepared from whole fish.[2] Promoted in an era of enthusiasm for the potential contributions of technology to human welfare, FPC and its technology inspired high hopes.

The most prevalent concept of malnutrition during this period was that of protein deficiency, which had its origins in the pioneering work of Cicely Williams in Africa during the 1930s.[3] The idea of protein deficiency led naturally to the concept of protein cure, which was corroborated by the effective use of skimmed milk in the treatment of kwashiorkor in Africa. The division between well and malnourished

Reprinted with permission from *Food Policy* 6:298-305 (November 1980). Published by Butterworth Science Ltd., Journals Division.

populations soon became known as the 'protein gap'.[4] During the 1960s the notion that the protein gap could be bridged by developments in food technology gained great appeal, creating a momentum in research and development efforts that proved to be inexorable.

Technological Imperative

The FPC technology was developed for two reasons. In the first place, because the idea, the technical capacity, and the will to create the product existed. This is the environment of basic research. Unfortunately, in this case, as in many other examples of technological development, the convergence of these factors created a 'technological imperative'[5] that became the driving force. Secondly, the technology was developed because it *could* be developed. In the ensuing rush of activity, critical questions concerning the practicality and applicability of the budget were often overlooked or ignored entirely.

The FPC technology was also developed, however, because it was envisioned that the product would serve a vital humanitarian function—feeding the hungry. Although this humanitarian goal was admirable, its meaning was often obscured in the course of political and technological disputes. Nutrition activists, politicians, regulatory agencies, and private industry came into conflict in a manner most often detrimental to the implementation of FPC as a nutrition supplement. Differing goals among developers and conflicting priorities within and between institutions severely constrained development, particularly in terms of the following issues:

Inadequate consideration was given to the social characteristics, cultural patterns, and nutritional needs of the group or groups for whom the product was intended. Insufficient attention was paid especially to the fact that any food consumed by a particular group is accepted only within a rigidly delineated cultural context, and any nutrition intervention that involves modification of food habits must carefully respect this. In the case of food made of fish, with its unique cultural connotations, this recognition becomes even more important.

Selection of product characteristics was directed toward the development of a universally acceptable product—namely, a greyish-white, odourless, tasteless powder. This orientation was self-defeating since it imposed technical, economic and olfactory constraints which profoundly affected the cost and applicability of the product.

The production of FPC developed into a 'high technology' enterprise, requiring massive inputs of capital, energy, and expertise. All of these conditions are characteristically lacking in the developing world, but were not adequately considered by the developers.

Given the expensive and esoteric requirements of FPC technology, the issue of how the production and consumption of the final product would be financed became critical. In the course of FPC development, however, the question of who would pay for the distribution of the product, once it had moved beyond the development stage, was never effectively addressed.

The principal development of FPC occurred within the public sector, due to the high risk and capitalization required. However, the notion of FPC as a 'public good' was never uniformly accepted. As a result, in those cases where government subsidy and political support were diminished or withdrawn, development efforts were curtailed or stopped entirely.

The concept of a nutritional supplement usually implies a product that is used *in addition to* something else. In the case of FPC, the product supplements the nutritional quality of a food but cannot, by itself, increase the quantity of the total diet when the target population has, to begin with, less than enough. This brings into question the usefulness of food supplementations which marginally affect the nutritional status of a target group but do not affect the group's absolute supply of food or food purchasing power. Experience has shown that FPC was never capable of affecting positively either of these critical dimensions of malnutrition.

The FPC story and, beyond this stance, the overall experience with food supplementation in developing countries, reveals that most of the important *positive* results which these endeavours have produced have translated primarily into long-range economic benefits for the industrialized countries in which the supplements were developed. The *negative* results of FPC and other new foods and food supplements, on the other hand, are of immediate significance to low income countries due to their failure, both as concepts and products, to alleviate chronic or acute malnutrition. Like FPC, these products have failed most often because they have been created in isolation from the locality-specific cultural and economic settings characteristic of the target populations in LDCs. While the positive effects are not insignificant, the negative aspects demand the serious attention of all those—policy makers, planners, and technologists—whose interests lie in improving the nutritional status of impoverished populations.

Positive Aspects of FPC Development

Extension of food resource base

Increasing population, industrialization, and urbanization have, of necessity, resulted in the development of mass food production and distribution technologies. Mass production and distribution of food, in turn, have reduced the variety and number of plant and animal species used in food manufacture. Goals of higher yield, disease resistance, better distribution, ease of husbanding, harvesting, and processing, as well as higher nutritive value per acre have all favoured certain species for utilization rather than others. Today, only a fraction of the raw materials suitable for the manufacture of food is utilized and acceptable as a food source. While this is particularly true for industrialized nations, production goals like those mentioned above are gradually being transferred to the food systems of developing countries as well.

For example, enough data exists on the present state of world fisheries to state that almost all the major, [i.e.] traditionally preferable species have been overfished practically everywhere in the world.[6] Data also exist,[7] that point to very substantial stocks of food-grade, schooling fish which, though harvestable by existing methods, remain inadequately utilized, principally as a result of market patterns in the industrialized world and rigidity of cultural preferences in industrialized [countries] and in LDCs.

The development of FPC—which can be produced from any edible fish species—or the development of new food supplements such as leaf and soya protein isolates from other unexploited raw materials, serve to indicate how the basic food resource base can be expanded. This is clearly progress in the right direction.

Utilization of fish in non-traditional forms

Fish in western countries has been traded and consumed in modern times primarily in its original and recognizable form, [i.e.] as whole fish. This has had the effect both of focusing fish harvesting efforts on species for which a known market demand exists, and of reinforcing the reluctance of food manufacturers to develop food processing methods designed to utilize fish in new or alternative forms as a food component similar to processed milk, egg, or wheat.

In attempting to resolve the widespread debate—particularly in the USA and Canada—over the controversial aspects of FPC development, wider possibilities for the use of fish as food became better known to food manufacturers and the general consumer. This shift in food preference patterns is demonstrated today, for example, by the widespread popularity of so-called 'fish-burgers' in the quick service food market.

The development of FPC or textured vegetable protein (TVP) has thus helped to broaden the attitudes of the western consuming public concerning what constitutes an appropriate food component. It has also helped to promote the idea that certain raw materials can be acceptable as invisible ingredients in processed or manufactured food products.

Regulatory attitudes towards novel food sources

One piece of tangible evidence supporting the wider use of new food resources in the USA is the endorsement by the Food and Drug Administration (FDA) of FPC as a food fortificant,[8] a logical decision in view of the restricted supply of traditional sources of protein. The general trend in food regulatory policies in the US, and other industrialized nations, has been toward a more liberal interpretation of what constitutes a human-grade foodstuff. This is indicative of a slowly growing recognition, on the part of regulatory agencies, that it should not be the responsibility of government to judge food on aesthetic and social grounds; the changing economics of food supply may cause periodic redefinitions of what is aesthetically and socially acceptable.[9] Moreover, increased interaction between cultures has introduced foods that were not previously an accepted part of a society's food consumption pattern. Continuing advances in the state of the art of food science have made available new products, for which there is no legal or administrative precedent, and consequently their suitability for human consumption must be judged solely on the basis of health, safety and functional properties alone, [i.e.] without indicating concerns about aesthetic aspects.

These tendencies towards a change in regulatory policy also have a direct impact on the developing world. Many developing countries closely model their food regulatory statutes on those of the USA or other developed countries, since they have neither the technical capability nor the funds to conduct the complex analyses necessary to establish their own regulations. National pride is also a factor that may act to prevent the use of a product in a particular country—no matter how appropriate its design—simply because it has not been approved for use in the country of origin.

Negative Aspects of FPC Development

Malnutrition ill-defined

During most of the research and development work on FPC, malnutrition was considered primarily as a protein deficiency disease.[10] The notion that the protein gap between well and malnourished nations could be bridged by developments in food technology had great appeal, and offered intellectual and moral support to developers of widely varying motivations in their search for funding and interest for FPC work. Intellectually, the prevalent scientific theory underlined the need for products like FPC and, morally, the humanitarian value of solving the problem of malnutrition was undeniable.

Just as developers were convinced then that the vast resources of the sea could be used to produce FPC, similar justifications are heard today that numerous other unutilized natural resources ([e.g.] plants, animals, micro-organisms) can be harnessed for the production of much needed foods or food ingredients.[11] The conceptual problem inherent in these statements is that, as in the case of FPC, important distinctions, such as those between food ingredients and final product or between nutritional need and effective economic demand, are still rarely drawn and even less frequently articulated.

The principal appeal of these suggestions is that they place few demands on any sector other than the technological one. This has been termed by many as the so-called quick and painless technological fix. Such solutions are appealing because they offer the hope that malnutrition can somewhat be alleviated without changing the fundamental social, economic, and political balance which, more often than not, constitutes the contributory environment for the problem's existence. Despite the fact that the definition of malnutrition has now been broadened to include not only protein deficiency, but also insufficient calorific intake and economic and social factors,[12] the appeal of the technological fix remains strong. This is particularly true in those situations where the idea of significant social and political change is unacceptable as a means of creating a more equitable distribution of income, and consequently, of food.

Food supplement design

Whether a particular food supplement will or will not be appropriate in alleviating protein malnutrition is determined, primarily, by the model under which the supplement is developed and applied. At the time of the FPC project, and perhaps still today in certain quarters, protein malnutrition was viewed largely in terms of the medical analogue, [i.e.] as a disease. As a result, developers attempted to produce a remedy or 'medicine' which, like any other curative agent, would be applicable wherever the 'disease' occurred.

It is apparent, however, that there are profound differences between products such as TVP, or single cell protein (SCP) and conventional medicines. For one thing, the very names of the new products indicate that the cloak of anonymity that surrounds the esoteric contents of most typical medication does not, and perhaps cannot for legal reasons, cover the origin of the food supplements. Although this problem could be overcome to some degree if current FDA regulations were modified, there remains a more fundamental obstacle overlooked in the development of FPC that must first be addressed.

While significant progress has been achieved in developing technological approaches to particular micronutrient deficiencies ([e.g.] vitamin A fortification, iodine fortification, etc.),[13] the attempt to devise technological solutions to macronutrient deficiencies such as protein entails problems of a completely different magnitude. Whereas micronutrient deficiencies require only periodic microdosages, and therefore lend themselves to a medical-type intervention design, macronutrient deficits (whether protein or protein-calorie) require consumption in relatively large, daily quantities. As a result, the medical-type intervention as a response to macrodeficits is rendered totally inappropriate. Protein or protein-calorie interventions can only be conceived to be what they actually are, [i.e.] sources of food, with all of the social, cultural, and economic preferences and constraints that this involves.

In addition, there are a number of other significant discrepancies between the typical curative agent and most protein and protein-calorie supplements. First, a protein concentrate must be consumed for as long as the protein deficiency exists, whereas medicines are normally required only for the duration of a disease. If the problem is long-term, chronic protein malnutrition—where large portions of the population are suffering from first or second degree deficiency, rather than acute, third degree malnutrition precipitated by famine or other disasters—it would be necessary for individuals to consume the protein for an indeterminately long period of time. That is, the need would continue until the social, economic, political, and environmental factors responsible for the lack of adequate, nutritious food supplies had been altered.

Second, protein concentrates are either mixed into a staple food that reaches all of those in need or are added, often incorrectly, by the final consumer, whereas medicines can either be administered in a central location or taken by the patient in pre-measured dosages.

Finally, whereas most consumers accept on faith the positive benefits of drug components, a protein concentrate may encounter distinct problems in this regard. That is, public knowledge of the product's raw material origin may be a significant impediment to the supplement's general acceptance.

Thus, we would argue that protein concentrates, even when conceived as a partial response to the putative problem of protein deficiency, are unable, by their very design, to have the universal application of a curative agent. Indeed, many of FPC's most problematic functional properties were determined as a consequence of the decision to produce a curative agent. For example, decisions that the supplement was to consist only of a high-grade, native protein with organoleptic properties suitable for combination with a wide variety of foods without changing their appearance, odour, or flavour, all occurred as a de facto result of adherence to the medical model.

Such rigorous characteristics required the development of complicated, capital-intensive, large-scale processing technologies (including chemicals, equipment, control mechanisms, etc.), the training of sophisticated and highly paid labour, and the elimination of a variety of serious bureaucratic, political, and economic obstacles. These requirements drove the cost of the finished product to unanticipated, and ultimately unacceptable extremes. The 'curative agent' approach demonstrated a significant failure on the part of the developers to grasp the true complexity of designing a product capable of helping malnourished populations with widely varying needs and in widely differing localities.

Critical areas of neglect

In the course of both the humanitarian rhetoric and actual development of food supplements, the realistic cultural, social and nutritional profiles of the populations are often overlooked. For example, little attention is usually given to the designs of the food products in which the supplements are to be incorporated, or to the specific nutritional requirements and cultural habits of the people who will eat them. This was clearly the case in the development of fish protein concentrate.

Food supplements are developed generally for those with the greatest nutritional need, [i.e.] infants, small children, and pregnant and nursing women. These are typically segments of the low income population that are the most passive and powerless. Thus, any serious attempt to define the nutritional needs of these target groups should raise important questions about the political, economic and social conditions that are the root causes of nutritional deprivation and largely determine whether a particular food supplement will be appropriate.

In addition, any thorough consideration of the anticipated consumers of a new food or food supplement will reveal that nutritional needs include not only quantitative dimensions ([i.e.] the need for enough food to provide sufficient energy for calorie expenditure and for environmental and emotional stress) but also qualitative dimensions. These include, most importantly, the cultural patterns that determine the food habits which exist in any group, no matter how poor or politically powerless. In general, the less industrialized or urbanized a population, the more conservative its food consumption system will be. Any attempt to make changes in that system will require a thorough knowledge of its rules. But this type of concern has rarely been considered in the course of food supplement development, much less been given major emphasis.

Ironically, the food consumption habits that were most attended to in the development of FPC technology were those of consumers in the USA whose interests were allegedly represented by the US Food and Drug Administration. In fact, it was in overall response to the demands of this regulatory agency that many of the cost-increasing aspects of FPC technology were added, despite the fact that this resulted in an unnecessarily refined product which was inappropriate for low income consumers with an established preference for the taste and smell of fish in their diets.

In addition to considering the food habits of the target populations, developers must also take into account the overall cultural significance of the raw material from which the supplement is manufactured. Many food resources have strong and persistent cultural and social connotations that play an important role in the acceptance or rejection of a new food product. For example, FPC is today known not simply as a protein concentrate but as a *fish* protein concentrate. The identification of the product with fish is still inviolate, and emphasis in discussion usually rests more upon fish than protein. The cultural connotations of fish bear ample evidence of the more general fact that any food, while having a clear biological function, also contains important aesthetic and social characteristics which vary with the consuming group. Any attempt to introduce new foods or ingredients which does not take these aesthetic and cultural functions into account has only a remote chance of success, especially in the least industrialized countries where food consumption habits tend to be the most conservative and tradition bound.

Relevance of technological applications to malnutrition

Experience with the development of FPC reveals that this product did not possess the capacity to alleviate malnutrition, even as it was then defined. This is not to suggest that FPC did not fulfill other, less emphasized objectives. It did demonstrate, for example, that it was possible to utilize fishery stocks, should they exist, that might otherwise go unused, and to provide employment in the fishing and fish processing industry. Some have even argued that the product shows the potential to return a profit under certain, limited conditions.[14] But none of these justifications can begin to compensate for the fact that FPC failed as a means of alleviating protein malnutrition, which was its principal acknowledged purpose for existence.

The important point here is that FPC programmes did *not* fail as nutrition interventions because of their myriad technical, political, economic, and human shortcomings, although all of these factors had a significant individual and synergistic impact. In reality, FPC failed because it was a technological application conceived at a time when the industrialized world was relatively free from constraints on capital, resources, and expertise. Yet, this product is intended ostensibly to be applied in the developing world where all of these constraints exist in abundance.

Whatever their intentions, such high technology protein supplements are only token palliatives offered by wealthy nations or local ruling elites in lieu of addressing the basic social and political factors underlying malnutrition. But attention to these problems often requires a politically and economically unacceptable reallocation of capital resources and reordering development priorities. In our opinion, however, there is little hope that technological fixes, such as FPC, can ever obviate the need to confront these difficult but fundamental concerns for social equity.

When designed in technologically advanced countries, products like FPC will, almost inevitably, address a different set of concerns in the course of development ([e.g.] in terms of processing, market structure, means of distribution, and so on) from those which exist in the developing world. Thus, the transfer of most expensive and elaborate technologies for the purpose of nutrition intervention will probably fail; if it does not, it will likely serve to perpetuate the gap between developers and recipients.

We are struck, in the final analysis, by the relative infrequency with which these facts have been recognized and acted upon by policy makers. As a result, we note with concern the continuing proliferation of high technology nutrition interventions aimed specifically at protein-calorie malnutrition. Like fish protein concentrate, they too may be doomed to failure by their intrinsic conceptual myopia.

Notes

1. E.R. Pariser, M. Wallerstein, C.J. Corkery and N.L. Brown, *Fish Protein Concentrate: Panacea for Protein Malnutrition?* MIT Press, Cambridge, MA, 1978.

2. Known until 1962 as fish flour, FPC differs from fishmeal in that it denotes a product with a higher protein content (about 75%, frequently above 85%), a lower lipid content (below 1%, frequently in the vicinity of 0.1%), and a lighter colour than that typical for fish meal. An important further distinction is that FPC is manufactured from edible grade raw material by methods satisfying food processing standards, whereas fish meal is prepared from any available fish by crude production methods utilizing equipment not usually suitable for the production of food for human use.

3. C.D. Williams, 'Nutritional diseases of children associated with a maize diet', *Archives of the Diseases of Children*. Vol.8, No.423, 1933; C.D. Williams, Kwashiorkor; 'Nutritional diseases of children associated with maize diet', *Lancet*. Vol. 2, pp. 1151–1152, 1935.

4. AID. *The Protein Gap - AID's Role in Reducing Malnutrition in Developing Countries, 1970; Strategy Statement on Action to Avert the Protein Crisis in the Developing Countries.* Report of the Panel of Experts on the Protein Problem Confronting Developing Countries. ST/ECA/144 E/5018/REV 1. Convened at UN Headquarters 3-7 May 1971 (UN Department of Economic and Social Affairs New York) 1971.

5. J. Ellul. *The Technological Society*, Alfred Knopf. New York. 1964.

6. J.E. Bardach and E.R. Pariser, 'Aquatic proteins' in Scrimshaw and Wang. eds., *Protein Resources and Technology; Status and Research Needs*. AVI Publishing Company, Inc. Westport, CT. 1978. p. 427.

7. Ibid.

8. In June 1974, the US Commissioner of Food announced that 'due to rapid advances in food technology . . . animal protein such as milk protein, *fish protein concentrate* (emphasis added), and egg protein can be used in the fabrication of a protein product and should be permitted. *Common or Usual Name for Plant Protein Products; Withdrawal of Textured Protein Products Proposal; Notice of Proposed Rule Making*, Federal Register 39, 110. p. 205893. 14 June 1974.

9. In a public statement by Stephen H. McNamara staff member in the Office of the General Counsel, Food and Drug Administration, it was noted that 'Our traditional perceptions of 'filth' and 'unfit' for food may be expected to change as the world's food supply shrinks in relation to the world's population. Aesthetic considerations increase costs and reduce available

food supplies . . . where safety is not a factor, at some point considerations of aesthetics must give way to considerations of human need.' (Stephen McNamara, 'Some Legal Aspects of Providing New Foods for Hungry Populations', *Food Product Development*. March 1975. pp. 57-59.

10. K.S. Rao et al., 'Protein malnutrition in South India', *Bulletin of the World Health Organization*, Vol. 20, pp. 603-639, 1959; W. Taxay, 'Some diseases associated with protein malnutrition as seen in Jamaica', *Gastroenterology*. Vol. 39, No.2, pp. 172-177. August 1960; S. Frank, 'Some aspects of protein malnutrition in childhood', *Federation Proceedings*. Vol. 20, No.1, Part III, pp. 96-101, March 1961.

11. C. Waslien, J. Myers, B. Kok and W. Oswald, 'Photosynthetic single-cell protein', in Scrimshaw and Wang, eds. *Protein Resources and Technology; Status and Research Needs*, AVI Publishing Company, Inc, Westport, CT, 1978, p.522. S.R. Tannenbaum, C.L. Cooney, A.M. Demain, and L. Haverberg, 'Non-photosynthetic single-cell protein, in Scrimshaw and Wang, eds. *Protein Resources and Technology; Status and Research Needs*. AVI Publishing Company Inc., Westport, CT 1978, p. 502.

12. A. Berg. *The Nutrition Factor - Its Role in National Development*. The Brookings Institution, 1775. Massachusetts Avenue, Washington D.C. 1973; D.M. Hegsted, A deprivation syndrome or protein-calorie malnutrition', *Nutrition Reviews*. Vol. 30, No. 3, pp. 51-53, 1972.

13. F.J. Levinson, 'Food fortification in low income countries - a new approach to an old standby', *American Journal of Public Health*. Vol.62, No.5, pp.715-718, May 1972, F.J. Levinson and A.D. Berg, 'With a grain of fortified salt', *Food Technology*. Vol. 23, No.9, pp. 70-72, 1969. J.C. Bauernfeind et al., 'Nutrification of foods with added vitamin A', CRC *Critical Reviews in Food Technology*. January 1974, pp. 338-375; J.C. Bauernfeind, 'Carotenoid vitamin A precursors and analogs in food and feeds', *Agricultural and Food Chemistry*. Vol. 20, No.3, May/June 1972, pp. 456-473.

14. Type B, FPC is produced in Norway by Orsildmel. Norsk Sildolje-Og Idemelindistris Salfslaf A/L, 5001 Bergen, Norway. Substantial quantities of the product are reported to have been utilized in several countries with considerable success.

38

Definition of the Nutrition Problem— Poverty and Malnutrition in Mother and Child
(excerpts from
Nutrition and Agricultural Development)
Fernando Mönckeberg

The findings regarding nutrition intervention of the previous authors (Chapter 37) are reinforced by Fernando Mönckeberg. In an excerpt from a chapter he wrote for *Nutrition and Agricultural Development*, Mönckeberg discusses several nutrition intervention programs for preschool children, the group most affected by malnutrition. The author argues that the effects of malnutrition cannot be alleviated by simply providing food; environmental factors (psychological and social stimulation) must be improved as well.

It is evident that malnutrition cannot be considered in isolation from the many other factors conducive to poverty and marginal existence. The prevention and treatment of sociobiological damage must be directed at the whole environment. Even assuming a theoretical circumstance in which the infant population could be adequately fed without improving other environmental factors, there might be no improvement in intellectual capacity or in social adaptation. Recent studies done in the slum areas of Cali, Colombia, confirm this assumption (1). Nutritional supplementation and health care improved nutritional status for the children, but produced no significant changes in their intellectual and social capacities. On the other hand, it is important to point out that when the sociocultural situation is so poor, any program designed to prevent malnutrition is inefficient, especially if it is applied to masses of individuals. Unsanitary conditions, poor dietary habits, cultural taboos and beliefs that prohibit consumption of a variety of foods, and limited education of the parents—all come between the theoretical program and the child. This has been shown in Chile, where a program of free milk distribution has existed for more than 20 years. The program, started in 1951, consisted of giving powdered milk to every child under two years of age, in amounts covering more than the

Reprinted with permission from *Nutrition and Agricultural Development* edited by Scrimshaw and Behar. 1976. Pp. 13–23.

total protein requirements and over 80% of the calorie requirements. In 1958 the program was extended to reach children up to 15 years of age, with distribution of 48 million kgs of powdered milk per year. In spite of this enormous effort, which cost over 60 million U.S. dollars every year, there have been no substantial changes in the nutritional status of the population attributable to this program.

It is clear that the only real, short-term possibility for preventing sociobiological damage is the development of integrated programs, consisting of improved nutrition and health conditions, as well as modification of the sociocultural environment by means of direct psychomotor stimulation activities. . . .

At present, an integrated program is being carried out with children from birth to two years of age in Santiago. This includes medical care, milk distribution, nutritional education, and psychomotor stimulation in the child's home twice a week. Progress has been very satisfactory thus far, and although there are no definite conclusions, after one year of intervention the growth and intellectual levels attained by these children are similar to those of peers in a higher socioeconomic group. Programs of direct intervention must necessarily be continued during all of the preschool years, otherwise the children will experience retardation consequent to the negative influence of the sociocultural environment they continue to live in.

Positive results have also been observed in another similar study of preschool children, carried out in Cali by McKay, McKay, and Sinisterra (1), in which children three to five years of age are given a diet covering every nutrient requirement, health care, and cognitive stimulation. The latter consists of five intervention techniques with the objective of teaching (a) improvement of verbalization and an elementary understanding of quantity and quality; (b) time and space relationships; (c) hand (manipulation) skills; (d) concentration and attention at work and improved memory; and (e) achievement of independent decision-making.

The conclusions of this experiment, which has now been conducted for four years, may be summarized as follows: An adequate feeding and health care program, combined with a psychological and social stimulation program, can produce remarkable changes in social and cognitive development, reversing almost completely the sociobiological damage induced by poverty. When children began participation in the study at age three, their achievement record was very similar to that found among children in higher socioeconomic groups. Even so, recent memory continues to be somewhat impaired in children from poor homes. This also illustrates the need for early introduction of the intervention program in the child's life. Neither nutrition alone nor medical care programs without improved nutrition suffices to improve the results of the different tests measuring the development of intelligence and degree of mental ability in general.

It is probable that the sociobiological damage produced by poverty and its consequences during the infant period, and later during the preschool years, disables the individual for his subsequent integration into society. We now know that learning capacity for such children is very seriously limited during the school years because the child is unable to adapt himself to the demands of his environment. In another recent study a significantly lower school efficiency was observed in children who had been exposed to both nutritional and cultural deprivation. In Latin America, for every 100 children starting primary education, only 20 are able to finish it. It is evident that sociobiological damage is the main cause of this high level of school dropouts (Table 38.1). Children who are able to finish primary education are those whose environments have been sufficiently generous to allow them to express the greater part of their genetic potential during their growth period. The individual who is not able to complete his primary education is definitely left in the fringes of society. This means that he must be resigned to obtaining menial employment,

TABLE 38.1. School "Alto Jahuel," Santiago, Chile

| | Grades (primary school) | | | |
	1 and 2	3 and 4	5 and 6	7 and 8
Number of students	403	260	160	80
Height deficit for age (average)	10%	7%	7%	3%
Weight deficit for age (average)	15%	8%	9%	3%
Calorie deficit for age (average)	16%	10%	10%	+2%
Animal protein deficit for age (average)	32%	20%	17%	6%
IQ (Wisc.) (average)	81	87	92	101
School performance	50	57	60	66

at very low wages, or even to unemployment, perpetuating the vicious circle of poverty, disease, and lack of progress from one generation to another, with very little hope of escape.

It is urgent to prevent this damage, because impairment suffered by the individual affects, not only him, but society as a whole. It is especially important to those countries where the great majority of the population lives under these conditions. To fight poverty requires completely new kinds of planning, and great efforts to create integrated programs directed toward populations at risk in the less developed countries. This concept must be clearly understood by economists, sociologists, teachers, and physicians. The complexity of modern society demands more and more everyday of the individual if he really wants to contribute to it and enjoy the benefits of human knowledge. Poverty and hunger have accompanied and hampered man during his whole history, but today the increasing gap between those able to enjoy society's benefits and those who are not is all too evident.

Notes

1. McKay, II., McKay, A., and Sinisterra, L., 1973, Behavioral intervention with malnourished children, in: Nutrition, development, and social behavior; A review of experience, D. Kallen (ed.), U.S. Department of Health, Education, and Welfare (NIII) Publication No. 73-242, p. 121.

Part VII

DEVELOPMENT AND UNDERDEVELOPMENT

39

Miracle Seeds and Shattered Dreams in Java

Richard W. Franke

The Green Revolution, the development of new varieties through genetic breeding, was introduced to developing countries over twenty years ago. It was in the early-1960s that the potential importance of the Opaque-2 gene in corn was discovered. According to Richard Franke, the green revolution in Indonesia resulted not only in improved crop yields but also in increased political repression and social inequality.

Culturally, politically, and economically, Java is Indonesia's most important island. It is also one of the world's richest agricultural regions. Streams, carrying an abundance of soil rich in nutrients, flow from the more than thirty active volcanoes along Java's central ridge. From time to time the volcanoes erupt, spewing out lava that eventually turns to fertile soil in the warm and humid valleys and on the coastal plains.

For hundreds of years Javanese farmers have ditched, terraced, plowed, planted and weeded this marvelous confluence of natural elements to produce the rice on which their lives depend. So rich is the soil, so dependable the water supply, so excellent the climate, that for centuries the population has increased, and the land has supported not only farmers and their families but also princely dynasties, courts, traders, armies, and eventually even the industrial development of Java's recent colonial rulers, the Dutch.

But the outcome of the island's history has not been a happy one for Java's peasants. By the turn of the twentieth century, the strains of population growth and the expropriation of rice lands by Dutch sugar interests had begun to produce the paradox so common in the underdeveloped world today—increased profits for the wealthy few and a declining standard of living for the mass of producers. Throughout the depression of the 1930s, the Japanese occupation during World War II, the war for independence from the Dutch in the 1940s, and to the present day, this decline has continued. It has brought the people of Java to the verge of famine and created ever worsening conditions for the vast majority of the island's 80 million inhabitants.

With an annual per capita income of less than $80 in 1969, Javanese peasants are among the poorest in the world. Nutritional standards are declining at an alarming rate. In 1960 the average Javanese consumed 1,946 calories per day, 200 short of United Nations minimum recommendations. By 1967 consumption had dropped to 1,730 calories. Protein intake is declining as well. Minimum adult recommendations call for 55 grams of protein per person daily. In 1960 the Javanese consumed 38.2; by 1967 this had fallen to an average of 33.4, meaning that millions of the poorest farmers and laborers subsist at even lower levels.

In Javanese villages and in the sprawling urban slums of the island's largest cities, the results of this undernourishment are obvious even to the casual observer. Children stare dully, unable to focus properly. Many persons have reddish hair and distended bellies, both signs of various stages of malnutrition. High rates of influenza, dysentery, tuberculosis, and more recently, outbreaks of cholera constantly plague a population physically too weak to resist disease. Cuts and burns heal with exasperating slowness, adding to the risk of infection. Even the body size of Javanese has been declining over the past fifty years, a result of the worsening diet. Java, it would seem, has received far too little help from the wealthy nations of the world.

Yet this island has been the object of one of the most elaborate food production schemes of the past two decades. Between 1967 and 1972 the government of Indonesia and its Western allies spent well over $100 million, mostly on Java, in an attempt to produce nationally 15.4 million tons of rice—the amount needed for self-sufficiency—by 1973. By the 1972 harvest, however, the program was clearly failing; the 12.2 million tons produced in that year were at least 2.1 million short of the need. With international food supplies at their lowest levels in years, the Indonesian government was able to purchase only 1.5 million tons abroad, leaving a 600,000 ton deficit, which in turn increased local rice prices by 30 percent in just a few months.

To make matters worse, the government has almost ignored soybean poroduction, which has undergone an absolute decline, causing protein intake to drop even below the disastrous levels of 1967. In the countryside of Java and in the urban slums, this will mean a further decline in nutrition for an already badly undernourished people.

How has this tragedy come about? Why have all these millions in expenditures failed to stem further impoverishment among the majority of Javanese? The answers lie in the blindness of development theorists to the social and political realities of Java and in the nature of aid programs from the wealthy nations—programs based on these faulty theories.

The program that was to have overcome the food shortage on Java is called the Green Revolution. The product of more than two decades of scientific research, the program is part of a broad and optimistic experiment occurring in several developing countries. Under the auspices of the Rockefeller Foundation, a seed research laboratory was established in Mexico City in 1944. Within several years, technicians had produced new varieties of corn and wheat with yield potentials far above those of local Mexican varieties.

By 1962 the Ford and Rockefeller Foundations united to establish the International Rice Research Institute at Los Banos, the Philippines, hoping the successes with wheat and corn could be duplicated with rice.

Sooner than expected, a genetic cross was achieved between a variety of rice from Indonesia and one from Taiwan. The result was a strain, IR-8, capable of doubling the yields of most local Asian rices. So profitable did the germ plasm from the new seeds seem that experts eagerly fostered their dissemination across the fields of southern Asia. By 1968, India, Pakistan, Thailand, the Philippines, Taiwan,

South Vietnam, and Indonesia had begun large-scale planting of IR-8 and associated varieties of "miracle seeds."

With such a technological boon in hand, agricultural development planners began to revise their outlook on the development process. They now began to view as simpler, and more strictly economic, problems they had once seen as the results of psychological barriers, set up by "traditional" peasants unaccustomed to the idea of innovation, and institutional barriers, such as the outmoded labor and tenancy arrangements. If the new seeds could offer tremendous production increases at the level of the family farm, then perhaps all that was necessary to achieve their acceptance was the assurance that individual planters earn a high rate of profit.

Such a position is represented in the highly influential study by Chicago economist Theodore Shultz, *Transforming Traditional Agriculture* (1964). In looking for ways to lower production costs to farmer-producers, thus increasing the profits from the farming enterprise, Schultz argues that if outside lending institutions can provide finance that will lower risk and if outside research and development organizations can pay for and even execute trials and experiments, then nothing should stand in the way of widespread acceptance of the new technology.

Economic planners were quick to take the cue from Schultz's proposals. During the 1960s, development programs and the discussions that surrounded them emphasized the construction of dams, irrigation works, harbors, markets, and roads. They advocated the provision of loans for fertilizer, pesticides, and above all, for new seeds.

With this new philosophy, the miracle of the Green Revolution should have been easily transmitted from the laboratory of the geneticist to become the major force for development in much of the impoverished world. Or so it seemed. The recent history of agricultural development programs on Java, however, reveals how poorly the theory and the seeds have fared.

Interest in agricultural development in Indonesia dates from the early 1950s. Reacting with a first flush of nationalism against the half-hearted agricultural extension system of the Dutch, the head of the national extension service proposed a way of intensifying contact between farmers and technicians. In each administrative unit, made up of about 15 villages, a five acre farming plot was set aside where both farmers and technicians could experiment with different planting and growing techniques. Practical and imaginative in its conception, the program failed primarily for lack of government funds.

By 1959 planners had fashioned a new program. This experiment, known as the "paddy center," consisted of large areas of almost 2,500 acres each, served by a central facility for credit, fertilizer, seed distribution, and education. The program began to show signs of failure by 1962-63, chiefly because rice produced in these centers had to be sold to the government, and the government kept its price lower than the open market price. Farmers resented the loans, while planners felt that they were too easily available and were undermining the farmers' "sense of responsibility."

As the government continued to introduce new but ineffectual programs, some Javanese farmers took the initiative for change into their own hands. Under pressure from a growing movement of peasant and workers' associations the government was forced to pass a series of land reform acts, beginning in 1960. Within months, however, the makeup of local land reform committees was so embroiled in politics that other kinds of agricultural programs were also likely to become engulfed. By 1964, tensions between landowners and landless had become so great that violent confrontations were frequently reported from the countryside.

With the peasants becoming involved in politics, an elite group within Indonesia's upperclass university system made their own plans. In 1963 some idealistic students and teachers at the College of Agriculture of the University of Indonesia, noting that their history of service to farmers and food production was somewhat less than illustrious, came up with the idea of personally aiding the farmers. The students planned to go into the villages, live with the farmers, teach and learn from them, and take their experiences back to a following group of students who would do the same.

The first year of the program was a heady success. Starting out in an area not far from the university, twelve students lived in three villages, worked in the fields with the farmers, offered suggestions for improved cultivation techniques, listened to farmers' points of view, and interceded with local government and private institutions on the farmers' behalf as only elite students—and perhaps radical political organizations—would dare to do at the time. Per acre yields rose 50 percent over regular plots, from 1,984 to 2,866 pounds per acre (before processing), and this happened before the introduction of the miracle seeds from Los Banos.

With only their own ideas, enthusiasm, and dedication, Indonesian students and farmers were doing with locally bred improved seeds what experts and advisers from outside were later to claim required the services of aid organizations, private foundations, and multinational corporations.

By the next rainy season, enthusiastic administrators from the Department of Agriculture had taken over the program from the University. More than 400 senior students from nine different schools lived and worked with farmers in more than 200 villages, amounting to 27,000 acres of paddy land. Despite difficulties in supplying some villages on time and some decrease in talent and enthusiasm due to the program's rapid expansion, another kind of success was achieved.

Students won the confidence of farmers as the government had never done. The potential of their actions showed itself in one village where local officials had stolen fertilizer intended for the project. The students responded by sending a well-documented letter to the officials threatening that if the fertilizer was not made available to the farmers, copies of the letter would find their way to even higher officials. The fertilizer came.

As the program expanded, it did not just involve greater numbers of students and farmers and larger amounts of land. Peasant leagues and radical political movements were growing in east and central Java, and the new program to increase rice production became entangled in the web of Indonesian politics. What the students at Indonesia's top agricultural college were discovering in their first few seasons with the farmers, Indonesia's Communist party had begun to learn and teach years earlier.

In 1953 the party had called for its workers to live in the villages and study the social and economic conditions there, working at the same time to win the confidence of smallholders and farm laborers. The program's slogan was "three togethers": eat together, live together, work together; and organize to help small farmers and farm laborers overcome their fear of action. By these methods the party hoped to surmount what it considered the major obstacle to Indonesia's economic development—social and political control by a powerful ruling group.

At the same time the party was giving the farmers technological advice. In addition to attacking the powerful bureaucracy as "feudal remnants" and "imperialist forces," radical leaders urged farmers to adopt the "five principles": plow deeply, plant closely, use more fertilizer, improve seedlings, and improve irrigation.

The Communist party and student activists came to regard technology and strong political organizations for the poor as joint necessities in any attempt to bring about a more efficient use of resources on Java, both natural and human. Unlike most

Western theorists, they rejected a simplified view of technology alone as the means to greater food production.

Javanese politics gave them precious little time, however, to test their theory. In September, 1965, as 1,200 students were starting the program for the rainy season, the long-smoldering struggle between landowner and landless, between Moslem storekeeper—religious official and Javanese Buddhist-Hindu farmer, between the Indonesian army and the Communist party, finally broke out into the open and ripped apart the fragile coalition that Indonesia's first president, Dr. Sukarno, had vainly tried to patch together. The army won.

During much of the rainy season of 1965-66 Indonesian society was embroiled in a protracted slaughter of known or suspected Communists. On Java alone, between 200,000 and one million persons were killed and radical peasant and workers' organizations destroyed. Little was done that year to increase the production of food.

By the dry season of 1966, the slaughter had come to an end in most areas. Despite the enormous social dislocations, the government expanded the area planted in rice from 27,000 to 415,000 acres, and this occurred in the first dry season that had ever been made a target of the rice production increase idea.

Dry season planting, however, was not the only innovation. At the invitation of the new military regime, American and West European advisors, most of whom had been thrown out of the country in 1963-64, now returned in large numbers to help put together a new development effort in Indonesia. In June, 1967, the government contracted with CIBA (Chemical Industries of Basel, Switzerland) to have this giant multinational corporation provide the technical apparatus for an experimental project to increase rice production in a small area in south Sulawesi (Celebes), to the northeast of Java.

Although no evaluation of the project was made, contracting with Western corporations continued at a rapid pace. By the rainy season of 1969-70, the West German companies Hoechst and A.H.T., the Japanese Mitsubishi, and a new, unknown company called Coopa were also offering the new agricultural technology, which for the first time included the miracle seeds from Los Banos. Together these companies provided fertilizer, miracle seeds, pesticides, and management advice for 2,470,000 acres, more than 20 percent of the entire wet-rice land of Indonesia.

Even from the start this massive program ran into difficulties. The new pesticides, untried on Indonesian fields, killed not only the harmful rice stem borer and various grasshoppers, as they were intended to do, but also the fish in the irrigation canals, an important source of protein in the peasant diet. One critic of the program asserted privately that one of the German companies was spraying onto the fields and into the canals the very chemical that had previously killed millions of fish in the Rhine, but the government never investigated this charge. Above and beyond all the stories and complaints, one fact was evident: farmers were not repaying the loans they had been granted.

Complaints continued. Students reported that in many areas the packages of fertilizers, seeds, and pesticides were not arriving. Then the latter part of 1969, just about the middle of the 1969-70 planting season, the nature of Coopa, the mysterious corporation, became clear. Reporters for *Indonesia Raya*, a major muckracking newspaper in Jakarta, discovered a company letter dated in Vaduz, Liechtenstein, on the same day as the day of its arrival in Indonesia. Company officials had claimed registration was in Italy, but this was only part of the problem for, as the paper reasoned, "even the most modern airplane in the world cannot carry a letter from Liechtenstein to Indonesia in less than one day." When further evidence came in, the only question remaining was which generals secretly owned the company? At a cost of more than 150 million rupiahs (equal to $400,000 at the time), Coopa failed to deliver the technology for which it had contracted, and when evidence began to link the company's operations with members of President Suharto's personal staff, the President announced that the entire affair would be handled out of court. The development planners' idyllic rate of profit seemed to have become highly elusive.

Scandal ridden as it was, the total program of multinational corporation agriculture rolled on into the dry season of 1970 before the real reaction came. Continuing reports of unsatisfactory harvests were added to stories of inefficiency and corruption. Even in the best agricultural area, harvests had fallen off from 2 1/2 tons per acre in 1965 to 2 tons per acre in 1968-69; in many regions crops were almost entirely lost because pesticides and fertilizers never arrived. Some government offices reported harvests of as little as from 220 to 882 pounds per acre, and a major famine occurred on the north coast of Java involving 100,000 persons.

Various international lending institutions, including foreign embassies, commissioned private studies of the program, and all agreed that no matter how perfect it looked on paper, something was not working. That that "something" was intimately related to the destruction of peasant and student political power and the rise of a bureaucratic military state was apparently outside the realm of development theory. The example of the students who once forced the government to deliver fertilizer was lost in the midst of theories that saw political action from below as insignificant, perhaps even threatening, in comparison to the power of technology.

Since the program was failing, something new had to be tried. By the rainy season of 1970-71, American and Indonesian planners launched a new program, incorporating many features of the pre-1965 experiments. First, interest rates on farmer loans were reduced from 3 to 1 percent. Secondly, the program was not packaged: a farmer could choose his own fertilizer and pesticide dosages without endangering his chance of getting seeds or a preharvest cost-of-living loan. Aerial spraying of pesticides, a major source of farmer opposition to the foreign companies' program, was discontinued altogether. Finally, to insure that the rate of profit would not be disturbed by price instability, the United States provided surplus rice that could be alternately injected into, or withdrawn from, regional markets. Farmers, it was hoped, would finally begin to see a profit from their harvests. The new plan, however, was doomed to failure by factors at the village level.

Like the national society of which they are a part, Javanese villages are highly stratified, with access to production resources distributed most unequally among different groups. A village along the north coastal plain of central Java illustrates this problem well. Excellent soil, good irrigation, nearby transportation, milling facilities, markets, and a long history of farmer acquaintance with new technology through their experience with the sugar factories should have made this a perfect place for a Green Revolution success story. Most farmers, however, cultivate plots of less than one acre, too small to support their families. They are forced, therefore, to supplement their farming with outside jobs. Since not enough jobs are available, many of the farming households ought to go bankrupt, but they do not. In the village a group of large landowners, government officers, and town employees command capital for the small farmers. The capital takes the form of loans against the future labor of poor farmers, a form of debt-bondage in which the farmers must give up their option for outside jobs and be permanently on call to their patrons.

The mechanism is simple. During the pre-harvest period, small-holder families may run out of cash or food. If unable to find work outside the village agricultural economy, they are forced to attach themselves to a wealthy family by asking for a loan. Since they have nothing to offer in repayment—their next harvest will be no more effective in bringing them even a minimum of subsistence (much less a surplus) than was the last—they become permanently indebted, accepting a 30 to 50 percent cut under the market wage for farm labor arrangements outside the village.

In such a situation, miracle seeds might seem highly beneficial. In addition to improving everyone's production of food, raising the standard of living, releasing the central government from its dependence on food imports, and lowering food prices, the productivity increases of from 50 to 100 percent on local farming plots of smallholders might eventually offer them the opportunity to reassert their independence from the lenders. That, however, is just the problem.

The wealthier families have clearly perceived the danger of too much technical progress of this sort, and during the rainy season of 1970-71 and the dry season of 1971, they used various means of preventing the smallholders from gaining access to the loans or to the technology. In some cases meetings to publicize government loans were never called, but notice of bank loans was passed along lines of kinship and neighborhood, thus kept within the circles of the village elite. In some cases subtle hints were delivered to small farmers; not much is needed to convince a family on the brink of starvation that they are better off with the security of the wealthy patron than striking out on their own even if the chances of success seem to be high. Failure to a family farm is not quite like bankruptcy for a modern business; there are no courts to handle starvation proceedings.

By the end of the dry season in September, 1971, the new technology was being utilized only on about 40 percent of the available paddy land, representing only 20 percent of the 151 households in the village. Poor families were totally absent from the list of participants. For them the promise of economic development meant only an increase in the wealth and lending potential of their patrons, and an opportunity for more of their class compatriots to fall into permanent debt and servitude.

In other parts of Java, the relationship between the social classes has deteriorated beyond the increased debt-labor bondage. In South-central Java, wealthy households are using the increased productivity of their fields to actually buy up paddy land from poorer families, driving the latter into the already jobless urban areas. In west Java, a region where landholding differences are even more extreme, some wealthy farmers have even begun buying Japanese-made rice-field tractors and home milling facilities, thus pushing an even greater number of landless and smallholding households out of the remnants of the rural labor market. The very possibility of technological success is creating a human disaster. For the poor, the Green Revolution in Java offers only the choice between servitude and homelessness.

What will the development theorists say about all this? Their answer lies in their actions: the programs continue as before with no substantial changes. The technology advocates, the rate-of-profit theorists, the military dictators, and the large landowners are attempting to produce enough food for the people of Java. They are failing. Their optimistic plans and programs have created only increased human suffering and promise more of the same. Perhaps solutions will come, not from the development experts, but from the small farmers and landless laborers of Java.

40

Latin American Farming:
The Peasants' Lot Is Not a Happy One

An Anonymous Author

As this article from *The Economist* indicates, land reform, i.e., redistribution of land resources, is not sufficient to ensure a productive food production system. Land reform is important (indeed, it is a prerequisite to most agrarian reform programs), yet access to credit, fertilizer, irrigation and agricultural training programs is also necessary. The government must be supportive of its peasantry—a tall order for many of the countries in Latin America.

Mexico is one of the richest countries in Latin America. its agrarian reform programme dates back to the peasant revolution of 1912. Fifty years later scientists at the International Maize and Wheat Improvement Centre in Mexico helped to invent the "green revolution" which led to the doubling and trebling of grain yields. But the Mexican peasant has very little to show for it.

About 3m rural families in Mexico cannot grow enough food to meet their daily needs. Some earn as little as $100 a year. True 80m hectares of land have been redistributed under the land reform programme, but owning a small, unproductive plot without access to credit, fertilizer and irrigation is next to useless.

Since 1973, the government has invested $1.4 billion to help the rural poor. The International Fund for Agricultural Development (Ifad) an aid agency with a mandate to lend to poor farmers, has chipped in with $17.5m—small change in comparison, but its largest loan in the region. Although the government's spending on poor farmers has now reached $350m a year, production of staple foods is falling. In the second half of 1982, agricultural imports rose by over 30% while agricultural exports fell—an experience common to oil producers in other areas. Mexico is now a net importer of beans, its national dish.

The peasant's lot is worse in central and South America's half-dozen poorest countries—Haiti, Honduras, Bolivia, Nicaragua, El Salvador and Peru. Half of their total population of 40m works in the countryside. Haiti is the most rural, with 74% of its labour force in agriculture. Most of the cultivated land is so steep, the cruel story runs, that Haitian farmers commit suicide by falling off their fields. Soil erosion is widespread, water scarce.

Reprinted with permission from *The Economist*: 67-68 (9 January 1982).

Haiti has no cash of its own to invest in agriculture. Foreign aid to its farming is now worth $20m a year, or about $5 a head for its people on farms. But foreign aid programmes become tangled in Haiti's government. Typical of this are problems with a joint $7m loan from Ifad and the Inter-American Development Bank, aptly named the Cul-de-Sac project. The objective was to increase food production and incomes for some 3,700 families. Personality conflicts, inflation, and high wage costs have delayed the scheme. Canada has cancelled a $3m grant for another programme intended to benefit 36,000 families, because of blunders and delays by local officials.

Although it has 63% of its workforce in agriculture, Honduras grows less food per head than any other country in Latin America. Agrarian reform in 1974 made way for land distribution and the encouragement of co-operatives. Until recently, the ministry of agriculture was run by the Liberal party while the institute responsible for implementing reforms was in the hands of the Nationalists. Their rivalry brought government investment in agriculture to a halt.

The government of Honduras has encouraged poor farmers and rural migrants from the shanty towns to settle in the Aguan valley on the Atlantic coast. The area produces pine oil, grapefruit, maize and cattle and includes a banana plantation abandoned by the Standard Fruit Company (a subsidiary of America's Castle & Cooke multinational) and now run by a co-operative. The valley could be one of the richest tropical agricultural zones in central America. But hospitals and schools stand empty or half-finished for lack of money. The construction of dykes and drainage canals is behind schedule. Heavy rains wash away roads and ruin crops. The United Nations and the World Bank are paying for costly research into ways of preventing the flooding, but nobody knows if there will be any money available to do anything about it. The peasants sink deeper into debt.

Since the withdrawal of the Standard Fruit Company from the valley, production has fallen by nearly a third. Standard Fruit still buys bananas from the co-operative, and saves on labour costs. Many plantation workers now earn less than 50% of their old "colonial" wage. Co-operatives in Honduras with fertile land are becoming greedy, restricting their membership and hiring casual labour to push up profits. Successful co-operatives in Mexico, Bolivia and Peru are doing the same.

"Radical" reform of agrarian laws is no guarantee of progress. After 1969, Peru's military government tried to shift political power to the landless and peasant farmers. One third of all privately owned land changed hands, but training, research and investment were inadequate. During the 1970s, Peru had the worst record of agricultural non-improvement in Latin America. The civilian government has allowed the sale of inefficient co-operatives since 1980, has given tax concessions to agri-businesses and allowed land to be used as a guarantee for bank loans.

The new policies still do not seem to be working. Banks do not want to invest in agriculture, except in the grandiose national plan for the development of jungle areas. And the almost total paralysis of the bureaucracy undermines any attempt at change. The World Bank has made an $80m loan dependent on whether the ministry of agriculture draws up a sensible list of priorities.

Neighbouring Bolivia has similar problems. Bolivia overhauled its land tenure 30 years ago, when the government created a ministry of peasant affairs. Today the mainly Indian peasantry has the lowest calorie intake and life expectancy in Latin America. An Ifad-World Bank loan of $9.3m to give credit to 95,000 Indians has made little impact. Since the loan agreement was signed in 1979, there have been four different governments and four project directors. Bolivia is short of the money it needs to pay for local costs, and inflation is eating away at the value of the loan.

Bolivia would be healthier, though poorer, if it grew more food instead of cocaine. The cocaine trade is worth between $800m-1.2 billion a year and involves some

70,000 small farmers. No other crop earns so much per hectare. Harvesting of legitimate cash crops suffers as cocaine farmers entice away seasonal labour with pay of up to $40 for a night's work.

Since the overthrow of Nicaragua's Somozas, a family who dominated the country's politics for four decades, the Sandinist government has pursued rapid agrarian reform. The Somoza family's own farms, amounting to 23% of all agricultural land, now belong to the state, 62% of land is still in private hands and 15% is farmed by co-operatives and poor peasants. Such sudden land reform often brings tears. Time will tell. The Sandinists took over an economy geared to production of export crops. While they still support the export sector for its foreign exchange earnings, there is more emphasis put on producing food for Nicaraguans.

Immediately after the revolution in 1978-79, agriculture was in a mess. Total farm output was about 37% down, some export crops like coffee as much as 80% lower than before the revolution.

According to the national institute of agrarian reform, the production of basic foods such as maize, beans, rice and sorghum is now 20-25% higher than under General Anastasio Somoza. This has been achieved by labour intensive farming. Productivity per person has fallen, but this is accepted as a necessary consequence of depending more on peasant farmers.

Still, there is some concern among aid donors that they may be rewarding peasants for supporting the revolution by handing out development capital in cash. Up to 40% of $70m in credits to the new government for agricultural development from Ifad and the Inter-American Development Bank and other donors has been made available in cash.

Many peasants have used part of the money as income, not as capital to improve their farms. Some aid donors worry that the Nicaraguan experiment may go the way of other agrarian reform programmes, like Peru's. Other development agencies, however, are privately delighted that they have at last found a government in the region which shares their preference for backing the peasants.

41

The Other Energy Crisis: Firewood
(excerpts from *Losing Ground: Environmental Stress and World Food Prospects*)
Erik P. Eckholm

Erik Eckholm warns that the development process will be impeded unless attention is given to deforestation and concomitant erosion problems in developing countries. Lack of access to firewood is reaching crisis proportions in developing countries. As a result, the productivity of the land is being undermined (the problem as it exists in the United States was discussed in Chapter 24). Reforestation projects are discussed as a possible solution to the firewood shortage. However, just as we have seen with nutrition intervention and agricultural development projects, they need to be implemented using local community involvement and democratic decision making.

Dwindling reserves of petroleum and artful tampering with its distribution are the stuff of which headlines are made. Yet for more than a third of the world's people, the real energy crisis is a daily scramble to find the wood they need to cook dinner. Their search for wood, once a simple chore and now, as forests recede, a day's labor in some places, has been strangely neglected by diplomats, economists, and the media. But the firewood crisis will be making news—one way or another—for the rest of the century.

While chemists devise ever more sophisticated uses for wood, including cellophane and rayon, at least half of all the timber cut in the world still serves in its original role for humans—as fuel for cooking and, in colder mountain regions, home heating. Nine-tenths of the people in most poor countries today depend on firewood as their chief source of fuel. And all too often, the growth in human population is outpacing the growth of new trees—not surprising when the average user burns as much as a ton of firewood a year.[1] The results are soaring wood prices, a growing drain on incomes and physical energies in order to satisfy basic fuel needs, a costly diversion of animal manures from food production uses to cooking, and an ecologically disastrous spread of treeless landscapes.

Reprinted with permission from Worldwatch Paper #1, from *Losing Ground: Environmental Stress and World Food Prospects*; by Erik Eckholm. Copyright (c) 1975 by the Worldwatch Institute.

The firewood crisis is probably most acute today in the countries of the densely populated Indian subcontinent and in the semi-arid stretches of central Africa fringing the Sahara Desert, though it plagues many other regions as well. In Latin America, for example, the scarcity of wood and charcoal is a problem throughout most of the Andean region, Central America, and the Caribbean. . . .

The costs of firewood and charcoal are climbing throughout most of Asia, Africa, and Latin America. Those who can, pay the price, and thus must forego consumption of other essential goods. Wood is simply accepted as one of the major expenses of living. In Niamey, Niger, deep in the drought-plagued Sahel in West Africa, the average manual laborer's family now spends nearly one-fourth of its income on firewood. In Ouagadougou, Upper Volta, the portion is 20 to 30 percent.[2] Those who can't pay so much may send their children, or hike out in the surrounding countryside themselves, to forage—if enough trees are within a reasonable walking distance. Otherwise, they may scrounge about the town for twigs, garbage, or anything burnable. In many regions, firewood scarcity places a special burden on women, who are generally saddled with the tasks of hiking or rummaging for fuel. . . .

It is not in the cities but in rural villages that most people in the affected countries live, and where most firewood is burned. The rural, landless poor in parts of India and Pakistan are now feeling a new squeeze on their meager incomes. Until now they have generally been able to gather free wood from the trees scattered through farmlands, but as wood prices in the towns rise, landlords naturally see an advantage in carting available timber into the nearest town to sell rather than allowing the nearby laborers to glean it for nothing. This commercialization of firewood raises the hope that entrepreneurs will see an advantage in planting trees to develop a sustainable, labor-intensive business, but so far a depletion of woodlands has been the more common result. And the rural poor, with little or no cash to spare, are in deep trouble in either case. . . .

Trees are becoming scarce in the most unlikely places. In some of the most remote villages in the world, deep in the once heavily forested Himalayan foothills of Nepal, journeying out to gather firewood and fodder is now an entire day's task. Just one generation ago the same expedition required no more than an hour or two.[3]

Because those directly suffering its consequences are mostly illiterate, and because wood shortages lack the photogenic visibility of famine, the firewood crisis has not provoked much world attention. And, in a way, there is little point in calling this a world problem, for fuel-wood scarcity, unlike oil scarcity, is always localized in its apparent dimensions. Economics seldom permit fuel wood to be carried or trucked more than a few hundred miles from where it grows, let alone the many thousands of miles traversed by the modern barrel of oil. To say that firewood is scarce in Mali or Nepal is of no immediate consequence to the boy scout building a campfire in Pennsylvania, whereas his parents have already learned that decisions in Saudi Arabia can keep the family car in the garage.

Unfortunately, however, the consequences of firewood scarcity are seldom limited to the economic burden placed on the poor of a particular locality, harsh as that is in itself. The accelerating degradation of woodlands throughout Africa, Asia, and Latin America, caused in part by fuel gathering, lies at the heart of the profound challenges to environmental stability and land productivity reviewed in this book— accelerated soil erosion, increasingly severe flooding, creeping deserts, and declining soil fertility. . . .

In the Indian subcontinent, the most pernicious result of firewood scarcity is probably not the destruction of tree cover itself, but the alternative to which a good share of the people in India, Pakistan, and Bangladesh have been forced. A visitor to almost any village in the subcontinent is greeted by omnipresent pyramids of hand-molded dung patties drying in the sun. In many areas these dung cakes have been the only source of fuel for generations, but now, by necessity, their use is spreading further. Between three hundred and four hundred million tons of wet dung—which shrink to sixty to eighty million tons when dried—are annually burned for fuel in India alone, robbing farmland of badly needed nutrients and organic matter. The plant nutrients wasted annually in this fashion in India equal more than a third of the country's chemical fertilizer use. Looking only at this direct economic cost, it is easy to see why the country's National Commission on Agriculture recently declared that "the use of cow dung as a source of non-commercial fuel is virtually a crime." Dung is also burned for fuel in parts of the Sahelian zone in Africa, Ethiopia, Iraq, and in the nearly treeless Andean valleys and slopes of Bolivia and Peru, where the dung of llamas has been the chief fuel in some areas since the days of the Incas.[4]

Even more important than the loss of agricultural nutrients is the damage done to soil structure and quality through the failure to return manures to the fields. Organic materials—humus and soil organisms which live in it—play an essential role in preserving the soil structure and fertility needed for productive farming. Organic matter helps hold the soil in place when rain falls and wind blows, and reduces the wasteful, polluting runoff of chemical nutrients where they are applied. Humus helps the soil absorb and store water, thus mitigating somewhat the impact on crops of drought periods. These considerations apply especially to the soils in tropical regions where most dung is now burned, because tropical topsoils are usually thin and, once exposed to the burning sun and torrential monsoon rains, are exceptionally prone to erosion and to loss of their structure and fertility.

Peasants in the uplands of South Korea have adopted a different, but also destructive way to cope with the timber shortage. A United Nations forestry team visiting the country in the late 1960s found not only that live tree branches, shrubs, seedlings, and grasses were cut for fuel; worse, many hillsides were raked clean of all leaves, litter, and burnable materials. Raking in this fashion, to meet needs for home fuel and farm compost, robs the soil of both a protective cover and organic matter, and the practice was cited by the UN experts as "one of the principal causes of soil erosion in Korea." Firewood scarcity similarly impairs productivity in eastern Nigeria, where the Tiv people have been forced to uproot crop residues after the harvest for use as fuel. Traditionally, the dead stalks and leaves have been left to enrich the soil and hold down erosion.[5]

The increasing time required to gather firewood in many mountain villages of Nepal is leading to what the kingdom's agricultural officials fear most of all. For once procuring wood takes too long to be worth the trouble, some farmers start to use cow dung, which was formerly applied with great care to the fields, as cooking fuel. As this departure from tradition spreads, the fertility of the hills, already declining due to soil erosion, will fall sharply. In the more inaccessible spots, there is no economic possibility whatsoever of replacing the manure with chemical fertilizers.

And so the circle starts to close in Nepal, a circle long completed in parts of India. As wood scarcity forces farmers to burn more dung for fuel, and to apply less to their fields, falling food output will necessitate the clearing of ever larger, ever steeper tracts of forest—intensifying the erosion and landslide hazards in the hills, and the siltation and flooding problems downstream in India and Bangladesh.

Firewood scarcity, then, is intimately linked in two ways to the food problem facing many countries. Deforestation and the diversion of manures to use as fuel are sabotaging the land's ability to produce food. Meanwhile, as an Indian official put it, "Even if we somehow grow enough food for our people in the year 2000, how in the world will they cook it?" . . .

The firewood crisis is in some ways more, and in others less, intractable than the energy crisis of the industrialized world. Resource scarcity can usually be attacked from either end, through the contraction of demand or the expansion of supply. The world contraction in demand for oil in 1974 and early 1975, for example, helped to ease temporarily the conditions of shortage.

But the firewood needs of the developing countries cannot be massively reduced in this fashion. The energy system of the truly poor contains no easily trimmable fat such as that presented by four- to five-thousand-pound private automobiles. Furthermore, a global recession does little to dampen the demand for firewood as it temporarily does in the case of oil. . . . Fortunately trees, unlike oil, are a renewable resource when properly managed. The logical immediate response to the firewood shortage, one that will have many incidental ecological benefits, is to plant more trees in plantations, on farms, along roads, in shelter belts, and on unused land throughout the rural areas of the poor countries. For many regions, fast-growing tree varieties are available that can be culled for firewood inside of a decade.

The concept is simple, but its implementation is not. Governments in nearly all the wood-short countries have had tree-planting programs for some time—for several decades in some cases. National forestry departments in particular have often been aware of the need to boost the supply of wood products and the need to preserve forests for an habitable environment. But several problems have [generally plagued tree-planting programs].

One is the sheer magnitude of the need for wood and the scale of the growth in demand. Population growth, which surprised many with its acceleration in the post-war era, has swallowed the moderate tree-planting efforts of many countries, rendering their impact almost negligible. Wood-producing programs will have to be undertaken on a far greater scale than most governments presently conceive if a significant dent is to be made in the problem.

The problem of scale is closely linked to a second major obstacle to meeting this crisis: the perennial question of political priorities and decision-making time-frames. With elections to win, wars to fight, dams to build, and hungry people to feed, it is hard for any politician to concentrate funds and attention on a problem so multi-dimensional and seemingly long-term in nature. Some ecologists in the poor countries have been warning their governments for decades about the dangers of deforestation and fuel shortages, but tree-planting programs don't win elections. . . .

Even with the right kind of political will and the necessary allocation of funds, implementing a large-scale reforestation campaign is a complex and difficult process. Planting millions of trees and successfully nurturing them to maturity is not a technical, clearly defined task like building a dam or a chemical-fertilizer plant. Tree-planting projects almost always become deeply enmeshed in the political, cultural, and administrative tangles of a rural locality; they touch upon, and are influenced by, the daily living habits of many people, and they frequently end in failure.

Most of the regions with too few trees also have too many cattle, sheep, and goats. Where rangelands are badly overgrazed, the leaves of a young sapling tempt the appetites of foraging animals. Even if he keeps careful control of his own livestock, a herdsman may reason that if his animals don't eat the leaves, someone else's will. . . .

In country after country, the same lesson has been learned: tree-planting programs are most successful when a majority of the local community is deeply involved in planning and implementation, and clearly perceives its self-interest in success. Central or state governments can provide stimulus, technical advice, and financial assistance, but unless community members clearly understand why lands to which they have traditionally had free access for grazing and wood gathering are being demarcated into a plantation, they are apt to view the project with suspicion or even hostility. With wider community participation, on the other hand, the control of grazing patterns can be built into the program from the beginning, and a motivated community will protect its own project and provide labor at little or no cost. . . .

Whatever the success of reforestation projects, however, the wider substitution of other energy sources for wood can also contribute greatly to a solution of the firewood problem. A shift from wood-burning stoves to those running on natural gas, coal, or electricity has indeed been the dominant global trend in the last century and a half. As recently as 1850, wood met 91 percent of the fuel needs of the United States, but today in the economically advanced countries, scarcely any but the intentionally rustic, and scattered poor in the mountains, chop wood by necessity anymore. In the poor countries, too, the proportion of wood users is falling gradually, especially in the cities, which are usually partly electrified, and where residents with any income at all may cook their food with bottle gas or kerosene. Someone extrapolating trends of the first seven decades of this century might well have expected the continued spread of kerosene and natural gas use at a fairly brisk pace in the cities and into rural areas, eventually rendering firewood nearly obsolete.

Events in the last two years, of course, have abruptly altered energy-use trends and prospects everywhere. The most widely overlooked impact of the fivefold increase in oil prices, an impact drowned out by the economic distress caused for oil-importing countries, is the fact that what had been the most feasible substitute for firewood, kerosene, has now been pulled even farther out of reach of the world's poor than it already was. The hopes of foresters and ecologists for a rapid reduction of pressures on receding woodlands through a stepped-up shift to kerosene withered overnight in December, 1973, when OPEC announced its new oil prices. In fact, the dwindling of world petroleum reserves and the depletion of woodlands reinforce each other; climbing firewood prices encourage more people to use petroleum-based products for fuel, while soaring oil prices make this shift less feasible, adding to the pressure on forests. . . .

Fossil fuels are not the only alternate energy source under consideration, and, over the coming decades, many of those using firewood, like everyone else, will have to turn in other directions. Energy sources that are renewable, decentralized, and low in cost must be developed. Nothing, for example, would be better than a dirt-cheap device for cooking dinner in the evening with solar energy collected earlier in the day. But actually developing such a stove and introducing it to hundreds of millions of the world's most tradition-bound and penniless families is another story. While some solar cookers are already available, the cost of a family unit, at about thirty-five to fifty dollars, is prohibitive for many, since, in the absence of suitable credit arrangements, the entire amount must be available at once. Mass production could pull down the price, but the problem of inexpensively storing heat for cloudy days and evenings has not been solved.[6] The day may come in some countries when changes in cooking and eating habits to allow maximum use of solar cookers will be forced upon populations by the absence of alternatives.

Indian scientists have pioneered for decades with an ideal-sounding device that breaks down manures and other organic wastes into methane gas for cooking and a rich compost for the farm. Over eight thousand of these bio-gas plants, as they are called, are now being used in India. Without a substantial reduction in cost, however, they will only slowly infiltrate the hundreds of thousands of rural villages, where the fuel problem is growing. Additionally, as the plants are adopted, those too poor to own cattle could be left worse off than ever, denied traditional access to dung, but unable to afford bio-gas.[7] Still, relatively simple and decentralized devices like solar cookers and bio-gas plants will likely provide the fuel sources of the future in the poor countries. . . .

Firewood scarcity and its attendant ecological hazards have brought the attitude of people toward trees into sharp focus. In his essay "Buddhist Economics," E.F. Schumacher praises the practical as well as esoteric wisdom in the Buddha's teaching that his followers should plant and nurse a tree every few years.[8] Unfortunately, this ethical heritage has been largely lost, even in the predominantly Buddhist societies of Southeast Asia. In fact, most societies today lack a spirit of environmental cooperation—not a spirit of conservation for its own sake, but one needed to guarantee human survival amid ecological systems heading toward collapse.

This will have to change, and fast. The inexorable growth in the demand for firewood calls for tree-planting efforts on a scale more massive than most bureaucrats have ever even contemplated, much less planned for. The suicidal deforestation of Africa, Asia, and Latin America must somehow be slowed and reversed. Deteriorating ecological systems have a logic of their own; the damage often builds quietly and unseen for many years, until one day the system falls asunder with lethal vengeance. Ask anyone who lived in Oklahoma in 1934, or Chad in 1975.

Notes

1. Keith Openshaw, "Wood Fuels the Developing World," New Scientist, Vol. 61, No. 883 (January 31, 1974). See also Food and Agriculture Organization, Wood: World Trends and Prospects, Basic Study No. 16 (Rome: 1967) for a brief overview of world fuel wood trends.

2. J.C. Delwalle, "Disertification de l'Afrique au Sud du Sahara," Bois et Forets des Tropiques, No. 149 (Mai-Juin, 1973), p. 14; and Victor D. DuBois, The Drought in West Africa, American Universities Field Staff, West African Series, Vol. XV, No. 1 (1974).

3. See, for example, Lila M. and Barry C. Bishop, "Karnali, Roadless World of Western Nepal," National Geographic, Vol. 140, No.5 (November, 1971), p. 671.

4. Government of India, Ministry of Agriculture, op.cit.; S K. Adeyoju; and E.N. Enabor, A survey of Drought Affected Areas of Northern Nigeria (University of Ibadan, Dept. of Forestry, November, 1973), p. 48; U.S. Dept. of the Interior, Bureau of Reclamation, Land and Water Resources of the Blue Nile Basin, Ethiopia, Appendix VI, Agriculture and Economics (Washington D.C.: 1964), p. 12; Leslie H. Brown, Conservation for Survival: Ethiopia's Choice (Haile Selassie I University, 1973), pp. 63, 64; FAO/UNDP, Forestry Research, Administration, and Training, Arbil, Iraq, Technical Report 1, "A Forest Improvement Programme," FAO/UNDP, IRQ-18 TR, IRQ/68/518 (Rome: Food and Agriculture Organization, 1973); Republica del Peru, Oficina Nacional de Evaluacion de Recursos Naturales, and Organizacion de los Estados Americanos, Lineamientos de Politica de Conservacion de los Recursos Naturales del Peru (Lima: May, 1974), p. 18; and J. Alden Mason, The Ancient Civilizations of Peru (Harmondsworth: Penguin, 1957), p. 137.

5. FAO/UNDP, Agricultural Survey and Demonstration in Selected Watersheds, Republic of Korea, Vol. 1, General Report, FAO/SF: 47/KOR7 (Rome: Food and Agriculture Organization, 1969), p. 17; and Donald E. Vermeer, "Population Pressure and Crop Rotational Changes among the Tiv of Nigeria," Annals of the Association of American Geographers, Vol. 60, No.2 (June, 1970), p.311.

6. See "Potentials for Solar Energy in the Sahel," interview with A. Moumoumi, Interaction (Washington, D.C.), Vol. III, No.10, (July 1975); National Academy of Sciences, Office of the Foreign Secretary, Solar Energy in Developing Countries: Perspectives and Prospects (Washington, D.C.: March, 1972); Farrington Daniels, Direct Use of the Sun's Energy (New York: Ballantine, 1974; reprint of 1964 edition); Dennis Hayes, "Solar Power in the Middle East," Science Vol. 188, No. 4195 (June 27, 1975), p. 1261.

7. C.R. Prasad, K. Krishna Prasad, and A.K.N. Reddy, "Bio-Gas Plants: Prospects, Problems and Tasks," Economic and Political Weekly (New Delhi), Vol. IX, Nos. 32-34 (special issue, August 1974); and Arjun Makhijani with Alan Poole, Energy and Agriculture in the Third World. (Cambridge, Mass: Ballinger, 1975), esp. ch. 4.

8. E.F. Schumacher, "Buddhist Economics," in *Small is Beautiful: Economics as if People Mattered* (New York: Harper & Row, 1973).

Additional Sources

"Beating a Drought, Organically." *Organic Gardening and Farming*, January, 1975.

Dhua, S.P. "Need for Organo-Mineral Fertilizer in Tropical Agriculture." *Ecologist*, Vol. 5, No.5 (June 1975).

Eckholm, Erik P. *The Other Energy Crisis: Firewood.* Worldwatch Paper No.1. Washington, D.C.: Worldwatch Institute, September, 1975.

———. "The Firewood Crisis." *Natural History*, Vol. 84 No.8 (October, 1975).

FAO. *Fuelwood Plantations in India.* Occasional Paper No.5. Rome: December, 1958.

———. *Organic Materials as Fertilizers.* Report of the FAO/SIDA. Expert Consultation, Rome, December 2-6, 1974; Soils Bulletin 27. Rome: 1975.

Carg, A.C.; Idnani, M.A.; and Abraham, T.P. *Organic Manures.* Technical Bulletin No.32. New Delhi: Indian Council of Agricultural Research, 1971.

Horvath, Ronald J. "Addis Ababa's Eucalyptus Forest." *Journal of Ethiopian Studies*, Vol. VI, No.1 (January, 1968).

Lamoureux, C.H. "Observations on Conservation in Indonesia." In Kuswata Kartawinata and Rubini Atmawidjaja, eds., *Papers from a Symposium on Coordinated Study of Lowland Forests of Indonesia.* Darmaga, Bogor, July 2-5, 1973. Sponsored by SEAMEO Regional Center for Tropical Biology and Bogor Agricultural University. Bogor, Indonesia; 1974.

Sagrhiya, K.P. "The Energy Crisis and Forestry." *Indian Forests*, Vol. 100, No. 9 (September, 1974).

Swaminathan, M.S. "Organic manures and Integrated Approaches to Plant Nutrition." Presented to Consultative Group in International Agricultural Research, Technical Advisory Committee, Eighth Meeting. Washington, D.C., July 24-August 2, 1974.

Thulin, S. "Wood Requirements in the Savanna Region of Nigeria." Savanna Forestry Research Station, Nigeria, Tech. Rep. 1. Rome: FAO, 1970.

"World of Forestry." *Unasylva*, Vol. 26, No. 105 (Summer, 1974).

42

The Sahel's Uncertain Future
Howard Schissel

In one sense, the reasons for the development problems facing the Sahel region of Africa are unique—the Sahel occupies a very fragile ecological zone characterized by frequent periods of extended drought (see "Sahelian Drought: No Victory for Western Aid" by Nicholas Wade in *Science* 185: 234-237 [19 July 1974] for an extended discussion of how misguided development efforts have exacerbated the problems caused by drought). Yet on almost every other count, the problems in the Sahel are typical of developing countries everywhere: colonial legacy, the need of expanding towns for cooking wood and charcoal (thus hastening deforestation), deterioration of terms of trade and increasing foreign debt, emphasis on cash crops in agricultural production, agricultural policies to keep domestic crop prices as low as possible, inefficient bureaucracies and unstable governments with military regimes.

Two solutions have been offered to solve the Sahel's seemingly myriad problems: development projects and food aid. Unfortunately, the development projects are sometimes misguided and may have disastrous consequences on local economies. Likewise, food aid is often counterproductive, reducing the incentive for local production. And yet, famine persists and aid is needed. During the 1968-1973 drought and famine, foreign assistance was essential for human survival. Now another prolonged drought promises even greater human suffering. One thing is certain—unless "aid" agencies recognize the farmers and herders as the principal resource of the region, chronic underdevelopment will continue.

[For a most comprehensive and detailed account of the experience of famine suffered in sub-Sahara Africa by the Hausa peasantry of Northern Nigeria, see *Silent Violence* by Michael Watts (Berkeley: University of California Press. 1983). Watts discusses not only periods of acute food shortage, but also the chronic crisis of low food and feed production experienced routinely by the peasantry. Watt's arguments are placed in a historical context, focusing on class relations.]

"When I was a student at Boutilimit in 1953," remarked Mogdad Ould Dahane, director of transport at the Mauritanian Commission for Food Security, "we welcomed General de Gaulle at this fort, which was then surrounded by a flourishing forest

Published by permission of Transaction, Inc. from *Africa Report*, Vol. 29, No. 4, copyright (c) 1984 by Transaction, Inc.

and agricultural plots." Just 30 years later, the ecological situation has radically changed for the worse. In early 1984, Boutilimit, the capital of the Trarza region—some 130 miles southeast of the capital, Nouakchott—was a picture of desolation: the old French fort was in ruins, the surrounding area was practically denuded, agricultural activities were restricted to the cultivation of a few watermelons, and wind-blown sand dunes were threatening to engulf the once active trading and religious center.

The extent of environmental degradation, caused in part by the persistent dearth of rainfall in the Sahel region of West Africa, is perhaps nowhere better observed than in the Mauritanian hinterland. In a traditional grazing area like the Trarza region, trees were literally being suffocated by advancing sand dunes and pastureland was virtually dried out. Over the past decade, in fact, almost two-thirds of the rugged acacia trees within 60 miles of the Mauritanian bank of the Senegal River have disappeared; palm groves in oases such as Chinguetti and Ouadane have been abandoned.

The impact of the drought on the population has been severe. With traditional agro-pastoral activities in decline since 1970, there has been a massive influx of destitute herders and uprooted farmers into the towns. Mauritania's demographic makeup has been inverted. Only 25% of the population lived in urban areas in 1970; by this year, the figure had risen to close to 75%.

Because of its geographical position, Mauritania is an extreme case. Yet the negative trends so evident in this country have also made themselves felt, with varying impact, in the other Sahelian states. A decade after the great drought (1968-1973) that ravaged the area and resulted in unprecedented foreign assistance, the Sahel still has not gotten back on its feet. None of the adverse trends identified has been stopped, let alone reversed. It is certainly not an exaggeration to say that time is growing short for the Sahel.

The word *Sahel* is derived from Arabic meaning shore or border; and in West Africa, it applies to the border of the Sahara desert and constitutes the transitional zone to the better-watered areas to the south. Geographically, the Sahel is a 200- to 350-mile-wide belt stretching across West Africa where both nomadic cattle raising and sedentary agriculture are practiced. Although suffering from the vagaries of climate, the Sahel was once the seat of the great medieval empires of Ghana, Mali, and Songhai. Even today, it possesses the resources to offer a decent standard of living for its population.

Eight countries, members of the Ouagadougou-based Interstate Committee for Drought Control in the Sahel (CILSS), are generally considered to constitute the Sahel: Cape Verde, Gambia, Senegal, Mali, Mauritania, Upper Volta, Niger, and Chad. Guinea-Bissau has recently applied for CILSS membership, and the northern parts of Cameroon, Nigeria, Togo, Ghana, Benin, and the Ivory Coast also have a Sahelian climate.

The heart of the Sahel's dilemma lies in the fact that the factors of production in the rural areas have not been improved. In sum, the last two decades have been marked by the trend of extending production of cereals like millet and sorghum, instead of intensifying output. Thus, neither farmers' productivity nor the yield per acre has risen in recent years: average millet and sorghum production remains extremely low. Rainfall or subsistence crops account for some 95% of cereals production in the Sahel. The seed varieties utilized have not been renewed, and only a small percentage of total cereals output is farmed with animal traction and fertilizers. Five percent of cereals are produced with irrigation, but yields are much lower than in other parts of the Third World, and conversely, production costs are higher. Paradoxically, it is less expensive for Senegal or Mali to import rice from Thailand than to produce this crop themselves.

Climatic hazards make the Sahelian production system terribly vulnerable. Where land has become scarce, farmers have reacted by reducing the length of the fallow period, which reconstitutes soil fertility. The need of expanding towns for cooking wood and charcoal has accelerated deforestation in the Sahel. An increase in the herd size and a thoughtless policy of drilling large numbers of boreholes for cattle have also contributed to the degradation of the Sahelian environment. These elements are part and parcel of a cycle that is building up steam and progressively sterilizing a growing portion of the Sahel land mass.

More ominous in the long term is the fact that a fourfold increase in the Sahel's urban population over the last 20 years has coincided with a similar growth in rice and wheat imports. With the projected doubling of urban population by the end of the century, the Sahel is likely to become progressively more dependent on imported cereals, a good share of which will come from food aid. Thus, the rural agricultural zones are not only less and less capable of supplying the towns, but they are even losing their ability to assure mere sustenance for the farmers and their families.

The negative factors affecting livestock raising are similar to those operating in the case of cereal crops. Although herds have been largely reconstituted since the mid-1970s, they have failed to match population growth. Thus, livestock no longer plays the same role in Sahelians' food supply and exports as in the recent past. First, the average person's meat intake has fallen from 37 pounds in 1968 to an estimated 29 in 1977. Second, herd structure has changed. There are fewer cattle and more goats, sheep, and camels. Export markets for this type of livestock in the richer coastal states are limited. Sahelian exports of cattle must now also face stiff competition from frozen meat imported from South America. Urban dwellers require produce that cannot be provided by traditional methods, increasing dependence on imports.

The Sahel, especially Gambia, Senegal, and Mali, was once a major exporter of groundnuts. But the Sahel's output is on the slide. From 1.5 million tons a year in the early 1960s, the region barely produces a million tons a year today. Not only is the volume of groundnut exports declining, but its position on the world market, compared with other sources of edible oil such as maize and soya, has been constantly deteriorating. Some years ago, it could be justified economically for countries like Senegal and Gambia to grow groundnuts and import rice; now, however, the deterioration in the terms of trade makes it of dubious value to specialize in this one crop. Yet only limited efforts have been made to diversify agricultural production.

In contrast to cereals and groundnut farming, the development of cotton cultivation has resulted from a full-scale conversion of farming methods, including the introduction of seed varieties suitable for the Sahel, fertilizers and pesticides, and use of animal-drawn plows. The results have been spectacular—there has been a fivefold growth in yields per acre over the last two decades. This gain demonstrates that Sahelian agriculture can be radically altered for the better. Cotton is a valuable cash crop that has received top priority from governments and development agencies. However, there does not seem to be the same incentive to invest in upgrading cereal farming or traditional livestock raising. Moreover, cotton has tended to grab much of the best land, to the detriment of food crops.

Criticism has increasingly been focused on the agricultural policies of Sahelian, and indeed most African, governments, which since independence have chosen to keep grain prices as low as possible to satisfy non-producing, but potentially troublesome urban populations. All studies underline the insufficiency of profit margins for rural producers, who are therefore not interested in boosting output. The need for more effective food strategies to raise incentives for producers and reduce state control over the cereal market has been recognized.

The revision of Mali's food strategy has been the most comprehensive in the Sahel. When Mali turned to the World Bank in 1980, the solution advanced by its agricultural experts was simple—the grain trade must be liberalized by ending the official monopoly granted to the parastatal authority, OPAM, and by augmenting producer prices to encourage farmers to grow more.

Results were quickly seen. OPAM's market share for grains plummeted from 30% to a mere 5%. It was thought that village cooperatives would take over part of OPAM's role by buying grains from farmers at official prices at harvest time and then reselling the cereals to rural people in the months preceding the new crop season at a price lower than the one prevailing on the free market. Unfortunately, things did not work out as planned. Cooperatives often lack funds to buy up surplus grain, and private traders have reasserted their hegemony over the grain market. For the most part, these traders seek to pay farmers as little as they can for the grain and to resell it in the months preceding the new harvest, when demand is at its peak, at the highest possible price. Thus, the majority of Mali's farmers have not been paid more in real terms since the new government policy was announced; and, of course, they do not have the financial incentive to work harder. The result of this policy, tailored according to suggestions in the World Bank's Berg Report, has been to take the surplus that can be extracted from the rural economy and transfer it from the state bureaucracy to the private sector, without any noticeable benefit to the rural population. Solutions are obviously not as easy as meets the eye, even those of the reputed development experts.

Foreign aid has often been misdirected, either through lack of sufficient study and preparation of projects, or through simple self-serving initiatives by the donors. A good example of the former is the case of the reafforestation efforts to stop the southward march of the desert. On paper the so-called green belts of eucalyptus trees looked attractive, but in the field the experience has turned out to be yet another costly failure. As one forestry expert in the Sahel explains: "[The eucalyptus tree] needs cultivating. It needs water. It needs all the management skills that these people do not have."

Examples of development projects serving the interest of the sponsoring country are legion. One of the prime examples is the Dire solar energy scheme in Mali, financed by France. In 1980, the French Ministry of Cooperation sang the praises of this project, which was designed to pump water from the Niger River to irrigate agricultural land near the town. The solar energy installation cost over $1 million and never succeeded during its functioning life of just one month in pumping more water than two diesel pumps costing $6,000. Today the ruins of this complex are a stark reminder of where misguided development plans lead.

Food aid is certainly necessary to avoid having malnutrition among the Sahelian populations turn into widespread famine, as in 1973-74. If emergency food aid is essential, the same cannot be said of institutionalized aid packages meant more to dispose of agricultural surpluses in the industrialized countries than to encourage an amelioration of the rural economy in the Sahel. Cheap imported cereals depress market prices in the Sahel and consequently eliminate the economic incentives for farmers to produce larger food crops. Paradoxically, it can be said that food aid as it is currently disbursed by most Western donors is counterproductive, discouraging efforts toward food self-sufficiency in the Sahel, as well as in other parts of Africa and the Third World.

The fragility of the Sahelian administrations and economies is such that many are not capable of absorbing new projects, let alone maintaining the old ones. It is estimated that for each new acre of land brought under cultivation in Mali, another one goes out of production for lack of upkeep. In spite of the efforts of the Club du Sahel to coordinate donor efforts, many still tend to pursue their own goals. Sahelian governments, desperately short of skilled personnel, can hardly hope to coordinate the influx of aid schemes and assess their viability. According to a source in Ouagadougou, there were some 340 different aid missions to Upper Volta in 1981. Moreover, new projects generate very heavy recurrent budgetary costs, which the Sahelian countries are largely unable to support, and so projects quickly deteriorate.

Bureaucratic and business interests also condition development planning. After years of delays, the Senegal River Valley Authority (OMVS) has finally begun building the two dams that are intended to harness the river and allow an extension of irrigated farming. Many experts believe that this $1 billion-plus scheme will become the Sahel's "white elephant." For one, it was probably not necessary to build two dams; studies showed that only one upstream in Mali would have been sufficient. But Senegal wanted "its" dam too, and if the two-dam solution had not been adopted, then the OMVS program would not have gotten off the ground. In addition, the OMVS project is capital-intensive, and past experience vividly demonstrates that state agricultural agencies like SAED in Senegal and SONADER in Mauritania are inefficient vehicles for mobilizing rural populations for higher productivity. But a more grass-roots approach had the "disadvantage" of providing fewer blandishments for foreign companies and state functionaries.

The Sahel, like other Third World regions reliant on the production of primary products, has been severely affected by recent trends in the world economy. The region has mineral resources, but falling demand in the industrialized countries and soft prices have played havoc with Sahelian finances. Mauritania's iron ore exports are down to their lowest level in a decade; Niger's uranium mines are in the doldrums; and Senegal's phosphates are having a hard time attracting customers. Upper Volta has been incapable of raising financial support for its proposed manganese mines. The deterioration in the terms of trade for these minerals has been dramatic. If a country needed 100 units of phosphates or iron ore to purchase 100 units of manufactured goods in 1975, 205 units of phosphates and 116 units of iron ore were necessary in 1982.

Since the Sahel consumes more than it produces and the rate of economic growth is too low to finance new investment, its trade balance and balance of payments have gone permanently into the red. These deficits have been financed by disbursements of foreign aid, capital transfers, and recourse to foreign borrowing. The result has been a steep increase in foreign debt. In absolute terms, the Sahelian countries' foreign debt is certainly not a threat to the international financial system, but in relation to their present economic potential, most Sahelian states are more heavily indebted than Mexico or Brazil. Debt service for most Sahelian countries is comparable to the most heavily indebted countries of the Third World.

All these factors combine to make Sahelian political systems terribly brittle. Chad is in a permanent state of instability. Only the Senegalese military intervention saved President Jawara's government in Gambia. Radical young officers took power last year in Upper Volta. President Seyni Kountché had a close call when dissidents attempted to seize power at the end of 1983. President Moussa Traore's regime in Mali, in office since 1968, is threadbare. Mauritania's national sovereignty is increasingly threatened by the conflict in the Western Sahara. Democratic Senegal under President

Abdou Diouf is an exception, but the economic situation is precarious and unrest in the Casamance region could raise the political temperature.

"The start of a solution to the Sahel's multiple problems," stresses Abdel Wedoud Ould Cheikh, sociologist at the Mauritanian Institute of Scientific Research, "can come only from the Sahelians themselves." The principal resource of the Sahel region is its farmers and herders and their remarkable adaptability to a harsh environment. But little attention has been paid to the wishes and needs of rural communities by distant bureaucracies in Sahelian capitals or abroad. Moreover, when rural populations have attempted to set up and manage their own institutions on the local level and turn them into authentic vehicles for development, their efforts have often been undermined by state administrations jealous of their authority. Unless Sahel farmers and herders can organize for greater political and social strength, the possibilities of altering the present pattern of under-development will be increasingly remote.

The Sahel may never offer the economic potential of the more fortunate coastal states, but it can provide an acceptable way of life for its inhabitants, reduce its dependence on foreign assistance, and augment its export capacity. Sahelian development must be viewed with a long-term perspective, with grass-roots schemes like basic health care and education, as well as village-oriented projects, playing a greater role than grandiose prestige projects. With more efficient utilization of limited local resources, these will be the essential factors necessary for the Sahel to escape its present development impasse. Alternatives are limited. As Ould Cheikh notes: "Unless we mend our ways, the Sahel at the end of the century will, at best, be very similar to what it is today, or in a more pessimistic scenario, the region will become the backwater of Africa."

43

International Food Aid
Kenneth L. Robinson

Kenneth Robinson takes an evenhanded approach to discussing the purposes and consequences of international food aid and, in particular, the United States food aid program, PL 480. He notes that the United States has been the major contributor in international food aid, being more successful in alleviating food shortfalls in the Indian famine of the mid-1960s and less successful in providing timely emergency food aid following the Sahelian drought of the early-1970s.

International food aid has played an important role in reducing hunger in food deficit countries since the end of World War II. Such aid has made it possible to prevent millions of deaths from famine such as occurred in the nineteenth century and between the two world wars (Aykroyd 1975). But a large proportion of the world's population still suffers from chronic malnutrition. Under these circumstances, should the United States and other countries that are fortunate to have food surpluses be offering more food aid, and if so, how much, in what form, and under what conditions? Should food aid, for example, be used as an instrument of foreign policy, and how can one minimize the potential adverse effects of food aid on incentives to produce in developing countries or to carry out reforms that may be needed to deal with the fundamental causes of malnutrition? This paper addresses these and other issues related to food aid.

Food Aid Needs

Estimates of the number of hungry people in the world vary widely (Poleman 1981), but there is no doubt that widespread hunger and malnutrition persist. The lack of accurate data regarding current levels of consumption of food in developing countries makes it impossible to determine with any degree of precision just how much food would be needed to eliminate world hunger. It is even more difficult to project future food-aid requirements. Clearly the results depend on assumptions made regarding future trends in production, and the average rate of growth in population and income, all of which are subject to a wide margin of error. The International Food Policy Research Institute has made several projections of import

Reprinted with permission from Papers on World Food Issues. 1984. Ithaca: Distribution Center, Cornell University.

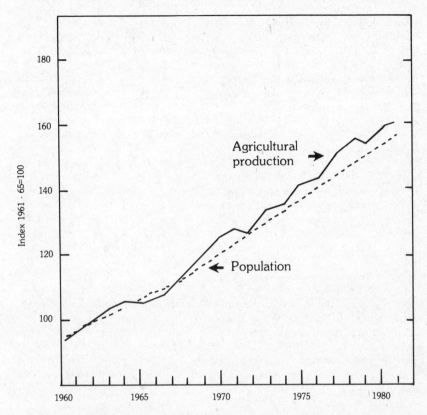

Figure 43.1. Index numbers of agricultural production and population in developing countries, 1960–81. [Source: USDA, *World Agricultural Situation*, Dec. 1981, and preceding issues]

requirements of low-income developing countries based on alternative assumptions regarding the growth of production and income. According to their estimates, grain import requirements by such countries could increase by anywhere from 25 to 80 million tons by 1990.

Projections made in the mid-1970s of an impending world food crisis have proved to be much too pessimistic, at least thus far. Aggregate food production in the developing countries has continued to rise a bit more rapidly than the growth of population (Fig. 43.1). This has permitted a slight improvement in per-capita food availability in Asia and Latin America but, unfortunately, not in Africa where food production continues to lag behind the growth of population. Despite higher levels of production, grain imports have continued to rise in many developing countries. This is attributable to the rapid growth of urban population, rising incomes, and an accompanying increase in demand for livestock products.

Rising import requirements during the past decade have been met mainly by purchasing grain on world markets rather than through international food aid. The volume of such aid in recent years has averaged just under 10 million tons annually, which is less than a tenth of the total volume of food imported by developing countries. The oil-rich nations, including Iran, Saudi Arabia, Nigeria, Indonesia, and Mexico, are now importing much larger quantities of food than they were a decade ago. Korea and Taiwan are typical of another small group of countries that have been able to pay for increased food imports by exporting more industrial products.

The most critical countries from the standpoint of potential food-aid needs are those with a large population and limited capacity to earn foreign exchange. Included in this group are India, Bangladesh, Pakistan, Egypt, and possibly China. Approximately two-thirds of the population in developing nations live in these five countries. There also is widespread poverty and malnutrition in many countries located in sub-Saharan Africa, Central America, the Andean highlands, parts of Brazil, and the Caribbean; but the population in most of these countries is relatively small, and consequently, food deficits for individual countries are likely to be modest in comparison with those in countries like India, Bangladesh, or Indonesia. India alone has nearly 100 times the population of most countries in the Sahelian zone of Africa.

Wars and conflicts within developing countries have added an element of unpredictability to food aid requirements during the past decade. Civil war in Cambodia (now Kampuchea) and the subsequent invasion by Viet Nam led to serious disruption of food supplies and the need to provide large amounts of food aid to refugees. The conflict between Ethiopia and Somalia over the Ogaden and internal strife in Uganda have compounded the problem of food shortages in East Africa. International organizations have been called upon to provide a high proportion of the food made available to families displaced by these conflicts. Future food-aid needs obviously will be influenced by the magnitude and duration of the refugee problem, as well as the incidence of drought and other natural disasters.

There are too many unpredictable factors to make even intelligent guesses as to future food-aid needs. About all one can conclude, based on our experience during the past decade, is that the demand for food aid is likely to vary greatly from year to year and from country to country. This suggests the need for flexibility in funding and programming food aid shipments.

Major Contributors

The United States has been by far the largest contributor of food aid during the past 25 years. In the mid-1960s, in response to the Bihar famine in India, the Unites States alone provided nearly 10 million tons of food aid. Very little was donated by other countries at that time. But beginning in the late 1960s, countries other than the United States and Canada began to make modest contributions. These contributions, mainly by the European Community, Japan, and Australia, have grown over the past decade and in 1982/83 accounted for around 45 percent of all the food aid provided in the form of grain (Fig. 43.2.). The emergence of large surpluses of wheat in the European Community in recent years accounts in part for the upward trend in contributions from that region.

U.S. food aid contributions during the 1970s ranged from a high of over 9 million tons in 1970-71 to a low of less than 4 million tons in 1973/74. Appropriations for food aid declined slightly during the mid-1970s; however, the principal reason for the drop in food aid shipments in 1973/74 was the rise in world grain prices. Less than half as much grain could be bought with the same appropriation in 1973/74 as in 1970/71.

Food aid contributions from the United States are provided mainly under terms spelled out in Public Law 480 (usually referred to as P.L. 480). The original act, approved by Congress in July of 1954, was designed mainly to dispose of surpluses accumulated as a result of price-support programs. P.L. 480 has been extended and amended every 2 to 4 years since 1954.

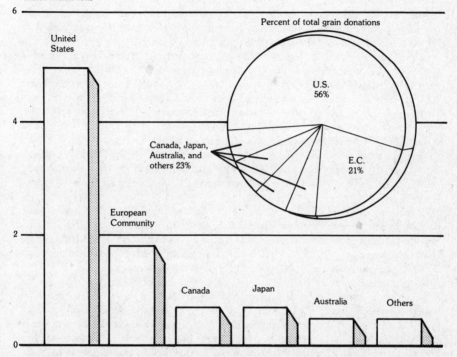

million metric tons

Percent of total grain donations

United States

U.S. 56%

Canada, Japan, Australia, and others 23%

E.C. 21%

European Community

Canada   Japan   Australia   Others

Figure 43.2. Projected food aid contributions in the form of grain, 1982–83. [Source: USDA, *Farmline*, Sept. 1982, p. 10]

Throughout the life of the act, Congress has given priority to sales of commodities rather than donations. The objective of many supporters of the original act was to provide a mechanism that would enable foreign countries to become commercial customers—hence the emphasis on sales and on using private trade channels to handle the actual shipments. This philosophy is expressed in the preamble to the 1954 act, which states that it is the policy of Congress "to make maximum efficient use of surplus agricultural commodities in furtherance of the foreign policy of the United States . . . by providing a means whereby surplus agricultural commodities . . . may be sold through private trade channels."

Between 65 and 70 percent of all the commodities provided under P.L. 480 in recent years have been sold to foreign governments rather than donated. Title I of the act authorizes sales of commodities under long-term and very generous credit arrangements. Recipient governments have a great deal of freedom in deciding what to do with the commodities acquired in this way. In some instances they are donated or sold at subsidized prices to particular "target" groups, but in other instances they are simply resold to commercial handlers or millers. Recipient governments are obligated to repay in dollars (or currencies convertible into dollars) over a 40-year period; however, it is doubtful if many governments who have received commodities under Title I will be able to repay on schedule owing to their chronic balance of payments problems. In 1977, a new title was added (Title III), which permits using the money countries are obligated to repay to finance approved development projects. This, in effect, converts P.L. 480 loans into development grants.

Donations of commodities are authorized under Title II. These may be made directly to foreign governments, or to international agencies such as UNICEF, the World Food Program (administered through the United Nations), and to private charitable organizations such as CARE and church-supported groups. In recent years 30 to 35 percent of all P.L. 480 commodities have been donated under Title II.

One of the important changes made in P.L. 480 legislation in the 1970s was to require that a minimum percentage (now 75%) of all sales made under Title I go to low-income countries, specifically those falling below the World Bank poverty line. This policy was adopted at the insistence of those who wanted to ensure that the bulk of food aid provided by the United States would be used to further humanitarian purposes rather than to serve foreign policy objectives or to build commercial markets.

Commodities Provided

Food aid provided by the United States and other countries during the past decade has consisted overwhelmingly of wheat and rice. In addition smaller quantities of corn, sorghum, soybean oil, skim milk powder, and so-called blended-foods have been made available to recipient nations. Blended foods consist of mixtures of grain (usually corn meal or wheat flour) and a protein supplement such as soybean meal, skim milk powder, or a combination of the two. They are frequently used as weaning foods or as a gruel for child-feeding programs. The emphasis on distributing whole grains is warranted. They are cheap sources of calories, are relatively easy to store and transport, and are less subject to pilferage or diversion to black markets than higher-valued foods such as soybean oil and skim milk powder.

Nutritionists now generally agree that it is unnecessary to provide high-cost protein products to those who are short of food. The principal problem in most countries is a shortage of calories. Whole grains, especially if supplemented with a little vegetable protein, will satisfy a high percentage of the nutritional requirements of children as well as adults.

Potential for Increasing Food Aid

The United States alone could provide enough grain to more than double food aid contributions over the next few years if Congress deemed it essential or desirable to do so. Less than 3 percent of total U.S. grain production has been distributed under P.L. 480 programs during recent years. Only a modest diversion of grain from commercial exports to high-income countries (where it is used mainly to increase livestock production) or from grain now fed to animals in the United States would be required to double current levels of food aid. Diversion of grain from livestock feed to other uses can be achieved simply by raising the price of grain and making it uneconomical to convert it into livestock products. The effectiveness of price rationing as a device to limit grain feeding was clearly demonstrated in 1974-75. Between 1972 and 1974, grain prices doubled. As a result, during this 2-year period, grain use by livestock was cut by around 40 million tons.

The principal barrier to increasing food aid during the 1980s is not likely to be the availability of grain, but rather political and economic constraints. The United States once again has accumulated large reserves of grain; consequently, farmers would welcome an increase in food aid. The willingness of the public (and their representatives in Congress) to appropriate more money for food aid is a major constraint. Logistic problems and the limited capacity of many countries to handle and distribute food aid, as well as concern about the dangers of becoming dependent on imports and the possible adverse effects subsidized food may have on internal production, are more likely to impose a ceiling on international food aid than a shortage of grain.

Achievements and Limitations of the U.S. P.L. 480 Program

Food aid provided by the United States has made a significant contribution over the past 25 years in alleviating food shortages caused by temporary shortfalls in agricultural production. One of the most notable successes was in helping to avert famine in India in the mid-1960s. The United States and other countries were less successful in providing timely emergency food aid following the Sahelian drought of the early 1970s; however, the loss of life would have been much greater if such aid had not been provided.

Title I commodities have proved to be extremely useful to recipient governments as a source of revenue. By selling the commodities obtained from the United States, even at reduced prices, recipient governments have been able to avoid raising taxes and, at the same time, damp down inflation. In a few countries, most notably in Brazil and Peru, revenue obtained from the sale of P.L. commodities has been used to subsidize internal production of wheat and rice (Hall 1980). P.L. 480 imports also have provided a relatively inexpensive source of grain to distribute through government-sponsored or licensed distribution centers. Finally, the availability of imported commodities offered on concessional terms has helped to ease the balance of payments problem of food-deficit countries or has enabled them to use foreign exchange for other purposes.

Although the availability of P.L. 480 commodities has helped to ease temporary food shortages, the program has made only a modest contribution to solving the problem of chronic malnutrition. A high proportion of the commodities sold to foreign governments under Title I has been used to augment commercial supplies, thereby helping to hold down food costs in urban areas. The principal beneficiaries in many instances have been civil servants and middle-income families. A high proportion of the commodities donated under Title II also has been used to meet the emergency food needs of refugees or the victims of drought or floods. Relatively little has been used to aid those who are chronically poor, such as the landless or those living in urban slums. One of the important contributions of Title II food aid has been to enable private charitable organizations to implement "food-for-work" projects, and to supply food for school feeding programs or to maternal and child health centers.

Criticisms of Food Aid

Few question the desirability of making food available to offset temporary shortages created by natural disasters. But not everyone is convinced that the United States and other potential donor nations should stand ready to provide food aid to countries with chronic food deficits. The principal objections to providing massive food aid on a continuing basis are that such aid is expensive, disruptive of commercial trade, and possibly counterproductive if it reduces incentives to increase agricultural production within food-deficit countries. Undue reliance on external aid, it is argued, also may lead planning authorities to neglect population-control programs or to assign a low priority to schemes designed to increase agricultural output, such as irrigation and drainage projects. The availability of food aid also may adversely affect the incomes of farmers who make up the bulk of the population in developing countries. The President's Advisory Committee on the World Food Problem succinctly summarized these arguments as follows:

Continued indefinite expansion of concessional sales by the United States is not in the best interest of either the donor or recipient nations. . . . Recipient nations may use such imports as a crutch to avoid the consequences of unchecked population growth, an unproductive agriculture, and irresponsibility in accelerating domestic economic growth.

Precisely how much effect food aid has had on incentives to produce food in developing countries is difficult to determine, but Blandford and von Plocki (1977) suggest that it was quite modest in countries like India, partly because the food was distributed in such a way as to insulate it from commercial markets. Furthermore, it was made available mainly to those who would not have been able to purchase additional food in the absence of the program. But in a number of Latin American countries P.L. 480 commodities probably have displaced food that might otherwise have been produced domestically.

Most countries would prefer not to become dependent on food aid simply because of the political risks involved. Food aid may not be available in the quantities needed in a particular year because of an adverse crop season in potential donor nations. Other conditions that may restrict food aid include dock strikes, a shortage of cargo vessels, or inadequate appropriations to finance additional shipments. Congress might decide to cut appropriations or limit shipments to certain countries because of disagreements or disenchantment with some of their policies. Experience during the mid-1970s when prices shot up and surpluses disappeared served to reinforce the conviction of most countries that undue reliance on food aid would leave them in an extremely vulnerable position.

International food aid has also been criticized because it tends to create demands for "exotic" foods, thus making countries more dependent on imports. Families in refugee camps or participants in school feeding programs often acquire a taste for commodities such as wheat that are not indigenous to the area. Nutritionists have been especially concerned about encouraging the use of skim milk powder or blended foods for weaning because programs that make use of these foods tend to reinforce trends away from breast feeding and the use of locally produced crops such as sorghum, millet, and cassava. Those who have come to depend on donated foods may become even more vulnerable if the program is cut back. Inhabitants of refugee camps, for example, are often reluctant to leave, thereby perpetuating the problem. Thus, the availability of food aid can have serious long-run consequences if substantial numbers of families are induced to alter diet preferences.

Other exporting nations have complained that food aid shipments have in some instances reduced their sales. When the United States provides wheat and rice to Indonesia or India, this may substitute for rice that might otherwise have been purchased from Burma or Thailand. Providing food aid to countries like Egypt may enable them to devote more of their arable land to export crops such as cotton, thus indirectly competing with the United States and other cotton exporters. In at least one instance, the United States cut off food aid because they discovered that the imported food was being used to free resources for export crops, which were then being sold to finance the purchase of arms.

Logistic and Management Problems

One of the problems in distributing food aid is the lack of adequate port and internal transportation facilities in food-deficit countries. India and China are among the few countries that have the capability of importing and distributing large quantities of grain, and even in these countries, adding to the present level of imports would be difficult. In Africa, port facilities are already congested, and long delays in unloading ships are common. Internal transportation facilities are even more limited. Few of the countries in the Sahelian region are served by railroads, and truck transportation is both difficult and expensive because of shortages of equipment and fuel and the absence of all-weather roads. Truck transportation becomes almost impossible in the rainy season. Similar problems are to be found in Bangladesh, a low-lying country with many rivers without bridges and few hard-surfaced roads. Imported food is likely to remain in warehouses in Chittagong or Dacca simply because it is so difficult to move it up-country to where it may be needed, especially in the monsoon season. Where the population is dispersed or nomadic, as in much of Africa, getting food to those in need is even more difficult.

In emergency situations, timing is of critical importance. Long lead times are required to arrange for procurement and delivery of food. An effective delivery system also may necessitate purchasing additional vehicles and arranging for their maintenance. Spare parts and fuel must be procured as well. The problems involved in attempting to mount a successful relief effort were well illustrated in our experience in Africa during the 1970s. Donor response to the drought in Ethiopia and in the Sahel was delayed partly because of inadequate information regarding current production and storage stocks. Accurate crop reports were simply not available, and in some instances governments were uninformed themselves or were reluctant to disclose the seriousness of the situation. When it became clear that a famine was imminent, there was insufficient time to get the food assembled and delivered to where it was needed. Because of the time required to arrange for shipping and delays in port handling, several months elapsed between the time the crisis became apparent and food aid was actually delivered. In some instances food aid arrived after the emergency had passed or when a new crop was being harvested, thus depressing prices and compounding normal storage problems.

Financing Food Aid

Money to finance food aid shipments now limits the amount of food that the United States can provide in any given year. U.S. contributions to food aid in the past have been strongly influenced by the availability of surpluses. Congress cut the appropriation for food aid during the mid-1970s when surpluses were no longer available. Additional commodities could have been purchased through normal channels, but this would have required an increase in appropriations and probably would have added modestly to inflationary pressures prevailing at that time.

Since the mid-1970s, Congress has appropriated between $1 and $1.5 billion per year for food aid. This has enabled the United States to provide between 5 and 7 million tons of food aid each year at an average cost of around $200 per ton. The cost per ton would be much higher if more blended and processed foods were provided rather than whole grains. The U.S. government subsidizes the cost of transporting P.L. 480 commodities to the port of entry, but relies on recipient governments to handle internal costs of Title I commodities. Private charitable organizations or international agencies usually finance the cost of transporting and distributing Title II commodities within recipient countries.

Doubling food aid appropriations to around $2.5 billion per year would add only about .2 of one percent to the total federal budget. P.L. 480 appropriations have been small, not only in relation to the total federal budget, but also in relation to expenditures on domestic food subsidy programs, which have averaged around $14 billion annually in recent years.

Conclusions

Political and logistic problems rather than shortages of grain are likely to constrain food aid shipments over the next few years. Only modest increases in production in food-exporting countries would be required to sustain a doubling of international food aid. If food-aid requirements were to rise above this level, additional incentives to increase production might be required, or alternatively, grain might be diverted from livestock feed simply by raising prices and, thereby, reducing incentives to convert grain into livestock products.

Future food-aid requirements are highly uncertain. Flexibility in funding would be desirable to enable the United States and other surplus-producing nations to respond to what are likely to be widely fluctuating requirements from year to year. Creating special reserves of wheat and rice (as the U.S. already has done with wheat) that can be used only to meet the food needs of low-income food-deficit countries would improve our response capability. The development of automatic rules for dispensing food aid in emergencies and an improved early-warning system to provide the lead time necessary to organize relief efforts also would be helpful.

The United States and other exporting nations have done reasonably well at meeting emergency food needs during the past two decades; we have done less well at solving the problem of chronic malnutrition, which is closely linked to poverty, landlessness, urban migration, and unemployment. P.L. 480 frequently has been used as an instrument of foreign policy or a device to get rid of surpluses rather than to provide food for those most in need. Thus, one of the issues that needs to be addressed in the United States is whether to continue to emphasize sales to foreign governments under Title I or to reallocate more of what aid is provided to international agencies and private voluntary organizations.

Another issue is what strings or conditions should the United States and other donor countries attach to food aid. Should the United States, for example, offer food aid to countries that suppress individual rights, discriminate against certain minorities, or fail to implement family planning programs? The more strings we attach to food aid, the less likely food-deficit countries are to accept such aid. The alternative is to provide food for hungry people, regardless of the political orientation of the government in power and whether or not we approve of their policies. Food aid obviously presents difficult moral choices. Managing food aid, even with the best of intentions, is not an easy task.

Discussion Questions

1. What are the principal factors that now limit international food aid, and what might be done to overcome these constraints?

2. How much would doubling the current volume of U. S. food aid cost, and would this require a major change in U.S. diets?

3. What might be done to ensure that more of the food aid provided by the United States and other donor nations actually gets to those most in need?

4. What conditions, if any, should we attach to food aid contributions?

5. Who should pay for food aid?

References

Aykroyd, W. G. 1975. The conquest of famine. Chap. 15, pp. 135-42. Readers Digest Press, New York.

Blandford, D., and J. A. von Plocki. 1977. Evaluating the disincentive effect of P.L. 480 food aid: The Indian case reconsidered. Cornell Int. Agric. Mimeo. 55. NYS College of Agric. and Life Sci., Cornell Univ., Ithaca.

Brown, L. R. 1974. By bread alone. Chap. 16, pp. 226-37. Praeger Pub., New York.

Hall, L. 1980. The effects of P.L. 480 wheat imports on Latin American countries. Cornell Int. Mimeo. 76. NYS College of Agric. and Life Sci., Cornell Univ., Ithaca.

International Food Policy Research Institute (IFPRI). 1977. Food needs of developing countries: Projections of production and consumption to 1990. Res. Rept. No. 3. IFPRI, Washington, D.C.

Jackson, T. (with D. Eade). 1982. Against the grain: The dilemma of project food aid. Oxfam, Oxford, U.K.

Lappé, F. M., and J. Collins. 1977. Food first: Beyond the myth of scarcity. Houghton-Mifflin Co., Boston, Mass.

Poleman, T.T. 1981. Quantifying the nutrition situation in developing countries. Food Research Institute Studies, vol. 18, no. 1, pp. 1-58.

Rothschild, E. 1977. Is it time to end food for peace? N.Y. Times Mag., Mar. 13, pp. 15, 43-48.

U. S. Department of Agriculture (USDA). 1977. P.L. 480 concessional sales. Foreign Agric. Econ. Rept. No. 142. Washington, D. C.

———. 1981. World agriculture: Outlook and situation. WAS 27. Washington, D.C.

———. 1982. World food aid needs and availabilities, 1982. Washington, D.C.

Part VIII

SOLUTIONS?

44

World Food: Myth and Reality
(excerpts)
Thomas T. Poleman

In Section V of his article "World Food: Myth and Reality," Thomas Poleman presents some guidelines that should be followed by food and agriculture agencies. He makes the distinction between developed countries' problems (e.g., managing reserve supplies) and developing countries' problems (e.g., expanding production quickly), and argues for food aid to target groups. Easing trade barriers might be an even more appropriate way to assist countries in (or rather, remove the obstacles to) their economic development.

Can Food Planning Become a Reality?

With the developing world seen as more hungry for jobs than food, what guidelines ought to be followed by the multiplicity of agencies concerned with food and agriculture? I venture to conclude with a few which may not be on everybody's list:

1. It would be helpful if the notion of a *world* food problem were played down. Problems there are aplenty, but the extent to which those of the West and the LDCs impinge on each other is minimal. In the industrialized nations they revolve around the perennial questions of managing reserve stocks, price maintenance, and in many capitalist countries, holding down production. In the developing world the need is to expand production quickly. That the requisites of the latter are pricing and investment decisions which may prove politically painful should be emphasized, something that the FAO and the World Food Council are only beginning to do. Just as the trumpeting of global disaster by Western doomsayers has misled, so many LDC politicians have for too long been allowed to ignore their country's food problems.

2. To the extent that food aid is pursued as a means of surplus disposal (or conscience assuagement), steps should be taken to minimize the effect on producer price incentives. An ideal mechanism for doing this, and simultaneously for improving nutritional well-being and the prospects for population control, would be to channel this aid through maternity and child health clinics.

Reprinted from *World Development* 5(5-7): 383–394 (1977) by Permission of Pergamon Press.

3. The real aid from the West, however, should take the form of technical assistance to agricultural research institutes and credits to underwrite the capital works needed to complement the new varieties—irrigation systems, fertilizer plants and the like. To a maximum degree these works should be designed to benefit the smaller farmers. But no matter should they not. Probably the best way the West can improve the lot of the disadvantaged of the LDCs is not—as seems the aim of recent modifications in the US aid legislation—to invest solely in projects oriented toward them. Rather it would be to reduce the incredibly high tariffs on processed and manufactured items which have prevented the LDCs from exploiting their one true comparative advantage in labour-intensive manufactures.

4. A final activity where minimal investment could bring high returns would be a crash programme for the generation of reliable statistics. Not until we are in a position to truly understand the situation of the LDCs can policy planning be confidently undertaken, and not until then, I fear, will we hear the last of the food myths.

45

Unvarnished Africa

An Anonymous Author

This article from *The Economist* begins with a barrage of pessimistic socio-economic statistics on African countries. According to the World Bank, small landholders need more financial support and governments need to establish more incentives for producers through fairer marketing practices, taxes and prices for domestic and export crops. Again, developed countries must offer more liberal trading opportunities as well as aid backed by policy reforms.

Sample some of black Africa's social statistics: life expectancy, at 47 years, is the lowest in the world; some 15-20% of the children die before their first birthday; safe water for only a quarter of the population; barely 30% of adults are literate. And now check the economic background; average annual incomes of only $330 or so (excluding big, oil-rich Nigeria); in the 1970s, falling real incomes in 15 countries; external debt up from $6 billion in 1970 to $32 billion in 1980.

Faced with this abundance of gloom, the World Bank's Africa report concentrates most of its attention on agriculture. Four out of five Africans earn their living off the land, and their tale has been a depressing one. Only three countries—Kenya, Malawi and Swaziland—managed to increase their agricultural production by more than 4% a year in the 1970s; seven registered falls. For many, the real disaster was their failure to boost agricultural exports. Taking the continent's 30 main exports, their volume rose just about respectably during the 1960s, but then fell in the 1970s; the biggest falls occurred in the oil-exporting countries. Nor was this due to declining demand: African exporters lost market shares in all but three crops (coffee, tea and cotton).

Taking food alone, production rose by about 2% a year in the 1960s, then only 1 1/2% a year in the 1970s. Adjusted for population growth, food production per African fell by about 20% between 1960 and 1980. And increases in output were due largely to more land being brought into use; yields per acre hardly changed. Africa became more dependent on imported food: commercial imports rose from 1.2m tons a year in 1961-63 to almost 5m tons a year in 1977-79, with a further 1m tons a year coming as food aid.

So what is to be done? Even without research breakthroughs that would help African farmers to conquer some of their natural enemies, the World Bank sees three policy areas badly in need of change:

Reprinted with permission from *The Economist*: 45-59 (4 September 1982).

* Support for smallholders. Most countries have gone for big, government-operated estates—and thus, usually, for disaster. By contrast, Kenya opted for the small man, who quickly took to growing tea, coffee, sugar cane and the other crops once thought to be the preserve of large estates. One Kenyan survey found that, on farms of less than half a hectare, output per hectare was 19 times greater and employment 30 times greater than on farms of eight hectares or more.

* Marketing. Through parastatal bodies, African governments generally control the marketing of export (and other) crops, as well as the supplies of fertilizers and seeds for farmers. And an expensive job they make of it: in Kenya (which is generally praised for its agricultural policies), parastatals charged farmers anywhere between 23% and 48% of the final price of their crops for marketing, storage and transport.

* Prices. Governments in most African countries fix both farmgate and consumer prices for basic foods. They also decide how much food to import. Almost invariably, farmers lose out: in the small free markets that exist, prices are often two or three times higher than official prices. Governments also tax export crops, a prime source of revenue. Again, farmers lose: export taxes have averaged 40-45% in Africa.

Exchange Rate Blues

The low prices that farmers receive for export crops are part of a general failing in African economies—overvalued exchange rates. Studies have shown that most African countries have resisted devaluing their currencies to compensate for their above-average inflation. Exporters are hit because world prices translate into a fixed amount of increasingly worthless domestic currency. "Several African countries", concludes the World Bank, "now find that producers of traditional export crops cannot be paid enough to cover the costs of production (for example, cocoa in Ghana, sisal in Tanzania and coffee in Madagascar)." Result: they stop growing the stuff or, if possible, smuggle it into neighbouring countries where prices are higher.

As exchange rates become overvalued, governments impose a battery of tariffs and quotas on imports—often, again, at the expense of (actual or potential) exporters. Upper Volta has a 66% tariff on animal-drawn ploughs; the cost of cans made in Kenya exceeds the price of canned food produced in the Gulf, thus excluding Kenyan farmers from the rapidly growing trade in canned food.

The administrative costs of organising protectionism are considerable—especially as trained administrators are all too scarce in Africa. Despite the high price of public goods and services, virtually every African government has taken on new responsibilities. During the 1970s, spending on public administration and defence rose almost four times as fast as gdp. To reduce the budgetary drain that this requires, the World Bank stresses the importance, wherever possible, of using private suppliers—entrepreneurs in road transport, for example, and self-help schemes to build schools and clinics.

Although Africa cries out for domestic policy changes, outsiders have a big role to play as well. First, says the World Bank, by offering more liberal trading opportunities. The rich world is happy to import most of Africa's raw materials, but it slaps a big tariff on those same commodities once they are even partly processed in Africa. Example: free entry for raw cotton, but a 13.7% EEC tariff on cotton clothing and a 13.2% one in Japan. Or America's 14.4% duty on leather goods, compared with nothing on hides and skins.

The second area for a foreign helping hand is aid. In real terms, aid to Africa grew by 5% a year in the 1970s, and accounted for 22.5% of all aid programmes. The World Bank argues that should be increased—provided it is backed by policy reforms. A "big" increase, it reckons, would involve aid rising by 6 1/2% a year in real terms during the 1980s, compared with a "small" rise of 2 1/4% a year.

What difference would the bank's strategy make? Without policy changes, and only a small rise in aid, the bank predicts that Africans will grow poorer in the 1980s. At the other extreme, policy reforms plus plenty of aid would raise average incomes by 2.1% a year. That would make Africans a quarter less poor by 1990 than they are now.

46

The Caribbean Basin Initiative
John P. Olinger

How, then, should trade barriers be reduced between the developed and developing countries? President Reagan's proposal for easing trade relations between countries, plus promoting aid and investment, was entitled "The Caribbean Basin Economic Recovery Act" (or Caribbean Basin Initiative— CBI). John Olinger, writing for Bread for the World, expresses some concern about the motivations and consequences of the CBI. In particular, Olinger argues that there may be increased production of export crops (since, for example, the CBI trade section incorporates strong incentives for expansion of sugar and beef exports) to the neglect of staple food production. Often, staple food producers have to compete with export crop producers for credit, irrigation, fertilizers, seeds, etc. In short, resources are devoted to crop production and land ownership is concentrated among a minority. Staple crops must be imported, the prices of which are extremely unstable; the countries are then vulnerable to the vagaries of world market prices for staple foods. Furthermore, there is no consideration given to long-term development and more importantly, changing the economic and social structure in which poverty and hunger are entrenched.

President Reagan launched the Caribbean Basin Initiative (CBI) in an address to the organization of American States on Feb. 24, 1982. The CBI is part of the administration's response to the crisis in the Caribbean and Central American region, a crisis most visible in the El Salvador conflict but which is rooted in the social and economic inequalities of the region.

The President noted that the countries in the region were under "economic siege" and proposed as a solution *"an economic program that integrates trade, aid and investment; a program that represents a long-term commitment to the countries of the Caribbean and Central American region, to make use of the magic of the marketplace, the market of the Americas, to earn their own way toward self-sustaining growth."*

The CBI recognizes the importance of trade and investment policies, and their usefulness in encouraging economic development. This basic idea represents an important step in the U.S. approach to the economic problems of developing countries.

Reprinted with permission from Bread for the World Background Paper #61. July 1982. Washington, D.C.: Bread for the World.

The CBI's trade-based approach is the administrations' strongest acknowledgement up to now that social unrest may be caused by something other than communist influence and is a step in the direction of recognizing the link between hunger and global security.

For these reasons, Bread for the World Education Fund has closely examined the CBI and its possible implications for hungry people in the Caribbean. The CBI gives us the opportunity to raise questions about trade relations between developing and developed countries and the impact of these relations on poverty and hunger in developing countries.

This paper first explains the context in which the CBI emerged and gives an overview of the initiative. The trade section of the CBI is then explained in more depth and finally the land and hunger implications of the CBI trade incentives for export crops are examined.

The Crisis in the Caribbean Basin

The Caribbean Basin is in fact two distinct regions — the Caribbean islands and the Central American isthmus.

Many countries in both the Caribbean islands and in Central America are affected by the same social and economic problems. The prevalent social problems include widespread poverty, malnutrition, high infant mortality and illiteracy. Economic problems include inequitable land distribution and heavy dependence on exports of primary commodities.

A large proportion of the population in the region receives incomes below the absolute poverty level. The absolute poverty level has been defined by the World Bank as the income level below which a person cannot afford a minimal nutritionally adequate diet and essential non-food items, such as clothing and shelter.

Not surprisingly, this poverty is accompanied by high levels of malnutrition. In El Salvador, according to the most recent data (1973), 72 percent of the population received less than the recommended number of calories for a nutritionally adequate diet as defined by the Food and Agriculture Organization of the United Nations and the World Health Organization.

In Guatemala the percentage of the population who were undernourished was 69 percent, in Honduras 60 percent, in the Dominican Republic 58 percent and in Panama 51 percent. Infant mortality rates in these countries are correspondingly high (See Table 46.1).

Poverty and malnutrition in the region are rooted in the unequal distribution of resources, in particular land. In the rural areas many people have no access to land (landless) or have access to only small amounts of land that are inadequate in size or quality for their needs (near-landless).

A Cornell University study estimated that in 1978 in Guatemala 85 percent of rural households were landless or near-landless, in El Salvador 80 percent, in the Dominican Republic 68 percent and in Costa Rica 55 percent.

In the eight countries in the region for which data are available, farms of 125 acres and greater represent only 2.2 percent of the total number of farms, yet account for 62.3 percent of all farmland.

Because these societies are based primarily on agricultural activity, such inequalities in land access seriously undermine the prospect for equitable economic growth and the reduction of hunger.

Most of the countries in the region are heavily dependent on exports of agricultural commodities such as sugar, coffee, beef and fruit to the industrialized world in order to pay for their economic growth. Some countries, such as Trinidad and Tobago,

TABLE 46.1. Poverty and Infant Mortality in the Caribbean Basin

Percent of Population Below
Absolute Poverty Income Level

	Rural Population	Urban Population	Infant Mortality per 1,000 Live Births*
Dominican Republic	45%	43%	96
El Salvador	20	32	53
Guatemala	21	25	69
Haiti	55	78	130
Honduras	14	55	103
Jamaica	N.A.	80	16
Nicaragua	21	19	122
Panama	21	30	47

*The infant mortality rate in the United States is 13 per thousand live births.

Guyana and Jamaica have exploited mineral resources. However, there has been little industrial development in the region.

In the 1970s, the world market for many of these agricultural commodities was unstable while at the same time the world prices for oil and for manufactured imports from the industrialized countries increased sharply.

When the prices of agricultural commodities declined, or increased less rapidly than the prices of oil or manufactured goods, the Caribbean countries had to produce and export more commodities just to maintain the ability to pay for existing levels of imports. Any possibility of expanding efforts for economic development had to be reconsidered in the light of the unfavorable world market for export crops.

The region's increasing international debt is the clearest sign of the much deeper economic problem. The region will need $4 billion—almost 10 percent of the regions gross domestic product—to meet its debt payments this year.

But it was not economic problems that attracted the attention of the U.S. government. In the late 1970's the U.S. government began to look at these two regions in a unified way under the stimulus of a sudden increase in political unrest.

In March 1979, a coup brought a socialist government to power in the tiny island of Grenada in the Eastern Caribbean. In July 1979, at the other end of the Caribbean, the Sandinistas overthrew the government of Anastasio Somoza in Nicaragua.

This was followed in October 1979 by a coup in El Salvador that replaced one military junta with another. Violence in El Salvador increased throughout 1980. In Jamaica in 1980 the parliamentary elections, which brought to power a more conservative government, were marked by extreme violence.

During the late 1970s the U.S. government's major response was to encourage more private investment in the region. President Reagan formalized this approach in the CBI.

U.S. Response to the Crisis: An Overview of the CBI

The Caribbean Basin Economic Recovery Act was introduced in Congress on March 18, 1982 as S 2337 in the Senate and HR 5900 in the House. Its three sections provide economic assistance, tax incentives for investment in the region and the creation of a free trade zone, which the president called the centerpiece of the legislation.

The CBI approach to *economic assistance* is straightforward and controversial. The administration wants to provide $350 million for economic assistance to the region in the form of Economic Support Fund (ESF) appropriations. ESF provides rapid financial assistance to friendly governments to pay for imports and reduce trading debts. It is not tied to development projects. (See Background Paper #60.)

The section of the CBI that deals with *investment* provides tax incentives for investment in the region. These incentives would take the general form of a 10 percent investment tax credit for U.S. corporations that make new investments in the region. In other words, a corporation would be able to reduce its total taxes by 10 [cents] for every dollar invested for specified purposes in the region.

The essence of the *trade* section is the creation of a one-way free trade zone for exports from the region to the United States for a period of 12 years. This means that, with some exceptions, exports from the Caribbean would be able to enter the United States duty free.

At the present time, 87 percent of exports from the region already enter the United States without duty anyway under the previously approved trade guidelines, the Generalized System of Preferences (GSP). The new legislation would affect another 5 percent of the region's goods.

Textiles and apparel are not included because of the perceived need to protect U.S. production of these goods. Some of the products that the CBI would allow to enter duty free include beef, veal, rum, tobacco products, footwear and miscellaneous other manufactured goods.

In addition, the CBI gives duty free treatment to all sugar exports from the Dominican Republic, Guatemala and Panama, three countries which do not enjoy such treatment because of the high levels of their sugar exports to the United States. These three countries could be given quotas for exports to the United States which would allow them to increase their shipments by about 10 percent over existing levels.

Criticism of the trade section has taken several forms. Some have said that the proposal would achieve little because most of the goods from the region already enjoy duty free status. Textiles which could serve as a basis for manufacturing growth and employment are excluded.

During congressional hearings it was estimated that overall there would probably be no more than a 1 percent increase in the region's exports within three years. This represents only about $100 million in new trade.

Labor unions have opposed the trade provisions because of the potential damage to U.S. industries. In a time of record unemployment, they argue, it is irresponsible to encourage countries to develop industries that might cause the loss of more U.S. jobs. This is an especially potent argument in light of the absence of trade adjustment assistance or incentives to retrain workers in the United States.

Little congressional attention has been given to the implications of the trade section on hunger in the region. The BFW Educational Fund is concerned particularly with those trade provisions which provide incentives for expanded export crop production. Examination of these provisions raises important questions about the impact of trade relations on poverty and hunger in developing countries.

Export Crops and Hunger

Many developing countries have pursued a development program based on export cropping—the production of crops, such as sugar, coffee, cocoa, cotton and tropical fruit, for export and sale to the developed countries. The revenues earned in the form of foreign exchange are used to purchase imported manufactured goods, as well as raw materials for the development of local manufacturing industries.

In the past decade many of these countries have had to import more and more food to feed their population. One of the main reasons for this is that governments in developing countries have not paid sufficient attention to the problems facing producers of staple food crops.

Often staple food producers have had to compete with export crop producers for credit and other agricultural inputs such as water, fertilizer, and improved seeds. In many cases the governments have been inclined to allocate resources to export crops to ensure continued foreign exchange earnings.

The unstable world markets for export crops, the necessity of many of the countries producing export crops to import food and, in many cases, accompanying high levels of malnutrition have led many people to question the validity of economic policies based on export crop expansion.

The BFW Educational Fund shares this concern. Each case of export crop expansion must be looked at to determine how export crop production affects the incidence of hunger and poverty and the concentration of land ownership. If export crops are produced under conditions of equitable land ownership and adequate production and distribution of domestic foodstuffs, then export cropping can be a useful and important way for developing countries to earn needed foreign exchange.

But in countries where land ownership is concentrated in the hands of a small minority of the population, or where there is widespread hunger, evidence indicates that continued reliance on export crops in situations where hunger would increase should be strongly resisted.

Export Cropping in the Region

Central America has long been an important source of agricultural products for the U.S. market. Many of these products are produced on large plantations or ranches owned either by local landowners or multinational corporations. The pattern of landholding is skewed toward large farms.

In Costa Rica, 14.4 percent of the farms account for 79.7 percent of total farmland, in El Salvador 1.1 percent of the farms account for 49.3 percent of the land (before the recent and uncompleted land reform), in Honduras 4.1 percent of the farms account for 55.5 percent of the farmland, in Panama 8.1 percent account for 63.5 percent of the farmland, in the Dominican Republic 2.4 percent of the farms account for 57.2 percent of the farmland and in Jamaica 0.4 percent of the farms account for 52.1 percent of the farmland.

The expansion of large farms growing export crops has led to the displacement of people from the land as large farmers have taken advantage of export market opportunities. This expansion has also led to a change in the relationship between the landowners and the tenants who work on the land, as in El Salvador. Salvadoran farm workers lost the right to farm small plots that produced basic foodstuffs. Instead some work for wages and have to buy their food in the market, many others are unemployed. This development is one of the causes of the social unrest in El Salvador.

Livestock raising has been another important export-oriented activity in Central America. In the 1970s 13.5 percent of U.S. imported beef came from Central America.

A report prepared for the U.S. State Department estimates that about two thirds of the region's arable land is devoted to livestock raising. Yet despite increased

TABLE 46.2. Import Content of Cereal Consumption in Carribean Basin

	Average Cereal Consumption per Person: 1977-1979	Import Content of Consumption
	kilograms/year	percent
Costa Rica	183	16
Dominican Republic	127	41
El Salvador	184	16
Guatemala	171	15
Haiti	151	23
Honduras	200	18
Jamaica	179	96
Nicaragua	162	17
Panama	173	19

production of beef, the regions per capita meat consumption dropped in the 1960s and 1970s.

The CBI Encourages Export Cropping

The CBI trade section incorporates significant incentives for expansion of sugar and beef exports. The impact of increased sugar and beef exports on production, land use, land ownership and hunger in the region needs to be explored.

If the CBI were adopted the Dominican Republic, Guatemala and Panama would be eligible for duty free sugar exports to the United States. Several questions need to be raised.

Would duty free treatment be an incentive for sugar producers to produce more sugar? If so, would the increase come from using more efficient production methods or would it come from planting more land in sugar? Would there be enough land in the countries to support such increases?

The CBI would also affect beef exports to the United States, which currently represent nearly one half of the value of the products eligible for benefits under the legislation. The elimination of duty on beef will increase exports by an estimated 3.5 percent to 7.5 percent.

The range land in the area is already overgrazed and it is unlikely that ranchers would be able to graze more cattle on the existing pastures. Will they have to clear more land for pasture, and increase the already severe pressure on land in the region?

The possible diversion of productive resources, in particular land, to cattle and sugar would have harmful effects on the poor and hungry people in the region. All of the countries affected by CBI now import a significant amount of their cereal consumption (See Table 46.2). A decrease in domestic food production would increase this dependence.

Also, these incentives for sugar and beef may encourage further consolidation of land ownership. Any program which might increase the number of landless or near-landless people must be seriously questioned.

The CBI: Problems and Possibilities

It is encouraging that the administration wants to address some of the serious economic problems of the region. The emphasis placed on trade reform is important and must be supported. Nevertheless, several broad reservations in terms of reducing hunger must be noted.

* A One Shot Deal—The approach to economic assistance is basically a one shot deal. While a quick infusion of money may help some countries pay for some of their imports, it will do little in the long run to assist their development.

* Private Sector, Non-structural Approach—The thrust of the CBI is toward the private sector, using U.S. companies to spur growth in the region.

There is no doubt that U.S. companies have played and will continue to play an important role in determining the economic structure of the region, but this approach ignores the need to develop social structures such as roads, health care, sanitation and schools, which are unprofitable for private investors. The private sector has not been involved in developing these services in the past and is unlikely to become involved now.

* No Anti-hunger Focus—Most important, the legislation does not deal significantly with the problem of hunger in the region and may actually worsen the problem. This is particularly true of the free trade provisions for agricultural commodities.

The CBI raises many questions regarding export crop development, trade and its effect on hungry people. Although some members of Congress have shown interest in these questions, the CBI has proceeded without much debate on hunger issues. The administration has not attempted to provide an analysis that would explore the possible influence of its proposed trade program on hunger in the region.

Any trade legislation which affects export crops should take these considerations into account and provide strong safeguards to ensure that it does not leave people hungry. The CBI is an encouraging first step in the process of treating trade relations as an integral part of the development process. Now the relationship between trade policies, particularly with regard to export crops and hunger, must be clearly recognized and taken into account when these policies are designed.

The general direction of the CBI is not toward strengthening staple food crop production, but toward continued reliance on export crops. Unless appropriate safeguards are incorporated, the incentives for sugar and beef exports could have detrimental effects on land use and land ownership patterns, thereby worsening the already considerable problems of poverty and hunger in the Caribbean.

If the CBI addressed more directly the problems of staple food producers, its potential for helping hungry people would be greatly enhanced.

47

It's Time to Give
Foreign Aid a Good Name
Richard Critchfield

Richard Critchfield has spent the last ten years with Rockefeller and Ford Foundation support monitoring village developments in developing countries. This article summarizes impressions gleaned from a five month tour as a consultant on Javanese village culture to the U.S. Agency for International Development (AID).

The author asks "[Is it] time to give foreign aid a good name." Richard Critchfield believes that this is a rhetorical question. Critchfield repeats the conventional wisdom of U.S. AID: of course the poor are richer than ten years ago, and American aid is working with American knowhow and "first-class American irrigation engineers." Critchfield believes that we should export development, in particular, green revolution technology.

Well, which is it? Does foreign aid just help the rich and not the poor? Or does it help everybody and play a key part in narrowing the world's North-South gap?

What matters about this question is why it gets asked at all. Of course foreign aid helps everybody. The best aid is the gift of useful knowledge. And Western, and most often American, scientific and technological knowledge is fast changing the face of village Asia.

Americans are less generous aid donors than they once were. The 2 percent of gross national product the United States provided at the height of the Marshall Plan in 1949 is down to a niggardly 0.22 percent; although real per capita American incomes have quadrupled in the past 30 years. That means the average American is giving only 1/40th as much of his income in aid as the earlier generation did.

Even so, the real problem is not money. The real problem is a knowledge gap. The poor nations need to possess a lot more scientific and technological knowledge than they do. And Americans need to know a lot more about what is going on in the world's 2 million villages, where 80 percent of the third world lives.

Ever since Vietnam, a *faddish*, pessimistic, anti-technology populism has developed that badly fogs the way we see the third world. It seems to be based upon (1) a disbelief in economic growth and (2) a belief that "participatory democracy," i.e.

Reprinted from *The Christian Science Monitor*: p.13 (13 July 1979) by permission of The Christian Science Publisher Society, Boston.

organizing the poor to fight for their rights, is somehow better than the informed and extended freedom of choice that Americans fought for and won in 1976 and fought for and lost in Vietnam.

Both mistaken notions threaten to do real harm to US relations with developing countries. Take Indonesia, which had only one Ph.D. and no university when it won its final freedom from the Dutch in 1949. In what is the world's fifth-largest nation, there is a desperate shortage of trained scientists, managers, and technicians.

This writer has just ended a five-month contract as a consultant on Javanese village culture and development to the US Agency for International Development (AID) mission in Indonesia. The job was to visit villages on the world's most crowded island, Java (87 million people, 1,600 to the square mile), and make an independent outsider's assessment of whether (1) the poor are richer or poorer than 10 years ago and (2) whether American aid is working. When the assignment ended in mid-May, I had visited 35 villages, interviewed 250 to 300 villagers, and written a 250,000-word report for AID's use.

The agency by law is not allowed to publicize its work. Now, no longer bound by this and a free-lance reporter once more, I feel free to interpret.

I came away making three main recommendations to the Agency for International Development in Jakarta:

1. Invest as much as you can in village irrigation.

2. Try to help village women, who have the babies and make the key cultural adjustment to change, improve their practical knowledge and incomes.

3. Try to give just as many Indonesians as possible higher education in science and technology at American universities.

These might sound uncontroversial. But so many buzz-words like "small is beautiful," "the poorest of the poor," "appropriate technology," and "basic human needs" have been substituted for real knowledge of the world's villagers that most of the key committees in Congress now oppose any form of aid to higher education.

What is most worrisome is the increasingly evident drift from dynamism of American leadership in Asia. One symptom is the way some American scholars in Indonesia claim—against all evidence—that the poor are poorer than 10 years ago and that the new high-yield rice technology is to blame.

What might be just an academic question to be chewed over at endless university seminars becomes a serious question of practical politics when Congress, the World Bank, AID, and others involved in development start believing it and framing policies on it (all this "help the poorest of the poor" nonsense.)

When you go out to villages yourself and look and ask and observe, you get a very different picture. Let us take Java and 35 villages scattered across its 620-mile length and 125-mile breadth. Two-thirds of Indonesia's villagers live on Java, and Indonesia is the world's seventh-biggest aid recipient, just after Egypt, India, Israel, Bangladesh, Syria, and Pakistan. (Note the politics of aid; it is either to preserve peace in the Middle East or help the three poor countries of the Indian subcontinent, which really are poor.)

* In just the past 3 to 5 years, 30 percent of all homes in the 35 Javanese villages have been rebuilt from bamboo huts to masonry houses. The average village now has 11 TV sets and 46 motorcycles. In the 35 villages, there was a total of 40 minibuses, 21 trucks, and 12 privately owned cars (something unheard of 10 years ago).

A landless laborer usually lives in a bamboo hut with an earthen floor and palm-fiber roof, sleeps on mats, uses oil lamps, and takes water from a spring or river. But in the past 3 to 5 years he has bought a bicycle or transistor radio and a flashlight.

The rich are getting richer faster; but the poor are getting richer, too. I put the question to several hundred villagers, including some of the poorest landless laborers I could find: "Well, are you better or worse off than you were 10 years ago?" Without a *single* exception, they said they were better off. Some laughed that anyone would be so foolish as to ask.

* The spread of irrigation and multiple cropping of the new high-yield, fertilizer-intensive, quick-maturing dwarf rice (with short, stiff stems so it won't fall over) has meant many more workdays for everybody.

As a result, large numbers of families with three people working 180 to 250 days a year have gone from a combined earning to 180 kilos (396 pounds) of rice (deemed "destitute") to just above the 320-kilo (just over 700 pounds) "poverty" line.

* Migration to the cities by landless, unskilled villagers is down to one-third of what it was in 1969.

* Infant mortality, always a good indicator of how the poorest are faring, is dropping. So is fertility.

* Rural industries have doubled or tripled in the past 10 years, in terms of craftsmen employed, volume of goods sold, and incomes.

* Village primary school attendance has shot up from about 10 percent to 50 percent as 31,000 new schools were built, 196,000 new teachers hired at quadrupled salaries, and 200,000,000 new textbooks handed out in the past five years.

So much is happening at once in village Java that it's as if the Red Queen, after it took all the running she could do to stay in one place, suddenly whooshed ahead. The main cause of this new prosperity is the rice revolution.

But the rice crop could be better. Go to any Javanese village with a really first-class American irrigation engineer and you'll find that almost nowhere does water get down properly to the bottom users, because of antiquated bamboo-tube paddy-to-paddy systems. With modern irrigation technology, land use, which now is 120 percent on Java, could easily go up to 200 percent or 300 percent.

Yet if you double-cropped only 50 percent of the 6.1 million irrigated hectares (15.1 million acres) and got 4 tons per crop (and Java's average is now up to 3.1 tons), Indonesia would have rice coming out of its ears.

Not surprisingly, "improved irrigation" was given as the main need, by far, in all 35 villages visited. It was followed, in order of priority, by roads, schools, credit, electrification, non-rice crop technology, pure drinking water, and more technical training. Villagers also said irrigation was the primary reason for more work and high incomes.

What is happening in Java and all over the rest of Asia is part of a movement of agricultural technology that began in the Fertile Crescent 6,000 to 7,000 years ago (the invention of irrigation); moved to Europe 1,000 years ago (the invention of the heavy moldboard plow and manorial farming)—briefly to England; then to America about 80 years ago (since the 1930s, new seeds, irrigation, mechanization, and massive use of fertilizer); and to the third world, especially India, China, and Indonesia in the past 10 to 15 years (tropical grain, irrigation, electrification, and multiple cropping).

By now one would not think it necessary to need to defend the "green revolution." Ever since the new grain was introduced to Asia in 1965, it has spread rapidly, from 34 million acres in 1969 to 130 million acres now. (Irrigation has spread almost as fast, especially in China, which now has 76 million of the world's 156 million irrigated hectares—385 million acres.) In rice alone, China, Japan, and Taiwan grow dwarf varieties almost exclusively.

In the same way, use of the birth-control pill and intrauterine devices has spread as fast. Repeatedly village women told me, "We would have had fewer children long ago but we didn't know what to do."

The multitudes of villagers can't be wrong.

So why is there so much gloom and doom in America about development? (After this Java survey, which confirmed in detail impressions I had had right across Asia in 1977-78, I'm not a bit worried about the villagers; they're doing just fine.)

It has to be the psychological hangover from Vietnam. Foreign aid has been under almost continuous attack ever since. First, aid was bad because it led to intervention and anyway helped the rich and not the poor. Then came predictions the planet, at present population, production, and consumption rates, would reach "overshoot and collapse" in less than a century.

Then the environmentalists got into the act, warning that the world's oil, mineral reserves, and fresh water would stretch only so far (especially since Americans, with only 6 percent of the planet's people, were consuming 32 percent of those resources every year to support luxurious life styles unseen since imperial, plutocratic Rome).

Suddenly Americans were being told to stop aiding and stop growing and stay home where they belonged, minding their own business and looking after endangered species like the bald eagle.

What is happening in village Asia is indeeed "a revolutionary enterprise of the most momentous consequence," as a recent piece in The New Yorker described it. It is nothing less than a movement of agricultural technology, with all the power and wealth that eventually go with it, certain to change the planet's geopolitics completely (the rise of the East?).

To stop, or even slow down, the provision of money, training, and technology, transferring resources, techniques, and information at this point (it was never simple) would be like trying to stop the rise of Europe in A.D. 1000. We are up against something very, very big.

If Asia's villagers need knowledge more than anything else, the U.S. needs more knowledge, too—of them.

Americans are still the leading power for dynamism and technological advance on this planet and could rather easily lead the rest of its inhabitants toward a decent world society and abundant food.

But it means sharing their technology as best they can and not keep looking for fashionable, and in the end, shoddy and fake, reasons for not giving the right kind of aid.

48

Filipinos Turn Back from Green Revolution

An Anonymous Author

The Green Revolution may be working for some villagers in Java (see Chapter 47) although certainly not everywhere (see Franke's discourse in Chapter 39), but Filipino specialists say that the Revolution has run its course. Although large-scale farmers have prospered from the new technologies (indeed, the country has periodically been virtually self-sufficient in rice), the small-scale farmers cannot afford the expensive inputs. Thus, a seed retrieval program has been established with broad-based farm support.

MANILA, May 15—Two decades after the Green Revolution arrived here, its miracles in high-yield cereal and vegetable production have lost their luster, and Philippine specialists are conducting a nationwide search for indigenous varieties that have become scarce.

A seed-retrieval program was ordered recently by Prime Minister Cesar Virata for the purpose of establishing a germplasm bank. Specialists from the Ministries of Agriculture and Energy and the Land Bank, aided by trained personnel and students, are searching for indigenous varieties of rice, corn and vegetables that became scarce because new, high-yield seeds were bred and sown during the Green Revolution.

Government figures show that, in two decades, 75 percent of the country's rice lands, or an area of 6.4 million acres, was switched to high-yield seeds requiring heavy doses of chemical fertilizers and pesticides. This resulted in the country's becoming self-sufficient in rice and even exporting some surplus last year, but small farmers have gone into debt keeping up with the cost of fertilizers and other farm chemicals.

"The seed-retrieval program seeks to rebuild the national genetic pool of plants geared to small farmers," the project director, Domingo Panganiban, said in an interview. The program also has the endorsement of the Philippines' biggest farm group, the National Congress of Farmers Organizations.

At present costs, the Filipino farmer has to invest about $42 in chemicals for every acre of land planted in the Green Revolution's high-yield variety. He cuts this cost by 66 percent if he uses an indigenous rice seed.

Reprinted with permission from The New York Times (16 May 1982). Copyright (c) 1982 by the New York Times Company.

If it is a good season, the farmer who is able to afford the fertilizers required for the high-yield variety harvests twice as much as the poor farmer who uses the local variety. But if the highly susceptible high-yield variety is attacked by rice blast or some other disease, the loss is much greater.

"Aside from retrieving endangered seeds," Mr Panganiban said, "we will also seek out and propagate medicinal plants and special trees useful in increasing incomes of small farmers."

Domingo Abadilla, president of the Earthman Society, which is cooperating with the Government in the seed-retrieval program, said of the Green Revolution:

"True; it increased yields, but it also contaminated the environment. How many fish no longer swim in farm streams because these are poisoned by chemicals?"

The Asian Development Bank, in a published study on the social and economic impact of the Green Revolution in Asia, noted that the cost of expanding the Green Revolution area was rising.

"Productivity gains in cereal production are coming more slowly and more expensively than they did during the past decade," the report said.

One result of the seed search has been the discovery by specialists of the hanga, or petroleum nut tree, which yields a high-octane oil when its fruit is squeezed between the fingers. Philippine tribal people have long used this oil as fuel for their wick lamps. Various proposals for mass utilization are now under study.

In addition, Mr. Panganiban said, specialists have found that a type of margosa known locally as the neem tree is a natural source of pesticides.

Local varieties of the winged bean are also being propagated. The plant's pod, eaten as a vegetable, has an unusually high content of protein along with vitamins and minerals.

Philippine tribal people have served as guides in the effort to seek out original varieties. The Ifugao tribe of the northern Philippines has long treasured an indigenous variety of rice called lugt bang, which is reddish in color and soft and glutinous when cooked.

49

Multiple Cropping: Centuries-Old Technique Gets New Results
(excerpts from *Reaching the Developing World's Small Farmers*)
Carroll P. Streeter

For Carroll Streeter the potential benefits from multiple cropping outweigh the possible problems. With support from Rockefeller Foundation and other agencies, multiple cropping is being promoted in developing countries. It is a logical extension of the Green Revolution, and requires irrigation, fertilizer, pesticides and machinery inputs. Streeter does note that some of these may not be available to Asian farmers. Other problems with multiple cropping are noted and yet the pros seem to outweigh the cons. Let's hope Streeter's predictions fulfill at least some of the hopes held by the harbingers of the Green Revolution.

In Taiwan, the heavy concentration of people in a limited land area has produced an agricultural phenomenon: never have I seen more intensive use of land. Not only is every bit of crop space used laterally, but as far as possible it is used vertically as well. For example, A-shaped trellises span irrigation and drainage ditches too deep for rice, and cucumbers are grown in the space over the water. Vegetables are planted under the branches of young fruit trees. Grapes hang in profusion from a wire latticework five or six feet above ground but by no means are they allowed to occupy the ground alone. In the winter when the grape leaves drop off, letting the sunshine through, a bountiful crop of staked-up tomatoes, cabbages, or some other vegetable comes on.

Two crops of rice a year are standard in Taiwan, one from early March to early July, the other from early August to November. That leaves a span of forty days between the crops in summer and ninety days in winter. But the fields are never empty; vegetables take over both times.

It might seem impossible to grow jute, which needs 120 days to mature, in the forty summer days between rice crops. But the farmers of Taiwan do it by letting the plants spend their first forty days in a separate small seedling bed. During the

Reprinted from *Reaching the Developing World's Small Farmers* Chapter VII by Carroll P. Streeter by permission of the Rockefeller Foundation. Pp. 63–68.

second forty days it is interplanted in the summer rice crop. The last forty days, after the rice is harvested, it grows on the field alone, shooting up to a height of ten or twelve feet before it is hustled off to make way for the next rice crop. It has had its full 120 days, although it occupied the field alone for only forty.

Taiwan probably raises more food per acre than any other place in the world. As a consequence her small farmers eat very well themselves . . . supply city people with a good diet, and provide the nation with substantial agricultural exports.

The island now produces a surplus of rice and winter vegetables, so many small farmers are turning to other crops—mushrooms, bananas, litchi nuts, citrus fruits, pineapples, guava, hogs, poultry, and pond-grown fish—anything that commands a good price. Sizable quantities of wheat, soybeans, and feed grains must be imported, but of the crops and livestock that can be grown under intensive methods she has more than enough.

The small farmers of Taiwan are experts at a technique that has been used for centuries in crowded Asia: multiple cropping.

Multiple cropping means raising three, four, or even five crops a year on the same ground instead of only one or two. This practice uses to the fullest the advantages of the tropics—a twelve-month growing season and more heat and solar energy than ever reach the temperate zones. Additional heat hastens plant growth. Sweet corn, for example, needs the same quantity of heat to mature no matter where it grows. In the Philippines it gets the required amount in sixty days; in Iowa it must have eighty-five to ninety.

Adding New Technology

A year-round warm climate, then, is fundamental to this method: by itself, however, it is not enough —as witness the fact that the Chinese and South Asians have been multiple-cropping for a thousand years without exceptional results. What is responsible for phenomenal gains in output is the new technology: new short-season varieties of rice, wheat, and other crops; ingenious systems for overlapping planting and harvesting dates to exploit land and sunshine to the utmost; and the proper use of fertilizers, insecticides, and other chemicals.

Taiwan has had more experience with modern multiple-cropping than any other area and now practices it almost universally. India has fifty-one pilot projects under way and has made dissemination of the system one of the major objectives of the current Five Year Plan. In northern Thailand the Ford Foundation is sponsoring a multiple-cropping project, and at the international Rice Research Institute in the Philippines Dr. Richard Bradfield of the Rockefeller Foundation has not only developed new multiple-cropping systems but is teaching them to trainees from all over Asia. As a result the new version of the ancient multiple-cropping method will probably spread through tropical Asia in the next few years.

The Green Revolution was based on greatly increased yields of individual crops. The prime examples of varieties responsible for these gains are the dwarf wheats developed in Mexico and the dwarf rices from IRRI, both of which were soon followed by even better varieties. Multiple-cropping emphasizes a second approach—taking in more harvests per year. "By going down both roads at once," Bradfield says, "we can multiply food production in the irrigated parts of Asia by four- to sixteenfold, depending on local circumstances. Even in many areas that depend only on rainfall we can double or triple it."

Bradfield's Many Harvests

Bradfield concentrates on five crops—rice, grain sorghum, soybeans, sweet potatoes, and sweet corn. Each has an excellent reason for being in his program.

"In Asia you have to start with rice," he explained as we walked around his plots. "You must talk to a farmer about his rice before you can discuss anything else. It is the best-adapted crop in a monsoon country where 60 to 120 inches of rain may fall within three or four months. More people in the world eat rice than any other grain."

Grain sorghum follows only rice and wheat as the world's most important human food. Both the grain and the stalks make an excellent livestock feed as well. The crop has two special merits: first, it is a good dry-land crop because it is resistant to periodic droughts; second, it ratoons—that is, after a crop is harvested a second, sometimes even a third crop will spring up from the stubble. These harvests are often as good as the first.

Soybeans put protein in the rotation. They contain more protein than any other crop. From the ripe beans processors make soy milk, soy flour, meat substitutes, and a variety of soybean oil derivatives. Soybean meal makes a fine protein food for livestock and poultry. Or the pods can be harvested green. Boil them for five minutes and they shell readily. With a pinch of salt they are considered a delicacy all over Asia.

Sweet potatoes not only yield big tonnage and supply bountiful calories but are especially rich in Vitamin A. "There are children within ten miles of this institute who have gone blind from lack of Vitamin A," says Bradfield. "There are said to be a hundred-thousand of these children in the Philippines. Yet one sweet potato a week would provide a child with all the Vitamin A he needs. Believe me, we intend to do something about that."

Sweet corn is the most profitable crop of the five. "We can sell all we can raise, right out of the field." Bradfield told me. "People here go crazy over it; they'll fight to get some. Our worst problem is pilfering. Around our plots we have a seven-foot fence with three strands of barbed wire at the top, but people go over and under it, even when armed guards are stationed there."

From this five-crop rotation Bradfield gets two to four metric tons of rice per acre, ten tons of sweet potatoes, and one ton of soybeans—these three alone totaling thirteen tons—plus eighteen thousand ears of sweet corn and six thousand pounds of green soybean pods. "On this succession of crops a lot of people can eat well—really well," he points out. By way of comparison, an above-average farmer in Illinois feels good if he raises 4.5 metric tons of maize (176 bushels) an acre. A top wheat grower in the Great Plains produces about 1.75 metric tons (65 bushels) an acre if he gets enough rain.

Bradfield's rotation is also valuable nutritionally. Philippine standards call for 2,600 calories and 55 grams of protein per man per day. On that basis one of his acres would provide enough calories in a year for twenty-nine men and enough protein for fifty-three.

Bradfield, of course, can achieve high yields partly because he can have all the water, fertilizer, pesticides, herbicides, machinery, and labor he wants. But many Asian farmers could do at least half as well, and those without irrigation but with forty inches or more of rainfall could do one-third as well. What this could mean is shown by Bradfield's estimate that if every farmer in Asia provided for his own family and one other, the continent would have a 40 percent surplus of food.

The Technical Package

To raise five crops a year a farmer must do several things:

—Choose short-season varieties. For example, Bradfield uses a rice that matures in about 100 days, while most rice requires 120 to 150.

—Interplant crops. A month or so before one is harvested the next is planted between the rows. Interplanting requires that the crops be compatible. Starting a short-season crop like sweet corn with a slow-starting one like sweet potatoes, for example, will conserve space and sunlight, since the fast grower will mature and be taken off by the time the slow starter is well under way. It is also good to grow deep-rooted and shallow-rooted crops together, to avoid varieties that sprawl excessively, and to avoid planting two crops in succession that are subject to attack by the same insects and diseases.

—Harvest some crops before they mature—sweet corn and green-pod soybeans, for example.

—Include a crop that will ratoon, such as grain sorghum, and get two or three harvests from one sowing.

—Fertilize adequately. Soils that work all year must be well fed.

—Spray as often as necessary. With so much vegetation growing, insects flourish.

—Minimize the tillage operations on each crop and use small power machinery for as many of them as possible. Bradfield uses a six horse-power walking tractor to complete the work rapidly and on schedule. "Any multiple-cropping farmer with as little as five irrigated acres could pay for one in two or three years out of the extra crops he would raise," Bradfield says.

In trying to cut down the tillage operations with rice, Bradfield is challenging centuries-old methods practiced in much of Asia. Farmers commonly plow a field under water several times, slogging behind a water buffalo. The theory is that this plowing "puddles" the soil to make it hold water better. Then the farmers transplant rice from seed beds to the flooded paddy, handling one plant at a time—an operation that requires a tremendous amount of stoop labor. But by keeping water on the field farmers hold down weed growth, and weeds are a tremendous problem in the tropics.

Bradfield and some of his associates at IRRI concede that puddling may be necessary in light, sandy soils that otherwise won't hold water. But they believe that on heavier soils rice can be sown much more easily and quickly with a drill—the field flooded later by irrigation or rainwater. Weeds could be sprayed out with chemicals. This is the way rice is grown in the United States, as well as in Australia, which has the highest per acre yields in the world.

"One trouble with puddling in nonirrigated regions," Bradfield says, "is that a farmer has to wait until he gets five or six inches of rain within forty-eight hours. He may wait two or three months for that. Meanwhile he could raise an additional crop of something."

The Timetable

Figure 49.1 shows how the Bradfield team manages to schedule its five crops in one year. The total growing days is 416, yet they are all crowded into one year thanks to intercropping. With a slightly different rotation Bradfield has actually farmed the equivalent of 450 days a year.

His simplest pattern consists of only rice and grain sorghum. On a field shaped in cross-section like Numbers 1 and 2 in Figure 49.1, the rice goes in the flooded

Crop	Date of Planning	Date of Harvest	No. Days in Growing Season	Tillage Operations
1. Rice	June 1 Field is shaped as shown, with depressed middles and ridges forty inches apart. The rice is sown with soybeans (no. 5 below) four weeks before the beans are harvested. Later the rice will be flooded.	Sept. 10	102	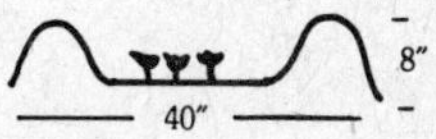
2. Sweet potatoes	Aug. 25 Rice middles are drained and sweet potatoes planted on ridges three to four weeks before the rice is harvested.	Dec. 5	102	
3. Soybeans for grain	Dec. 22 The depressed middle, which raised the rice in no. 1 above, has now been elevated. The ridges that raised sweet potatoes (no. 2 above) have become furrows. This is a simple tillage job.	March 17	85	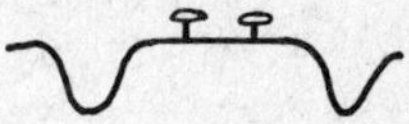
4. Sweet Corn	March 1 Corn is interplanted in soybeans (no. 3) two to three weeks before beans are harvested. Furrows have been fertilized and irrigated for corn and will later be filled in as corn is hilled, forming ridges for the soybeans (no. 5) to follow. Soil for this comes from the middle, which is again depressed in the process.	May 5	65	
5. Soybeans for green pods	May 1 Interplanted in sweet corn a few days before the corn is removed.	July 1	62	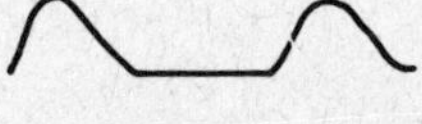

Sow rice again June 1 about a month before the soybeans (no. 5) come off, and repeat the cycle. The secret of intercropping, or growing two crops at once, is in handling their slow-growth period. Most crops start off slowly, then have a period of rapid growth, then slow down again toward maturity. The trick is to overlap the slow growth toward the end of one crop with the slow starting period of the next. The growth curve in Figure 2 illustrates:

Figure 49.1. Intercropping system.

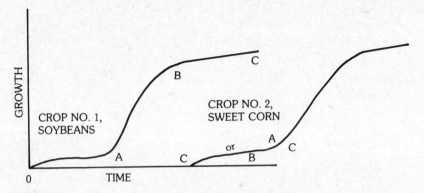

Figure 49.2. Growth vs. time: sweet corn and soybeans. Crop no. 1 (soybeans) grows rapidly from O to A, then spurts rapidly to B, slowing off to C at maturity. Crop no. 2 (sweet corn) starts slowly from B to C, overlapping the slow growth period of the soybeans.

middles. Two rows of sorghum are planted on the ridges as soon after the rice harvest as possible, usually about October 1st. The first crop of sorghum is taken off eighty-five days later, about Christmas. Then the ridges are fertilized with fifty pounds of nitrogen per acre, the weeds are cleaned out and the field is irrigated if necessary. No new seeding is required. The first ratoon crop of sorghum comes off March 10th to 15th. The field is again fertilized, weeded and irrigated, and the second ratoon crop is harvested about May 25th—the third crop from one sowing— just in time to seed rice again. The best yield so far has been 23,100 pounds of grain per acre (5,000 of rice and 18,100 of sorghum), or a little better than ten metric tons per acre.

In rain-fed areas of Asia many farmers settle for one rice crop a year and nothing else. Much of the time their little paddies stand dry and weedy, growing nothing. Bradfield is showing how to substitute grain sorghum for weeds and get at least one sorghum crop on the moisture left by the rice cultivation. With timely rainfall it is sometimes possible to get a ratoon crop as well.

Bradfield explained all this as we stood in his sweltering little fields at IRRI. he told me how he had divided his fields into twelve plots and raised four or five crops a year on each. This let him harvest something about once a week.

"And you know," he said with a chuckle, "I believe we could add livestock to this picture, putting meat, milk, and eggs within reach of a lot of people who are going without right now. At the same time the small farmers of Asia would make more money.

"Some of my economist friends scoff at that. 'Dick,' they say to me, 'you know as well as anybody that it takes several pounds of grain to make a pound of meat and that Asia can't afford this. It has to have the grain for people, not animals.'

"But what they forget is that half a crop is made up of stalks and vines and leaves that people can't eat but that animals can. At IRRI we've produced more than ten tons of good green forage per acre, in addition to all the grain and vegetables we've taken off. If we're not going to waste all this we will have to have animals to convert it into something people can eat.

"More farmers over here ought to have a small pond or reservoir to save some of the monsoon water. If it were deep it wouldn't take much land. They could put a few head of livestock right alongside the pond so the manure could run into it—

the kind of manure lagoons a lot of farmers in the United States now have. The manure could fertilize the algae in the pond and help them grow at least a ton of fish per acre, and the manure wouldn't hurt the fish for eating. The overflow water could irrigate a bit of land, carrying a little soluble fertilizer with it. Such a simple setup could be a regular little protein factory."

I know this is no wild dream, for I have seen small farmers in Malaysia with almost exactly this arrangement. They had snails on the bottom of the pond, fish in the water, ducks on the surface and hogs alongside.

Multiple-Cropping In India

India, with her population growing at a rate of more than a million people a month, in 1971 won her long struggle to achieve self-sufficiency in grain. With the world watching anxiously to see whether this success is permanent or only temporary, India is now trying for a new breakthrough in production through multiple-cropping.

By 1966-67 her farmers were double-cropping 14 percent of the cultivated land. Since then they have sharply increased such acreage thanks largely to the appearance of new short-season varieties that allow more crops to be squeezed into a year. Wheat, for example, has become an important crop for the first time in four of the most densely populated states of east India—West Bengal, Assam, Orissa, and Bihar—because new short-season varieties of rice are harvested there by October, in time to sow wheat, instead of in January as before. Bihar has tripled its wheat acreage in the last three years while raising as much rice as ever, and West Bengal had 800,000 acres of wheat in 1971 although it had practically none the year before. In the state of Maharashtra in western India, farmers with at least 100,000 acres whose only crop had been cotton now get an additional crop of soybeans.

India has a vigorous multiple-cropping drive in motion under the direction of Dr. Akrim Singh Cheema, agriculture commissioner in the Ministry of Food and Agriculture. Cheema was one of a party of Indians who visited Bradfield in the Philippines and toured rural Taiwan a few years ago. They came home determined that India would do something similar.

Today India has fifty-one multiple-cropping demonstration projects under way in various parts of the country. Some of the most exciting research is being done at the Indian Agricultural Research Institute on the outskirts of New Delhi. An irrigated field here formerly yielded one wheat crop a year and lay fallow the rest of the time. The IARI scientists are now using it to grow four crops in twelve months—wheat, maize, mung beans, and either mustard or potatoes. In other plots they have various sequences of forage crops, pulses, soybeans, grain sorghum, cotton, and vegetables.

One interesting experiment involves sugar cane, a profitable crop that covers millions of acres in irrigated parts of India. But it is a slow starter and occupies the land for nearly a year. To the late Dr S.S. Bains and his associates it seemed that the land and the sunshine could surely produce more than that. Hence while the cane is small and growing slowly the scientists at IARI are planting eight kinds of vegetables between the rows—radishes, potatoes, beans, onions, cowpeas, tomatoes, eggplant, and a species of melon. All ripen quickly, after which the cane grows up to make a normal yield. In other experiments wheat and cane are growing together, in still others cotton and cane. In much of irrigated India sugarcane farming may never be the same again.

Some of the unirrigated sections of the country can also benefit from multiple-cropping, although of course to a lesser extent. Those that receive twenty-four inches of rainfall a year may be able to harvest one additional crop, and those with fifty inches or more can sometimes get two extra crops. Among the crops best adapted to multiple-cropping in rainfed areas are pearl millet, finger millet, grain sorghum, peanuts, castor beans, and the grams.

Problems of Markets and Storage

The potential of multiple cropping for increasing production is beyond question. Its progress in the future will depend not so much on the availability of technology or the industry of farmers as on (a) whether the farmers can get the credit to buy the inputs they need, including water, power, and labor, and (b) whether it will pay them to raise the additional food. The profitability will depend on whether farmers can find an assured market for what they raise, whether they will be able to get their crops to that market, and whether they can get a fair price.

The problem is most acute with vegetables, which are highly perishable. Before he plants, a farmer needs to consider how many vegetables he can sell, to whom, and at what probable price; otherwise he may find a heap of rotting vegetables on his hands. In Taiwan some of the local farmers' associations conduct well run community markets that help solve the problem. The associations maintain quality standards, and their markets have enough volume to attract a good many buyers who bid competitively. Even then, of course, total supply cannot exceed total demand without a disastrous effect on prices.

Grain farmers are not in quite such a precarious position because their crops can be stored. Their problem usually is that they have to sell at harvest, when prices are lowest. They need storage facilities and longer-term credit to hold their crop a few months longer. Buyers with storage facilities and capital are making easy profits—after the grain has left the farmers' hands.

Because of such problems, farmers who are new to multiple-cropping would do well not to commit all their resources to the system in the first year. They should adopt it gradually as markets, labor supply, and their own energy allow, stepping up the pace when feasible. Meanwhile they could at least provide their families with more and better food and might begin to sell something. Often they could furnish their own market for grain and forage by feeding their own livestock and poultry—grain chiefly for hogs and chickens and forage for cattle and buffaloes. Usually there is no problem in selling meat, milk, or eggs at any reasonable price, and of course their own families will consume some.

Despite all the problems, multiple-cropping carries more promise of a better life for more people in the tropics and subtropics than anything else now on the horizon. These areas could far outperform the temperate zones, where most of the world's food is now raised. And these are the areas that need food most—where there are the largest numbers of poor and hungry people.

50

What Is Oxfam America?
(an update)

An Anonymous Author

Some of the previous authors in this section have advocated aid for the developing countries . . . with Rockefeller money . . . with U.S. Agency for International Development sponsored programs. The alternative agents of development are relatively small and private volunteer organizations with no vested interests. Some organizations such as CARE (Cooperative for American Relief Everywhere) and CRS (Catholic Relief Services) have been heavily subsidized by the U.S. government. Others (Church World Service, American Friends Service Committee, Oxfam) are funded with mostly private donations. Some information on one such group, Oxfam America, is presented below. The group recognizes that the political and economic causes of hunger cannot be ignored; local participation and self-reliance are encouraged and developed.

In its most recent fiscal year, Oxfam America attracted more than $5.6 million in contributions. Most came from individuals and private religious, civic and school groups. (Table 50.1 details Oxfam America's income and expenditures for the last fiscal year. A certified audit statement of the agency's financial condition is prepared each year by the firm of Kendig, Shannon and Company, and is available upon request.) Oxfam America neither seeks nor accepts funds from any government agency.

At Oxfam America, we look for projects where a few dollars go a long way—projects which set an example or create changes that reach far beyond the project itself. Our funds go directly to people overseas; we work with them to get results. And we constantly look for ways to keep fundraising and operational costs down. That is why we have an international reputation for economy and efficiency.

Although Oxfam America concentrates on funding self-help projects, we also provide aid when disaster strikes—as in Bangladesh, Kampuchea (Cambodia), Somalia or the Sahel—when development is simply not possible. Then we follow up with programs designed to promote self-reliance. In 1979, for example, we sent thousands of tons of desperately-needed food to Kampucheans. Today, we are one of only a

Reprinted with permission from Oxfam America Newsletter (September 1983). Boston: Oxfam America.

TABLE 50.1. Financial Figures for Fiscal Year 1983*

CONTRIBUTIONS AND OTHER REVENUE

A.	Family and Individuals	$3,402,473	60.5%
B.	Groups	761,705	13.6%
C.	Foundations	1,108,692	19.7%
D.	Miscellaneous	348,825	6.2%
		$5,621,695	100.0%

PROGRAM EXPENDITURES

A.	Program Grants	$3,105,742	55.2%
B.	Project Administration & Technical Services	606,110	10.8%
C.	Development Education	547,444	9.7%

SUPPORTING SERVICES EXPENDITURES

D.	Fundraising	1,046,415	18.6%
E.	General Administration	342,652	6.1%
		$5,648,363	100.4%

Note: Expenditures exceeded income by $26,668. These figures are unaudited. A complete copy of the audited financial statement is available upon request.
*May 1, 1982 to April 30, 1983.

handful of agencies working in that country providing seed, tools and training for development. When a disaster is over, Oxfam America is still there working.

Oxfam America is a non-profit corporation and all contributions are tax-deductible.

How Do We Pick Projects?

People often ask us how we find and select the projects we support. For most projects, this process begins in the field, where the local people meet and exchange ideas with an Oxfam America Projects Officer who knows their region and its problems well.

Oxfam America usually works with a grassroots organization that has identified a community need and is developing practical ways to meet it. Our partners in the project may be members of a farmers' union, women's association, village council or community development group. Formal project proposals grow out of thoughtful give-and-take between an Oxfam America representative and these local leaders.

Grant requests are also referred to us through the worldwide network of Oxfams and by other international agencies. And local groups that are familiar with Oxfam's work design and submit proposals independently.

Here in the United States, applications are discussed by our staff in light of Oxfam's regional policies and overall program goals. Finally, the overseas Projects Committee—a volunteer group of development professionals—meet with the staff to assess each proposal.

Project Criteria

We try to ensure that the projects we fund in some way address certain criteria. They should:

* work with low income groups (the overwhelming majority should be rural) and give special attention to women and other especially disadvantaged groups.
* build self-relience by improving long term food and livelihood security, and by increasing people's capacity to organize for social and economic change.
* increase economic and social equity.
* encourage local participation in all phases of the project.
* meet an important need of the local community (clear goals should be set at the start).
* encourage local self-management.
* relate in a constructive way to past or ongoing development efforts.
* set an example and put in motion changes that reach far beyond the project itself.

Some Current Overseas Projects

AFRICA

Cape Verde
Scholarships for literacy program for National Women's Organization.

Mali
Rebuilding 40 wells used by nomadic herders.

Mauritania
Training for improved management of surface water.

Mozambique
Agricultural tools for communal villages of Southern Niassa.

Senegal
Training and support for village health projects in remote Kedougou region.
Rural agricultural training center.

Somalia
Sand dune stabilization program.
Solar pumps for and repair of nomadic herders' wells in Nugal region.

Sudan
Technical and financial assistance to rural communities.

Tanzania
Agricultural projects in the isolated Kigoma region.

Upper Volta
Expansion of savings and credit associations to rural areas.

Zambia
Self-reliant farm and refugee center for refugees from South Africa, and Namibia respectively.
Day care center for children of women refugees from South Africa.

Zimbabwe
Funding food distribution and transportation and storage in rural drought areas.
Construction of well and irrigation facilities for small farms.

ASIA

Bangladesh
Organization of 60 new economic opportunity groups in the Jamalpur Women's program.

India
Support for the mat-makers' cooperative at Pennathur.
Establishment of a sapling nursery and mobilizing women toward reforestation in Doon Valley.
Silkworm culture and silk spinning in 50 Rajasthan households.
Aid for organization, credit and marketing for artisans in the Self-Employed Women's Association of Delhi, expansion of SEWA to Bhaglapur and Haryana.

Kampuchea (Cambodia)
Materials for repair of two large and important irrigation stations in Prey Veng to expand rice production.
Repair of rice mills in Battambang province.
10 solar irrigation pumps and 300 tool kits for farmers to repair wooden parts of traditional pedal-powered pumps.

Sri Lanka
Support for Anuradhapura Development Education Institute.
Pilot project in people's malaria control program.

Vietnam
Relief assistance for victims of Typhoon Nancy.

LATIN AMERICA AND THE CARIBBEAN

Antigua
Dam construction and livestock program expansion for cooperative farm in West Antigua.

Bolivia
Village-based agricultural training program in three communities in Cochabamba District.

Dominica
Technical assistance to fishing, farming, artisan and cottage industry cooperatives throughout the island.

El Salvador
Assistance to displaced Salvadorans including emergency aid, community health, family relocation and food production projects.

Grenada
Education and training for agricultural cooperative members.

Guatemala
Demonstration and training in agricultural production.
Health care for Guatemalan refugees in Chiapas, Mexico.

Honduras
Coordinating assistance to Salvadoran refugees.
Health and nutrition education and training program in Mesa Grande refugee camp.

Rotating credit fund for 256 local agricultural cooperatives in southern Honduras.

Nicaragua
Emergency flood relief.
Small farmer extension program to reach isolated farmers.

Peru
Marketing and commercialization program for Amuesha Indians.

51

The Plenty Project:
Inside the Hippie Peace Corps
(excerpts)
Lillie Wilson

A perhaps unlikely agent of development is a group of longhaired hippies from The Farm in Summertown, Tennessee. They are as committed to economic development at home (e.g., the South Bronx) as they are to villagers in the Guatemalan highlands. They pay no executive salaries, no personnel salaries; overhead costs have never exceeded five percent of their entire budget. They practice an appropriate technology ever mindful that the tremendous and ubiquitous political repression in the developing countries cannot be denied. Hopefully, repressive societal structures will change as people gain more control of their lives.

On a sunny day in April a bright purple Greyhound Semicruiser decorated with large yellow whales pulled up in front of the United Nations building in New York City. Out poured an unlikely-looking delegation of diplomats: their long hair and colorful clothes (vintage Haight-Ashbury 1968) seemed out of place at the UN Plaza, with its imposing architecture and air of staid respectability. But these visitors were here on official business. They had set up a meeting with a few local financiers, various UN representatives, and members of the press to discuss the plans of a unique international relief agency known as Plenty.

Certainly the group's name was not unfamiliar, to the reporters, since the media had recently acclaimed Plenty's South Bronx project, which was saving lives in the most notoriously crime-ridden area in the city; nor was it new to the UN associates, since the UN had several years ago granted Plenty "N.G.O." (non-governmental organization) status, thus conferring official recognition for its foreign activities and giving it access to UN information and functions. Later that year, in fact, a board would meet to consider elevating Plenty to "consultative" status, the next rung on the UN ladder, which would give its opinion and reports hearing in international policy discussions. Yet for many of those present this was their first opportunity to meet the Plenty people firsthand and see these self-proclaimed "hippies" up close.

The first item on Plenty's agenda was a buffet for all present, an array of dishes prepared with soybeans grown on the Farm, Plenty's 1,800-acre home base in Tennessee. During the meal, Plenty's guests got a chance to talk with the unusual delegates, and before long it became apparent that these visitors were not just different, they were exceptional. It wasn't only that they smiled more than most people, or looked you straight in the eye, or were so free of big-city nerves, even though all of that was true. The main thing was that they seemed to share a tacit, thorough belief in everything they were saying and doing. . . .

Plenty: The Spirit of Abundance

In 1974, as soon as the people at the Farm had enough—minimally enough—for themselves, their refrigerated truck started going out with food for the hungry. That same year, they initiated the Plenty project, even though most of their newly built cottages didn't have running water yet and the community itself wasn't completely out of the woods, literally and figuratively. But the conviction that "there's PLENTY right now" led them to help others seek food self-sufficiency. Once it was incorporated, Plenty was eligible to accept tax-deductible donations, but the Farm's own resources would remain the organization's mainstay for the next several years.

Plenty's first food drives went to local areas in Tennessee, where the Farm had already seen the need up close: Memphis, Nashville, Mount Pleasant, and a few rural areas. As they picked up news (on the Farm ham radios) of more distant places that were in trouble, the Farm truck fanned out its itineraries and went as far as Los Angeles and the refugee communities in Miami. Then construction crews headed out when they heard about flash floods in Colorado and a rash of tornadoes in northern Alabama, to clean up the wreckage and rebuild housing.

Rarely has Plenty had to put up with the bureaucratic rigamarole or elaborate fund-raising and budgeting schemes characteristic of other charities. "We just keep our ears open and look around and see where and what the need is," says one of Plenty's directors, David Proviance. "Usually, we can just pile into a bus or truck and go there and start in. It's a very effective way to help."

"We deliver more cents on the dollar than almost any charity in the world, because none of our people are paid anything," says Gaskin. "We have no executive salaries and no personnel salaries, so we can get a very high percentage of our resources straight to the people on the other end who need it." Plenty's overhead costs have in fact never exceeded 5 percent of its entire budget, a figure that other organizations—especially those with ad budgets, bureaucracies, and expensive downtown offices—could scarcely hope to emulate. Money given to Plenty never languishes awaiting implementation; it goes straight to those in need.

So far, nearly 200 people from the Farm have been Plenty volunteers on one project or another, a number that is about one-fourth their total adult population. But the line between those who work directly on the projects and the rest of the Farm folks isn't clearly drawn, because everyone on the Farm is working to make Plenty possible, and whenever funds are flush, the money goes into projects, not pockets. Even now, a few Farm dwellings are without running water and nobody brings home any fancy groceries. Feelings of "sacrifice," however, just don't seem to be there.

"What are we doing this for?" wrote Gaskin in Mind at Play (1980). "I hope this isn't too pretentious an answer, even at the risk of sounding foolish. We are doing this because it's the hope of the world. The mainstream culture is far wrong and has lost the essential human values, and we're trying to grow a little culture of the essential human values. We happen to have been thrown into a fertile field where we can grow, and we have an obligation to all those seeds that were thrown in all those places where they couldn't grow because the ground was too rocky or the government too mean."

Plenty Around the World

We recognize the fact of our essential oneness as a religious reality. We have founded our community on those premises. What affects any of us affects all of us. We share a vision of a world where there really is enough to go around.

—Farm press release

By 1976 Plenty was reaching out to foreign countries, where its volunteers have ministered to some of the most desperately needy people in the world. Their Bangla Desh project, begun in 1976, included work on a clinic and orphanage, and Plenty's electronic team designed a solar-powered CB radio system for use in the Bangla Desh countryside, where lack of communications facilities is a big problem. (Regrettably, the govenment was wary of the invention and Plenty wasn't allowed to distribute the radios.)

In 1979 Plenty began work in Lesotho, an area near the tip of southern Africa where unemployment is rampant and malnutrition endemic, a result of the South African minority government's disastrously oppressive economic and political policies. The volunteers here learned how to build Lesotho's traditional-style huts from local masons, administered emergency food and medical aid, and went to work on the agricultural problems. Already they have created an entire irrigation system, brought in drought-resistant trees to remedy the soil erosion, and begun a village-owned garden and fruit orchard. Perhaps most significantly, they have taught the villagers soy agriculture and are supervising a local tofu and soymilk operation run by native trainees. Still in the works are an extensive community building project and the construction of public washing facilities, complete with solar heaters. When a meeting was called to inform the local women that they were going to get warm-water showers, they stood up and started to dance.

The Haiti project got going just last year. It has been truly a blessing for a country so poor that three-fourths of its children will either grow up crippled or mentally disabled from malnutrition, or not survive childhood at all. Plenty's soy technician arrived there last December, following the other volunteers, and within a month produced 50 gallons of soy milk for Port-au-Prince's hungry children.

Possibly the most demanding and instructive of Plenty's overseas projects has been that undertaken in the Guatemalan highlands. When Farm carpenters showed up there after the 1976 earthquake to help reconstruct the demolished villages, they soon realized that the people were hurting more than the property, and that they were suffering not so much from the earthquake as from chronic disease and hunger.

The poverty in Guatemala was much more extreme than anything they had ever expected to see. The country, they realized, is actually composed of two societies: the wealthier Latinos and the poor Indians. The good arable land is largely planted with export crops (cotton, sugar, and coffee), which forces the poorer population up into the highlands, where the soil is poor and mere survival difficult. Since there is so little good land left for domestic food production, the prices in the local markets tend to be prohibitive, out of reach even for the employed migrant workers on the export-crop plantations. It's a situation typical of much of Latin America, where the increasing wealth of the food exporters and the expanding agribusiness has swallowed up the food-producing countryside and effectively wiped out entire indigenous villages.

Unable to cope with the magnitude of the problems they found, Plenty's volunteers called on the Farm for more help. "We were being brought dying babies," Gaskin remembers, "and we felt we had to start up right away with the nutrition and health care so we could get upstream and catch some babies before they got that skinny and sick." Plenty's agricultural team brought in a special variety of soybean that would be able to thrive at the highlands' altitude, and began teaching local farmers how to grow them. Meanwhile, components for a complete soy dairy— capable of making large quantities of tofu, soymilk, and "ice bean" (soy ice cream)— was crated down to the highlands, where Plenty set it up with the help of its future owners, the townspeople who would eventually take it over as a communally owned business. The dairy now provides free food for the town's hungry and there's still enough left over to sell at the local market cheaply and profitably.

The Farm paramedics also noticed that a large proportion of the Guatemalan children had intestinal parasites from drinking contaminated water, and so they began talking with the villagers, who felt they needed a water system that could provide clean water. It was to be one of Plenty's biggest undertakings, but more than a hundred local people turned up to help when construction started. Together, they laid 26 kilometers of pipes, and by August 1980 four villages had clean running water coming out of household taps for the first time, providing a total of 50,000 gallons a day.

At the same time, however, Guatemala's political climate was becoming increasingly dangerous, and the Plenty workers' position there was precarious. Anyone who worked with the poor was in danger of being considered an "organizer" by the violent, right-wing government, which makes short work of its enemies. When one government official found out that Plenty was planning to leave, he urged them to reconsider, fearful of how embarrassing it might be should the fact become publicized that this small relief organization had fled the country because of the threat of violence. Wisely, all the Plenty workers did leave by the end of the year, but there remained a significant bequest—not only the soy dairy and water system, but also 1,200 houses, twelve schools, and four clinics.

While Plenty was still in residence, Stephen and Ina May Gaskin visited Guatemala, and what they saw there affected their perspective profoundly. "We learned their language." Ina May says, "Spanish first, then the Indian languages, and we got to be close friends with the people, with the Indians. I got to know a lot of them because I worked at the clinic and delivered their babies, and a few times I was with a family when somebody died, and these are very, very gentle people."

"Earlier on, the terror was in the background, but as soon as the politicians down there figured out that Reagan might really win the election, the repression started to escalate. Then when the Republicans won, the terror really broke out and there were death squads just shooting Indians wholesale. Now they're hunting down literacy workers, nurses—anyone who's helpful to these very poor people. [I]f a man finds out he's on a hit list and runs away and hides, the soldiers come to his house and machine-gun the women and kids. We have eye witnesses to this. It really is happening."

"And it has its start when someone like Haig announces that 'Human rights are not going to be a priority for this administration'" adds Stephan. "You've got to realize that when Washington says something like that, it goes down the line very fast and at the other end there are peasants getting shot and poor folks watching their kids die."

"We were in the 'hot' area of Guatemala, where all the Cuban Communist organizers were said to be, and believe me, there wasn't any big Cuban presence there, not for miles and miles around, and the Indians didn't know anything about communism or socialism or Soviet intervention or Cuban intervention or anything else like that, that has everybody at the top so excited. A fellow from the government came to one village and wrote "Death to Communism" on a wall and the Indians didn't understand what he was doing. They're very simple people and such pure Indian that they don't grow beards, so when they see someone with a beard they figure he may be a Cuban or a European or some other outsider, but it's all the same to them. And you know how they always say that the death squads are hired by some militant wing to the right of the government? Well, I've been there, and there ain't no *room* to the right of that government!"

"I've had the privilege of having gotten around and of having seen things" Gaskin concludes, "and now that I'm back in the United States I just have an obligation to say what I saw. And this is one of the strongest things I have to tell people: that we must realize how truly poor some of these people are, and the reasons for that poverty, which is that we're eating their food back here in the United States—the crops grown on their land which are shipped out and packaged and sold. And they have less and less—they just can't possibly afford the food we're eating—because the multinationals have reached the state of the art where they can get more and more money off poorer people, and they're getting better at it all the time, so that now it's at a point where they can make another one-half percent profit by taking it out of the ebb and flow in a foreign country. And every time they do that, it's coming directly off the tail of some poor people somewhere in the world."

"This is a *direct* relationship, not a conceptual or theoretical or hypothetical one—that profit is coming *directly* off those people. In Guatemala, they have even less now—less beans and less corn—than they did when we first got there in 1976. They boil coffee leaves from the plantations because they can't afford food grown in their own country, and people are starving."

The Plenty workers' experiences in Third World countries like Guatemala and Africa have left them with a heightened sense of what exploitation really means, and their humanitarian concerns have necessarily opened their eyes to the political ramifications of their work. "Everybody talks about the balance of power between the United States and Russia," says Gaskin. "because there's a big economic structure around them that has everyone afraid. But take a little closer look at the 'balance of power' in the world and then see what balance there is between the United States and some tiny country like El Salvador. Russia and the U.S. are just stomping all over the rest of the world in this contest they've got going between them. The real distance isn't between the U.S. and the Soviets or between communism and capitalism. The real distance is between somebody who drinks bottled water from a spring on another continent and people, who have to carry unsanitized water up a hill on their backs."

Bringing It All Back Home

The more deeply the Plenty volunteers delved into local issues, the more their concerns broadened, and ultimately their focus circled back on problems closer to home. "Our experience in Guatemala made us more sensitive to what was going on with our own indigenous populations back in the States," says a volunteer who went to the highlands after the earthquake. In recent years Plenty has established an Amerindian Affairs office in Washington, D.C. and has helped out with food supplies and an ambulance service at Native American gatherings in Washington and the Black Hills of South Dakota. Not long ago, they raised funds for the Mohawk to buy back their own land, and they plan to serve as a liaison for Indian groups at the U.N. once they get consultative status.

Plenty's radio technicians have also helped out Greenpeace, the activist group fighting seal and whale slaughters on the Canadian and European coasts, by installing a whole new communications system in their ship *The Rainbow Warrior.* Plenty volunteers were on board last year when Greenpeace was arrested in both Iceland and Spain for being too effective in its intervention techniques, and this spring they were on hand to participate in the *Warrior's* disruption of the harp seal hunt in Newfoundland.

Some of Plenty's heaviest confrontations to date have taken place in the antinuclear arena. Plenty's lawyers, for example, have taken on the cases of victims of atomic testing; suing the government for compensation. And last January the Farm's band, the Nuclear Regulatory Commission, itself became the plaintiff in Plenty's legal fight to shut down the Tennessee Valley Authority's nuclear plant at Sequoyah. The suit's official name is—what else?— NRC vs. NRC.

Perhaps the most widely publicized—and effective—program that Plenty has undertaken in this country is their project in the South Bronx. This April it received the American Institute for Public Service's special Jefferson Award, a citation given "to honor the highest ideals and achievements in the field of public service."

The project got going two years ago when some people on the Farm saw shots of the South Bronx on a Bill Moyers television special and thought "the place looked like it had been atom-bombed." After the volunteers arrived and studied the problems, they decided that the most desperate need was for a reliable, free ambulance service. The city's public ambulance was notoriously slow and undependable, and private ambulances could cost as much as $90 a trip—a fee far beyond the means of the area's impoverished inhabitants. By late 1980 the Plenty Ambulance was averaging more than a hundred calls a month, with a response time of seven minutes—considerably faster than that of the city ambulance. And the volunteers now provide on-the-spot paramedic care; they're equipped with emergency life support systems and can offer transport to the hospital of the patient's choice—all for free, of course. They've also instituted a training program in emergency medical techniques for Bronx residents, free to anyone who wants to take the course. Some of their "graduates" have gone on to get jobs with other medical teams.

Everywhere that Plenty has ventured, it has made a point of working with the religious groups in the area—and it has also made a great impression on them. In 1980 the local chapter of the Church of the Seventh-Day Adventists praised the Plenty Anmbulance Service as the one group which "did the most to improve the quality of life in the South Bronx." Their work there also put them back in touch with the Missionaries of Charity, a group of nuns who work with Mother Teresa: they'd already worked side by side in Guatemala and Haiti (the sisters actually helped get Plenty's Haitian project started by welcoming volunteers at their Home for the Destitute and Dying in Port-au-Prince). When the Plenty crew in the South Bronx discovered that Teresa's sisters ran a home for battered women only a quarter of a mile away from their headquarters, they naturally went over to see if they could be of assistance and they then spent several nights guarding the home until a good security system could be installed. "We're naturally telepathic with them" says Ben Housel, Plenty's South Bronx director, noting that he and one of the sisters were friends as "flower children" in San Francisco over a decade ago. "They understand what we're about."

The connection brings up an interesting question: Are Plenty's projects primarily an extension of the high ideals of the '60s? Gaskin feels that the Farm has gone much further. "People want to keep on connecting me up with the '60s," he says, "and sure, those were good times, but all that's *way* back. We've got to take care of the '80s now, and the old '60s retreads aren't going to work." What *is* going to make the difference in the '80s, as Plenty is amply demonstrating, are the people who don't stop at talking "politics" but go out and get the work done.

Plenty's projects *have* drawn the epithet "political," but Gaskin doesn't think it's apt. "Doing stuff about whales and the Indians and the nukes and the poor folks isn't political," he told Lex Hixon in a radio interview during his visit to New York. "That's just stuff that's right or wrong that we should be doing right. It's not political to recognize right and wrong."

Out of the Woodwork and into the Cracks

The crowd that convened in the UN conference building had heard of some of Plenty International's accomplishments before. But as they watched *The Plenty Video* (an expertly done documentary on Plenty's projects, produced by the Farm's media crew, VideoFarm), it became clear that they hadn't been prepared for everything they were seeing. By the time Gaskin got up to talk (he was introduced as he usaully is, as the Farm's "spiritual teacher"), he was speaking to an audience with a collective lump in its throat. People stood up not to ask questions so much as to express admiration.

"You have shown us the most valuable thing we could see," said one man, "which is a living example. What you are doing is something for us all to emulate." Another man asked Gaskin if he'd read Alvin Toffler's *Third Wave* "I've just read it," the man said, "and it's uncanny how everything he talks about as being the wave of the future is just what you're doing now. There have been committees and studies and planners here working on doing projects like yours for years and years, but you people have just gone out and done them.

"The reason we exist at all," Gaskin told the crowd, "is that there is a lot of work to be done that nobody's doing. There are a few other groups like ours, but it's fallen to us because you guys with the neckties just aren't doing it. If the people in charge aren't taking care of the changes, they're not going to stay in charge for long. Because the changes are going on, and *if* it's the hippies doing it all, who's minding the store?

"There are some real advantages to our being hippies," he continued. "One of them is we don't get blamed for American foreign policy. The countries we go to all know that back at home we aren't the ones pulling the strings and doing all the bad things to them. Another one is that we can get in through the cracks. We've never had to worry about being respectable or about how we look to the higher-ups. So we can go to foreign countries and just do what we see needs to be done.

"We've gotton down to the most practical stuff, both at the Farm and on our Plenty projects, and that's taught us a lot about how to live with each other and what the real work is. And when you do this, you start to see that it's the meek who really do inherit the earth."

This attitude—a hopeful, positive outlook based on firsthand experience—is noticeable in all the Plenty volunteers. They know for a fact that when even a few people care, things start to happen and the most desperate situation can begin to change.

"I really believe that the job we have in front of us isn't all that impossible," Ina May Gaskin has said. "We are going to have to make some things clear to people who don't want to look at such stuff, but I don't feel the American people will let it go down once they understand what's happening."

There's a great faith among the Plenty workers, and throughout the Farm, that their ideals are shared by enough Americans to turn the country around once people get together. They speak enthusiastically of the strength and confidence they get from having their own land, their own livelihood, and complete independence from the profit system. But without exception, everyone I spoke with felt that while the communal support that they receive might make it easier for them to act, there are equally important opportunities for change all over the country.

"There's a whole network out there of, well, I call them short-haired hippies," Gaskin said, "and they already understand what the issues are. Most of them came through the Vietnam years, and they're a trained peace group that we have waiting in the wings. But now they are ten years older and stronger and maybe trained in a profession, and this time they'll realize that they're not powerless.

"It's just a matter of having everybody come out of the woodwork. We already know how to cooperate and make coalitions and do the grass-roots work, and there are enough of us to make real changes. But you've got to remember that democracy doesn't mean a thing on the page if people aren't out there participating. Don't get discouraged if you go to one meeting that doesn't work out. Go to another one and say to yourself, 'Hey, I'm one of the people who is going to close this nuclear plant, or save this village, or change this election.' Just get out and participate!"

The Hippies Win an Alternative Nobel Peace Prize

When the likes of Richard Nixon and Henry Kissinger started wining the Nobel Peace Prize, more than a few people realized that something was seriously awry. Fortunately, one of them was a wealthy young Swede named Jakob von Uexkull, who had not only the impulse but also the wherewithal to do something about it. He sold some of his valuables (or so the story goes) and set up the Right Livelihood Foundation, for the purpose of awarding an annual prize to the truly deserving. On December 9, 1980 (not quite accidentally the day before the Nobel ceremonies), the first Right Livelihood presentation took place and the $50,000 award was split equally between two winners: Hassan Fathy, an Egyptian architect who has worked all his life to provide cost-free housing for the poor, and a group called Plenty International, which Von Uexkull singled out as "an example of that Spiritual Revolution which is working to save and change the planet."

52

The Roots of Appropriate Technology
(excerpts from
Experiences in Appropriate Technology)
R.J. Mitchell

In *Experiences in Appropriate Technology*, the basic tenets of appropriate technology (AT) as, for example, practiced by the hippie peace corps (see Chapter 51) are identified. One of the main goals of AT is to assist people in gaining more control of their own development. "Trickle down" theories of development are dismissed since the majority of the population does not directly participate in it. Communities are allowed to define their own problems, form their own solutions and thus gain greater control of their lives, all the time cognizant that land reform, education policies and a host of broader issues must also be addressed.

The concept of appropriate technology emerged from Third World development projects of the 1960s. In response to the low impact and often negative consequences of insensitive applications of imported technology, many people began to question the choices of technology and the way these choices were made. Even the most optimistic observer had severe doubts when faced with the discarded tractors that farmers could not maintain; broken and abandoned water pumps; new city hospitals which treated disease in the absence of clean water supplies which could prevent it; the small diesel-powered rice hullers that put millions of women out of work; the promotion of powdered milk formulas as a substitute for breast feeding. Well-documented cases of inappropriate and, in some cases, ruthless choices abound. Many choices of technology simply didn't work in a particular Third World environment; some choices increased the gap between the rich and poor; many were positively harmful. The fenced enclaves of modern industry have provided very few jobs and demanded heavy dependence on foreign advisors, capital, and governments. The social costs appear to be greater than any benefits.

The 1970s were marked by a growing awareness of related problems in highly industrialized countries—environmental pollution, unemployment, alienation, dependency on non-renewable energy, low-income communities on the fringe of rich societies. Many people perceived the development of a global economic system which

Excerpted with permission from *Experiences in Appropriate Technology* edited by Robert J. Mitchell. 1980. Ottawa: The Canadian Hunger Foundation. Pp. 3–8.

Development is a process of social, economic, and political change and growth where people's needs for land, food, shelter, education, health care, energy supplies, and improved techniques are methodically being satisfied.

Underdevelopment is a process of growth where the benefits are accruing to a minority; the needs of the majority are not being met. It is a particular form of malignant growth bearing the seeds of poverty, injustice, and conflict.

The Third World refers to the people in any country who are excluded from development.

---

removed the ability of individuals and communities to serve their own needs; a system whose growth was becoming increasingly expensive, tenuous, irrational, and inequitable.

These problems are both local and international in scope. New actors (OPEC, Third World governments) have appeared on the global stage to assert their rights and gain more control over their own development. Local communities have united to address local issues. Solving these problems has met with some success but in many cases neither the global economic system nor local political systems serve the needs of the majority nor allow them access to information on and participation in decisions on the choice of technology. Such decisions are usually made from the "top down" for people rather than with people. The poorest majority are somehow supposed to select and maintain better technology, and not hold these decision-makers accountable for any failures. The links between low-income communities and the few engineers, bureaucrats, corporations, and politicians who make such choices are weak. Rich people make demands on high market and political systems. Low-income communities are both poor and powerless. In many cases the local community is too weakly organized to make decisions which would give it access to better services and increase its bargaining power with central· authorities. In other instances such organization has been ruthlessly suppressed.

A number of groups formed which promoted alternative technical choices and development policies from different perspectives. Some strongly advocated smaller-scale, non-polluting, locally-made technologies. Their critics initially viewed them as anti-technology or anti-progress. In the face of formidable resistance, these alternative technologists tended to over-promote their cause. Hand, wind, and solar power became panaceas. In retrospect, these advocates generally agree that their emphasis on small-scale was only part of the solution. A network of development issues—land reform, education policies, decentralized decision-making, suitable consultants, and agricultural and industrial strategies among others—must also be addressed.

Much of the activity in developing the hardware of AT, particularly in North America and Europe, has focused on renewable energy technologies (using solar, wind, water, or wood energy), future energy supply options, and the environmental and political implications of these choices. Some of these technologies are suitable for low-income communities; others are not. Solar water heaters, a popular and cost-effective technology reintroduced into North America, are, paradoxically, not very relevant to most communities with greater solar radiation nearer the equator. There, more often than not, the problem is access to water itself.

In the early 1980s AT practitioners form a motley crew: pragmatic technologists, commune-based activists, development economists, anti-nuclear advocates, adult educators, small businessmen and farmers, anti-government conservatives, development professionals, alternate energy consultants, designers, and craftspeople both inside and outside scientific research institutions and corporations. They often move alongside, not with the mainstream of their chosen trade. These people inquire into the choice of everything from a village hand pump to nuclear power plants in large cities, and offer options. Initiatives by groups of craftsmen and entrepreneurs world-wide, who are already making the best use of local resources and skills, go unrecorded.

Behind the diversity of these people there are some unifying perceptions. They seriously doubt the wisdom of conventional international development strategies whose bankrupt practices, while more evident in many Third World countries, are being questioned in industrialized countries.

AT practitioners are dubious that the benefits of investment in technical research and development in demonstration centres, laboratories, universities, or corporations will "trickle-down" to marginal income groups without accompanying financial and political incentives to link this research with the needs that local people express. In the 1960s investments in development projects based on economic theories for integrated economies generally assumed that somehow the benefits from these investments would eventually reach a broad majority. These theories have proved false and are now largely discredited. In many cases the benefits have accrued to a small minority.

Another concern of AT practitioners is that communities be allowed to define their own problems, use their ability to find solutions, and ultimately assume more control of their development. There is a strong anti-bureaucratic element in AT, belief in greater decentralization. Among the professionally trained practitioners, there is also a recognition of the limitations of their brand of "expertise" and the importance of expanding their narrow training and experience by listening to local people. AT is not something to be practised on people by experts, for if it is, its participatory, self-reliant basis disappears.

Finally, AT practitioners are concerned with choosing technologies, providing a wider range of options and benefits, and supporting local organizations in selecting these options.

Technology and Appropriate Technology

Technology is used here to include not only techniques, products and tools, but also the less tangible aspects—knowledge, management and organization of work. All are interconnected and do not exist in a social vacuum.

The term "appropriate technology" has been used very loosely. In the last five years many organizations have jumped on the AT bandwagon, some because it is now fashionable, others because they are seriously grappling with answers to the questions it addresses. Critics have dismissed it as an extremist, anti-modernization or anti-industrialization ethic. It is none of these. AT does ask what style of progress or industrialization is wanted, what balance between large and small-scale production is needed, what choices of technology will promote development, and who will participate in the selection of options. People involved in AT will not accept that the choices be monopolized by bureaucrats, consultants and corporations.

It has been only in the past 10 years that these questions have been asked on such a scale. Previously it was assumed that the most modern technique was universally suitable. This has rendered many countries dependent on foreign advisors and capital, and made local communities vulnerable to the whims of central

The Dimensions of AT: An Approach to Development

(a) A technology designed, developed, or chosen in conjunction with local users to increase their productivity and meet their immediate and longer term needs, without significantly increasing their dependence on outside sources of materials, energy, funds, and knowledge.

(b) A social and political process of integrating better technology into low-income communities.

(c) A style of development which recognizes the fact that the potential users of any technique have significant and necessary social, economic, and technical information and resources to contribute.

(d) A technology that can promote and strengthen local organizations and small-scale entrepreneurs so that they can increasingly assume more control over the choice of improved technology and adapt outside inputs to their own resources.

(e) An approach to designing technology that promotes local economic linkages between low-income users, institutional technologists, local craftsmen and entrepreneurs, and larger scale production.

(f) A technology that will work; that local inhabitants or organizations can afford and continue to maintain and improve.

---

governments or the marketplace. Many choices are based on political expediency, choices that cannot be justified technically, economically, or socially.

People have always searched for more beneficial technologies. More technical knowledge is potentially available than ever before, but the global disparities in social conditions render generalizations on what is suitable in a particular environment impossible. Transferring any technology from one social context to another is risky. Simply dismissing traditional technology as obsolete does not indicate what is a better choice. Should one jump all the way to the most modern techniques, half the way, a quarter the way? Often, as some of the case studies here show, the most beneficial and feasible technique can be a blend of modern and traditional skills and resources. These sorts of options are too seldom available to low-income communities. Such "intermediate" technologies are not intended to chain communities to an inferior technique but to increase local incomes and use local resources that can improve over time. The country or community becomes less dependent on outside knowledge. The engineer or agronomist should not present a technological "black box" to a remote village, leaving them dependent on his expertise and reliant on his services.

No technology, even proven ones, can be labelled "appropriate" before carefully explaining why in a particular context what options were considered, and how the choice was made. This is understandably the major omission in most descriptions of appropriate technology as choices are seldom presented for open discussion. The reasons for a particular choice are often hidden within a bureaucracy, or unclear even to the decision-makers.

The Approach to Appropriate Technology—
Linking Technology and Users

Approaches to implementing AT depend on the local situation. An ideal case would have well-organized users who have clearly identified the problem and have some proven technologies to choose from. Technical assistance in helping them adapt the technology to their conditions would be forthcoming. They can overcome outside influences which might block them from implementing their choices. What has been termed a "social carrier of techniques"[1] already exists, whether it be a farmer, an agricultural or building cooperative, a village water supply committee, a government agency, or a multinational corporation.

The reality is that, more often than not, the necessary social carrier does not exist in poor communities, as shown in this book. The case studies focus on the powerless but potential social carriers and their efforts to analyse their situation, acquire technical assistance which will respect the risks they have to take in choosing a particular technology, and promote their efforts in overcoming the barriers in their way. Many of the case studies here are rooted in community development and adult education techniques rather than engineering design.

AT groups now number in the thousands. Some work on specific technical problems in a local context; others promote socio-political conditions that might reduce the power of large organizations to impose choices that serve narrow interests and thwart the development of local solutions. Between these two groups are people aware of the need for sound technical and economic information, yet are also aware of the social and political aspects that ultimately determine choices.

It has been said repeatedly that one of the major constraints in promoting AT, perhaps the greatest, is the fact that different professional biases and bureaucratic structures hinder interaction between all the participants.

Given a specific problem, an engineer will usually ask questions different from those considered by a development economist or a community development worker. The desk-bound bureaucrat will have different perceptions and needs from the peasant in the countryside. As John Kenneth Galbraith said, "Farmers rightly sense that there is danger in the counsel of any man who does not himself have to live by the results." This problem is recognized, a great deal of lip-service is paid to it, but very little is, in fact, done about it. Even the call for "multi-disciplinary" approaches to problems implies a professional bias. This usually excludes low-income farmers from the ranks of professionals. Such an approach is too often divorced from the specific problems of a community whose plight is the focus of all this multi-disciplinary research, has had little input or say in the matter, and hence very little chance to implement these solutions.

Some Questions from Experience

Each case study presented here not only describes an experience, but also asks some questions. How do local people adopt better technologies? What helps or hinders this process? What style of technical, economic, or political assistance will help them? Can the organization or individuals at the local level control the choice of technical options?

Are the usual requirements of AT (low cost, labour intensive, local resources and so on) really sufficient to describe the full dimensions of choosing technologies that support local development? Who is the AT expert? Is the dictionary definition of technology itself sufficient to describe what is happening in many of these case studies?

The answers to the questions have to be analysed in a specific situation; global generalizations are risky and misleading; many questions remain unanswered and unasked. The images of the development process presented here are much more intimate than the computer-enhanced photographs from satellites 900 km above the

Earth[2] or the images at international conferences of development "experts." The case studies here focus on communities and "technology with a human face."

One case study from Tanzania shows that indigenous blacksmiths, who have always produced good farm implements, have until recently been excluded from rural development plans. The immediate problem is not to provide better workshops for them, but to change attitudes which dismiss their knowledge and products as backward, and to provide them with steel. In Canada, a remote Indian community is waging a long struggle to organize itself, do its own research, and install a more appropriate technology than the one imposed on it by the government. The community chose to hire its own technical consultants to help find technical options and negotiate with the government. Part of Cairo's garbage is effectively recycled by a low-income minority group operating in a sensitive social balance. Proposals to introduce "improved" waste disposal technology without an understanding of existing solutions could make this group even worse off. In Indonesia, potential users found a number of small-scale technologies neither reliable nor suitable, despite the fact that they had been labelled "appropriate" by outsiders. AT organizations in Papua New Guinea, the United States, and Ghana have developed a network of services to assess, design, deliver, and fund small-scale technical options that local people can choose from. In Lesotho the success or failure of some village water supply systems is based more on village and national politics than on providing suitable hardware. A rural development scheme in Newfoundland using intermediate-scale fishing boats will not be effective until traditional fishing techniques are revived and all sizes of boats share access to the limited stocks of fish. The other case studies amplify the basic premise of AT: people must find suitable assistance which will support their own efforts to adopt and control their choices in technology.

Notes

1. C. Edqvist and O. Edqvist, "Social Carriers of Techniques for Development," SAREC Report, R3 (Swedish Agency for Research Cooperation with Developing Countries) 1979.
2. See for example, "Economic Development," *Scientific American*, September, 1980.

53

Influencing Congress
Bread for the World

What can the individual citizen in the U.S. do? Bread for the World argues that we can influence Congress to enact more progressive legislation. Bread for the World members have worked for The Right to Food resolution, Food aid reforms, Emergency famine aid and an Emergency grain reserve. Although the motives of the various congressional representatives for voting for this legislation may have been somewhat different than those of Bread for the World, at least the legislation was enacted. In this short article we are told that each letter does make a difference. It is time for us to become more familiar with, and more active participants in, the legislative process.

Congress is a mystery to most U.S. citizens, and sometimes to members of Congress themselves. But because we are committed to working through the legislative process, it is important that we understand the workings of Congress, and how we can influence it for hunger concerns.

The Value of a Letter

The obvious question when confronted with a complicated governing system such as ours is, "How much difference can one letter make?"

Most congressional aides agree that even one well-written letter on a subject can start the staff thinking about that issue. These aides see each letter as representing the opinion of many people who did not write. Several letters on the same topic may prompt the assignment of a staff member to draft a position-paper for the congressperson, or even draw a personal response on the issue from the congressperson. Senators and representatives may receive one or dozens of letters on any given topic. But they don't ignore them. The pros and cons are counted and each letter can make a difference.

Communication with elected officials, by whatever means, is a basic privilege and responsibility for all U.S. citizens. It is respected and appreciated by the members of Congress. Even a letter disagreeing with a congressperson's action or stand is useful because it can help him/her to better understand the other side of that issue.

Reprinted with permission from Bread for the World Member's Guide: Influencing Congress. Washington, D.C.: Bread for the World.

How BFW Members Have Made a Difference

BFW members are the movement. Our participation in Bread for the World, our letters, visits and phone calls to members of Congress have prompted the enactment of these life-giving measures:

* The Right to Food resolutions. Congress made this a fundamental statement of principle.
* The U.S. farmer-held grain reserve. This reserve now plays a major role in moderating price fluctuations in grain to the benefit of consumers and producers alike.
* A "human rights and human needs" amendment. Passed in 1978, this legislation sought to improve lending practices of a special agency of the International Monetary Fund (IMF) when dealing with the poorest countries. Bread for the World played a smaller role in 1980 in securing a basic human needs provision aimed at all IMF lending.
* Food aid reforms. These amendments encouraged the use of food aid to help countries become more self-reliant.
* Emergency famine aid. Bread for the World proposed this amendment which increased urgently needed food aid by $42.8 million. A later BFW proposal added several million dollars to aid African refugees.
* Emergency grain reserve. This legislation sets aside four million tons of wheat for emergency food aid only.

Writing an Effective Letter

Writing a letter to your congressional representative may at first seem a rather difficult task. But you can do it and you can do it well. You need not be an expert on the issue to get attention. Nor do you have to be a master of the literary art. Here are three basic rules to follow:
1. Make one specific point or ask for one specific legislative action. Concentrate on one issue per letter.
2. Write your own views in your own words. As "unimpressive" as it may look to you, your letter will receive more attention than one which looks like the mass-produced product of a mail campaign, where people have simply copied letters.
3. Be brief. Rarely should your letter exceed one page in length. An effective letter can be as short as two or three sentences.

In addition to these basic rules, here are some other suggestions that will help insure that your letter will receive careful consideration:

* Be considerate. Don't threaten, scold or demand. Remember that members of Congress are persons. They should be treated with the respect every human being deserves, even in disagreement.
* Be constructive. If a bill addresses a problem in the wrong way, give your view without being unduly harsh.
* Be timely. Consult your newsletter to find out when to write.
* Ask for their ideas or for their response to some specific question.

* Act as a resource person. Provide information that will be helpful to your representative or senators.
* Consult your monthly newsletter. There you will find the numbers and descriptions of important bills, and updates on their progress.
* Be certain your address is on the letter as well as the envelope. Write legibly and spell names correctly.
* Thank your congressperson and/or aides for positive actions and responses.

One final suggestion: If possible, try to get together with other BFW members and write your individual letters in a group. There is motivation and support in numbers. If you've never written a letter to a congressperson, hearing of someone else's experience can encourage you to try your own hand at it. If you receive a negative response from your member of Congress, it helps to have a group forum to talk it over with. Maybe others have had similar experiences; perhaps another approach will work better. Persistence pays off.

Whatever the response, keep writing. Your efforts are important and needed. By them, you are expressing your concern for the millions who are hungry in the world today. As one member of Congress said, "Someone who sits down and writes a letter about hunger . . . almost literally has to be saving a life . . ."

Introducing Legislation

Bread for the World staff and membership work together to influence legislation at many points along the way. One of the first steps is the actual drafting and proposal of the bill.

BFW issues analysis constantly watch for proposals that would best promote the elimination of hunger. In addition, they draft legislation in consultation with the staffs of various congresspersons who share Bread for the World's concerns.

When a bill emerges out of this process, BFW members are asked to help find sponsors for the bill among their congresspersons. This is because legislation can only be introduced by members of Congress and because good sponsors help give a bill credibility among their colleagues. Once legislation is introduced by the sponsors, it is given a *reference number* (such as HR 1010 or S 901) and referred to the appropriate committee(s).

A bill or resolution may be considered by only one committee or by several committees.

Committee Work

Most legislation lives or dies by the action or inaction of committees. The effort to influence legislators during the committee process is for this reason important for BFW members. Committee work is not often covered in the press, so members should watch their newsletter carefully.

The committee's work includes research, debate, hearing testimony and revising the actual content of legislation. A bill may emerge from the committee process completely different from the way it was introduced.

BFW members can affect the committee process in two ways. First, BFW members may urge committee chairs to schedule consideration of the bill so that it will receive a respectful hearing and will be separated in the minds of the committee's staff from the great mass of other proposals that they are being asked to consider.

Second, at different times during the consideration of the bill, BFW members contact their congresspersons on the appropriate committee (or sub-committee) and stress their concerns regarding the bill.

To do this, you as a BFW member should learn on which committee your senators and representatives serve. Lists of committee members are in the back of this guide, and each time a new Congress convenes, a new list will be mailed to you. Often, you will find a committee list printed next to the action item in the newsletter.

Sub-committees and legislative aides are important in the committee process. Aides are sometimes able to make or break legislation by the research they do or advice they give on an issue. Subcommittees, usually listed with committees in BFW material, may do most of the committee's work.

54

India Goes It Almost Alone in Economic Development

William K. Stevens

That India is the world's largest "democracy" in terms of sheer quantity if not quality (see articles on sterilization abuse and population control in Part II) cannot be denied. That many constituents in that democracy participate in their own development is questionable. At least the official word was that the country's leadership (under Indira Ghandi) would tolerate only those foreign enterprises that contribute directly to India's development, i.e., foreign companies cannot (with a few notable exceptions, e.g., advanced computer firms) own a majority interest in the manufacture of goods unless a large percentage of production is for export. This is certainly a step in the right direction. Let the "trickle" in "trickle down" become a little more forceful, i.e., the global reach of the multinational corporations can be permitted only as long as more favorable profit-sharing arrangements (as, for example, in the People's Republic of China) are negotiated and the safety of workers is scrupulously enforced. (See "Union Carbide Fights for its Life" by J.H. Dobrzynski, B. Glaberson, R.W. King, W.J. Powell, Jr. and L. Helm in *Business Week* (24 December, 1984): 52-56.)

NEW DELHI - Five years have passed since Coca-Cola and the international Business Machines Corporation were forced out of India, one because it refused to give the secret formula for Coke to Indian bottlers and the other for refusing to cede a majority interest in its Indian operation to Indian Investors.

To those who rightly or wrongly saw that twin debacle as vivid proof of Indian inhospitality to American business, it must have come as a surprise when Prime Minister Indira Gandhi held out her hand in friendly invitation to American businessmen during her recent visit to the United States.

India, she told a group of industrialists in New York, has grown strong enough economically so that it can afford to lift or ease many of the controls long imposed on imports, foreign investment and free enterprise generally. Furthermore, she said, India must liberalize such areas of its economy if its development as an emerging industrial nation is to continue.

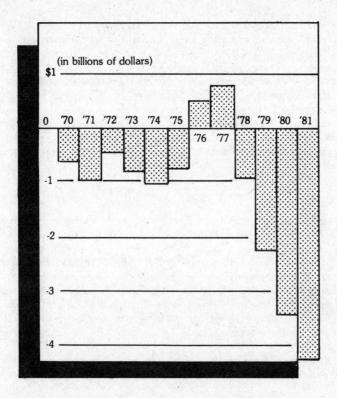

Figure 54.1. India's balance of payments. [Source: International Monetary Fund]

But she also left no doubt about the limits of foreign involvement. How, she was asked, can India develop the high technology that would enable it to join the ranks of modern economies if it cannot secure the help of companies such as I.B.M.? That, she said, depends on the attitude of those who want to come to India. "Obviously," she told the businessmen, "I cannot allow anything that impinges on our independence. Any kind of dominance in the economic field does impinge on our independence."

In that statement lies perhaps the main clue to India's economic stance in the world, to the rationale for a policy that sometimes seems vexing and contradictory to Westerners and to prospects for cooperation between the world's two largest democracies. In economics as in all else, India on the 35th anniversary of its liberation from the British crown projects an almost prickly air of independence that goes beyond simple nationalistic pride. One of the bedrocks of Indian economic policy is a conviction that the nation must go it alone, relying on its own resources as much as possible.

India long ago decided it would not live beyond its means by buying more abroad than it could pay for. Or at least more than it absolutely had to buy to promote basic development. Far better, India's planners reasoned, to avoid balance-of-payments deficits and to build slowly toward a self-reliance that in the long run would be more stable, even if it meant a relatively anemic array of consumer goods for Indian citizens in the meantime.

In the first years of independence, India spent more freely abroad. "We were in the very happy position of having large sterling balances accumulated during the war years," explains L.K. Iha, one of Mrs. Gandhi's main economic advisers. This money, he said, was owed to India for supplies it produced during World War II, "so we were in a position to import without worrying about how to pay for it. That situation led to the first spurt of very fast growth in which we allowed the import of plants and machinery almost at will."

But after 10 years, he said, it became clear that the reserves were being used up dangerously fast and that India was therefore "constrained to see that we used foreign exchange cautiously." Imported items regarded as luxuries were essentially prohibited in the world's 10th largest industrial economy.

Strings Attached

India, in effect, has been telling any foreign company seeking to operate here: You can come, but you must sell products that contribute directly to our development. This means, above all, the front-rank technology necessary to produce modern capital and the high-quality consumer goods that India largely lacks. Foreign companies cannot own a majority interest in the manufacture of goods unless a large share of production is for export. An exception is made for state-of-the-art technology such as advanced computers. Depending on how high a priority the Government places on the technology, the foreign company can be allowed to hold a majority interest. One of I.B.M.'s problems in 1977 was that it was purveying old, established technology.

These rules allow for a roughly equal partnership between foreign and Indian companies, and American diplomats here say that an outside company can do well if it ties up with a good Indian company, as many have already done. One estimate places the direct United States investment in joint ventures here at nearly $400 million. But some American analysts say this is considered peanuts—as is the $3 billion a year in trade between the United States and India, even though that figure last year made the United States India's biggest trading partner.

Other Headaches

One reason United States activity is not as high as it might be, American diplomats say, has less to do with India's stringent rules than it does with [the] country's legendary red tape and self-admitted bureaucratic rigidities. Power failures, port tie-ups, transportation breakdowns and spotty communications add to the headaches, they say. Mrs. Gandhi says that as part of the "liberalization" program, controls have been lifted on many imports of capital goods and raw materials. She maintains that red tape is being cut, and that the infrastructure is improving.

India insists, however, that the infrastructure cannot continue to improve unless present levels of low-interest loans from the World Bank are maintained. The United States cut contributions to the loan fund, but Mrs. Gandhi received assurances in Washington that India would get special attention. There were reports here last week that such aid would soon be increased from its 1982 level of $800 million.

Some Indians say that the effects of generations of colonial exploitation justify the country's need for financial concessions. They also point out that India's economic progress has been uneven, that large areas of the country and huge segments of the population remain desperately poor. India's main economic achievement since independence, it is believed, is that it has become essentially self-sufficient in food-grain production. But there is a widespread conviction among Indian leaders that in other areas the country's brand of state capitalism has fallen short of expectations. Liberalizing the private and trade sectors is seen as one way to increase efficiency, productivity and growth.

Why should it all matter to the United States? Because, say American students of the question, it is impossible to ignore a strategically vital, subcontinental nation of nearly 700 million people linked to the United States by democratic ideals and humanitarian considerations. In economic terms, they reply that there is much money to be made here if and when India achieves a truly modern economy. The India of the future, say some American diplomats, represents a huge market with an equally huge supply of inexpensive labor.

If that is true, there will be competition for it, and Mrs. Gandhi has made it clear that she will deal with whoever can provide India with what it needs. It is perhaps a straw in the wind that on her way back to India from the United States, she stopped in Japan. There, Prime Minister Zenko Suzuki said his country was ready to extend maximum economic and technological help to India.

55

Marking Revolution
Opposing Revolution
Walter LaFeber

Walter LaFeber questions what has happened to the ideals once shared by all Americans as embodied in the Declaration of Independence. The "inalienable right" (and now I quote Thomas Jefferson as well as Ronald Reagan) to self-determination seems to have been denied to people struggling for democracy in Latin America. No amount of letters (see Chapter 53) prevented the various U.S. military occupations of sovereign states throughout history. Actions speak louder than words—the hegemony of the superpowers may interfere with the development process. Perhaps all the more reason to keep writing those letters.

ITHACA, N.Y.—The Reagan Administration is commemorating the 207th birthday of the American Revolution by escalating United States military force against revolutionaries in Central America. Secretary of State George P. Shultz laid down the rule when he warned recently that the administration will not tolerate "people shooting their way into the government." Given George Washington's and Thomas Jefferson's dependence on American riflemen, it is well for Fourth of July celebrations that Mr. Shultz's law cannot be applied retroactively.

The first nation born of modern revolution is now the most powerful anti-revolutionary force in its own hemisphere. This contradiction is hardly new. Thomas Jefferson bequeathed it to us.

The great Virginian's declaration of American independence stated that when a government destroyed the rights of the governed, "it is the Right of the People to alter or to abolish it, and to institute new Government." That principle appeared first during Jefferson's lifetime when Latin Americans revolted against the corrupt Spanish empire. But it could now apply to the Sandinista rebellion against the Nicaraguan dictatorship, the revolution against a Salvadoran Government allowing more than 30,000 civilians to be killed without convicting one murderer and the uprising of impoverished Guatemalan Indians against a murderous regime.

Jefferson drew back from applying his own principle. As an author in 1776 he believed in "inalienable rights," but later as diplomat and President he also believed in the expansion of United States power. Thus, he confronted the contradiction:

What if people with inalienable rights in say, Central America, disliked United States influence? How could he reconcile his principles with his nation's power?

He tried to escape the dilemma with rationalization. First, he hoped the revolutions would fail. In the 1780's, he wanted the Spanish to hold their new world territory until "our population can be sufficiently advanced to gain it from them piece by piece." But Latin American revolutionaries moved ahead, even faster than the high United States birth rate and Jefferson next warned of ideological dangers. As Roman Catholics, the rebels might not qualify for certain inalienable rights. "History. . .furnishes no example of a priest-ridden people maintaining a free civil government," he wrote in 1813. In 1821, the influential North American Review laid it down as a "maxim" that only temperate climates allow good character.

Thus, North Americans both condemned the growing revolution and indicated why they had the right to instruct the revolutionaries. Over the next 150 years, the instruction was extensive, including United States military occupations of Cuba, Nicaragua, Haiti, the Dominican Republic and Mexico; the overthrow of governments in Guatemala, Costa Rica, Brazil and Chile; and the seizure of the Colombian province that became Panama, and of one-third of Mexico.

Time has sharpened the contradiction between Jefferson's principles and United States power. The revolutionaries only moved further to the left. Fidel Castro quoted the Declaration of Independence, but his political program came from such Cuban revolutionaries as Jose Marti, not Jefferson. The Virginian's politics, unlike his philosophical principles, no more fit Cuba in 1959 than North American style elections are suited to devastated, class-torn El Salvador in 1983.

As Fidel Castro seized power in 1959, Henry Cabot Lodge, the United States delegate to the United Nations, posed the key question in an Eisenhower Cabinet meeting: "The U.S. can win wars, but . . . can we win revolutions?" Mr. Lodge believed we could if we "focus on the Declaration of Independence." This past February Ronald Reagan apparently agreed: "People living today in Africa, in Latin America, in Central Asia, possess the same inalienable right to choose their own governors and decide their own destiny as we do."

But Mr. Reagan then doubled the number of military advisers in Central America and demanded increased aid for covert action against the Sandinistas. He now warns members of Congress that they could be branded un-American in 1981 if they oppose him on Central America.

Congress can avoid the contradiction that ensnared Jefferson, destroyed Lyndon B. Johnson's efforts in Vietnam and undermines Ronald Reagan's policies by following Mr. Lodge's insight: In revolutionary crises, it is better to "focus on the Declaration of Independence" than on United States power. Then, perhaps, American power would not contradict but instead conform to the principles of 1776. It should not be un-American to believe in the Declaration of Independence.

56

Asking the "Right" Questions
Gigi M. Berardi

The last essay in this volume appeared as a guest editorial in the *Journal of Environmental Education*. I wrote it in response to a National Science Foundation-sponsored Chautauqua course that I had attended. Intended primarily for educators, the course focused on the physical constraints of energy resource production, supply and demand almost to the exclusion of political economy considerations. Furthermore, the overall theme of scarcity and demand from uncontrolled exponential population growth was emphasized. Some of the data I used to counter the resource scarcity issue (see below) have not been adjusted to account for energy quality (see "Energy and the U.S. Economy: A Biophysical Perspective" by C. Cleveland, R. Costanza, C. Hall and R. Kaufmann in *Science* 225: 890–897 [31 August 1984]). Nevertheless, if the problem is scarcity then a possible solution should be to redistribute or increase supply, or decrease demand; only then will development be effected. Such solutions have not been tenable in the developing world. Scarcity is more a social than a physical phenomenon and the same repressive political and socio-economic structure that created that scarcity (or rather prevented full broad-based control of the production process so that resources—limited and marginal as they may be—could be managed for optimal output) will also prevent redistribution and increased production schemes from being effective in providing for the basic needs of that society.

It is unfortunate that problems are often presented very simplistically using metaphors (a good example is Garrett Hardin's lifeboats in Chapter 18) and such concepts as exponential growth models that have the power to "seduce and bewitch" (in the words of Julian Simon). The real issues are lost or conveniently forgotten, especially when their consideration involves critical examination of life style or, more importantly, U.S. foreign policy. And yet we must view resource "problems" in larger contexts, in order to identify the actual problem and its origins, articulate possible solutions, likely and unlikely, and most importantly, to be empowered with an intellectual framework that makes critical thinkers of us all.

Last year I attended a three-day Chautauqua course entitled "Energy and Society." The course was very good in its presentation of the components of energy demand, the generating characteristics of electricity, and basic information about renewable

Reprinted from *The Journal of Environmental Education* 15(3): 1–2 (1984).

and non-renewable resources. It provided an excellent overview of energy conservation, one of the instructor's particular areas of expertise.

There was, however, one problem. By the end of the course, participants were asking questions which were difficult to answer. Why, for example, in certain areas of the country, has there been a substantial decrease in the use of electricity, and yet rates remain high and are even increasing; or why is the price of gasoline lower now, in real terms, than 20 or 30 years ago (3)? If we are to believe that we are faced with limits to growth, that the danger of exponential population and resource-use growth will mean more and more human misery and/or increasingly higher prices for resources, why is it that indexes (1929=100) of labor capital input per unit of extractive output (1) are as follows (Table 56.1):

TABLE 56.1. Indexes of Labor Capital Input per Unit of Extractive Output (1)

	Total Extractive	Agriculture	Minerals	Forestry
1870-1900	134	132	210	59
1919	122	114	164	106
1957	60	61	47	90

The above evidence shows increasing, not diminishing, returns with the exception of forestry—cost per unit of product rose from the Civil War to World War I, but since then diminishing returns have given way to slightly increasing returns due to cost-reducing innovations, conversion of wood wastes into usable products, and a shift to wood substitutes. What is happening? Differential resource scarcities resulting in changes in relative costs allow for substitution of economically rational resources. This, together with economies of scale in the social production process and cost-reducing innovations, weaken the effect of increasing scarcity. Indeed, the idea of an absolute limit to natural resource availability is untenable when what is considered a resource changes so drastically over time.

This is not to say that technology has and will solve all our problems. However, it is foolhardy to think that we can portray the energy problem merely as one of scarcity—of exponential population growth and resource use.[1] If the problem is portrayed as such, then the logical solution is to increase supply or decrease demand, and the energy problem is then solved. Such a solution is untenable if we examine this logic in relation to food production and supply, something with which I am particularly familiar. If the world food problem is presented as one of scarcity (not enough arable land, low food production, high demand from rampant population growth, etc.), then we would expect decreasing demand or increasing supply to be the obvious ways to increase food availability. In practice, the former action results in population control campaigns which may lower the food-producing capability of a nation, depending on the percentage of the labor force employed in agriculture; the latter action has in many areas of the world resulted in a decrease in food availability. Statistics from Alan Berg (2) support this finding (Table 56.2).

It is simplistic and misleading to assume that a decrease in demand and/or an increase in supply will solve food/energy problems. *Social institutions and production process* must also be considered in understanding resource-supply problems and in trying to find appropriate solutions. If this is not given consideration in higher education then we, in our role of educators, will be unable to answer "difficult" questions, questions which make trivial our simplistic presentation of resource

TABLE 56.2. Production and Consumption of Beef in Central America (2)

Country	Production (000 tons)		Change in Production (%)	Consumption (Kg per person)		Change in Consumption (%)
	1961-1965	1970		1961-1965	1970	
Costa Rica	21.4	41.4	+92	12.3	9.1	-26
El Salvador	21.0	20.0	- 5	7.7	5.9	-23
Guatemala	41.0	57.4	+40	8.2	7.7	- 6
Honduras	16.7	29.6	+77	5.5	5.0	- 9
Panama	24.7	32.0	+30	20.9	21.8	+ 4
Nicaragua	32.2	56.4	+75	12.3	12.7	+ 3
Mexico	475.0	605.3	+27	10.9	10.9	0

problems. Of course, we may not have the answers to these questions, especially those of us with training exclusively in the natural sciences, but at least we should provide an intellectual framework within which our students begin to ask the "right" questions.

Notes

1. In fact, this "exponential-growth-fixation" has become so entrenched in environmental dogma, as the foundation for most environment-resource courses, that to investigate these assertions analytically is often times seen as heresy.

References

1. Barnett, H.J. and Morse, C. *Scarcity and Growth: The Economics of Natural Resource Availability.* Baltimore: The Johns Hopkins Press, 1963, 8. See also Simon, J.L. "Resources, Population, Environment: An Oversupply of False Bad News." *Science* 208 (June 1980): 1431–1437.

2. Berg, A. *The Nutrition Factor.* Washington, D.C.: The Brookings Institution, 1973, adapted from data on page 65.

3. Griffin, J., and Steele, H. *Energy, Economics and Policy.* New York: Academic Press, 1980.